With sincere thanks
and every best wish,

Ron Feldman

Sheila B Kamerman

THE COLUMBIA UNIVERSITY
SCHOOL OF SOCIAL WORK

A Centennial Celebration

THE COLUMBIA UNIVERSITY
SCHOOL OF
SOCIAL WORK

A Centennial Celebration

EDITORS

Ronald A. Feldman

and

Sheila B. Kamerman

Columbia University Press
New York

Columbia University Press

Publishers Since 1893
New York   Chichester, West Sussex

Copyright © 2001 Columbia University Press
All rights reserved

Library of Congress Cataloging-in-Publication Data
The Columbia University School of Social Work : a centennial celebration
/ editors, Ronald A. Feldman, Sheila B. Kamerman.
p.   cm.
Includes bibliographical references and index.
ISBN 0-231-12282-9 (cloth : alk. paper)
1. Columbia University. School of Social Work—History.   2. Social
work education—New York (State)—New York—History.   I. Feldman,
Ronald A. II. Kamerman, Sheila B.
HV11.7 .C64 2001
361.3′071′17471—dc21
00–065928

∞ Casebound editions of Columbia University Press
books are printed on permanent and durable
acid-free paper.

Printed in the United States of America
c 10 9 8 7 6 5 4 3 2 1

This book is dedicated to the social work pioneers of yesterday, today, and tomorrow.

CONTENTS

THE COLUMBIA UNIVERSITY
SCHOOL OF SOCIAL WORK

A Centennial Celebration

INTRODUCTION

Ronald A. Feldman and Sheila B. Kamerman

Social work is one of the youngest helping professions in the United States. It is generally agreed that American social work traces its educational roots to 1898, when the first formal courses in "social philanthropy" were offered under the auspices of the Charity Organization Society (COS) of New York City. Prior to that time, occasional lectures on related topics had been offered at various social service and educational institutions. They sometimes introduced certain of the principles that underlie today's social work profession. As documented in the June 21, 1898, edition of *The New York Times* (p. 7), the first formal course of the fledgling social work profession was offered in New York City:

> A class in practical philanthropic work was organized by Robert W. de-Forest, President of the Charity Organization Society, yesterday morning. The class will work from June 20 until July 30, and is open for graduate students from universities recommended by their instructors, and those who have had experience in philanthropic work.

The six-week summer course in "practical philanthropic work" grew into a full academic year in 1903–04 and by 1910 had become a two-year program. The institution that sponsored this program became known as the New York School of Philanthropy in 1904 and as the New York School of Social Work in 1919. Although the School had working linkages with Columbia University from its inception, it did not become affiliated formally with the University until 1940, at which time it was called the New York School of Social Work of Columbia University. In 1951, the School ended its formal affiliation with the Charity Organization Society and received its own New York state charter. It entered the Columbia corporation in 1959 and was designated as the Columbia University School of Social Work in the 1962–63 academic year.

1

Beginning in 1898 future social workers were exposed systematically and regularly to the latest scientific knowledge that could be garnered from university researchers and educators. Relevant social science knowledge was borrowed, adapted, and tailored to the emerging mission of social work. Concurrently, the foundation was laid for university-based scholars and educators to generate a discrete knowledge base that could be codified, applied, and advanced by social work professionals. The dual beginnings of social work education and social work practice were celebrated a century later in 1998, when the National Association of Social Workers, the largest professional association of social workers in the United States, with a membership of some 160,000 persons, declared 1998 as the centennial year of the social work profession. This landmark celebration of the profession traced social work's origins to the summer course in social philanthropy that had been offered by the New York City Charity Organization Society exactly one hundred years before.

Despite an illustrious hundred-year record of achievement, there are few well-documented histories of the social work profession and, especially, of the relationship between social work education and social work practice. Likewise, no systematic historical record exists of the century-long development of the Columbia University School of Social Work (CUSSW) or its myriad contributions to social work education. Only one published book even partially addresses the history of CUSSW, a monograph by Elizabeth G. Meier. Published in 1954 as part of the Columbia University Bicentennial History Series, it addresses only the first fifty years of the School's history. No published volume examines the second fifty years of CUSSW's history or the overall hundred-year record of the School. Accordingly, the present volume aims to deepen and extend the hundred-year historical record of this distinguished school of social work and, even more, to examine its linkages with contemporary social work education and the practice of professional social work. The book should thus give the reader a unique opportunity to view over time the growth and development of a school of social work that has integrally shaped social work education and practice since its inception. Likewise, the reader will become acquainted with a variety of pressing issues that must be addressed as social work progresses into a second century of education and practice. Even more, the reader will note also that certain of the issues that confront contemporary social work education have existed in one form or another since the birth of the social work profession.

This volume is set forth in six parts. Nearly all of the essays were written for the Centennial Celebration of the Columbia University School of Social Work, which was held in June 1998. Respectively, these parts are entitled Historical Overview, Methods of Practice, Fields of Practice, Doctoral Education, CUSSW and New York City, and The Future of CUSSW.

Part 1 presents two general overviews of the history of the Columbia University School of Social Work and its antecedents, namely the New York School of Philanthropy and the New York School of Social Work. The author of chapter 1 is Professor Emeritus Alfred J. Kahn. No other living individual is as well acquainted on a firsthand basis with the historical development of CUSSW. In 1948, he was the first recipient of a doctoral degree from the School of Social Work. Dr. Kahn has been a member of the Faculty of Social Work ever since. The second chapter bears dual authorship. The senior author is "WBM." Regrettably, the precise identity of WBM is unknown. Purely by happenstance, a 45-page double-spaced document authored by this individual was found recently in the files of the dean's office at CUSSW. It provides a succinct and, in some respects, elegant summary of the first fifty years of history of the New York School of Social Work. Each page of this document was imprinted with the initials "WBM," but it has not been possible to decipher the precise identity of WBM. It is likely that this document was authored circa 1960. With only minor editing, WBM's essay constitutes slightly more than half of chapter 2. The remainder of the chapter carries forward WBM's historical discussion through the present time and was written by the senior editor of this volume. Taken together, chapters 1 and 2 provide a framework for the more focused and detailed discussions that appear in parts 2 and 3 of this book.

Part 2 examines the five major methods of social work practice that distinguish the curriculum of the Columbia University School of Social Work. Respectively, these are Clinical Practice, Advanced Generalist Practice and Programming, Social Administration, Social Policy, and Social Research. Each essay discusses one of these five practice methods in terms of its historical development, present status, and current or emerging issues. By and large, the respective practice methods are viewed from the perspective of "yesterday," "today," and "tomorrow," thus reflecting the overall theme of the School of Social Work's centennial celebration: Celebrating the Past, Confronting the Present, and Visioning the Future.

Part 3 examines the seven fields of specialized practice that characterize the curriculum of the School of Social Work. Respectively, they are Family and Children's Services; Health, Mental Health, and Disabilities; Aging and Adult Human Development; the World of Work; International Social Welfare and Services to Immigrants and Refugees; School-Based and School-Linked Social Work Services; and Contemporary Social Problems. Each essay examines the focal field of practice in the context of its historical development, present status, and current or emerging issues.

Part 4 reviews doctoral education at CUSSW from an unique perspective, namely a review of the acknowledgment sections of selected doctoral dissertations, while part 5 discusses CUSSW's relationship to New York City from the particular perspective of settlement houses.

Part 6 examines developments at the School of Social Work that have occurred primarily in the last fifteen years. From this perspective, it identifies a wide range of issues pertinent to CUSSW's future. Many of them are of shared concern to virtually all schools of social work in the United States.

Taken together, the seventeen chapters of this volume update and extend the extant recorded history of the Columbia University School of Social Work. They augment such documents as the landmark book written by Elizabeth Meier (1954) and lesser known but nonetheless important documents such as a 1942 historical monograph by Saul Bernstein and colleagues and a series of seven monographs about various aspects of the School's history authored by Sidney Berengarten from 1987 through 1993. At the same time that these chapters chronicle key developments in the second fifty years of the School's history, they also shed light on trends and developments that are occurring throughout all of social work education. Hence, the present volume endeavors not only to celebrate the past history of the Columbia University School of Social Work. It seeks also to examine issues that presently confront both CUSSW and all of social work education and, further, to suggest ways to address some of these issues in the near future.

To the extent that the developmental histories of CUSSW in particular, and of social work education in general, are interdependent, knowledge about the one is bound to inform the efforts of the other. Social workers, perhaps more than other helping professionals, realize that "roots"—whether of a family, an institution, a community, or a profession—are powerful determinants of the future. Similarly, social workers' understanding and appreciation of their profession's past will be the best guarantor of their future.

REFERENCES

Berengarten, Sidney, ed. 1987. "The Columbia University School of Social Work: A History of Social Pioneering." Monograph 1. New York: Columbia University School of Social Work.

—— 1992. "The Columbia University School of Social Work: A History of Social Pioneering." Monograph 4. New York: Columbia University School of Social Work.

—— 1993. "The Columbia University School of Social Work: A History of Social Pioneering." Monograph 7. New York: Columbia University School of Social Work.

Bernstein, Saul, et al. 1942. *The New York School of Social Work: 1898–1941*. New York: Community Service Society.

Meier, Elizabeth G. 1954. *A History of the New York School of Social Work*. New York: Columbia University Press.

Part One

HISTORICAL OVERVIEW

Two essays comprise part 1 of the present volume. Chapter 1, by Alfred J. Kahn, is entitled "Themes for a History: The First Hundred Years." In this essay, Professor Emeritus Kahn traces out the dual heritage of the Columbia University School of Social Work (CUSSW). He discusses how a curriculum for a professional education was "invented" under the aegis of the Charity Organization Society of New York City, and how it subsequently evolved into the two-year curriculum that characterizes today's social work education program. Professor Kahn identifies the roles played by key faculty members in the historical development of the School. In particular, he discusses how the School of Social Work both responded to societal changes and occasionally helped to shape them. His essay examines, respectively, the first two decades (1898 to 1918), the 1920s, the New Deal and its aftermath, the war years and the 1950s, the years of the Great Society and the War on Poverty, the 1970s, the Reagan-Bush years, and the Clinton years. It is the most comprehensive discussion to date of the full hundred-year history of the Columbia University School of Social Work.

Chapter 2, "A Century of Curriculums and Celebrations," by WBM and Ronald A. Feldman, complements chapter 1 with descriptions of major historical developments and landmark celebrations at CUSSW and the New York School of Social Work. As noted in the introduction to this book, the first sections of chapter 2 are largely anecdotal descriptions written by an unknown author identified only as WBM, whose manuscript was discovered only recently in the "dead files" located in the dean's office. The original manuscript reviewed developments at the School only through the 1960s. The latter sections of the chapter record significant developments from the 1960s through the present. The period from 1898 through 1909 is viewed as one of "vision and audacity." The period from 1910 through 1929 is regarded as one of "progress and maturity." The years from 1930 through 1939 are viewed as the "decade of depression," while 1940 through 1949 are subtitled "new horizons." A separate section of this chapter examines the New York School at mid-century and another section treats the period from 1950 through 1998 as one of "expansion and consolidation." Chapter 2 concludes with a detailed description of the Columbia University School of Social Work's landmark centennial celebration in June 1998.

Chapter 1

THEMES FOR A HISTORY:
THE FIRST HUNDRED YEARS

Alfred J. Kahn

Two reports cover about half the history of what is now the Columbia University School of Social Work (CUSSW). Saul Bernstein of the faculty was allotted ten weeks to produce what was called a "resumé" of the history as needed by the Community Service Society's (CSS) new Institute of Welfare Research in connection with its program planning process (Bernstein et al. 1942). A limited number of duplicated copies were distributed. And in 1954, as part of the Columbia Bicentennial History Series, Elizabeth G. Meier completed a relatively brief history begun by Eduard Lindeman. Each is extremely interesting and useful. Neither is complete for its time, nor does either deal in detail with social-economic-political context or with the context of American social welfare, social work, social work education, or the university in which the school developed.

Therefore, when the assignment was proposed, it looked daunting—a major project involving perhaps one to two years of research. That, however, was not feasible. What was feasible was some primary research and considerable reliance on secondary sources—and even at that, the material seemed to demand at least a rather long paper or monograph. The time constraints were real, however. Hence, the title and subtitle. The essay offers a narrative and some judgments. The former is incomplete and the latter a string of hypotheses. The remainder of the volume adds substantially to the story and helps control for personal biases.

THE FIRST SCHOOL: A DUAL HERITAGE

We assemble on this hundredth anniversary for celebration and contemplation; but first we must deal with the question of what makes this school's centennial the beginning date for social work education in the United States and therefore the beginning date for the launching of professional social work. I start with a caveat: Robert Merton, citing Newton, has taught many of us about "the dependence of invention and discovery on the existing cultural base" (Merton 1957:558). In this instance the ground was prepared after the Civil War. State Boards of Charities and Corrections were increasing in number and being staffed. The Associations for Improving the Conditions of the Poor (AICPs), Charity Organization Societies (COSs), Children's Aid Societies, the State Children's Home Societies, and the sectarian family agencies were adding more paid staffs for agency administration or "friendly visiting," and there were similar developments in related fields. Where could they recruit if on-the-job training was not deemed enough? And in the Progressive Era politics after the 1893 depression, with the beginnings of modest federal regulatory action and of state social protection legislation, there was widespread interest in social reform, prevention, and the differentiation of socially engendered poverty from personally implicated "pauperism." Reformers and home visitors both needed knowledge.

At the meetings of the American Social Science Association, which began in 1865, and particularly in its 1874 spin-off, eventually the National Conference of Charities and Corrections, there was serious discussion about social problems, social reform, and also, in papers by Anna L. Dawes (1893) and Mary Richmond (1897), about the need to create an institution to prepare people for the work in these programs.

This was the soil in which we began. It was 1898, the year of New York City's consolidation into its present political form. The motor car and moving pictures were only three years old. Columbia in its beginning move from Forty-ninth Street and Madison Avenue had held its first classes on the Heights in October 1897. *The New York Times,* in its third year under Adolph Ochs, who turned it into the paper we know today, carried this item on page 7 on June 21, 1898 (a paragraph cited frequently in the centennial publicity and exhibit):

A class in practical philanthropic work was organized by Robert W. de-Forest, President of the Charity Organization Society yesterday morning. The class will work from June 20 until July 30, and is open for graduate students from universities recommended by their instructors, and those who have had experience in philanthropic work.

Meier provides an early chronology which is listed in appendix 1A.

From the 1870s, a number of universities had sponsored lectures and even lecture series about social problems, economics, the history of reform, and philanthropy. (As noted below, Betty Broadhurst [1971] provides fascinating detail.) There were also periodic lectures and training sessions elsewhere in COSs for their staff members in the 1890s. But nowhere but in New York was there a program for a selected group of enrolled students in what was designed as an ongoing program and which ran continuously as a summer school from 1898 and made the transition to a year-round program in 1904.

The basic sources are in agreement:

Lubove (1965:140–141)—"Social workers in other cities followed the New York lead" (following the 1898 pioneer course).

Hollis and Taylor (1951:9)—"The pioneer [of the "embryonic schools of social work"], the New York School of Philanthropy, was founded in 1898 as a six-week summer school . . . [and] became a full academic year in 1903–04 and by 1910 a two-year program."

Finally, Graham Taylor, who was one of the field's great pioneers and the leader of the University of Chicago social work education initiatives (a three-month course) in 1903, as well as the chair of the Committee on Training for Social Workers of the National Conference of Charities and Corrections, reported for his committee as follows to the 1905 meeting, by which time there were four one-year schools:

Training schools thus arose not only simultaneously but under re-markably similar conditions. The Charity Organization Society of New York was first in the field with its Summer School in Philanthropic Work which for eight years has succeeded in attracting students by its unique educational methods. (Johnson 1905:437)[1]

By 1904 the direction had become clear: The New York School of Philanthropy was conducting its one-year course; in Boston, Harvard and Simmons jointly created the Boston School for Social Workers (Harvard withdrew in 1912); there were Extension Division courses at the University of Chicago, and in 1908 a one-year full-time school was established; and in

St. Louis there was launched the School for Practical Training of Charity Workers. That same year there were schools in London and Liverpool. Amsterdam opened the first year-round school in the world in 1899 (U.N. 1958:107–115).[2]

After the first week of the year-round program in 1904, a gift of securities with an assured annual income of $10,000 from John S. Kennedy, vice-chair of the New York COS, who earlier had financed construction of the United Charities Building, made possible the formal establishment of a permanent institution. At the dinner honoring Kennedy, Daniel C. Gilman, president of the Johns Hopkins, discussed some of the work of the pioneer scholars who created the field (see below) and he then commented:

> Now New York comes to the front, larger, richer, and more venture-some than any city. The building was here, the leaders, the scholars, the ideas, the organization. Waiting for what? Endowment. So endowment enters . . . bearing a letter which is a sort of charter . . . a bill of duties, a summary of principles. (Gilman 1906, quoted by Broadhurst 1971:838)

A DUAL HERITAGE

Not that the pioneers knew exactly how social work education — or for that matter, social work — should look. Their domain was called "philanthropy" and they had a dual heritage: on the one hand, the "practical" work in the AICPs, COSs, children's agencies, corrections, and other programs, and on the other hand, the social investigations, reform, and emerging social science. But their energies were considerable, they were clearly a very able lot, and in the context of the Progressive Era, through World War I, their approach was empirical and optimistic. Moreover, they set up extraordinarily effective networks and communication links. Dr. Betty P. Broadhurst (1971) tells the story, particularly the academic side, in great detail and with rich quotations from correspondence, committee reports, and published papers in her remarkable but unpublished doctoral dissertation ("with distinction") at this school. Since the history is very relevant to an understanding of where the schools began, and what needed to be accomplished subsequently, it is essential to summarize some highlights.

This was the period before modern social science and its differentiations had taken its shape, when for many of its early leaders the mission was research to clarify and then solve social problems, develop broad social reform, and achieve effective administration of philanthropy. A new "scientific" education was being introduced into American universities, markedly different from the classical, and featuring economics, history, and psychological development as fields of study. A convening point for those who had begun the shift from traditional descriptive, deductive, and speculative approaches concerning social problems and what would today be called "social policy" to what Broadhurst (1) calls a "scientific formulation" was the American Social Science Association (ASSA), founded in 1865. This was not yet one of the learned societies, loci of an empirical methodology, that were to come. But it was a meeting ground for identification and clarification of differences among what we would now consider to be (1) a learned society, (2) a forum for objective study of problems and practices, and (3) an organization concerned with "practical" philanthropic work in agencies. From the ASSA eventually emerged the National Conference of Charities and Corrections (1874) and other specialized groups in prison work, public health, and urban planning, as well as the American Historical Association and the American Economic Association. Its discussions were a major spur to the development of sociology as a social science in the United States.

And it was at the Johns Hopkins in 1876 that the new type of social science school developed and attained its great impact. The operating unit was the professor who carried out social investigations, used his research as a base for teaching, and documented findings through publication. In the Progressive Era these were reformers who considered planned change possible. Some were "radicals" with regard to the economic system, as well. And these new social science scholars sent their own students into the field to collect data and/or to learn by observation. Eventually, some of those students also became COS volunteer "friendly visitors."

Broadhurst describes Hopkins as the "mother house," creating intellectual colonies which spread knowledge and enthusiasm for modern social science investigation and instruction and for student observation and data gathering to Wisconsin, Chicago, Ohio, Boston, Stanford, and at least another dozen colleges and universities before World War I. Philip W. Ayres, who went from Hopkins to Cincinnati and then Chicago (carrying knowledge of Ely's experience with field placements at Hopkins), arrived in New York in 1897 committed to the Summer School in Philanthropy and, as assistant director of New York COS, became the School's first program director.[3]

Despite the School's connection to the COS, it was committed by the Kennedy endowment as much to United Charities, AICP, United Hebrew Charities, the Society of St. Vincent de Paul, and to its relationship with Columbia as it was to the COS itself. Kennedy had elected to encourage ties with the "practical charity work of the city" rather than establishing a university department.

How were these two streams, universities and operating charities, to come together when the domain and scope of activity of what would eventually be known as "social work" was yet to be discovered?

From the practical side there was the influence of Zilpha Smith, with long staff training experience in Boston; Anna Dawes, also from Massachusetts; and Mary Richmond in Baltimore and then Philadelphia.

It would take us too far afield to speculate about why Johns Hopkins did not establish the first or any social work school and why one did not develop in Wisconsin or at Stanford despite important lecture series by the pioneers under the developing social science programs. Amos Warner, one of the most impressive of the Hopkins graduates and a man who would come to personify the connection between research and practice, had become the general agent of the Baltimore COS while completing his Ph.D. at Hopkins—a new-breed economist-social researcher who was interested in the practical. His *American Charities* (1894), a compilation of the new studies of charities and social problems, became the first social work text. Warner took what we might call the new applied social science path. Mary Richmond took over in Baltimore, groomed by Gilman, but not in the social science model. Eventually, she traveled to Philadelphia COS in 1900. Her *Friendly Visiting among the Poor* (1899) was the second text used by the pioneer Summer School in Philanthropy from 1899. There we have it: the two sources complemented one another to offer social science guided prevention and social reform and the "case by case" work of charity.

The Summer School in Philanthropy's lecturers were leaders of charity departments and organizations, public officials, university faculty (some from other cities)—and people like Mary Richmond, who traveled to New York from the beginning. By 1909 the new, philanthropically oriented Russell Sage Foundation had brought Richmond to New York to head its Charity Organization Department. She thus remained heavily engaged in lecturing at the School and influencing its policies.

The many lecturers were not paid between 1898 and 1907, and there were as many as seventy-five different people involved in 1906–07. By 1907–08, there were small honoraria (but not for summer lecturers or COS staff). The first full-time salary went to Mary G. Worthington, appointed in 1908 as the supervisor of the fieldwork program. The fieldwork component had gradually expanded and been formalized. The director argued that the students "shall spend relatively more time in the actual doing of philanthropic work under skilled direction and supervision than in lectures about it." The placements were as frequently related to housing, factories, and child labor reform as to individual work (Meier 1954:25, 28, 35).

Inventing a Curriculum

The social work school had yet to be invented. The new school in New York had to discover how to bring together in an organized program the training at the practical side with the learning about society, people, and social problems that came from the new academic work. And it was more than a "theory" versus "practice" issue. It was also a question of mission. The first students were interested in the direct practical work in COSs and children's agencies or in administration of social programs. That is, many of them were. Others had broader institutional and social reform goals rather than planning to work with individual families. No choice had been made between these two streams, and the notion of such choice had not been posed when the School was launched. The balance in favor of what came to be known as "casework" over what was generalized initially as "community organization" evolved only over a considerable period of time.

To illustrate, when the full year of study was instituted, the School listed itself as preparing students for service as

- "expert visitors for charity organization societies or other charitable institutions" (what would later be called caseworkers);

- investigation of social conditions or institutions;

- financial secretaries for private individuals (to implement their charitable work?);

- tenement house and factory inspection;

- executive secretaries of educational or philanthropic societies;

- probation officers;

- head workers and assistants in social settlements, institutions, churches, welfare departments of manufacturing and mercantile establishments;

- workers in the public service, especially those branches that deal with public welfare;

- members of boards and committees of philanthropic institutions;

- "friendly visitors" and volunteer workers (Meier 1954:24–25, citing the New York School of Philanthropy Yearbook, 1906–07).

(We shall note subsequently how much the list was to change.)[4]

Important leaders, practitioners, and professors from all streams gave individual lectures or lecture series on the subjects in which they specialized. School leadership attempted to suggest continuities.

One should not romanticize. One of the field's educational pioneers, writing about her experience in *another* school (Chicago) in the earliest days, has said "most of the courses were series of lectures on one subject given by almost as many different people as there were sessions in the series. One looks in vain for any semblance of a curriculum or an integrated program of study." She adds:

> Fortunately, the early leaders of the field laid a groundwork on which
> we should be able to build for many years to come. They recognized
> the necessity of preparing students to render the direct services for
> which people come to social agencies, to understand the findings of
> social research . . . and to participate intelligently in efforts to modify
> the social conditions which are inimical to the growth and develop-
> ment of the individual. (Wright 1954a, 1954b)

All this applied in New York, as well.

By 1910–11 much progress had been made. Instead of a series of lectures integrated by the director or a chair, there were regular courses meeting once or twice a week. There was a full-time faculty. There had been a "shakedown" of topics, too. (For example, cooking and public speaking were dropped as the curriculum focus was sharpened.) Students went on field visits, excursions, and carried brief agency case assignments under several patterns. In our current sense, curriculum and fieldwork had to be shaped over the years, first for the summer school (1898), then the one-year school (1904), and then the two-year program (1911). Most admitted students had B.A. degrees or "equivalent" experience, so the work was defined as graduate. From the beginning there was reciprocity between the School and Columbia which allowed free course enrollment and the earning of an academic M.A. with the social work diploma. But the content of the teaching of what would now be called "practice" still needed to be invented.

The period from 1898 to 1920 holds a fascinating story of trial and error, teamwork, learning from research (Richmond's 1917 *Social Diagnosis* reflected a systematic research process), experimentation, formulation, and reformulation as the school began to identify

- its main curriculum options for students;

- what would go into what would be seen as "technical courses" as contrasted with the social and behavioral science and social reform, which gradually reflected the developing sociology where there had mostly been political economy;

- how to organize fieldwork and connect it with the class;

- how to absorb and apply in practice the social and behavioral science material.

We have reproduced in appendix 1B the report by the School's director of the third summer's lectures, field observations and trips, and other activities. By 1904 the students could (according to the *Bulletin*) choose from among forty-one lecture courses grouped under the following headings (which hardly formed a coherent classification scheme):

- a survey of the field (social work, charity, social reform, industrial causes of distress, financing);

- the role of the state;

- "racial traits in the population" (race, ethnicity, immigration);

- constructive social work (health, industrial welfare, preventive programs);

- the care of needy families in their homes (scientific charity, etc.);

- child helping agencies;
- treatment of criminals.

A TWO-YEAR CURRICULUM: TO THE 1950s

Our review of the development of a concept of curriculum requires some mention of values and attitudes. Later, the Deweyite Eduard Lindeman (1921; also Gessner 1936) was to formulate and teach his democratic ethic. But as the two-year program was launched, Devine introduced one of his several essay collections, *The Spirit of Social Work* (1911), with the following:

> One of the extraordinary developments of the opening decade of the twentieth century is the extent to which the multitude of social workers, engaged in various occupations, enrolled under various banners, have made mutual discovery of one another's existence, have become aware of one another's common aims and aspirations. They have found themselves, so to speak, and in doing so have found that this social point of view, this mutual interest in social work, differentiates them not only from the exploiter but from the neutral and indifferent member of society.
>
> This new view of life and of human relations is at once conservative, constructive, and wholesome; radical, revolutionary, and disturbing; absolutely non-partisan, catholic, and social; comprehensive in its grasp and yet sternly practical and acquainted with the humility of the scientific and inquiring mind. It is a view which tempts to no violence and yet leaves no wrong permanently on the throne; a view which exalts the family, the state, religion, security of life and of property, and yet insists that all institutions are made for men and not men for institutions; a view which opens our eyes to the evils which are, but yet does not seek to make them, in some mystical sense, symbols of imaginary evils which are not.
>
> Social workers are not Utopians. They are sober citizens of a real commonwealth. Yet the community which they have in their mind's eye, as the not too distant goal of their diversified and yet co-ordinated endeavors, is one in which the premature death shall have been conquered, in which feeble-mindedness shall have been abolished, in which childhood shall be protected and nourished, in which neither

men nor women shall be exploited for gain, in which toil though it may still be severe will not be destructive, in which heredity and environment shall be joined in a holy wedlock of which high physical and moral character shall be the offspring, in which there shall be leisure and opportunity for the growth of the spirit, in which always and everywhere men shall rule things, being worthy to rule and under no domination save that of loyalty to the highest and best that the mind of man has conceived.

At the heart of the School is the curriculum. The basic architecture evolved over the first fifty years.

First, it was necessary to go from a large roster to a core. The early lists included an extraordinary range of activities and career goals just as the early National Conference of Charities and Corrections could claim a very broad domain which in a few decades would experience spin-offs and more consensus about focus. The School was sensitive to agency demands for staff, student interests, and successive faculty conceptualizations of curriculum as the society evolved and the decades passed.

Thus, the gradually evolving curriculum concept: What needed to be taught? How shall the curriculum be structured?

- Beginning with a one-year program, the School saw the need for a two-year graduate program.

- Beginning with co-equal divisions ("working with individuals and families"; "working toward social betterment through mass programs of social legislation and social action"), the School adjusted the balance to the demand. By the 1920s the vast majority of students were preparing for work with individuals, families, and groups. A "macro" division remained even if it was periodically redefined.

- Beginning with a curriculum structure that held methods, practice fields, and specialized background content all on one level, a sense of relationships among these components developed. By the 1950s and subsequently, there was a structure involving: method, background information, field or context; behavioral-medical-social science knowledge.

- After considerable specialization by field of practice, especially from the 1920s to the 1940s, various generic and generalist ideas arose. First, that the various branches of casework were essentially manifestations of one method (the 1920s and 1930s). Then, that there was a generic core to all social work methods (1950s) as well as an essential shared platform of background information and behavioral-social science, medical knowledge. These components were periodically refined and redefined (1940s, 1950s) and a common curriculum has existed since the 1950s.

• There was conviction throughout that class and field learning were both absolutely essential and required effective integration.

• There was conviction throughout that the social work learning model required substantial student individualization through selection, advising, and field supervision. Such experiences would prepare students to individualize their clients.

• It was understood from the beginning that the School should make the most of its locational advantage: a rich multicultural context, a diversity of agency and program types, constant and varied immigration, rich philanthropic-volunteer-public resources, and the supportive programs of the Russell Sage Foundation.

The remainder of this section offers illustration and selective highlights, 1910 to 1950, by which time the curriculum "architecture" was apparent.

As the two-year diploma program was implemented and there was a substantial full-time faculty, an attempt was made to define for the first year material basic for all social work (known for a while as "pre-vocational"), while the second year was to be elective and vocational. A distinction along these lines has persisted, although the vocabulary has changed.

By the end of World War I, as put by Meier, "two large divisions of social work were seen—that of working with individuals and families and that of working towards social betterment through mass programs of social legislation and social action" (Meier 1954:55). Extraordinary progress had been made in conceptualizing casework and how it would be taught. These had been and remained co-equal tracks in the School during the Progressive Era developmental years. When the *Charities and Commons* magazine of the COS launched its reform-oriented monumental survey of Pittsburgh, the prototypical industrial city of immigrants and company towns of the late nineteenth century, eight of fourteen investigators were or were soon to be associated with the School. The survey director was Paul Kellog, who had taken part in the summer program, and the School's courses on labor and industry made extensive use of the rich reports. Faculty members were among those active in the large social survey movement which was to follow.

The adapting and shaping continued. To jump ahead: according to the 1923–24 School *Bulletin,* courses were organized by five departments:

- Department of Social Casework
- Department of Industry
- Department of Social Research
- Department of Community Organization
- Department of Criminology

These were described as the "five major fields of professional social work," each leading to a diploma. About half the time in earning the diplomas was being spent in fieldwork; the class–field distinction was not considered a theory–practice division since "the two are combined in courses at school and in the field" (7).

This, however, does not fully detail the range of subject matter (1924–25 *General Announcement,* April 1924). By the end of the third quarter (first year), a student also was required to choose a "major field" for specialty concentration in the second year, meaning both fieldwork and a special seminar:

family casework
child placement
institutional supervision
juvenile delinquency
visiting teaching
hospital social work
psychiatric social work
penal, reformatory, detention work
parole
social organization
rural organization
recreation organization
research
statistics
personnel administration
factory inspection

Some of the earliest fields of practice (as we would now call them) were still present until the 1930s; others had already disappeared or decreased. Criminology has its own "professional" apparatus; industrial social work ended during the New Deal as "company unionism," only to be reborn under Reaganism. The methods were direct service, community development/ prevention—in our terms. And the Department of Social Casework—the largest by far—had begun to distinguish family casework, psychiatric casework, medical social work, and child welfare.

But the constantly present thrust to integration and the generic prevented full triumph of centrifugal forces (Bernstein et al. 1942:50–52). Porter Lee, the dean, along with Professor Mary Hurlbutt and Mary Antoinette Cannon, was a moving force in the Milford Conference (1923–1929), and Lee and Cannon were principal drafters of *Social Case Work, Generic and Specific* (AASW 1929), a major document in the profession's history. (Hurlbutt had left to work abroad.) The conclusions about the existence of a generic casework method shaped thinking at the School and curriculum changes early in the 1930s, even though the depression, the refugee situation, and the war work deferred full curricular reform until the late 1940s.

Beginning in the 1920s, training for child guidance work was expanded through the Bureau of Child Guidance (1922–1923), a service agency and training center created at the School by a Commonwealth Fund delinquency experiment. A second project (1928–1933) created the Institute for Child Guidance, with a large program of social worker, psychologist, and psychiatrist training. Dr. Berman Glueck, who came to the School in 1918, was the first director of the Bureau of Children's Guidance, and Dr. Marion Kenworthy, who came in 1921, was his associate. When Glueck resigned in 1924, Kenworthy took over and was a major force at the School until her 1956 retirement, the first psychiatrist in a full-time position in a social work school. In 1929, Porter Lee, the dean and a casework teacher, co-authored *Mental Hygiene and Social Work* with Kenworthy; it was the first psychiatric casework text.

New personnel on the faculty and many new electives represented the beginning of a new curriculum which, after World War II, involved basic required courses in human growth and development for all students. Until then, psychology and psychiatry had been chosen by the students, who after World War I were being prepared for Veterans Administration assignments in psychiatric programs, those in criminology and, then, child guidance. Always enjoying something of an élite status, psychiatric social work had become increasingly popular. The idea was accepted that psychiatry belonged in a foundation core along with some social science material and medical information. Contrary to some accounts, an eclectic psychiatric and psychological theory mix was available; the psychoanalytic monopoly did not come to the fore until the 1940s.

Thus the areas of attention in the curriculum both narrowed and grew. Social reform became community organization in its more narrow sense, and direct work with individuals and families predominated. Group work was added as an option in the late 1920s, with a developmental and socialization emphasis, and attracted a significant group in the 1930s. It added a therapeutic subspecialty in the 1950s. (Later, in the 1970s, casework and group work came together in what is now known as "clinical practice," in recognition of the family as a "group" and the experience that even the practitioners who concentrate on intensive individual work cannot manage without some group competence.)

To sum up the formulation of the 1930s, the School *Bulletin* for 1932–33 explains the offerings as follows:

- methods and procedures common to all forms of social work;

- the specific problems of the different fields of social work;

- subject matter essential to social work specifically adopted from social and behavioral sciences and from the practices of other professional fields;

- the combination of the technical, scientific, and philosophical phases of social work as a basis for practice.

In the School's curriculum work of the late 1940s, the Milford Conference notion that there was a generic core to all casework became the point of departure for another concept which had been mentioned earlier but was not enacted: there is a generic core to all social work. Now the idea of a foundation of required work for all students was standardized. The notion of the specialty chosen by the student on top of the foundation (the second year) was to evolve and fluctuate among method, field of practice, and professional functions.

Finally, the 1952–53 *Bulletin* sums up the postwar curriculum review. The considerable separation of courses of study by field of practice had given way to an integrated concept:

- Courses in one's primary method (4);
- Basic content required of *all* students:
    Field of social work
    Basic concepts and processes in practice
    Growth and development
    Psychopathology
    Medical and social problems of illness
    Socio-cultural basis of individual and community life;
- Government and social welfare;
- Courses in methods other than one's own;
- Research;
- General seminar;
- M.S. thesis;
- Field work.

The processes over five decades had reflected a sharpening, if narrowing, conception of social work, the emergence of a class–field balance, a differentiation by method (casework, group work, community organization, administration), and conviction about a large generic core. The next four decades added new elements to the mix.

So it went. A changing society, a developing profession, an evolving curriculum. The School was highly respected, its graduates were in demand, its faculty members were national leaders, and their books were widely used as texts. In 1950, 91 of 517 full-time faculty members in accredited schools of social work were New York School alumni, as were 20 of 53 deans, a proportion probably never again reached given the general expansion of social work education. A full assessment of all this would require an ambitious research undertaking, but much "case" evidence of the New York School's impact is at hand.

THE FACULTY BEHIND THE CURRICULUM

The School was fortunate in its faculty from the beginning. In a bootstrap operation, the School built its faculty out of the social science stream as described above, the fields of practice—especially COS and state board employees—and from among its own graduates. In a process that was to be repeated in the 1950s and 1960s with the doctoral program, the availability of graduate training had brought to the School highly experienced people who took time out for systematic learning and contemplation. They became leaders-teachers, deans, and directors—in New York and elsewhere. New York also was especially fortunate in its directors/deans.

To illustrate from earlier years, note the remarkable team of Porter R. Lee, director from 1919, Walter W. Pettit, his associate from the beginning, and Margaret Leal, initially called "Secretary" but a major force in the administration. Lee, a 1903 "summer school" student, came from the casework practice side, headed several COSs, came to teach in 1912, and introduced the case method of teaching. It was Lee who in 1919 convened the fifteen schools that created the American Association of Schools of Social Work. He saw the need for work on conceptualizing and teaching the technical aspects of direct practice. He was a major intellectual force behind the Milford Conference and in the drafting of its report and—in a widely distributed series of writings, especially *Social Work as Cause and Function* (1937)—prodded the field to think deeply about its mission and its relationship to social change. Walter Pettit (who came in 1915 from the community organization side, where he had introduced the case method of teaching to community organization) became director on Lee's death early in 1939, and Margaret Leal became the associate director—and, in 1947, acting dean. There was, in effect, a "dynasty" that provided continuity and strong leadership for almost thirty years. It was Pettit who negotiated the 1940 Columbia affiliation which enabled the School to shift from its "diploma" to the M.S. degree.

SELECTIVE HIGHLIGHTS FROM TEN DECADES: RESPONDING TO CHANGE, OCCASIONALLY HELPING TO SHAPE IT

The hundred years of the "New York School," now the Columbia School, coincide with the hundred years over which the modest and somewhat reluctant American Welfare State was proposed, then launched, developed, expanded, challenged, and now forced into new adaptations. The major periods over this time may be called the Age of Reform (Hofstadter 1955): the Progressive Era, the New Deal, and the Great Society.[5] In the space between them (especially the 1920s and 1950s) and after them (the 1970s and 1980s), reform became "function" and the new policies and programs were integrated and developed in a flurry of institution building and professionalization. There were also some retreats.

Social work education, and thus the organized profession, was born out of the major 1893 depression, but the ground was laid by the social and intellectual changes of the Gilded Age. Yes, there was the dominance of Social Darwinism, but there was also the challenge of Lester Ward and the Populist tradition. We already have referred to the social science and social welfare developments between the Civil War and the 1890s.

Modern social work, and this School, were products of the Progressive Era. But the societal context changed in major ways over the years, offering new tasks, obstacles, and opportunities. It was consistent with social work's dominant ideology that the field be open to change. But it is a fair judgment that social work was not one of the powerful forces in society, so its challenge was more often to find the right response for those who depended on it— rather than to move major societal innovation. But, as we should recall, there were exceptions here, too.

On the other hand, this first and always leading school had a powerful impact throughout on the profession and on social work education. It was in a central role in the creation of the American Association of Schools of Social Work (AASSW), the deliberations of the Milford Conference, the launching of the National Association of Social Workers (NASW): Nathan Cohen was the first president, Gordon Hamilton was the first editor-in-chief of its new journal, *Social Work,* and five of the twelve editors-in-chief thus far have been CUSSW faculty members or doctoral graduates. It played a large part, too, in the education of deans, directors, and senior professors for the expanding educational community. In the activities that developed the field, its faculty members were leaders: their texts were widely used, and they were visible in the conferences, organizations, associations, and debates that were to shape the profession's future.

In what follows, I point to some highlights which, at most, are notes for a history yet to be written or fragments of that history assembled by others. There is much more to cover, including relationships with Columbia, with social work, with the world of policy and action, and with the behavioral and social sciences. There were always faculty members and administrators who focused on core curriculum and educational refinements, while others looked at the society and wanted the School to reclaim a stronger reform role. Some of the faculty were national "actors"; others stayed closer to home. The School did not shape the society (what one institution has?), but it had great influence on social work education as it strengthened its own educational offerings.

The First Two Decades: From 1898 to 1918

I have told the story of the beginnings: the summer school and its lectures and lecture series covering the full range of as yet undifferentiated "charities and correction" concerns, and I have mentioned the evolving observation and field experience offerings. Although very much a COS activity, from the beginning the School had an ongoing Columbia connection in political economy and, then, sociology. Philip Ayres was the director until the one-year School began in 1904, when Edward T. Devine became the head. Both were Ph.D.'s in the new mold, scholars of social problems and reform—and with a commitment to training for "practical" work.

The stream of attention to social conditions led to the establishment at the School in 1906 of the Bureau of Research, a successor to statistics and research committees in the COS. Shortly thereafter, the newly established Russell Sage Foundation gave grants to four year-round schools to support social investigation for the Foundation and, in the New York instance, research training, postgraduate research fellowships, and research in Columbia's sociology department (Broadhurst 1971:866–867; Bernstein et al. 1942: 100–102).

After a spurt to 1912, the research activity declined. Broadhurst speculates that this may have been one of the periodic fluctuations in emphasis in the early years between the socioeconomic content and the practical direct work (see below). A young researcher at the Bureau of Social Research concluded her 1909–10 study of "Malnutrition in a Group of 107 School Children in P.S. 51" with the following note: "Until society adjusts itself and provides adequate incomes and adequate education to all its workers . . . ," there must be some recourse to the expedient of temporary relief for poverty. Her professor, the leading economist Simon N. Patten of Pennsylvania, teacher of Devine and Lindsay and lecturer at the School in 1904–07, 1911, and 1913, had predicted, in recommending her for the fellowship, that she would "acquire through her energy and brains an important position among social workers." Frances Perkins did not disappoint anybody, first as factory inspector, then as a New York State official, and finally as Franklin Roosevelt's Secretary of Labor, chairing the committee that wrote the Social Security Act (cited by Meier 1954:37).

This was the era in which the School was seeking its footing among what was to become differentiated as the social reform and social science materials, on the one hand, and the "practical" work and skills it was established to teach, on the other. In the 1905–06 curriculum, as the one-year program began, the emphasis was on work with individuals. In a gradual process, this being the era of muckrakers and social reforms, the courses on economic problems and proposed reforms, sociology, and other general required lectures and electives came to completely dominate the offerings. While we lack a full accounting of what went on, clearly there were debates, tensions, controversy, which involved administrators, teachers, and the COS board. Samuel McCune Lindsay, student of Patten, had replaced Devine as director in 1907. His 1912 resignation letter, reprinted by Bernstein et al. (1942:26–28), refers to communications from Richmond and Glenn and the inability to arrive at agreement on educational policy. To Lindsay, the options were the law school, the medical school, and Teachers College (a university graduate professional school), or a "training school, much more limited in scope, devoted to the development of a finer technique in a few lines of work—perhaps exclusively in the activities of a charity organization society"—more like a business college or a nurses' training school in a hospital.

Devine, still director of New York COS, returned to the School's directorship as well. Leading people from the practical end were recruited for what was a growing full-time faculty. The need for technical practice courses was highlighted—and progress was made (Berengarten 1987:2–4 and note 7). As suggested in the above curriculum review, however, Lindsay was not all wrong in his view of what was going on. By the 1950s, the School looked as much like the model he preferred as the alternative he rejected. This would be a graduate professional school, not narrow vocational training.

The critical accomplishments of these two decades have been mentioned earlier: the progress in the conceptualization of casework and how it is to be taught (see Richmond's *Social Diagnosis* [1917] and *What Is Social Case Work?* [1922]); the major progress in formulating a curriculum; the recruitment of an exemplary faculty, stable and paid; progress in sorting out what were essential background subjects and what were the techniques. But much remained unresolved.

Many oversimplified accounts describe the COS people as "charitables" who were unaware of economic context and who contested settlement "radicals," or assume that COS was strictly Social Darwinist, but the record shows this view to be an exaggeration, if not an outright error. Early students were encouraged (and at many points even required) to spend some time visiting or working in settlement houses. Richmond, who experienced the 1893 depression at the Baltimore COS, understood and talked about the interdependence of "mass betterment and individual betterment" (Broadhurst 1971: 529; Richmond 1917, 1922; Simon 1994, ch. 4). Debating those whose curriculum views differed from hers and fearful that the "academic" would overwhelm the "practical" in a university setting, she certainly saw need for both and called for environmental interventions beyond cash assistance (Broadhurst 1971:533).

Devine, the director, worked his views out in a changing societal context. Trained by Patten at Pennsylvania, he had adopted the radical Patten views of the economy and called for a more equitable distribution of the economy's surplus "to the people of the community in which it is created" (Devine 1910: 148). His own little book about poverty, in the spirit of the era's distinctions between poverty, the main issue, and pauperism, called for development and opportunity in terms which would not have been out of place in Lyndon Johnson's poverty war (1907 essay, in Devine 1910). He described the social work ideal as securing the recognition of normal standards of comfort, activity, and life, and "to sweep away the obstacles which prevent the realization of these standards by ordinary human beings." [6]

To the extent that the record here has been reported, the School was apparently not very active—Devine aside—in some of the major Washington social welfare initiatives of the Progressive Era. Devine urged a White House Conference on Children, advocated for the Children's Bureau, and was active on child labor reform and antituberculosis efforts. But others, particularly Chicago social workers, were the leaders in the Children's Bureau, juvenile court campaigns, mothers' pension laws, and the enactment of the Shepperd-Townsend maternal and child health program. In effect, New York concentrated on the private sector until the 1930s, whereas Chicago put the public in focus—and they debated.

Devine did not escape from his age and held some views that have not fully disappeared in our own day. While poverty is "the larger and more important problem," to be dealt with through social reform, health care, housing, and administration of justice, "pauperism" is biologically primitive, presenting a distinct social problem—as do criminals, prostitutes, inebriates, *monopolists,* and *revolutionaries* (Devine 1916; emphasis added). He favored segregation for paupers, whom he described as often mental defectives, alcoholics, or drug users, but he also argued for their humane treatment (1916).

Devine and his academic colleagues were from the beginning active in service on what we would now call the "macro" side—people who could at the call of governors and presidents take on responsible tasks and missions: a Red Cross assignment after the San Francisco earthquake of 1906 and the Ohio floods in 1913. He led Red Cross relief work in France during World War I. He helped convince Theodore Roosevelt to call the 1909 White House Conference on Children. (I note, parenthetically, a similar series of roles for social work leaders during the New Deal and during and after World War II, and wonder whether it is the field's more recent recruitment patterns or social work's current status that has made such roles—perhaps best exemplified by Harry Hopkins—virtually disappear.)

Devine was only one among the faculty members with special wartime roles. Mary Hurlbutt, who joined the faculty in 1914, worked in Czechoslovakia and subsequently had a series of top-level assignments for the National Board of the YMCA and others in the immigration field. She built competence in ethnicity and work with immigrants that served the School well into the 1950s. As much could be said for Clara Kaiser. During the war the School offered a free course for Red Cross emergency services. In 1919, it offered a one-year course for Red Cross Home Services.

The 1920s

In 1919 the School became the New York School of Social Work. Its relationship to New York COS was unchanged. Its ties to Columbia were "less close." This was for the country a time of withdrawal to private concerns, and end of the prewar reform, if perhaps a "seedtime" for the next wave (Chambers 1963).

The postwar heritage of casework above the poverty line, e.g., casework where the starting point was not necessarily a relief application, and family casework which explored the psychiatric theme, created an era of great professional development, expansion, and institution building. The national service agencies and social work professional associations took their more mature shape: family welfare, child welfare, school social work, medical social work, travelers' aid, and psychiatric social work. It was the era of specialization, enrichment of fieldwork, and progress in conceptualizing supervision. As we already have seen, it was an era of major curriculum development at the School.

The survey movement, launched in Pittsburgh, had transferred its major energies from exposure of the societal price of the industrial system to social welfare needs studies. Community welfare planning and coordination became important—and, therefore, grew in the schools. The New York School recruited, developed new courses, and was clearly in the lead here, too, as it was in casework. It also was among the schools which began to develop group work.

Then, as the economic problems hit at the end of the decade, faculty reported on the developing economic crisis and the inability of the voluntary sector to cope. Klein looked at the geography of economic need in New York City in his 1932 *Some Basic Statistics in Social Work*. Klein's 1938 "second" Pittsburgh survey was a comprehensive "needs" study.

Pressed by a heavy flow of applications from the early '20s, a significant increase in the student body was made possible by expansion of space available to the School in the COS building (105 East Twenty-second Street). The Russell Sage Foundation provided a library reading room. Then in 1931 the Foundation completed the building space constructed for it and the School moved across the street (122 East Twenty-second Street) to its own quarters. The next move was to be in 1949.

Lee's important "cause and function" paper at the 1929 National Conference of Social Work (Lee 1937) is evidence that the School leadership, observing the 1920s, wondered how social work could both retain a societal change commitment, as in the Progressive Era, and continue its progress as an established societal institution with standardized administrative and service delivery responsibilities.

The integration of the School's education program with others is exemplified by the fact that by the early 1930s, under defined circumstances, some New York School courses were credited at Columbia for M.S. degrees, as they had been from about the beginning; under defined circumstances some NYSSW courses were credited for half the requirements of an M.S. degree at the New York University School of Education; there was a 1925 cooperative arrangement with the Yale Divinity School for a student to earn a B.D. degree and a NYSSW diploma in three academic years, one of which was spent in

New York. From the fall quarter in 1925 there also was a cooperative arrangement with the then-existent Training School for Jewish Social Work. Students spent a full year at the New York School, preceded and followed by a summer at the Training School. The joint degree and related "major" arrangements which have been available since the 1970s and 1980s represent an update of these practices.

The New Deal and Its Aftermaths

Immediately available accounts do not document the role of School faculty and administration as the Great Depression deepened. Some public leaders and social welfare groups urged a larger public role in responding to the crisis. What is well documented, if not elaborated here, is major service by faculty members and administration in helping Washington, cities, counties, and states as they moved to implement both the federal emergency measures and the later provision of the Social Security Act, particularly the public assistance and child welfare titles (Bernstein et al. 1942:76–77). And, of course, Francis Perkins chaired the cabinet committee which prepared the Social Security recommendation for President Franklin Roosevelt, and Jane Hoey, awarded her diploma in 1916, was the major federal official charged with implementing the assistance provisions. It is therefore no surprise that the "social investigation" in public welfare came to resemble the COS case study — a practice not questioned at CUSSW until the income transfer discussions and changes of the late 1960s and 1970s.

On the curriculum side, public welfare appeared slowly, focusing on public–private roles; it was late in the 1930s (1936–37) before there was a full array of courses about the new programs and public welfare administration. One new course, called Government and Social Welfare, was the first required offering designed to acquaint all students with the new public safety net. Among the instructors were Robert Lansdale, subsequently the New York State welfare commissioner, and David Adie, who taught part-time while holding the commissioner post.

If the core curriculum was only gradually impacted, there being little expectation at the time of a larger movement of diploma graduates to these new public programs, there was a major in-service, part-time, evening-course effort to upgrade the large group of new civil servants who had been recruited to staff programs in New York and neighboring states.

But the nature of the change was increasingly appreciated and discussed. During most of the 1930s the School's *General Announcement* (hereafter *Bulletin*) devoted one issue each year to a report of that year's alumni conference. The May 18, 1933, conference dealt with Constructive Planning in Retrenchment. Communities were feeling the depression. The alumni issue of July 1934 featured a conference keynote by Ruth Taylor, commissioner of public welfare in Westchester County, who made her message clear: "I am speaking of *permanent* public welfare developments" (emphasis added). The October 1935 *Bulletin* carried a report of M. Antoinette Cannon's year of leave working for the Texas Relief Commission: "An Experiment in Providing Instruction for Relief Workers." The July 1937 alumni conference report is one of the few indicators, apart from the publication by the School of Fisher's book, that the social work radical "rank and file" movement (Fisher 1936) was being heard at the New York School. The workshop topics were as follows: workers' education in the Works Progress Administration, social change and social casework, group work, government responsibility for social welfare, and social action.

The intellectual ferment created in casework by its new role in public welfare and the new worker-client-agency configuration is covered by others in this volume — including the diagnostic-functional schism, in which the New York School carried the diagnostic view lead. Gordon Hamilton's (1940) *Theory and Practice of Social Case Work* confronts the application of the casework method as it had been developed during the 1930s to the new social welfare world. It became the leading text for its era.

The New Deal changed the School in other ways as well. The Federal Emergency Relief Administration (FERA) financed a considerable expansion of social work education to meet the needs of the new programs. Registration at all schools peaked in the fall of 1934. The New York School grew. Moreover, a process under way for some years was much accelerated: the gradual change of the social class composition of the student body to include more from lower middle class and working class backgrounds, and more males. This process was reinforced immediately after World War II as well.

Finally, shortly after Porter Lee's death, Walter Pettit, the director, completed the long-explored process of affiliation with Columbia. The inheritance of the 1890s had never fully disappeared, but by then the AASSW had decreed that all new members had to have university affiliation. New York had been "grandfathered" in. As of October 6, 1940, the School became formally affiliated with Columbia University. Thereafter (and for some people retroactively), the M.S. degree took the place of the diploma. The University Council (on which there was now School representation) assumed jurisdiction over the School's course of study. Two Columbia professors joined the council. Columbia's president became ex officio president of the School. But all of this was continuous with the past. The School had long listed itself as "conducted by the Charity Organization Society of New York." Now it was the NYSSW "of the Community Service Society of New York," the COS having joined with AICP to create the CSS.

The War Years and the 1950s

The *General Announcement* for 1942–43 states that "the faculty is engrossed with considerations affecting the responsibility of the profession with respect to the War" and will "strive to maintain standards." Individual faculty members and students took on war-related assignments, again a subject requiring fuller documentation. The School protected the integrity of the two-year program while implementing a special program for workers with war leaves. The "community organization" faculty was involved in the needed social service developments in war-impacted communities. Dr. Marion Kenworthy, in her role as consultant to the surgeon general of the United States, was influential in the development of a special classification for military social work, something that had been developed by the field of psychology in World War I. Further, her extensive correspondence with her former students, now in the military, offered very effective stimulation and support as these students developed, tested, and taught the new social work roles in several branches of the military (Maas 1951).

Leiby (1978:352) interprets the professionalization of the 1950s as resuming a process diverted by the New Deal and the war. Certainly this was the case at the New York School.

The new faculty cohort of the late 1940s and the 1950s was proportionately more male and had more doctoral-level trained people than earlier cohorts, as well as people with training and experience in military social work, Veterans' Administration psychiatric programs, child guidance, research, and social science. Welcomed by their senior colleagues—leaders of the development of earlier decades, many of them giants in the field—the new arrivals participated in a series of curriculum development and curriculum change processes which shaped the subsequent decades. If the Progressive

Era, the Great Depression, the New Deal, and the war years were periods of change and ferment, the 1920s (as already suggested) and the 1950s were periods of curriculum and practice development and education advancement. The School concentrated on improving and enriching itself and, in the process, had major impacts on social work and social work education. Here the occasion permits only a summary listing:

- The evolution of the generic concept. The core message of the Milford Conference about casework was extended to cover all of social work. While casework, group work, and community organization had their differences, these were less important than the knowledge, values, and elements of methods which they shared. The curriculum did not have to be developed through parallel but completely separated fields of practice: medical social work, school social work, psychiatric social work, child welfare, family social work, or even group work and community organization. Rather, students would learn about generic methods and processes, about the profession's history and value orientation. A core of behavioral, social science, research, and social policy knowledge could be taught for all students. The specialized "field" courses would be few—and there would be electives. The generic "premises" did not of course wipe out "fields." Psychiatric social work in fact received an important boost as an élite choice as fellowship funding from the 1946 Mental Health Act reached the School. On a smaller scale, child welfare training funds and, later, special initiatives in probation-parole-police-institutional care with children were also important and recognized in the 1950s and 1960s.

  Of course this could not be worked out and taught all at once. Details of developments from the late '40s to the early '60s appear in other essays in this volume. The profession's complete adoption of this perspective— there having been initiatives in several places—came in the "Working Definition of Social Work Practice" (Bartlett 1970).

- The rethinking of the behavioral and social science base. The elaborated prewar psychiatric sequence had been aimed at "psychiatric social workers," but the generic orientation now called for basic psychodynamic understanding by all students. The fundamental courses (Growth and Development and Psychopathology) were now shared by all and were part of a cluster of requirements that included "medical" and sociocultural foundations.

- The enrichment of the social science base along the lines of a widely used text edited by Herman Stein and Richard Cloward (1958) and concerned with family structures and ethnic patterns, social roles, values, social stratification, deviance, and bureaucratic structure. This drawing upon social and behavioral science represented (as put by Gordon Hamilton in her foreword) an attempt to strengthen the hand of the practitioner in the course of study, diagnosis, and treatment. It built upon the precedents of Mary Hurlbutt, who had brought her understanding of ethnicity, strengthened by work with immigrants and refugees, into course work on cultural elements in practice. It was a major departure from the role of social science in the "reform" aspects of curriculum at the turn of the century. Now social science enriched understanding of and direct work with clients. A sequence of faculty seminars and a special project with field supervisors, led by Stein, were part of a systematic and successful curriculum reform (Berengarten 1992).

- Following the faculty curriculum revision in the late '40s, there was perceived need to move further. A general curriculum review, financed by the Carnegie Corporation and led initially by Gordon Hamilton, was the occasion for a thorough review of the behavioral and social science components of the curriculum, the research, the social policy, and the basic training for the methods. After Hamilton's retirement in 1958, Stein became the study director and wrote its final report (Stein 1960). The work of the '50s had been systematized and integrated.

This also was an era in which doctoral training came to the School. It was long discussed. The major faculty members in several relevant fields constituted a formidable core. Eveline M. Burns, who came to the School in 1946, was already known and respected in School and University. In July 1943, she talked to the Alumni Conference about "Security, Work, and Relief Policies," the major economic and social planning report for which she had taken the lead at the (short-lived) National Resources Planning Board. Her Social Security assignments had been highly respected. Once on the faculty, Burns was assigned the lead in the exploration and negotiation of a doctor of social welfare degree. The course of study was designed to parallel the Ph.D. requirements and the specifics were negotiated with the executive committee of that faculty. Moreover, Arts and Sciences was built into the educational, examination, and dissertation process. However, the social work faculty decided that a Doctor of Social Welfare (D.S.W.) would do more for the status of social work than a Ph.D. The permission to develop a program was given in 1946, implemented in 1950, and the first degree was awarded in 1952. Eight social work schools already offered the doctorate at the time. After a slow start, the program hit its degree-granting pace in 1959–60 and was soon awarding half the social work doctorates in the country. Its graduates became influential faculty members and deans in leading schools. The scale of influence changed only as, in subsequent decades, many schools began to offer doctorates and the numbers grew substantially. Almost fifty years after the degree's inception, a shift was made to the Ph.D., with little curriculum change, because of the importance of a standard degree in the academic culture and the alleged competitive disadvantage which has evolved for the D.S.W.

But for the 1950s and 1960s, the doctoral program led to a much closer School relationship with the University than ever. Students and faculty were exposed to the considerable social science ferment at Columbia, especially in sociology. This was no small factor in some of the developments already described.

The Russell Sage Foundation (RSF) also made a major contribution to the doctoral program. The RSF had been important to the School from the beginning, setting up the 1906 research center as well as taking on the original Pittsburgh survey. It had also provided a reading room and then a building and its library to the School in the 1930s. All along, the RSF had enriched the program by making its many staff specialists in labor, surveys, charity organization, and many other fields available as lecturers and teachers. In 1956, as part of a broader program intended to bring together the social professions and the social sciences in mutually beneficial interaction, the Foundation funded the recruitment of several social scientists, as well as funding doctoral fellowship programs, at both the New York School and the Michigan School of Social Work. This program brought to the New York School, for various periods, Lloyd Ohlin, criminologist and collaborator with Richard Cloward in the '60s; James Bieri, clinical psychologist; Robert Bush, statistician; Eugene Litwak and Lee Wiggins, sociologists; and Katherine Spencer, the anthropologist who was important to Stein's work. The RSF also provided the fellowships to Howard Polsky, Hope Leichter (Teachers College), and Otto Pollack (Jewish Board of Guardians), whose important work helped stimulate the entire social science development and encourage the integration of behavioral and social science and the attention to a wider range of personality theories than had been the case earlier.

During this period, the "research center" joined class and field as a major program vehicle at the School. I have already mentioned the initial 1907–1912 effort funded by Russell Sage, but it did not continue. Several faculty members had significant projects in the periods before and after World War I, especially Kate Claghorn, long the sole full-time research instructor, and Philip Klein, a 1913 graduate who joined the faculty in 1927. Another five-year effort under a research department headed by Klein continued from 1927 to 1932 and carried out several explorations designed to build knowledge for use in the curriculum (Bernstein et al. 1942:104 ff.). Klein also served as research director for the White House Conference on Children, 1939–1940. Now, in the '50s, a new initiative heralded the School's changed relationship to the University and its commitment to scholarship on a par with that of academic social science departments. The process began in the fall of 1956, when an anonymous donor made the first two grants to create a research center. The fund ensured the infrastructure for eight years, but the program was to be project driven. Through a series of projects and a number of leading faculty members as directors, the center developed a strong record. It facilitated financing, implementation, and access to the education program projects over a wide range of topics. For example, the report to the dean of 1960–61 listed eleven projects under way, or about to begin, funded by a diversity of sources, each autonomous with its own director. The center also played a role as a training base for M.S.W. and D.S.W. students.

In the '60s, the center was renamed the Center for Research and Demonstration, as a series of demonstrations was added to the research mission (the Experimental Welfare Center and the Bird S. Coler demonstration of a medical social service program in a hospital for the chronically ill). The Center continued to play its umbrella facilitating role until superseded by a series of autonomous centers which continued to keep the School in the forefront of several areas of research and demonstrations.

Under the direction of Sidney Berengarten and with the sponsorship of Marion Kenworthy, the School was the site from 1947 to 1954 of the Pilot Study on Selection of Students. A series of three interviews was conducted with each applicant in an effort to identify the presence of "personality equipment . . . suited to professional growth and the assimilation of theory and technique." Project staff felt that they had learned a good deal and there was sharing with other schools and, eventually, the creation of a national roster of interviewers. The approach was eventually dropped in view of changed admission requirements and recruitment policy (Berengarten 1987).

A full record of the School's social service and income security commitments and aspirations in the 1950s is reported in *National Policies for Education, Health, and Social Services* (Russell 1955), the record of a Columbia Bicentennial Conference for which the School assembled an impressive roster of U.S. and international scholars and public officials. The proposals are "liberal" in the New Deal sense (pro-Welfare State) and carry a view of social work continuous with the broad conceptions of 1898. Nathan Cohen's summary concludes that the social worker must not only be skillful in the diagnosis and treatment of the individual and group problems met in day-to-day practice, but also must be able to speak with knowledge and understanding of the wider social issues involved and the possible courses of action and development for society as a whole (Russell 1955:240).

The '50s, then, was a period of academic progress, integration into the University community and—fittingly—in 1950 the full separation from the Community Service Society and the receipt (1951) of a charter from the New York State Board of Regents. In 1959 the School entered the Columbia Corporation and transferred its endowment and some component of autonomy. For several years thereafter it was known as "The New York School of Social Work of Columbia University." In 1962 it was renamed as the "Columbia University School of Social Work." The '50s had positioned it for the Great Society.

The War on Poverty and the Great Society

The '60s was a period of major cultural transformation and a social policy watershed (Chalmers 1991; *Journal of Policy History* 1996). The changes began with John F. Kennedy and continued through the first Nixon term. The School's closest prior association with political activism after the Progressive Era had been the involvement of some of its faculty and alumni with the social work "rank and file" movement of the depression years and the radical social work unionism before World War II. Now there was awareness and some support of the increasingly militant civil rights movement, then the Poor People's movement, and finally the anti-Vietnam War protests of the decade.

The School's first policy response to the Kennedy Administration was a project supported by the Marshall Field Foundation, the results of which were eventually published under the title *Public Welfare: Time for Change* (Wickenden and Bell 1961). At a time of attacks on Aid to Dependent Children (ADC) as encouraging illegitimacy and malingering, the project probed many of the debated aspects of public assistance policy and developed recommendations for major reform. Its report contributed to the case for what became the 1962 Amendments to the Social Security Act, converting Aid to Dependent Children to Aid to *Families* with Dependent Children and increasing funding for public welfare services.

This effort—a policy-analytic and program development strategy—was characteristic of Burns's earlier work and of subsequent policy efforts by faculty. The War on Poverty generated a quite different process. Here, the School's greatest influence was in helping to shape the War on Poverty's program strategy—community action—which in turn supported considerable militant action with regard to welfare, education, health, housing, and the other systems critical to poor people. This is not the place for detail, but I note the national influence of the Mobilization for Youth (MFY) program, a research/demonstration effort in delinquency, which eventually developed into a prototype for the War on Poverty community action program. The MFY legal services program, later freestanding, also had enormous national impact. Other related projects were located at the School—Peace Corps and Vista training, especially. Out of these activities came a new model for community organization—a shift to grass-roots organizing and "cause-directed advocacy," away from the citizen enabling, consensus building, and local community planning that had characterized traditional social work community organization (Kahn 1960). The School leadership for these programs (Richard Cloward, Francis Piven, George Brager, James Hackshaw, Mitchell Ginsberg) made major marks on national developments. One spin-off from the Peace Corps training experience was a several-year exchange relationship between CUSSW and the social work schools of Colombia, South America.

The rapid changes and institutional realignments of the era led the School into other experiments and evaluations: an experimental welfare center in the Bronx and responsibility for operation of a medical social service program in a hospital for the chronically ill (Bird S. Coler) and at the Harlem Hospital Center. These projects had both program developmental and training facets. The welfare center and Bird S. Coler program were discontinued after several years: "insurmountable administrative complexities" led to the reconsideration. The Harlem program was later cut back and modified.

In terms of faculty involvement in the wider sphere of Great Society initiatives, they tended to be monitors of developments and sometimes, either individually or in their various associations, participants in the policy debates; but they were not shapers of the new social provision and safety nets: civil rights, voting rights, Medicare, Medicaid, the Elementary and Secondary Education Act, the Higher Education Act, food stamps, Model Cities, the Older Americans Act, and (later) the indexing of Social Security and the development of the Supplemental Security Income program. Nonetheless, these developments of the Great Society—the monumental series of social legislation initiatives which constituted the third stage in the shaping of the American Welfare State after the Progressive Era and the New Deal—were rapidly incorporated into social policy teaching, and students were helped to understand the new commitments of the society and the new opportunities and rights of their clients.

The activist environment of the Great Society, especially as the war protest phase accelerated, inevitably made educational institutions, defined as part of the "establishment," targets of their students as well. After a series of campus confrontations in the spring of 1968 and a one-week class strike, social work faculty and students negotiated a series of agreements involving "sharply increased student participation in the policy-making bodies of the School, an acceleration of the recruitment of minority students and faculty members, and curriculum innovations" (Berengarten 1967–1969:1).

By the fall of 1968 there were courses in black and Puerto Rican culture. A massive recruitment effort over the next period expanded very substantially minority representation in the student body. The governance reform took a bit longer but gave the student organization a significant role which persists after thirty years. (Similar reforms have been phased out over the years in many other faculties.) In addition, a series of task forces developed recommendations in all areas of curriculum which reflected the new policy context and cultural milieu of the late 1960s (Berengarten 1967–1969:1).

The School's internal program did not give up its long-range continuities, however. For example: a large grant from the U.S. Children's Bureau in mid-1964 led to the establishment of the Child Welfare Research Project, initially led by David Fanshel, to conduct a major developmental study of foster care, but then to carry out a series of separately funded studies and spin-off studies involving Fanshel, Shirley Jenkins, and a group of outstanding child welfare researchers whom they recruited. Continuing a tradition that went back to Henry Thurston in the 1920s and continued with Leontine Young, Elizabeth Meier, Carol Meyer, Brenda McGowan, and Mary Goldson, this work had a major impact on child welfare policy, practice, and training.

The expanded and more rigorous practice research of the late 1950s continued and was extraordinarily productive in the 1960s. At the center of this development were Florence Hollis and a number of Columbia doctoral graduates who worked both at Columbia and elsewhere. There was renewed support for the social work clinician-researcher role and for more eclectic practice models (Berengarten 1993).

Among the other curriculum developments of the '60s was the transition in the concept of policy training in the M.S. program, which progressed from "Government and Social Welfare" to "Social Policy and Social Welfare."

The 1970s

If we think of the Great Society as extending through the Nixon first term, a notion justified by the policy developments and the scale of public social welfare expenditure, the '70s was a brief period—Nixon's second term, including Gerald Ford's administration, and the Carter years. Yet for the School, as for social welfare generally and social work education, these were busy years. The work of the '60s, realigning social work and social work education with new programs and ideologies, continued, and there was no sharp delineation from the earlier era.

Although the Center for Research and Development remained as a token overhead structure, a process begun in the '60s was accelerated: now externally funded discrete specialized programs, centers, or projects covered a wide range of fields and missions, and several positioned the School in a leadership role in the United States or sometimes internationally—and often beyond the social work profession itself. While its educational functions of course continued as the School's central mission, several of these programs became major components of the institution, consistent with its role in social welfare. Space constraints permit only a one-time roster here, not including faculty leadership or those who joined the School in connection with these activities. The School's *Bulletin* for 1979–80 provides one such convenient listing. A more recent illustration is included subsequently:

Aging project;
Adoption training project;
Drug use projects;
Cross-National Studies (of social service systems and family policy);*
Industrial Social Welfare Center;*
Working mothers' research project.

Several were time-limited projects. The two marked with (*) remained active in the '90s as their developing programs received renewed and new funding. The Industrial Social Welfare Center, focused on the world of work, created widespread interest and became the center of a national development in schools of social work, reviving a social work practice field which had closed down during the New Deal. The Cross-National Studies program was in a visible leadership role here and in Europe in clarifying and creating interest in comparative family policy.

The community organization concentration, propelled by the MFY experience, had shifted to training for activist organizing and advocacy in the 1970s. It was a program concentration at the School early in the '70s. However, by the late '70s, paid jobs for graduates of the concentration had dwindled. Grass-roots leaders and participants had taken over the role. As mentioned earlier, the group work concentration had been combined with casework in a direct practice sequence, as practice teachers learned from their experience that "caseworkers" often had to work with families as a whole as well as other types of groups.

The agency realignments and new student interests led to a further curricular reconceptualization of methods in the mid-1970s. The academic year 1974–75 saw a transition to a system of three concentrations:

1. "[the] study of concepts, principles, and methods of social casework, social group work, and community organizing which are essential to provision of social services to individuals, families and groups";

2. "concepts, principles, and methods applicable to community organizing, program and social policy development, . . . coordination and administration";

3. "for the student who seeks a professional research career in social work."

At the same time, the "advanced standing" (after undergraduate social work study) and "reduced residency" (experienced social workers and those with degrees in related fields) statuses were recognized.

Within a year or two a sharper distinction was needed between those who wanted intensive clinical experience (1), those essentially headed to careers in planning or administration (2), and those people who wished to be generalists in basic direct service and program development (3). The option for research majors remained. These distinctions persist—with an even sharper focus in concentration 1 on clinical practice.

Especially interesting, the mid-1940s stress on generalist training after an era of full specialization in course sequences by field of practice was now once again reversed. Electives apart, students were now required to select a field of practice platform course and a field-of-practice-related methods course as a degree requirement. This development was generated by the demands of employing agencies and the proliferation of "fields," as a consequence of the expanding number of categorical service programs developed as part of the Great Society expansions and by subsequent congressional action from the '70s on (to today). Moreover, faculty had come to believe that generic theory must also include a "theory of practice specifics," e.g., a theory of how abstract, general notions are applied to real programs and service systems (Kahn 1965; Kamerman 1995).

The Field of Practice/Social Problem Area listing in the 1979–1980 *Bulletin* (18) serves to illustrate. (The most recent of the periodic updatings appears subsequently.)

Health and mental health (including mental retardation);
Family and children's services;
Aging;
Corrections and court services;
Drug addiction and alcoholism;
Industrial social welfare;
Education.

By far, the first two covered the majority of the students. It was generally understood that unless "mental health" meant only psychiatric programs, it could be applied as well to many programs in the other "fields," but the internal alignments among faculty and growing practice in the field made the designation a convenience—if a bit ambiguous.

An evolution in practice theory and in the relationship of that theory to behavioral science had begun at the School in the late '50s and was to reshape the 1970s and 1980s (see chapter 3, this volume). What it meant to the School, among other things, was more diverse recruitment, valuable internal debates about "models" and "paradigms," broader offerings to students, and great richness in the range of externally funded research (Mailick 1998).

Those elements of School ideology and value systems which were reflected in the '40s and '50s in strong commitment to humane and effective *public* social services and to a strong social work presence in *public* programs were not supportive of the spreading private practice (largely of casework counseling and treatment). There also was the opposition that grew out of conviction that social work should not give up its commitment to institution-based group practice and a tradition of accountable supervision. This did not change when the professional association, NASW, dropped its opposition and created a vehicle for private practitioner interchange in the late 1960s. Thus throughout the 1970s, despite evidence of growing private practice of social work nationally and even among our graduates, there was no place in the School curriculum in which either related practical or ethical issues were discussed — a kind of pluralistic ignorance. Indeed, leading members of the faculty often expressed disapproval and doctoral applicants for the advanced practice sequence did not list private practice as a professional objective. It was well into the 1980s before the overwhelming reality had its impact. NASW's newspaper was actively reporting all that the association was doing to protect the "third-party payments" status of private practitioner social workers. Going well beyond direct treatment, private free-standing practitioners were offering many other services (advice, consultation, contact-reports about one's elderly parents in other states, Alzheimer day groups, etc.). There is now present in all conversation at the School a realistic sense of the role of private practice in student plans and career pathways, but the curriculum is not explicitly impacted, nor has there been a decision that it should be. Unlike some social work doctoral programs, Columbia's does not prepare for the direct service (psychotherapeutic) practitioner role; its emphasis is on the scholar-researcher of direct practice, on the teacher, sometimes on the administrator. The privatization initiatives of the Reagan-Bush years placed the entire private practice development in national context but — as of the late '90s — it is yet to be dealt with at CUSSW explicitly.

On the other hand, the events of the late '60s and early '70s had created strong conviction about multidisciplinary practice, and the delivery systems were elaborating new roles and new forms of teamwork. A joint degree program for M.S. students with Columbia's Graduate School of Business was introduced in the autumn of 1974. Within a short time there were rules, procedures, and programs for either dual degrees or "minors" with the Division of

Urban Planning in the School of Architecture, the Jewish Theological Seminary, the School of Public Health (1979–80), Union Theological Seminary (1981–82), Columbia School of International and Public Affairs (policy analysis), the Special Education program at Bank Street College (1982–84), and the Columbia School of Law (1987–89). These arrangements, although developed de novo, recall the tradition of the first decade with Columbia University and the programs of the 1920s with Yale Divinity, N.Y.U. School of Education, and the Training School for Jewish Social Work.

In all these matters, as in the expansion of the behavioral and social science framework employed at the School, there was much play for faculty, administration, student, and alumni discussion and initiative. Very little stood still. Yet one also could discern a new note: while the School always had taken seriously and prepared appropriately for periodic reaccreditation from the Council on Social Work Education or its predecessor, there had never been any doubt about initiatives and program variations "not yet visible" elsewhere. The School was one of a group of leading schools at the cutting edge. It was followed, seldom led. However, action by the NASW in the late 1970s to accept graduates with undergraduate degrees as full members and the subsequent decision of the CSWE to admit and accredit undergraduate social work programs—all in the context of a voluntary "affirmative action" initiative in the early '70s—led to a major power shift in CSWE. Soon there were many more undergraduates than graduate members, and the by-laws and accreditation standards and procedures reflected concern with the undergraduate schools' definition of their missions and their preferred mandates for the graduate curriculum. This too brief and obviously debatable characterization of the process is offered only as a possible explanation of the fact that the CSWE has also become an inhibitant and has, for the first time in this long history, imposed curriculum requirements on a School which by virtue of its leadership has always been ipso facto in compliance. Other leading graduate schools have also shared this experience, but the graduate deans' group cannot respond adequately since too many of them also operate undergraduate programs. (In these too brief and debatable comments, I speak of course only for myself.)

The Reagan-Bush Years

As already suggested, many of the research and curriculum developments of the '70s continued into the 1980s and indeed into the 1990s. But now there were new problems and challenges for social work and social welfare as American society faced its first systematic effort to dismantle or cut back some of the social programs of the Great Society and the New Deal. Following passage of the Omnibus Budget Reconciliation Act of 1981 (OBRA 1981), social workers had reasons for concern about the well-being of clients dependent on public assistance programs (especially Aid to Families with Dependent Children, food stamps, and child nutrition), and social welfare agencies needed to master what came to be known as "cut-back" management.

Little was or could be done to stop OBRA 1981, given the political dynamics of the time, but CUSSW was one of several social work schools at which some faculty teams undertook research to learn what the changes in AFDC eligibility rules about work and the major decrease in AFDC work incentives did to clients. Subsequent reports from these studies heightened public concern and may have contributed to the series of minor adjustments legislated in several subsequent years. No large attacks on social programs succeeded in Washington after the 1982 election, but there was need for constant vigilance. Moreover, it soon became clear that a Congress constrained in social expenditures nonetheless could not ignore the public concern with child neglect and abuse, runaways, drugs, HIV/AIDS, domestic violence, homelessness, and the needs of the frail elderly. Bipartisan congressional action went where the president did not lead, and a large number of relatively small categorical service programs were enacted.

In all of this, the CUSSW dean, Mitchell Ginsberg, who was in a major leadership role in several national social work associations, together with several CUSSW faculty members, was active in various advocacy capacities, in congressional testimony, and in contributing to program development. The CUSSW presence was visible in the long campaign for child care legislation that came to fruition in the early '90s and in the truncated parental leave legislation twice vetoed by President Bush and finally signed by President Clinton.

Not an official activity of the School, but housed here and directed by Professor Richard Cloward, the organization Human Serve (in a sense a derivation from MFY but pursuing a new policy tack) conducted a voter registration campaign in the '80s, calling on voters to protect their social entitlements. Later, the motor-voter tactic was adopted by Human Serve, an effort to let people register to vote as they went to public offices to do other business (renew licenses, apply for public assistance). The federal legislation initiated out of this CUSSW activity was finally passed during the Clinton presidency.

Significant numbers of new voters have been registered: any impact on actual voting or on patterns of voting will now be observed.

The Adoption Assistance Act of 1980, passed at the end of the Carter years, gave legal status and resources for the "permanency" commitment in child welfare. Several of the studies which had come out of the CUSSW child welfare research were cited in the hearings and advocacy materials. This legislation was protected against an effort to "block grant" it in 1981, but it was underfunded and not adequately implemented by a constrained bureaucracy. In New York, a strong CUSSW child welfare faculty in various consultation, advocacy, and training roles helped public and private child welfare agencies move in the directions called for by the federal law and earlier state legislation.

None of this is intended to exaggerate: the *major* social legislation of the era was fought over and shaped by interest groups, lobbyists, and officials —with a not-very-influential presence of social work associations—and CUSSW was essentially observer, analyst, and instructor. I refer to the Social Security reforms of 1983, the tax reforms of 1986, the McKinney Homeless Act of 1987, and even the Family Support Act of 1988, as well as—during the Bush years—the Americans with Disabilities Act and improved housing funding.

But within the M.S. and doctoral programs, the policy developments were followed, analyzed, and taught. Further, the field of practice foundation courses and new specialized electives integrated the new programs and information into practice as taught. The method concentrations, as revised in the '70s, were made more realistic with experience and were described by the early '80s as follows: clinical social work practice; practice, programming, and supervision; social administration; and social research. Students from all concentrations share the two first direct-practice courses and are required to complete (single) courses in research, personality development, social science, social policy, and a field of practice. All else is elective.

In the mid-'80s, the school established an educational site at SUNY/Purchase to provide improved access for courses and fieldwork to students who reside north of the City in Westchester and Rockland counties and in Connecticut. The program has attracted highly qualified applicants and has been very popular. Also, in the late '80s, the School increased its flexibility and competitiveness by offering applicants an opportunity to complete degree requirements in a combined full- and part-time program over three or four years.

The pattern of research and demonstration activities, several very productive of research with obvious impact nationally and internationally, continued. A 1984–1987 listing included the following: the Brookdale Institute of Aging and Human Development, Columbia Community Services (a homelessness project), the Cross-National Studies Research program, the Industrial Social Welfare Center, the Child Welfare Training Project, Cognitive Behavioral Interventions for Child-Abusing Parents, the Maternal and Child Health Training Project, and the Westchester Department of Social Services Training Project. Beyond this, a large number of faculty members were involved in research related to their special competence—so that faculty names appeared regularly in the field's journals. The range of personality theories, social science orientations, and practice expertise in the faculty had continued to expand in the '80s, and with the arrival of Professors Steven Schinke and Robert E. Schilling in the late '80s, the School was the site of extensive behavioral studies research. At the same time, faculty-authored practice texts reflecting older and newer psychodynamic and "person-in-situation" traditions continued to appear and to have wide influence.

Before the review of the Clinton years and the concluding notes, the reader may find the perspective offered by numbers and lists in appendix 1C helpful.

The Clinton Years

From the point of view of training for practice and research and demonstration, much of the '90s, after the Bush administration, has been continuous with the '80s, but one or two highlights are especially relevant.

The School had never had a fully endowed chair. Efforts to create chairs in honor of some of the faculty giants of the past—Eduard Lindeman, Gordon Hamilton, Eveline Burns—had not been successful. The money raised was well used, but for other purposes. A chair in honor of Marion Kenworthy was only partly funded—until the '90s. A Brookdale chair in gerontology was financed for a limited time, but not endowed. Then came the present dean, Ronald Feldman: researcher, educator, social work leader, and (apparently even to his own surprise) expert fund-raiser. We now have ten endowed chairs, making a major contribution to the budget, faculty stability, and the substantive mission of the School. (Is a new building far behind?) Endowed scholarships, tight budget discipline, and successful alumni annual campaigns have added up to create an endowment of approximately $50 million (a five-fold increase in thirteen years) and a budget in the black—a comfortable situation for budgetary relations with the University.

A word about student and faculty diversity. CUSSW has had a strong record in African American and Puerto Rican student recruitment and a productive project for cooperation with historically black colleges since the commitments of 1968. Increasingly, however, the patterns of immigration and international recruitment have shifted in the direction of Asians and other Hispanics as well (foreign students, native born, new immigrants). The School educates a very diverse student body (now almost 35 percent "minority"), and the faculty is itself far more diverse than its predecessors. In the '60s and '70s the emphasis was on African Americans and Puerto Ricans. By the early '90s, the minority faculty was far more diverse. The author reviewed the 1997 and 1998 summer faculty and doctoral degree recipients and could only marvel at how "normal" developments have implemented the "diversity" theme of the past decade in our professional culture.

One result of all this has been some addition to the field of practice options in the M.S. program. In the current catalogue the list includes all those covered previously (with "Disabilities" added to Health and Mental Health), but also Contemporary Social Problems (homelessness, violence, and substance abuse) and International Social Welfare (including services to immigrants and refugees). School social work, which has come and gone in the past, has been reestablished.

Retirements and deaths have resulted in major faculty turnover from the mid-1980s, as the post–World War II faculty generation has gradually receded in size and a new, younger generation of faculty members has taken over their many roles and now is in the majority. Whether one judges by formal credentials or student-assessed classroom performance, by practice initiatives and innovation or published research, the "newcomers" are outstanding. The hundred-year tradition is in good hands. One is impressed with the richness, among other things, of practice elective course offerings. Where once the School was "diagnostic," in the Freudian tradition, courses now cover a diversity of practice models: psychosocial, cognitive-behavioral, life model, task centered, crisis intervention, and problem solving (Mailick 1998).

At the end of the 1980s, the Center for the Study of Social Work Practice was established and endowed at the School as a joint activity with the Jewish Board of Family and Children's Services, a high-quality multifaceted clinical setting which has long been a center for training and collaboration with the School. The founding director was Professor Shirley Jenkins, who was succeeded after her death by Professor Edward J. Mullen. In the tradition of clinical and casework research, the Center facilitates research collaboration by academics and practitioners, sponsors strategic national conferences, funds pilot research initiatives, conducts research, and publishes reports and newsletters.

Illustrative of the practice and practice–research diversity at the School is the work of the Robert Schilling–Nabila El-Bassel Social Intervention Group (SIG), a team of fifty funded by large federal research initiatives which has the goal of "inventing interventions" to cope with the most difficult of social problems and, ultimately, to test such interventions through clinical trials. It undertakes to work with people not in formal agency settings. The research plans call for a series of well-ordered steps, each with rigorous requirements, and for building on what goes before. The work is multidisciplinary in conceptualization and implementation, and like most other of the many faculty-directed studies at the School, offers opportunities for practitioners as well as assistantships and jobs for doctoral students.

The pioneers of 1898, or 1904, or 1911 (perhaps even 1950!) would not have conceived of a school in which faculty members in all specialities have doctorates and carry out research. They worked with a few research "specialists." This pattern began to change in the 1950s. In the last dozen years, funded research at the School has increased ten-fold over what was already a good base. What was in 1898 a School to teach the "practical" has also over the hundred years become a center that values and teaches scholarship while constantly improving the teaching of practice theory and how to practice. Ranking systems for schools are controversial, but if one attends not to the suspect "reputational" measures and looks at the objective ones (faculty citations in the indexes, per capita faculty publications in refereed journals, doctoral graduates and their publications), CUSSW has been first over the last four years in all but one ranking, where it was second (and where a case can be made that that, too, should be read as a first).

When the Republican Party took control of the Congress in 1994 and proposed to implement their "Contract with America," to which a large number of their members in the House of Representatives were committed, it generated protests, letters, testimony, and other expressions of sentiment. A faculty–student coalition at Columbia was active and instigated action elsewhere. Faculty members played important roles in various conferences and meetings. A letter from three professors at CUSSW was read by a New York senator during the debate. None of this stopped the basic "welfare reform" legislation, as revised to avoid a presidential veto, but it was part of a national reaction that for the time stopped a series of related initiatives. The social policy faculty had been strongly augmented in recent years by replacements for retired and deceased members as part of a general succession process at the School in the '90s—and almost all were or soon became engaged in research on the impacts of the legislative and budgetary actions, spillover effects, child welfare spillovers, and work-family issues.

In the meantime the Cross-National Studies Program received major funding from two foundations for an effort developed under the title "Confronting the Politics of Child and Family Policy." One component involved six expert consultation/miniconferences over an eighteen-month period to clarify options for states and the major national voluntary organizations in dealing with the results of P.L. 104–193. Six reports out of the work had wide national circulation. The other component was a multicity round table with thirty to thirty-five members that over a two-year period clarified issues created for the big cities, conducted six big-city case studies, and developed the content for a widely disseminated volume, *Big Cities in the Welfare Transition* (Kahn and Kamerman 1998).

In another initiative, two members of the social policy faculty, Irwin Garfinkel and Marcia Meyers, completed a simulation study on the potential impact of the federal legislation in New York, and circulated it—to wide publicity—at a time when it could influence the New York State plan.

None of this is mentioned to exaggerate impacts, most of which are unknown, but it does illustrate the relatedness of faculty research and teaching to the shifting social welfare scene and the continuity of a tradition that developed in the School's first decade: one cannot work with a child, family, or group without constant awareness of setting, resources, availability of services, and without a willingness to strive to be sure that these are in place.

It is not that the entire agenda always has attention. Much of the faculty research involves "basic" knowledge development with a strong social science component: some is policy related and directly "applied." Since the Reagan administration there have been devolution initiatives (the new or the newest federalism) as well as encouragement to privatization. The legislation of the Clinton years offers more opportunities to the "for profit" sector. Managed care is being explored and experimented with in child welfare. There are varied interests within the profession (NASW is expected to protect its members who wish to be properly treated as providers by managed care companies), in the local social service communities (nonprofit agencies require public funding of the bulk of their budgets), and in some fields (the desire to encourage employer or union employee assistance programs or day care). These are all visible topics; some appear on CUSSW research and action agendas. The private practice debate of the '60s has not had a full CUSSW response—but clearly a larger framework will be needed—or at the least some faculty members will need to develop, analyze, and debate, thereby encouraging student understanding.

It will be recalled that the School has had a relationship with Columbia University from the beginning. Columbia faculty were among the early lecturers in the summer school of 1898–1904 and the one-year courses of 1904–1911. Two of the early directors, Devine and Lindsay, had Columbia appointments. There were reciprocal arrangements for course attendance for Columbia and social work students. In the 1920s some social work courses were credited for a Columbia M.S. But it was in 1940, with the academic affiliation, that the current era began. In 1950 the School was separated from CSS and obtained a state charter in 1951. It joined the Columbia Corporation in 1959 and moved to the campus in 1970.

I have already discussed the importance of the doctoral program in facilitating fuller integration of the School with the University. As much should be said about participation from the 1950s, first in the University Council and then the senate—and the involvement of faculty members and administration in task forces and committees and projects, ranging from the publications committee of Columbia University Press, to the Human Subjects Review Committee, to the boards of the Bureau of Applied Social Research and its successor, the Social Science Center. Faculty members participate in the rich program of University seminars—and involve members of other faculties in seminars generated by our projects. Our Ph.D. students are active with and eligible for fellowships from an interdepartmental social policy consortium which we helped create. Our faculty members lecture in courses in other schools and departments and sometimes co-teach. The decision to award social work Ph.D.'s by the Graduate School of Arts and Sciences involves joint appointments for a significant number of social work faculty in that School. The new Child and Family Policy Institute, with the School in a central role, has joined many departments and university units in research, seminars, and joint educational efforts focused on young children and their families.

With all this has come accountability to Columbia standards and policies and—most important for faculty—integration into the University's procedures for the granting of tenure. In effect, the University's criteria and priorities with regard to research, teaching, professional ethics, and school/community service become the School's criteria too, unless variations can be negotiated. The rules and procedures have become increasingly important and have caused some tension and stress since University policy has its own dynamic and the School is but one unit. It is unnecessary to list the advantages of the School's affiliation with a great research university—but it also has a countable price. It is not the price that the School leadership worried about when it deferred university affiliation for more than four decades, however, for it has proven possible to balance the practical and the theoretical; the fieldwork and the lecture-technical courses in social work methods have been developed to a level that commands respect. Access to behavioral and social science and professional courses in other faculties is extraordinarily enriching. There is no longer any question about affiliation—nor has there been for fifty years—but understanding the price is part of understanding the School today.

CONCLUSION

In short, this is a centennial story of consolidation and integration after broad and even diffuse roles at the beginning; of definition and redefinition of core base and specialty as the experiences of the profession changed; and, then, with the watershed social policy developments of the Great Society, the many categorical—if fragmentary—initiatives vis-à-vis the social problems of the 1970s and 1980s, and the add-ons required by a changed accreditation process. If the long and complex lists of lectures and concerns of 1898 and 1904 seemed diffuse and—given what was to develop— occasionally misdirected, the *Bulletin* of 1997–98 also seems very complex, but not diffuse, offering increasingly specialized sequences (once again?), and it is very rich in the opportunities it offers individuals in the context of what has become a much more pluralistic occupation of direct services to individuals, programming and administration, and scholarly policy analysis. The distinctions between the "practical" and social science "theoretical" of the early decades do not apply to the faculty members in this professional school of the late 1990s and early twenty-first century. They practice and teach social work but are also sophisticated researchers, and behavioral-social scientists in the domains relevant to their concentrations.

As numbers go, "100" is an attractively round one, but in the history of a live, vital institution with an urgent mission and a record of leadership, it signifies only one of many milestones for what I have called "celebration and contemplation." Indeed we are early in a new era which may be summed up with the terms "economic globalization" and "the information revolution." Already under way internationally is a reexamination of social protection and social benefit systems and an updating of the personal social services. There is work to be done by social workers in all this. Fortunately there are faculty members and researchers here at CUSSW who understand this and who are prepared to act—as well as able students who are interested and committed.

The agenda must also include issues about privatization, practice through public funding and/or market mechanisms, the future relationship with an also changing university, full integration of the faculty-student-client diversity trends into our program—and some societal threats to the values that have represented a constant throughout our history. These matters I leave for future discussions.

APPENDIX 1A

Chronological Outline of the School

1898   The first training course in philanthropy is established under the auspices of the Charity Organization Society, 105 East 22nd Street. The Summer School in Philanthropic Work remains the primary source of training until 1904. Philip W. Ayres, Ph.D., is its Director. Robert W. de Forest is President of the Charity Organization Society and Chairman of the Committee on Philanthropic Education.

1904   Establishment of the New York School of Philanthropy is made possible through a grant from Mr. John S. Kennedy. Edward T. Devine, Ph.D., becomes its Director.

1905   Kennedy Lectureship is established.

1907   Samuel McCune Lindsay, Ph.D., is appointed Director of the School upon the resignation of Edward T. Devine, who continues as General Director of the Charity Organization Society, of which the School is a part.

        The Bureau of Social Research is established through a grant by the Russell Sage Foundation. It continues in operation until 1912.

1911   Initiation of the two-year program is made possible by an endowment of one million dollars from the will of John S. Kennedy.

1912   Dr. Lindsay resigns and Dr. Devine reassumes the directorship.

Source: Elizabeth G. Meier, *A History of the New York School of Social Work.* (New York: Columbia University Press, 1954), 141–142.

1917   Porter R. Lee is appointed Director upon the resignation of Edward T. Devine.

1919   New York School of Social Work becomes the new name of the institution.

            Porter R. Lee calls a meeting of representatives of the schools of social work which results in the formation of the Association of Training Schools for Professional Social Work.

1922   Establishment of the Bureau of Children's Guidance is effected through a grant from the Commonwealth Fund for a five-year program.

1926–27   Robert W. de Forest resigns as Chairman of the Committee of the School of Social Work. Mr. Samuel H. Fisher is appointed Chairman; Mr. Morris Hadley, Vice-Chairman.

1931   School moves to 122 East 22nd Street.

1939   Walter W. Pettit, Ph.D., is appointed Director of the School following the death of Porter R. Lee.

            The Charity Organization Society merges with the Association for Improving the Condition of the Poor.

1940   The School is affiliated with Columbia University as one of its graduate schools; the Master of Science degree is awarded.

1946   The degree of Doctor of Social Welfare is authorized by Columbia University.

1947   Miss Margaret Leal is appointed Acting Dean upon Dr. Pettit's retirement.

            The Hearn Social Action Award is established by Judge Murray Hearn and his wife Norma, to be awarded for outstanding contributions in social action.

1948   The 50th Anniversary celebration of the School and the 100th Anniversary of the Community Service Society are observed.

1949   Mr. Kenneth D. Johnson is appointed Dean; Miss Margaret Leal, Associate Dean.

The School moves to the former Carnegie residence, 2 East 91st Street.

1950   Mr. Frederick Sheffield becomes Chairman of the Board of Trustees.

The School is separated from the Community Service Society.

1951   The School is granted a charter by the New York State Board of Regents. The size of the Board of Trustees is increased to nineteen members, later to twenty-five.

Dr. Walter W. Pettit is named Dean Emeritus.

1952   The first degree of Doctor of Social Welfare is conferred by Columbia University.

APPENDIX 1B

*Program of the Third Annual Session
of the Summer School in Philanthropic Work*

Conducted by the Charity Organization Society of the City of New York.

ARRANGED BY TOPICS

June 18–July 28, 1900

(The sessions of the class were held in the Library of the Society except on the occasions of visits to other societies and institutions.)

Opening address: Professor Francis G. Peabody, Harvard University. Mr. Robert W. de Forest, President, and Mr. Edward T. Devine, General Secretary New York Charity Organization Society.

Visits to the Joint Application Bureau of the Charity Organization Society and the Association for Improving the Condition of the Poor, United Charities Building, and an explanation of the societies in the United Charities Building.

The Treatment of Needy Families in their homes: Dr. Jeffrey R. Brackett of Baltimore in charge during the first week, Mr. William I. Nichols during a portion of the second week, Mr. Philip W. Ayres the third week.

Introductory Address: The Treatment of Needy Families in their Homes: Dr. Jeffrey R. Brackett.

First Considerations in a case of need: How to get at the facts, Mrs. F. P. Strickland, Superintendent Joint Application Bureau.

The Requisites of Good Investigation, Mrs. E. V. H. Mansell of the Charity Organization Society.

Source: Edward Devine, *The Practice of Charity,* 176–182 (New York: Lentilhon, 1901).

The uses and limitations of material relief, Mr. Frank Tucker, General Agent of the New York Association for Improving the Condition of the Poor. Discussion opened by Dr. Lee K. Frankel, Manager of the United Hebrew Charities. Dr. Frankel spoke to the School later upon Tuberculosis among the Jewish Immigrant Population.

Public Out Door Relief: Mr. Frederic Almy, General Secretary of the Charity Organization Society of Buffalo. Mr. Robert D. McGonnigle of Pittsburgh, took part in the discussion.

A visit was made to the Brooklyn Bureau of Charities established upon the abolition of out-door relief in Brooklyn.

The Problem of Finding Employment: Rev. William E. McCord, Headworker Union Settlement. Discussion opened by Miss Sybil A. Bliss of the Cooper Union Labor Bureau. Visit to the Industrial Building of the New York Charity Organization Society.

The Care of Families in which there is sickness: Miss L. L. Dock of the Nurses' Settlement.

An evening visit to the lower East Side.

The Inculcation of Thrift: Rev. Henry Mottet, D.D., Rector of the Church of the Holy Communion, New York City.

A discussion upon the work of the Penny Provident Fund was conducted by Miss Marian Messemer.

Visit to the Greenwich Savings Bank.

The Removal of Children from their Homes: Mr. Francis H. White, Secretary of the Brooklyn Children's Aid Society.

Co-operation in Securing Aid and Attention for Families: Miss Mary L. Birtwell, General Secretary, Associated Charities, Cambridge, Mass.

The Part of Personal Influence in Establishing Independence: Mr. William I. Nichols, General Secretary, Brooklyn Bureau of Charities.

The Causes of Criminal Tendencies among Boys: Mr. James B. Reynolds, Headworker University Settlement.

The Attitude of Non-Sectarian Agencies Towards Religious Teaching in the Home: Mr. Edward T. Devine.

Care of Dependent Children. One week, Mr. Homer Folks, Secretary of the State Charities Aid Association, in charge.

Institutional methods in dealing with placed-out children: Mr. Homer Folks.

The oversight of children in foster homes: Mr. Charles Loring Brace, Secretary of the Children's Aid Society.

Co-operation between public and private agencies in caring for children: Mr. Robert W. Hebberd, Secretary of the New York State Board of Charities.

The Board of Children's Guardians of New Jersey: Mr. Hugh F. Fox and Mrs. E. E. Williamson.

The Care of Delinquent Children: An estimate of the part that placing-out occupies: Mrs. Glendower Evans of Boston. Discussion opened by Mr. Mornay Williams.

Visits made to the following institutions caring for dependent children: Sheltering Arms, Institution of Mercy, New York Foundling Asylum, Hebrew Orphan Asylum, Hebrew Sheltering Guardian Society, New York Catholic Protectory, Infant Hospital and Schools on Randall's Island, House of Refuge.

Medical Charities: Dr. Silas F. Hallock in charge.

The proper sphere of Medical Charities in New York, Dr. Hallock.

Visits to the Presbyterian Hospital, Bellevue Hospital, Demilt Dispensary.

The Care of Contagion. Dr. George R. Keene, Superintendent of the State Hospital for the Insane, Providence, R. I. Discussion was opened by Dr. William H. Park of the Municipal Laboratory of the Department of Health of New York. Visit to the Manhattan State Hospital on Ward's Island and to the Municipal Laboratory.

Hospital and Dispensary Care for Children: Dr. Henry B. Chapin.

Institutional Care of Adults. Dr. Samuel M. Lindsay, University of Pennsylvania, in charge.

An address upon Municipal Care for Adults: Hon. John W. Keller, Commissioner of Charities, New York City.

Visit to the Municipal Lodging House, and the correctional institutions on Blackwell's Island.

Address upon Almshouses in England and the United States, illustrated by lantern photographs: Professor Herbert E. Mills, Vassar College.

The Development of the Almshouse: Miss Mary Vida Clark of the State Charities Aid Association.

Visit to the Almshouse on Blackwell's Island.

The closing week of the course in charge of Mr. Edward T. Devine, General Secretary of the Charity Organization Society, was devoted to a study of constructive social movements.

The purpose of scope of settlements: how far are their objects attained? Mr. James B. Reynolds, Head Worker University Settlement.

Visits were made during this week, and earlier, to the University Settlement, College Settlement, Hartley House, Union Settlement and Whittier House, to St. Bartholomew's Parish House and to the Hebrew Educational Alliance. At the last named addresses were given by Dr. David Blaustein, Superintendent, and Mr. A. S. Solomons.

Vacation Schools: Mr. Clarence E. Meleney, Associate Superintendent of Schools.

Visit to schools on the East Side.

Housing as a Municipal Movement: Dr. E. R. L. Gould, President of the City and Suburban Homes Company.

Parks and Playgrounds: Mr. James K. Paulding, President of the Social Reform Club.

Visit to the playground at Seward Park.

The development of the tenement house: An address with lantern photographs by Mr. Lawrence Veiller, Secretary of the New York State Tenement House Commission.

Three other addresses were presented:

The number and location of foreign populations in Manhattan and the Bronx: Miss Kate Holliday Claghorn, Ph.D., Secretary of the Collegiate Alumnæ.

The statistical method in social work: Professor Richmond Mayo-Smith of Columbia University.

Civil Service Reform with reference to charitable institutions: Mrs. Charles R. Lowell.

The following papers were presented by members of the School:

The commitment of dependent children in New York, Mr. Charles B. Allen.

The care and prevention of tuberculosis, Mrs. Edith P. Austin.

A study of private societies for material relief, Mr. C. C. Carstens.

Truancy in New York, Mr. Edward W. Capen.

The care of delinquent children, Miss Florence Ledyard Cross.

The effect of physical training upon the moral development of girls, Miss Mary A. Daniels.

Deserted wives, Miss Ada Eliot.

The supervision of children placed out in foster homes by New York Societies, Mr. Carl Kelsey.

An outline of amusements among the Italians, Miss Charlotte Kimball.

The social settlements in New York and vicinity, Miss Louise B. Lockwood.

A historical sketch of out-door relief in New York and Brooklyn, Mr. Elmer R. Park.

The study of dispensaries, Miss Elizabeth B. Tower.

The movement for parks and playgrounds, Mr. John P. Whitman.

APPENDIX 1C

Selected Lists and Tables

Short of a major research investment and for lack of essential archives, it is not possible to convert fragmentary data from different periods into fully coherent time series. Yet some numbers are essential for the story, and even limited numbers may raise questions, suggest trends, and sum up developments.

DEANS, NAMES, AND BUILDINGS

By way of orientation, we list the School's directors (to 1940), deans, and acting deans, 1898 to the present:

Philip V. Ayres, 1898–1904
Edward T. Devine, 1904–1907; 1912–1917
Samuel McCune Lindsay, 1907–1912
Porter R. Lee, 1917–1939
Walter Pettit, 1939–1947
Margaret Leal—Acting Dean, 1947–1949
Kenneth Johnson, 1949–1958
Clara Kaiser—Acting Dean, 1958–1960
Fred Delliquadri, 1960–1967
Sidney Berengarten—Acting Dean, 1967–1971
Mitchell Ginsberg, 1971–1980
George Brager, 1980–1986
Ronald Feldman, 1986–2001
Edward J. Mullen—Acting Dean, 1991–1992

The Summer School in Philanthropic Work (1898–1903), soon called the New York School of Philanthropy (1904–1919), and then the New York School of Social Work (1919), was operated as a department of the New York Charity Organization Society (COS) in its building at 105 East Twenty-second Street, still the home of the successor organization, the Community Service Society, and other social agencies. In 1931, the New York School moved across the street to 122 East Twenty-second Street, into a tower of the Russell Sage Foundation building that had been constructed for it. It shared what may have been the country's best (or one of the best) social welfare library. It also interacted with the many departments of the Foundation, which helped shape many major studies and initiatives in industrial relations, social surveys, health, and charity organization.

In 1949 the School moved, rent free, into the Carnegie Mansion at Ninety-first Street and Fifth Avenue, remaining there until 1969 when the Foundation felt it had outgrown the building. The Miller House on the grounds had been the location of an active research center from 1956. From the time of its academic affiliation with Columbia in 1940 it was known as the New York School of Social Work of Columbia University. In 1951 it ended its formal COS connection and received its own New York State Charter. In 1959, it entered the Columbia Corporation. By 1962–63 it was known as the Columbia University School of Social Work (CUSSW).

The Carnegie Mansion's horizontal floor plan, its spacious classrooms and seminar rooms, the wide corridors, the original Carnegie library, a large basement cafeteria which became a daily faculty–student gathering place, and the lovely garden combined to provide the School with an environment still fondly referred to by those who experienced it. It is sorely missed. In 1970 (after an interim year on 110th Street), the School moved "temporarily" into McVickar Hall on West 113th Street, then being vacated by the School of International Affairs. A first draft of a plan for a new School building had been prepared by the distinguished architect Edward Durrell Stone. There was a tentative site. But the politics of Columbia's relationship to its neighbors from the late 1960s and the lack of adequate funding pushed planning aside. Available funds were assigned to McVickar renovations (and further major investment was made in McVickar in the summer of 1996).

With good spirit, students, faculty, and staff have settled in, made the building serviceable and some of its newest features most attractive, and all have learned to compromise with an essentially inadequate vertical space. One doubts that this has affected the School's basic mission. The question of a new building is again high on the agenda, however.[1]

STUDENTS AND FACULTY

We begin, as they say, with the bottom line. The School has graduated about 16,000 men and women and has a worldwide alumni mailing list of 12,000, about 60 percent of whom are in the New York area. The School has provided more than its statistical share of deans, leading scholars and teachers, and leaders of the social work profession—but it would require a comparative research project to document and to specify this in full detail.[2]

Plans had been made for 15 students for the 1898 summer class, but 28 were admitted out of 40 applicants. Some were beginners, but among them were some agency executives and academics. By the second summer, there were two sections; those with advanced experience or who had participated in the first class were separated from the beginners. As will be noted in table 1C.1, from Bernstein et al. (1942), the total doubled to 59 by 1905–06 for the one-year program and jumped to 322 with the two-year program in 1910–11, falling back in a major way during the war and immediate postwar years.

These numbers do not tell the full story. Some students, while fully qualified, could not manage or were not sure they wanted or needed a full-time program. There were so few social work diplomas (or, later, degrees) that it was not a job requirement in many places, although it apparently had advantages. Some took part-time courses on the basis of job experience but did not meet full-time admission requirements (a college degree or specified experience).

Nonetheless, education and the supply of graduates created its own demand. Then came the private and (newer) public responses to the depres-

---

[1] Groundbreaking for a second building on 113th Street took place in October 2000.
[2] What follows is based on what is immediately available and accessible. Archives are limited, there are gaps, and I have had to define independent work on statistics as beyond my scope. Most all of this is "orienting" and "suggestive."

sion. The enrolled student total, much of it part-time and no-credit (see table 1C.1), soared to 671 in 1930–31, 812 in 1935–36, and remained at 832 for the start of the M.S. degree, in 1940–41.

From a long-term perspective, the key numbers to observe are the *full-time* enrollment, for the two-year diploma until 1940 and the M.S. degree thereafter, or the graduation totals (also see table 1C.2). The part-time and no-credit students were practitioners being upgraded and/or preparing to enter the diploma/M.S. program. The full-timers became the School's major contribution to social work professionalization. Here the School built its pace slowly, rising above 100 only in the mid-1920s, to 194 in 1933, and 230 in 1935–36. The pace, apparently, could have been faster. Applications outstripped space, faculty resources, and fieldwork opportunities from the mid-1920s to the early 1930s, according to the directors' periodic reports. A first solution was to increase classroom space at 105 East Twenty-second Street. A second was the 1931 move to the Russell Sage building. Ceilings were put on full-time enrollment (under a quarter plan). About half the applicants were being rejected in the 1930s. To keep the School nationally representative it was decided to limit New Yorkers to one-third of the acceptance pool. This apparently proved difficult. New York City students made up the following proportions of the full-time student body in the seven years from 1934 to 1940: 16.8, 27.4, 29.6, 37.5, 39.7, 43.7, and 48.3. The February 1936 graduating class had a New York City representation of 42.5 percent and additional state representation of 10.4 percent. By 1941 the New York City proportion was 49.4 percent and the additional New York State portion 9.3 percent. As had been the case from the beginning, the remainder was well distributed from around the rest of the country. The foreign contingent was barely visible in the pre–World War II years.

While the Bernstein statistical series extends only to 1940, it is clear from the dean's arrival reports, which usually reported enrollment or graduations, that the post–World War II period saw serious growth—and it was managed. Looking only at full-time numbers, the total reached 571 in the 1948–49 academic year (also 1,035 part-time students) under a deliberate policy of keeping under 375 full-timers per quarter. After the School shifted away from its quarter plan (1923–1951) to a semester plan (January 1951), the full-timers remained in the 300–400 range throughout the 1950s. A graduating class, typically, was 150–158. Several phenomena—the growth of new schools

TABLE 1C.1

Number of Students, Men and Women, Enrolled in First Term of Academic Year for Selected Periods, 1898 to 1925–26 and 1930–31 to 1940–41, Classified as Full-Time and Part-Time, with or Without Credit

NUMBER OF STUDENTS ENROLLED [a]

ACADEMIC YEAR	ALL STUDENTS			FULL-TIME [b]			TOTAL PART-TIME CREDIT AND NO-CREDIT			PART-TIME CREDIT [c]			NO CREDIT [d]		
	TOTAL	MEN	WOMEN	TOTAL	MEN	WOMEN	TOTAL	MEN	WOMEN	TOTAL	MEN	WOMEN	TOTAL	MEN	WOMEN
1898	28	6	22	28	6	22	—	—	—	—	—	—	—	—	—
1900	30	12	18	24	10	14	6	2	4	c	c	c	c	c	c
1905–06	59	5	54	35	4	31	24	1	23	c	c	c	c	c	c
1910–11	322	32	290	37	11	26	285	21	264	c	c	c	c	c	c
1915–16	256	44	212	74	21	53	182	23	159	c	c	c	c	c	c
1920–21	112	20	92	76	12	64	36	8	28	c	c	c	c	c	c
1925–26	364	26	338	114	18	96	250	8	242	143	7	136	107	1	106
1930–31	671	95	576	175	19	156	496	76	420	318	41	277	178	35	143
1931–32	721	89	632	194	31	163	527	58	469	391	48	343	136	10	126

1932–33	520	68	452	157	25	132	363	43	320	281	30	251	82	13	69
1933–34	497	55	442	175	24	151	322	31	291	292	26	266	30	5	25
1934–35	745	111	634	230	36	194	515	75	440	470	66	404	45	9	36
1935–36	812	119	693	221	40	181	591	79	512	561	78	483	30	1	29
1936–37	853	158	695	228	40	188	625	118	507	598	116	482	27	2	25
1937–38	903	155	748	232	42	190	671	113	558	637	109	528	34	4	30
1938–39	834	193	641	235	56	179	599	137	462	599	137	462	—	—	—
1939–40	732	158	574	241	54	187	491	104	387	491	104	387	—	—	—
1940–41	832	227	605	271	70	201	561	157	404	561	157	404	—	—	—

Source: Saul Bernstein et al. *The New York School of Social Work: 1898–1941* (New York: Community Service Society, 1942), 115.

[a] Six-week summer session in 1898 and 1900; thereafter fall semester or fall quarter.

[b] 1898 and 1900: students enrolled for the full program of the six-week summer session.

1905–06 to 1915–16: students registered for 15 or more points.

1920–21 to 1940–41: students registered for 10 or more points.

[c] Part-time students who met academic requirements for admission as regular students.

[d] Part-time students who did not meet academic requirements for admission as regular students, and students enrolled in extension courses which gave no credit.

[e] Figures not available.

TABLE 1C.2

Graduates, Men and Women, Classified by Type of Certification and by Year of Graduation

| ACADEMIC YEAR | GRADUATES | | | CUMULATIVE TOTALS | |
	MEN	WOMEN	TOTAL	2-YEAR GRADUATES	ALL GRADUATES
Total	273	1,363	1,636	1,508	1,636
1-Year Certificate					
1905–1911	28	100	128	—	128
2-Year Diploma					
1911–12	—	4	4	4	132
1912–13	3	5	8	12	140
1913–14	1	9	10	22	150
1914–15	1	10	11	33	161
1915–16	3	8	11	44	172
1916–17	5	9	14	58	186
1917–18	4	18	22	80	208
1918–19	—	9	9	89	217
1919–20	3	16	19	108	236
1920–21	4	19	23	131	259
1921–22	3	22	25	156	284
1922–23	2	19	21	177	305
1923–24	5	38	43	220	348
1924–25	2	28	30	250	378
1925–26	6	24	30	280	408
1926–27	3	19	22	302	430
1927–28	1	31	32	334	462
1928–29	—	12	12	346	474
1929–30	3	17	20	366	494
1930–31	—	24	24	390	518
1931–32	5	24	29	419	547
1932–33	6	57	63	482	610
1933–34	11	57	68	550	678
1934–35	8	57	65	615	743
1935–36	18	87	105	720	848

TABLE 1C.2
Continued

| ACADEMIC YEAR | GRADUATES | | | CUMULATIVE TOTALS | |
	MEN	WOMEN	TOTAL	2-YEAR GRADUATES	ALL GRADUATES
1936–37	17	98	115	835	963
1937–38	27	104	131	966	1,094
1938–39	24	149	173	1,139	1,267
1939–40	36	126	162	1,301	1,429
1940–41	11	35	46	1,347	1,475
M.S. Degree					
1940–41	33	127	160	1,507	1,635
Professional Certificate					
1940–41	—	1	1	1,508	1,636

Source: Saul Bernstein et al. *The New York School of Social Work: 1898–1941* (New York: Community Service Society, 1942), 116.

(especially in the New York metropolitan area), absorption of the postwar expansion, lower tuition in public schools, and changing demographics—had changed the picture.

Then, after some anxiety about applications, the 1960s saw an application increase that was again substantial. The School grew as it could, tried to be more selective, and began a transition once again to an application procedure which did not require personal interviews. The full-time enrollment was 449 (24 were doctoral students) in 1965–67. Since then, declines in federal social work fellowships, demographic fluctuations (college graduate totals), the status of social work in career planning, and the attractiveness of—or a fear of—New York City have created new fluctuation. One notes what became an anxiety-provoking application fall between 1976 and 1982 from approximately 1,300 to approximately 400 and then modest steady growth to the 600 level. In the face of this, without visible decline in student body quality, the enrollment declined (full-time) from 400 to 300 to 275 in 1989. As seen in Table 1C.3, the graduation totals in the mid to late '80s fluctuated in the low and mid-200s to the 300s, then rose to the high 300s, and have settled in the

TABLE 1C.3

CUSSW: Student Graduates by Degrees and Gender, 1983–1997

| YEAR | M.S.* | | D.S.W** | | | MALE AS % OF |
	MALE	FEMALE	MALE	FEMALE	TOTAL	TOTAL
1983	67	214	7	5	313	23.6
1984	38	168	12	12	230	21.7
1985	44	165	6	8	223	22.4
1986	47	247	4	3	301	16.9
1987	42	248	9	8	307	16.6
1988	54	245	8	11	318	19.5
1989	37	219	2	8	266	14.7
1990	50	265	6	9	330	16.9
1991	49	267	8	8	332	17.1
1992	40	282	1	6	329	12.4
1993	56	318	1	5	380	15.0
1994	52	307	1	10	370	14.3
1995	60	336	4	6	406	15.7
1996	62	333	2	6	403	15.8
1997	59	344	3	6	412	15.0

Source: Data from University Registrar.

*Includes a very few certificate students.

**Both Ph.D. and D.S.W. from 1994.

400s. The application pressure is once again severe. New York, Columbia, and CUSSW are in a period of high popularity, and circumstances produce a high-quality, multiethnic, international student body. Demography, the state of the economy, the shifting attractiveness of social work, and cost factors seem to determine the flow. Currently, with high application totals, the administration and faculty continue to protect the quality of the student body and the educational experience offered, and to be cautious about excessive growth.

In all of this, enrollment trends for CUSSW from the mid-1950s to the present generally follow those for graduate social work schools nationally as compiled by the Council on Social Work Education (CSWE): growth from the 1950s to 1978, a serious fall from 1975 to 1986, and a bottoming out to a

15-year low, followed by steady growth since 1986 and new highs in recent years as undergraduate colleges have produced larger cohorts.

During this century of enrollment, the United States has gone from 1 to 4 to 122 graduate social work programs. The New York metropolitan area went from 1 school to 8.

There are no minority data for earlier years under earlier "color blind" policies, but clearly African Americans and Hispanics were underrepresented among students and faculty. The African American/Hispanic subgroups in the student population grew significantly as a result of special recruitment efforts and some minority scholarships in the 1960s. The CSWE administered one such federal (NIMH) fellowship program as well. It would require a special data collection and analytic effort to allocate the growth among the changing applicant and recruitment pools, special efforts within the School (which were constant, and included special programs such as the Title XX minority training program, which brought welfare department people in for degree training), and other factors. In any case, the minority subgroup in the student body had reached a steady 15–20 percent by the '70s and has since maintained that level and grown. While categories have tended to be subdivided as the diversity of minority and foreign students increased, a relatively coherent picture can be drawn for the past two decades. (In what follows I combine with Hispanics Puerto Rican "islanders" and "mainlanders" and classify as Asian those students not identified specifically, as on student visas from Asian countries.) With some fluctuations and declines, the combined African American and Hispanic "minority" totals were in the range of 11.3 to 20.8 percent in the period 1983 to 1997, with the average at about 17 percent. During the earlier years, the African American proportion was almost double the Hispanic, reflecting the size of the eligible cohort. The gap clearly is narrowing. Students of Asian background were very few at first, then matched and sometimes exceeded the Hispanic group. As of 1997 they were a visible presence among minority students (African Americans, 13.5 percent; Hispanics, 7.3 percent; Asians, 12.2 percent; non-Hispanic whites, 66.5 percent). White students had been 80–85 percent of the total from 1983 to 1990, were between 75 and 80 percent to 1997, and, most recently, fell below 70 percent. We do not know whether the trend will be sustained. We do know (CSWE) that nationally minority enrollments have been in the 20–25 percent range, but the particular minority groups vary with the region and the subclassifications by university. The proportion of "white" students at Columbia tends to be within 5 percent of the CSWE pattern.

GENDER

The student body has been dominated by women from the start and the proportions have not changed much over the years. In 1925, 1930, and 1935 males constituted, respectively, 16, 10, and 18 percent of the classes. They ranged from the low 20s to the low 30s in the 1940s and 1950s except for an immediate post–World War II "G.I. Bill veteran" spurt, which quickly faded (46.1 percent in 1946). Males constituted 22.6 percent of a 1956 graduate census, and a third of the 1961 class. Whether one counts enrollees or graduates, they were 25–29 percent of the classes in the 1970s and 1980s, then reverted to the 1920s proportions in the 1990s—typically 15–16 percent of graduates; occasionally there were fewer (14.3 percent in 1994). CSWE data show similar trends for the country: males 17.2 percent in 1991, 17.5 percent in 1995, and 16.5 percent in 1996).

Throughout there have been gender differences in career lines. Of the 1941 graduates, 50 percent of the men and 62.9 percent of the women had concentrated in casework, and 12.8 percent of the men and 2.5 percent of the women in community organization. The men were also more likely to have been in group work (6.9 percent) and research (2.3 percent) than the women, for whom the corresponding proportions were 1.6 percent and 0.5 percent.

A 1956 survey of graduates found the men more heavily represented in executive and subexecutive posts than women graduates (56 vs. 27 percent).

The survey on 1989–1995 graduates did not report career lines by gender.

The academics who came from Johns Hopkins and other universities to teach in the new social work programs were all males, but by the time the School had a full-time faculty and taught the practical work, women were included. By the 1920s women had a numerical edge and have continued to outnumber the men, but not in proportions that match the student body. Indeed, the percentages have been close in some years or reversed. (Nationally, female graduate faculty have tended to outnumber male by a slightly higher margin—5 to 10 percent—than at CUSSW.) However, all the directors/deans have been males. There have been several very influential female associate directors/deans, from Margaret Leal (1937) to Grace White (1951), Gordon Hamilton (1952), Clara Kaiser (1958), and now, Peg Hess. Leal and Kaiser also served as acting deans, as noted above.

When the School had its own board, all the board chairs from the beginning were male, until the fifth, Mrs. George E. Brewer Jr., elected in 1955. By then there were 7 female trustees on a board of 20, an increase from 3 in 1948, 2 in 1951, and 6 in 1950. The board became an advisory council when the School joined the Columbia Corporation in 1959, and the female representation grew substantially.

The School began with a national and international student body and prided itself on this fact. Through the '40s, *Bulletin* covers often highlighted geographic representation on marked maps. Nonetheless, the majority of students derived from the Northeast. As the years went by and schools developed in other regions, the northeastern proportion grew. Applications far outstripped space, and we have mentioned the apparently not fully successful effort to limit New York students in the 1930s so as to remain "national."

With the depression and the Federal Emergency Relief Administration (FERA), government funds lent support for founding or expansion of undergraduate and some graduate programs in the Midwest in what had been the land/grant colleges. This affected the flow to existing schools. There was further expansion in every decade and every region thereafter as all universities considered social work and—in the 1930s and thereafter—most M.S. programs considered doctorates. While still more nationally representative than most, Columbia currently draws most of its students from the tri-state area: New York (57.1 percent), New Jersey (8.1 percent), Connecticut (8.1 percent)—according to an unpublished survey on 1989–1995 graduates by Professor Ada Mui and Samuel Cotton. California follows on the list, as it has for some time. The other students are from scattered locations around the United States or from other countries.

Foreign students were mentioned in annual reports from the beginning. In its second year as a full-year school, New York drew students from England and Canada as well as 15 states. By 1908–09, Cuba, Japan, Italy, Canada, and England were represented in the student body, as well as 21 states. The post–World War II foreign buildup was reflected in a special "foreign student" program in 1952 and accelerated by the important but short-lived Joseph Hirschorn foreign fellowship program, which financed 14 of that year's 40 foreign students. By the time of the 1956 graduate census, all states in the continental United States were represented among the 4,000 graduate respondents, with concentrations along the Atlantic Coast, in the Midwest, and in 26 foreign countries, with the latter counting only non-U.S. citizens.

As Europe developed its own social work education, largely undergraduates in the U.S. sense, the flow to the United States for basic social work professional education slowed considerably. A few Asian countries and Israel became major foreign student sources. The entire picture changed in the 1980s and now Southeast Asia is the major foreign origin for the substantial foreign student group (as it is in the rest of the University). We lack the basis for a precise analysis in the present context because University statistics have not consistently separated Asian American and immigrant Asians from Asian students on student visas.

CAREER LINES AND CURRICULUM CHOICES

Of recent graduates who responded to an unpublished mail survey (Mui and Cotton 1995) half had come to CUSSW as part of a career change, 8–12 years after earning a B.A. Those at the McVickar building averaged 31.5 years of age, those at Purchase 32.5.

Their M.S. concentrations had been as follows:

clinical practice	67.9%
generalist practice	25.5%
administration	6.1%
research	0.5%

They had chosen the following field of practice concentrations when in school:

family and children	43.5%
health and mental health	39.3%
world of work	7.9%
aging	6.7%
personal social services	2.6%

They were working in the following areas:

mental health	30.7%
family services	16.4%
medical social work	12.7%
youth services	11.3%
child welfare	10.3%
school social work	7.9%
geriatric services	7.3%

In the following settings:

hospitals	18.1%
social service agencies	12.2%
community mental health agencies	12.2%
schools	7.6%
criminal justice	7.3%
other	19.0%

Half of the pre-1956 graduates had been supervisors or executives. Only one-third were in public employment, despite the depression-era program developments. However, the biggest shift, seen in a 1994 graduate survey, showed 11.7 percent in private "for profit" employment. The 1989–1995 survey offers more detail: 3.4 percent in full-time private practice or consultation and 12.2 percent in part-time practice or consultation.

NOTES

1. According to Broadhurst (1971), at the 1895 meeting of the National Conference of Charities and Corrections there was "recognition of the need to bring theory and practice together in the teaching of scientific charity" (762). F. H. Giddings of Columbia was present as were participants from Harvard, Yale, and Chicago Theological. There were papers sent from Smith and Wisconsin. Ayres, who arrived in Chicago in 1895, set up a plan with Henderson, J. Lathrop, and G. Taylor for practical work experience for students from various universities near Chicago for the summer of 1896. There were six participants (two from Northwestern, two from Chicago, one from Michigan, and one from Wisconsin) (771). That fall the University of Chicago offered two extension courses in sociology "for the special benefit of those engaged in charity work" (principles of poor relief and problems of the poor in cities). Ayres, one of the two lecturers, responding to a board split and dissatisfaction, resigned and came to the New York COS, which he knew to be "favorable to a summer class." The focal point for education in social work shifted to New York and the COS, but Chicago "was not far behind" (785). As typical of the two-track development, Wisconsin eventually developed strong departments of economics and sociology while New York and Chicago developed schools for training social workers.

2. For treatment of the other early programs and models and the evolution of professional membership associations and educational associations in social work, see Kahn (1998).

3. Other major centers of influence were Pennsylvania's Wharton School (see below re: Simon N. Patten) and Harvard's Department of Social Ethics (Francis Peabody).

4. It is of some interest that as of late 1997 *The New York Times* reported that "more than 75 American graduate schools now offer advanced degrees in philanthropy," apparently concentrating on management of or fund-raising for nonprofit organizations — or preparation for board membership. There is a large Center on Philanthropy at Indiana University—Purdue University and a specialized library. (*The New York Times,* December 24, 1997, p. A15.) Unlike the philanthropy education that evolved into social work early in the twentieth century, many of these programs are business school based and think of themselves as focused on management, although some have broader ambitions. In addition, several centers (the Rockefeller Foundation, the Philanthropic Initiative [Boston], the Council on Foundations) conduct brief intensive training courses for foundation board members and staffs. (*The New York Times,* May 3, 1991, p. A1.) The initial Summer School in Philanthropy of 1898 attracted people with all these interests and much more.

5. Hofstadter, writing when he did, referred to Populism, Progressivism, and the New Deal. In current perspective, one can view the Welfare State as in fact successively shaped by the Progressive Era, the New Deal, and the Great Society.

6. A review of Devine's substantial writings and those of Porter Lee upsets all stereotypes about COS leadership in the Progressive Era and Social Darwinism. This essay allows no space for such a review. Devine pointed out in his "Organized Charity and Industry" (in Lee and Devine 1915) that the Pittsburgh survey and subsequent reporting in the *Survey* magazine pulled no punches in "giving continuous and searching attention to industry" despite the importance of J. P. Morgan as COS treasurer and J. D. Rockefeller and A. Carnegie as major contributors.

REFERENCES

American Association of Social Workers (AASW). 1929. *Social Case Work, Generic and Specific.* New York: AASW.

Austin, David M. 1986. *A History of Social Work Education.* Austin: University of Texas School of Social Work.

Bartlett, Harriet M. 1970. *The Common Base of Social Work Practice.* New York: National Association of Social Workers.

Berengarten, Sidney, ed. 1967–1969. *Report of the Acting-Dean.* New York: Columbia University School of Social Work.

—— 1987. *The Columbia University School of Social Work: A History of Social Pioneering.* Monograph 1. New York: Columbia University School of Social Work.

—— 1992. *The Columbia University School of Social Work: A History of Social Pioneering*. Monograph 4. New York: Columbia University School of Social Work.

—— 1993. *The Columbia University School of Social Work: A History of Social Pioneering*. Monograph 7. New York: Columbia University School of Social Work.

Bernstein, Saul, et al. 1942. *The New York School of Social Work: 1898–1941*. New York: Community Service Society.

Broadhurst, Betty Page. 1971. *Social Thought, Social Practice and Social Work Education: Sanborn, Ely, Warner, Richmond*. D.S.W. diss. New York: Columbia University School of Social Work.

Chalmers, David. 1991. *And the Crooked Places Made Straight: The Struggle for Social Change in the 1960s*. Baltimore: John Hopkins University Press.

Chambers, Clark. 1963. *Seedtime of Reform*. Minneapolis: University of Minnesota Press.

Devine, Edward. 1901. *The Practice of Charity*. New York: Lentilhon.

—— 1910. *Social Forces*. Various dated essays from the editor's page of *The Survey*. New York: Charities Publication Committee.

—— 1911. *The Spirit of Social Work*. New York: Charities Publication Committee.

—— 1916. *Pauperism: An Analysis*. A document in the series, Studies in Social Work. New York: New York School of Philanthropy.

Fisher, Jacob. 1936. *The Rank and File Movement in Social Work, 1931–1936*. New York: New York School of Social Work.

Gessner, Robert, ed. 1936. *The Democratic Man: Selected Writings of Eduard C. Lindeman*. Boston: Beacon Press.

Gilman, D. C. 1906. *The Launching of a University*. New York: Dodd, Mead.

Hamilton, Gordon. 1940. *Theory and Practice of Social Case Work*. New York: Columbia University Press.

Hofstadter, Richard. 1955. *The Age of Reform*. New York: Knopf.

Hollis, Ernest V. and Alice J. Taylor. 1951. *Social Work Education in the United States*. New York: Columbia University Press.

Johnson, Alexander, ed. 1905. *Proceedings of the National Conference of Charities and Corrections, 1905*. Columbus, Oh.: Fred J. Heer.

Journal of Family History. 1996. Special Issue: "Integrating the Sixties" 8, no. 1.

Kahn, Alfred J. 1960. "Social Science and the Conceptual Framework for Community Organization Practice." In Leonard J. Kogan, ed., *Social Science Theory and Social Work Research*. New York: National Association of Social Workers.

—— 1965. "Social Work Fields of Practice." In *The Encyclopedia of Social Work, 1965*, 750–755. New York: National Association of Social Workers.

—— 1998. *Themes for a History: The Origins of the American Social Work Profession, with Special Reference to its Professional Education*. Eleventh Annual Robert J.

O'Leary Memorial Lecture. Columbus: Ohio State University College of Social Work.

—— 1999. "The Social Work Research Domain in Historical Perspective: The First 100 Years." In Miriam Potocky-Tripodi and Tony Tripodi, eds., *New Directions for Social Work Practice Research*. Washington, D.C.: National Association of Social Workers.

Kahn, Alfred J. and Sheila B. Kamerman. 1998. *Big Cities in the Welfare Transition*. New York: Columbia University School of Social Work.

Kamerman, Sheila B. 1995. "Fields of Practice." In Carol Meyer and Mark Mattaini, eds., *Foundations of Social Work Practice*. Washington, D.C.: National Association of Social Workers.

Kenworthy, Marion E. and Porter R. Lee. 1929. *Mental Hygiene and Social Work*. New York: Commonwealth Fund.

Klein, Philip. 1932. *Some Basic Statistics in Social Work*. New York: Columbia University Press.

—— 1938. *A Social Study of Pittsburgh*. New York: Columbia University Press.

Lee, Porter R. 1937. *Social Work as Cause and Function and Other Papers*. New York: Columbia University Press.

Lee, Porter R. and Edward Devine. 1915. #1, "Social Work with Families and Individuals" (Lee) and #2, "Organized Charity and Industry" (Devine). New York: New York School of Philanthropy.

Leiby, James. 1978. *A History of Social Welfare and Social Work in the United States*. New York: Columbia University Press.

Lindeman, Eduard. 1921. *The Community: An Introduction to the Study of Community Leadership and Organization*. New York: Association Press.

Lowery, Lawson G. and Geddes Smith. 1933. *The Institute for Child Guidance, 1927–1933*. New York: Commonwealth Fund.

Lubove, Roy. 1965. *The Professional Altruist*. Cambridge, Mass.: Harvard University Press.

Maas, Henry S., ed. 1951. *Adventure in Mental Health: Psychiatric Social Work with the Armed Forces in World War II*. New York: Columbia University Press.

Mailick, Mildred D. 1998. "Clinical Practice: The Last One Hundred Years." *Currents*. New York City Charter, National Association of Social Workers, vol. 41, no. 1: 1, 4, 8.

Meier, Elizabeth G. 1954. *A History of the New York School of Social Work*. New York: Columbia University Press.

Merton, Robert. 1957. *Social Theory and Social Structure*. New York: Free Press.

Richmond, Mary. 1899. *Friendly Visiting among the Poor*. New York: Macmillan.

—— 1917. *Social Diagnosis*. New York: Russell Sage Foundation.

—— 1922. *What Is Social Case Work?* New York: Russell Sage Foundation.

Russell, James E. 1955. *National Policies for Education, Health, and Social Services.* New York: Doubleday. (See part 4, "Social Services and the Free Economy," and part 4, "Income Security for a Free People.")

Simon, Barbara Levy. 1994. *The Empowerment Tradition in American Social Work.* New York: Columbia University Press.

Stein, Herman D. 1960. *Curriculum Study.* New York: Columbia University School of Social Work.

Stein, Herman D. and Richard A. Cloward, eds. 1958. *Social Perspectives and Behavior.* New York: Free Press.

United Nations (U.N.) Department of Economic and Social Affairs. 1958. *Training for Social Work: Third International Survey.* New York: U.N. Department of Economic and Social Affairs.

Warner, Amos. 1894. *American Charities.* New York: Crowell.

Wickenden, Elizabeth and Winifred Bell. 1961. *Public Welfare: Time for a Change.* New York: New York School of Social Work of Columbia University.

Wright, Helen. 1954a. "Three Against Time." *Social Service Review* (March): 49.

—— 1954b. "Social Work Education: Problems for the Future." In Cora Kasius, ed., *New Directions in Social Work,* 181–182. New York: Harper.

Chapter 2

A CENTURY OF CURRICULUMS
AND CELEBRATIONS

WBM and Ronald A. Feldman

The first quarter-century of the school's development and of its role in social work education can be conveyed succinctly through an examination of its status at the time of landmark historic celebrations as well as at other historic junctures. One of the first major celebrations of the school's progress took place in 1923 at the time of its twenty-fifth anniversary. At this celebration, Professor Felix Frankfurter of Harvard University, later justice of the Supreme Court of the United States, paid special tribute to the "vision and audacity" of those who had conceived the idea of the school and had laid its foundations. This theme reflected the development of the New York School of Social Work in its earliest years.

1898–1909: VISION AND AUDACITY

The 1890s, when the first glimmers of professional social work began to shine, was an age of "charity" or "philanthropy." The average citizen thought of social work essentially as extending a helping hand to the poor and unfortunate. The very names of social work agencies then prominent—the Associations for Improving the Conditions of the Poor, the Special Visitors and Private Almoners, the National Association for Prevention of Mendicancy and Charitable Imposture—suggest the approach at that time of the vast majority of people toward welfare work. It was the age of the volunteer "friendly visitor." No one had as yet conceived of social work as a real profession.

The spiritual godmother of the New York School of Social Work, if not the actual originator of the idea, was Josephine Shaw Lowell, a Civil War widow of outstanding courage, intelligence, and determination who in 1882 was responsible for the establishment of the Charity Organization Society of New

York (later merged with the Associations for Improving the Conditions of the Poor to form the Community Service Society). Mrs. Lowell had a scholarly and analytical approach to the problem of philanthropy. In 1878, as the first woman commissioner on the New York State Board of Charities, she appointed a committee that reported that the expenditure of large sums of money on charity in New York City should be handled in accordance with sound business principles. On the basis of this report, Mrs. Lowell was appointed as chairperson of a new committee "to take such steps as they may deem wise to inaugurate a system of mutual help and cooperation" among the existing welfare organizations of New York City. The result was the Charity Organization Society. The efforts and the resultant COS organization laid the groundwork for the professional approach to social work.

In 1897, COS established its first Committee on Philanthropic Education. Headed by Robert W. deForest, then president of COS, it reported: "Charity is a vast social engine which should have competent people to work it. . . . A well-equipped school of philanthropy has become a necessity." The conclusions of the Committee were promptly adopted by COS, and early in 1898 the Society announced the first formal program of training for social work to be established in the United States. The name chosen for this division of the Society's endeavors was the New York School of Philanthropy and its declared purpose was "to fit men and women for social service in either professional or volunteer work." The first session of this "training school in applied philanthropy" was the six-week summer course, which opened on June 20, 1898.

The twenty-seven men and women who came together for the first time on that June morning must have shared the typical exuberance and expectation of students attending a new course at a new institution. One of them, Kate Holladay Claghorn, later a member of the School's staff, wrote:

> We were a heterogeneous group. Many of us had already done something or tried to do something for our fellowmen and two or three had already distinguished ourselves; some of us were young things just out of college. Our chief qualification was our interest in the subject.

They were identified as mainly college graduates representing fourteen colleges and universities and coming from eleven different states.

In the COS *Bulletin* for 1897–98, the following summary and evaluation of the new project appears:

A training class in applied philanthropy, consisting of 27 members, mainly college graduates, was organized under the immediate direction of the assistant secretary (Philip W. Ayres) and with the oversight of a special committee of the Central Council. No charge for tuition was made, but members of the class were required to enter the service of the Society for a period of six weeks performing such duties as might be assigned which were, however, in all instances for their educational value. At 8:30 each morning the class met for reports by members and a discussion of such reports. At 9:00 A.M. there was usually an address by some specialist, frequently the chief executive of some important charitable society or institution from New York City and vicinity, or more distant cities.

The *Bulletin* noted further:

Many of the progressive and instructive institutions of New York were visited with careful observation of their methods. At Sing Sing Prison a careful explanation was given by the warden. The institutions on Blackwell's and Randall's Island were visited besides several public and private homes for children and other dependents.

The immediate results of this course are all that was anticipated. . . . It is hoped that from this beginning a plan of professional training in applied philanthropy may be developed which will raise the standards of qualification and of usefulness throughout the entire field of charitable work. The Society cherishes the conviction that important results to the philanthropic work not only of New York and vicinity, but also of the country at large would follow the endowment of a school to which the best minds would be attracted, and from which specialists in the various forms of charitable work and corrections could be entered successfully upon their respective careers in life.

The founders of the New York School themselves considered the early sessions of the institution to be largely experimental (as, perforce, they had to be at a time when objectives, techniques, and training methods were still highly nebulous). What is extraordinary is that, even at this early date, the broad outlines of social work education as it was known in 1950 were so clearly defined and that many of the fundamental patterns which characterized the work of the New York School for its first half-century had already been established in the first courses offered by the COS.

From the beginning, the founders conceived of the institution as a postgraduate school for professional training comparable in every respect to the leading postgraduate schools of medicine and law. From the beginning, also, consistent emphasis was placed upon fieldwork. Theory was not enough. The student had to gain information and insight regarding the problems of the profession through actual, personal contact with those problems. Persistently, since the School was started, every effort has been made to make available through the School the knowledge and experience of the leading practitioners in the whole field of social work. During the School's first year, the student body was privileged to hear as lecturers such distinguished speakers as Arthur Twining Hadley, president of Yale; Felix Adler, Columbia professor and leader of the Society for Ethical Culture; Judge Ben B. Lindsey; Jane Addams of Hull House; Mary Simkovich, head worker at Greenwich House; and Lillian D. Wald of Henry Street Settlement.

The School has likewise followed vigorously its original concept of a national and international educational institution rather than that of an institution concerned primarily with local interests. The wide geographical distribution of the students that attended the School's first session may have been partially accidental, but through the years the School has taken positive steps to perpetuate a like result. Further, the School regarded itself from the very beginning as a professional school where men and women were to be trained in a life work.

It is evident from the early COS report that what the new School lacked was not vision, but the financial means to turn that vision into reality. COS had in mind a training course which would require a full academic year, if not two, but because the School was dependent upon private financial contributions, this objective could only gradually be achieved. In the second year of the School, a registration fee of $10 was charged for the first time and a new set of admission standards was announced. Applicants were required to have completed a course in social work at a college or university and to have had at least one year of philanthropic work.

In 1900, the program of field visits to agencies and institutions was enlarged and strengthened. Private charitable agencies were visited during the first week. Next came a series of observations at child welfare agencies. Public charities, almshouses, and hospitals were examined the third week. Medical charities represented the fourth classification of fieldwork, followed by visits to playgrounds, model tenements, and hotels for indigent transients. The sixth and final week included visits to police stations, magistrate courts, and prisons.

The enthusiasm for the School on the part of its student body was evidenced in 1901 when the graduates, as a spontaneous gesture, collected $84 in personal donations to be used as a scholarship fund the following year. This was followed, in 1902, by the organization of an alumni association which, since that time, has been an important adjunct of the School. An important step toward the Society's ultimate objective was taken during the academic year of 1903–04 when a winter session of the institution was for the first time inaugurated. Evening classes, to permit attendance by employed social workers, were a feature of the new curriculum, and these courses were well attended.

In October 1904, through financial support furnished by friends of Edward T. Devine, general secretary of COS and newly appointed director of the School, it was at last possible to establish the training course on the basis of a full-year program. In mid-November of the same year, the new program was made doubly secure through the generosity of John S. Kennedy, who offered to provide the School with an endowment that would produce an income of $10,000 a year. In accordance with the deed of gift, the capital fund donated by Mr. Kennedy was to be held as a permanent endowment for the School, the income to be applied to the needs of the institution under the direction of the Committee on Philanthropic Education of the Community Service Society, which, in effect, became the Board of Trustees of the School.

In a letter addressed to President deForest of COS, Mr. Kennedy explained his philosophy regarding the eventual development of the institution —a philosophy which has in essence been followed by the School ever since:

> I have also considered the possible desirability of establishing the School as a department of some university but have decided that it should preferably be connected with the practical charity work of the city in analogy rather to training schools for nurses which are connected to the hospitals than to any separate university department. I should hope it would affiliate its work, however, not only with Colum-

bia University, but with other educational institutions and have sought, by naming as ex officio members of the Committee the presidents for the time being of the more important societies dealing directly with the poor, not only to associate them in the direction of the School, but to emphasize my desire that the School shall give a training in the practice of that broad charity which is free from any limitations of creed or nationality.

Mr. Kennedy's three basic principles—affiliation with Columbia University on an informal basis, continuance of COS as the parent institution, and emphasis on training related directly to practical social work—were completely in accord with the thinking of COS leadership, and Mr. Kennedy's gift was promptly accepted. The informal connection with Columbia, designed to strengthen the educational opportunities of both institutions, continued until 1940, when a closer affiliation was arranged.

The School was beginning to come of age not only in the financial sense, but as an educational institution. The curriculum was materially strengthened and, by 1905, the School was offering study courses covering fifty-one subjects under the following major headings:

1. Survey of the Field
2. The State in Relation to Charity
3. Racial Traits in the Population—A Study in Sociology
4. Constructive Social Work
5. The Care of Needy Families in Their Homes
6. Child Helping Agencies
7. Treatment of the Criminal; Reformatory Methods; Probation

The care of needy families in their homes included a study of actual case records, and it was during this period that the term *casework* was first used in the publications of the School.

In 1907, two significant events occurred. The first of these was the appointment of Professor Samuel McCune Lindsay of the University of Pennsylvania as director of the school. The second was the establishment of the Bureau of Social Research, the School's first venture into organized research on a major scale. Both of these events presaged a change in direction for the School—a tendency to place greater emphasis upon the theoretical and academic aspects of social service education as opposed to the more practical and immediately utilitarian aspects.

The School continued to grow and to flourish. In less than a dozen years, it had transformed the field of education for social work from haphazard apprentice training to well-formulated standards of professional training. Fieldwork had been established as a basic element in a practical approach to a practical profession. The technical content of the School's curriculum had been expanded and vastly improved. Principles of selectivity in the admission of students had been worked out. The training course itself had grown from a six-week series of more or less disconnected seminars to a well-integrated program of education covering a full academic year. The sponsors of the institution had good reason to be gratified at the progress that had been made. Their audacity had been rewarded, even though their vision was still to be completely realized.

1910-1929: PROGRESS AND MATURITY

The twenty-year period between 1910 and 1930 was an era of growing maturity not only on the part of the New York School, but in the whole field of social work. Lilian Brandt of the Community Service Society of New York described the period leading up to World War I as "one of the golden ages of social work, as measured by creative contributions." A new interest was developing, she pointed out, in the economic basis of family life, and working conditions and wages were being scrutinized for their effect upon health, on mental and moral development, and on the general welfare. The whole world was experiencing what has been termed "a revolt of the individual." Perhaps even more significant was the growing influence of psychiatry in dealing with problems of the individual.

Early in its second decade of service, the New York School was able to take a vitally important forward step in its development. It announced that during the academic year of 1911-1912, the School would for the first time offer a two-year course in social work with an official diploma as the reward of graduation. The new course was not completely what the founders had envisaged, for only one full year of residence at the School was required. Credit for the second year's work could be obtained in one of several ways—by participating in practical service in an approved social agency; by taking approved courses at the School or at other specified training institutions; or by attending summer or evening sessions at the School.

This expansion on the part of the School was made possible by additional benefactions on the part of John S. Kennedy, who, by bequest in his will, left approximately $1 million to be added to the School's endowment fund, and by continued financial support from the Russell Sage Foundation. Although tuition at the School was increased in 1911 to $150, this did not begin to produce sufficient income to cover operating expenses, and the School continued to be financially dependent upon endowment income and COS support.

The first academic year on a two-year basis was significant, also, because it brought to a head the question of the basic orientation of the School and led to decisions which determined the School's philosophy through its first fifty years. Since 1907, the School had been under the direction of Samuel McCune Lindsay. Professor Lindsay's background and experience had been largely in university work. He felt from the beginning that the New York School should be developed as a university graduate school emphasizing the theoretical more than the practical aspects of social work. In this concept of the School and its objectives, Professor Lindsay found himself at variance with a majority of the members of the COS Committee on Philanthropic Education. In March 1912, therefore, he tendered his resignation, which was accepted by the Committee. The Committee promptly reappointed as director of the School Edward T. Devine, who had already served in this capacity from 1904 to 1907.

This change in directorship marked a return to channels which had been earlier charted by John S. Kennedy, wherein the emphasis had been placed upon practical professional training reinforced by limited university affiliation. The Committee's "mandate" was reflected in Mr. Devine's report for the year ending June 30, 1913. There had been, he stated, a revision of the curriculum so thorough as to "make the School practically a new institution." The General Announcement of the School, issued at this time, summarized its point of view in these words:

> The School of Philanthropy is primarily a professional training school, of graduate rank, for civic and social work. The word "philanthropy" is to be understood in the deepest and broadest sense as including every kind of social work, whether under public or private auspices. By social work is meant any form of persistent and deliberate effort to im-

prove living or working conditions in the community, or to relieve, diminish or prevent distress, whether due to weakness of character or to pressure of external circumstances.

Beginning in 1913, a full second year of residence at the School itself was offered to students. Under this new regime, the first-year course emphasized basic or generic material, while a high degree of specialization was expected during the second year. At the same time, a special entrance examination was instituted to screen out applicants who obviously had little aptitude for professional social work. These were both steps toward the high level of professional competence which the School was more and more expecting of its graduates.

How rapidly the social work field was expanding, in terms of job opportunities, was indicated in the 1915 School report. It was estimated, for example, that there were some 4,000 salaried jobs in volunteer welfare agencies in the New York metropolitan area alone as compared with only 1,200 ten years earlier. In the country as a whole, there were estimated to be over 20,000 professional jobs available. Salary averages, while below those prevailing in law and medicine, already topped those in the ministry and were on a par with those prevailing in the teaching profession. The School, in its General Announcement for 1915–16, was able to state:

> Social work is now recognized as a distinct profession, competing deservedly with other vocations for the interest of men and women choosing a career. A professional training will before long be as indispensable to the social worker as it is now to the lawyer, physician and clergyman.

As an indication of the changing attitude of the public toward welfare work and, specifically, of the would-be social worker toward his or her job, the student "Annual" for 1915–16 began to raise some very pointed questions with regard to the name of the School. "Did we come to the School of Philanthropy because of its name or in spite of it?" questioned the student editors. "Do we feel a sense of pride in telling strangers where we study? Or do we assume an apologetic air and explain that it is not as bad as it sounds? A medical college turns out doctors, a law school lawyers, a cooking school cooks. A school of philanthropy must, by all the rules of analogy, turn out philanthropists. Are we prepared to attach a label to ourselves?"

Apparently COS and the members of the School's faculty were also becoming conscious that the term *philanthropy* no longer represented the ideals and philosophy of social work in general or of the School in particular. In April 1919, it was announced that the name of the school had been changed to the New York School of Social Work.

Meanwhile World War I, with all its social and economic implications, had produced changes far more profound in the whole professional approach to social work. The Associations for Improving the Conditions of the Poor, in its 1918 report, stated:

> The draft has told us in unmistakable language that poverty and disease are robbing us of our birthright and our physical, economic and moral effectiveness. War has indeed paved the way for and made obvious our pressing obligation to make unrelenting warfare against disease and its accompaniment, poverty.

Many thousands of returning war veterans suffering from "shell shock" and from postwar maladjustment also made it clear that sickness, poverty, and other forms of distress were often matters more of the mind than of the body. It was during the war period that the School first inaugurated its Department of Mental Hygiene.

By way of specific war service, the School initiated, in April 1917, its Red Cross Training Course for Emergency Social Service. Three months later, a comprehensive program keyed to various war services was announced, including a series of special institutes for both volunteers and professional workers.

It was in 1917, also, that Edward T. Devine, who had piloted the institution through two difficult periods of growth, retired as director. He was succeeded by Porter R. Lee.

The first postwar peacetime year, 1919, released the energies of those connected with the School for concentration upon their primary responsibilities. In May 1919, a special conference of great significance was held at the School. It was attended by representatives of fifteen schools of social work, all of which had been established in the twenty-one years since the founding of the COS pioneer venture. The purpose of the conference was to discuss and define the status of professional education for social work. While the conference itself solved no fundamental problems, it had to its credit one major achievement—the establishment of the Association of Training Schools in Social Work—which has had a profound influence upon the creation of higher national standards of professional education for social work.

For the newly designated New York School of Social Work, 1919 marked the first comprehensive review of fieldwork and its problems in connection with the school curriculum. It was found that there was a lack of continuity in the fieldwork experience of the students and that fieldwork was not always adequately related to classroom teaching. Supervisors in welfare agencies used for fieldwork training had no formal connection with the School and little appreciation of the educational problems involved. Few of these agencies had an organized plan for supervising the work of trainees. In short, fieldwork at the School, that indispensable element in sound social work training, was neither well organized nor well administered. Immediate steps were taken to correct the most pressing fieldwork problems and the foundation was laid for remedying others. But the provision of adequate fieldwork opportunities in terms of maximum educational value to the social work student remained as a perennial challenge to the faculty of the School.

One immediate aftereffect of World War I was a greatly increased influx of foreign students at the School. A number of fellowships and scholarships were established especially for foreign students, and by this means the influence of the School as an international force in the field of social work was broadly extended. Between 1920 and 1926, the School had in residence students from no fewer than twenty-five foreign countries, as shown in table 2.1.

The Silver Anniversary of the School in 1923 afforded an opportunity for reviewing the progress of the institution over the period of its first quarter-century. During that time, more than six thousand persons had attended the School, including summer schools and institutes. In 1898, the student body consisted of twenty-seven students who attended a six-week summer course. In 1923, there were 175 full-time students enrolled for the School's two-year program, which included forty-five courses and fieldwork. The teaching staff in 1923 consisted of twenty-eight members, most of them full time, as compared with the body of volunteer lecturers that originally carried out the curriculum. The space occupied by the School had increased 40 percent, and student tuition fees had advanced from a nominal $10 registration fee to $350 for the two-year course. Most significant of all, however, was the marked increase in acceptance of the concept of social work as a true profession and of the New York School as the outstanding exponent of that concept.

The School did not let its anniversary year pass without engaging in some

TABLE 2.1

Countries of Origin of Foreign Students, 1920–1926

COUNTRY	NUMBER
Armenia	2
Australia	1
Canada	6
China	3
Czechoslovakia	2
Denmark	1
East Indies	1
England	3
France	5
Germany	3
Greece	1
Holland	1
Hungary	1
India	6
Italy	3
Japan	3
Mexico	1
New Zealand	2
Philippines	6
Poland	3
Rumania	1
Russia	3
Sweden	1
Switzerland	2
Turkey	4
Total	65

searching self-analysis. There was a growing feeling on the part of the faculty that the institution had gone too far in the direction of departmentalization and specialization. The second half of the two-year program featured seven specializations—Family Case Work, Mental Hygiene, Child Welfare, Hospital Social Service, Community Organization, Criminology, and Industrial and Social Research. Each department had its own courses listed and numbered separately in the School bulletins. Each had its own seminars, its own fieldwork, and its own prerequisites, and graduation was from a particular department rather than from one educational institution. In 1921, a group of students from one department were refused permission to attend seminars in another department. With approval of a department head, students were sometimes admitted directly to a second-year course without the basic training of the first-year program.

A special committee on instruction went to work on overhauling the curriculum. In 1927 the curriculum was reoriented and revitalized under four main headings:

> The Fundamental Techniques of Social Work
> Scientific Materials and Formulations of Human Experience
> The Practice of Social Work
> The Orientation of the Social Worker

This victory of integration over specialization was of vital importance to the future development of the School and to the growth of social work as a profession. It meant, in essence, that specialized knowledge in a particular field was not enough—that to the concept of the professional social worker had been added the significant requirement that he or she must have a broad understanding of social work and practice in general before attempting to become expert in any individual branch of the profession.

In 1927, a further step was taken to strengthen the fieldwork program by the establishment of a centralized Field Work Department headed by a director and guided by a standing committee. Executive responsibility for arrangements with social agencies and with students was assigned to the director, who also assumed responsibility for keeping track of students' progress in this division of the School's program. A review of the plan, made two years later, confirmed that substantial progress had been made.

As the golden age of the 1920s drew to a close, another important event took place at the School. In March 1929, more than 250 graduates of the institution gathered together for the first Alumni Conference, which was keyed to the general topic: Why Train for Social Work? The conference immediately became an annual event which reflected, in discussions and formal papers, the main currents of thought and practice in the social work field.

1930–1939: DECADE OF DEPRESSION

Few of the New York School graduates that attended the Alumni Conference in the spring of 1929 could have envisaged, any more than did the nation's economists and business leaders, the devastating era of the Great Depression which was soon to overpower the world, bringing financial ruin, catastrophic unemployment, and untold misery in its wake. Nor could they have foreseen that other concomitant of the depression era—the tremendously awakened interest on the part of government and private citizens alike in all phases of social work.

Work relief, unemployment insurance, old-age pensions, and many other forms of social security are today so commonplace and so fully accepted as a part of the social scene that it is difficult to recall the days when these forms of protection for the individual against economic adversity were still theoretical concepts for the professional social worker to argue about.

When the depression broke in the early 1930s, the immediate need for an increasing number of skilled social workers was apparent. The demand for trained social work employees on behalf of government and private agencies, coupled with a host of would-be trainees who sought to break into a profession which held so much promise in a world of economic chaos, resulted in unprecedented pressure upon the School. Veteran social workers and neophytes alike attempted to storm its citadel.

Many of the applicants for admission to the School were willing to accept part-time courses. Had the School been willing to compromise its high standards, thousands of extra social workers might have been graduated during the '30s. But the School refused to compromise. Even with endowment income sharply reduced, with public officials calling upon the faculty for increasing measures of counsel and assistance, with high enrollment straining every teaching facility, the School stuck to its basic idea of practical professional education on levels that had been established over a period of three decades.

The New York School never regarded mere size as a virtue. On the contrary, the School has consistently utilized the growing demand for its facilities not as a means to create a larger student body, but as a means to improve the quality of the student body through greater selectivity. As early as 1930, suggestions were made in the director's annual report regarding limitations on enrollment, and in 1934 positive steps in this direction were taken. By 1935 the pressure of applicants from New York City had become so great that the national and international characteristics of the School were being threatened. Reluctantly a new policy was adopted—the number of applicants admitted from the metropolitan area would be limited to approximately one-third of the total student population.

In spite of efforts to keep the student enrollment within bounds, the School had by 1931 outgrown the space available for it in the United Charities Building, where it had functioned since 1898. A move was therefore made to a new home at 122 East Twenty-second Street.

One result of increased selectivity was to raise the already high caliber of first-year students, but there was no escaping the fact that hundreds, possibly thousands, of qualified applicants had to be refused admission simply because there was no room for them, either in classes or in the placement agencies, which played such an important part in the fieldwork program.

The dilemma was equally acute where courses for part-time students were concerned. In the spring quarter of 1935 there were, for example, 572 registrants and only 300 places available, and additional sections of courses were yet to be arranged. At the same time there was a corresponding influx of applicants for evening courses. Preliminary explorations were made to determine the consequences involved in permitting a part-time registration of one thousand students. When it became clear that this number could not be handled satisfactorily, the plan was dropped.

During the depression no-credit extension courses were given for the New York Home Relief Bureau and for other agencies. Numerous institutes, including a four-week summer session on the administration of unemployment relief, were set up. Requests for extension courses and regular courses came from all sections of the country. There were even requests that branches of the School be established in particular communities. Anxious as it was to justify the great faith shown in it, the School could fill only a few of the requests for help. To have done more would have been to weaken and adulterate its teaching standards; and that, the School was not willing to do.

Outside activities of the faculty during this period were an impressive demonstration of the School's sense of responsibility to the total community. Staff members worked with the President's Emergency Committee for Employment, the New York State Temporary Relief Administration, the Federal

Emergency Relief Administration, and many other local, state, and national groups.

Despite the constant pressure on the faculty, there was no diminution of effort in the search for an ever-improved curriculum. A new type of required course in social research was instituted in 1932, aiming at understanding of research rather than the acquisition of the specialist's skill. The subject of social work administration assumed increasing importance. And there was a notable trend toward emphasis on courses in group work and public welfare.

It remained for an intensive faculty study in 1936 to focus on specific needs and to state more clearly than had ever been done before the School's concern for a teaching philosophy that integrated all aspects of social work. The last vestiges of specialization were buried. Henceforth, primary emphasis was to be on the important concepts common to all the varied fields of social work.

In 1938, after eleven years of service as director, Porter Lee resigned his post due to ill health. He was succeeded, as acting director, by Walter Pettit. A year later Mr. Lee died and Mr. Pettit became the fourth director of the New York School.

1940–1949: NEW HORIZONS

The New York School entered the decade of the 1940s by an act which symbolized its maturity and gave new recognition to the high professional standards it had created and maintained for so many years. On October 1, 1940, after forty-two years of informal relationships with Columbia University, the School entered into a formal affiliation with the institution whose rise to world stature under Nicholas Murray Butler in many ways paralleled the growth of the one-time School of Philanthropy.

Columbia assumed no financial responsibility for its newest graduate school, but undertook to provide degrees to properly qualified graduates. The School gained representation on the University Council and in turn invited Columbia representatives to sit on the School Council. Greatly simplified arrangements were made to permit students at either institution to take courses at the other.

The times permitted little basking in the glow of the new imprimatur on the School's record and its work. Already more than a year old, the Second World War within a single generation had made it clear that there would be unprecedented demands upon professional social workers. This feeling was confirmed in July of 1941, less than six months before Pearl Harbor, at the School's annual Alumni Conference. Social Work in the Present Emergency was the theme and there was general agreement on two major premises. Social work, the delegates contended, had survived and developed in previous crises. Further, there was unanimity in the conviction that the social upheavals already caused by World War II meant that "the people we serve will be more in need of our services."

Once again, as in the dark days of the depression, the curriculum facilities of the School were taxed to the breaking point. The demand for trained social workers in private agencies, in public programs, and in military establishments reached new peaks. At the same time some members of the faculty were being inducted into the armed forces, while others were being drawn away from the School to develop and execute special projects.

Many other schools in the field discussed, and a number of them adopted, "speed-up" systems of instruction patterned on accelerated programs in other educational areas. The New York School had been operating on a four-quarter-a-year plan of operation since 1923. It rejected the suggestion that the six quarters normally required for the M.S. degree be shortened. "War," director Pettit pointed out in his report for 1942, "merely accentuates social problems with which social workers have been dealing right along and that the training for social work in war time must be fundamentally the same as in time of peace."

While the School would not compromise its standards, it did increase enrollment moderately, organized additional fieldwork units, and made special arrangements to assist the United Services Organization (USO), the American Red Cross, and other units vitally concerned with wartime social problems. During the first year of the war, even with enrollment expanded to three hundred full-time students, the School was able to accept less than 60 percent of those who sought admission.

Pressure on the faculty was intense throughout the war. Each year was marked by special "institutes" or lecture series, such as two courses for twenty-five French women who were planning to return to France and help in postwar rehabilitation; a four-week institute for workers in recreation, civilian, and war agencies; and special meetings with representatives of nine metropolitan colleges to develop criteria for undergraduate curricula.

Long before "demobilization" became a headline word, a special postwar committee was at work on plans designed to help returning veterans catch up on the latest developments in the welfare field. As frequently as possible, mimeographed letters from the School and from individual faculty members went out to graduates and others in the armed forces who had been associated with the School. The concern always was to help these men and women retain their professional interest and status in an expanding field and to provide a sound base for their postwar work. As so often in the past, the School continued to emphasize as its ideal a combination of technical specialization and broad awareness of the cultural and social backgrounds against which techniques must be applied. "Social work today," Mr. Pettit wrote in 1944,

> is faced with the question of how can social workers be prepared for positions requiring a high degree of specialized technical training and at the same time develop a sense of responsibility for leadership in economic and social developments . . . Social work, as it achieves professional status, must have a basis of common philosophy, knowledge and practice out of which specialization develops.

Evidence of this continuing search for a balanced approach to training for professional social work was the work of a special committee assigned to explore the relationship between fieldwork and classroom instruction in the School curriculum. By 1945, when the committee's report was submitted, 136 agencies were providing fieldwork opportunities for School degree candidates. Fieldwork supervision accounted for nearly 20 percent of the total budget, exclusive of many charges assumed by outside agencies themselves. The Community Service Society alone provided fieldwork for an average of sixty students and carried the costs in its own budget.

To provide a "uniform pattern in preparation for professional social work," the curriculum committee suggested that classroom teachers from time to time supervise a limited number of fieldwork students and that fieldwork supervisors be assigned classroom responsibilities. The imperative need was clear: the curriculum should be unified and interrelated, and success in achieving this goal depended on faculty participation in more than a single aspect of a student's program.

The end of the war brought many hints that a worldwide "unified" approach to professional social work might be in sight. Notable among these was the first Pan-American Congress of Social Service in Santiago, Chile, to which Dr. Pettit was accredited by the State Department as a member of the

U.S. delegation. Another was the signing of the United Nations charter; the U.N. Economic and Social Council derived fundamentally from awareness of global aspects of human welfare problems. At the New York School itself, applications from candidates for admission from overseas surpassed all previous totals.

The New York School celebrated its fiftieth anniversary in 1948. In the same year the Community Service Society, its parent organization, marked its hundredth anniversary. The occasion, as sentimental as it was practical, was made to order for an objective analysis of the progress made in professional training for social work.

The scope of subjects covered in the School's three-day anniversary symposium at New York's Hotel Roosevelt and the Academy of Medicine was previewed by Dean Pettit in his final annual report when he retired in 1947. In his last message as dean, he summarized his beliefs and his observations. The most important concept upon which social work rests, he wrote, is "the fundamental value of human personality." Many before him had groped for such a telling phrase. None had struck a truer note. Related to this basic idea, he continued, is the necessity on the part of all social workers to be interested in and to have a liking for people, irrespective of class or race.

Training for social work is still in the experimental stage, he pointed out, noting the frequent reorganization of educational practice in even the older, more securely established institutions. He emphasized again the dilemma of trying to develop men and women who are both trained specialists and culturally and economically literate.

Social work, both public and private, requires understanding and support of the community, he declared. Too rapid progress in development of methods or too much emphasis on esoteric differences in philosophy tends to confuse essential community sources of approval. Many problems involving the possibility of cooperative training with other professional schools in the same university remain to be worked out, Pettit suggested. And he noted briefly that schools of social work have often been more successful in developing practitioners than in furnishing the field with administrative and executive personnel.

Pettit pointed to the need for continuing work on the problem of selective admissions. He concluded with a tribute to outside agencies, whose role in providing fieldwork opportunities makes professional training realistic and productive. "No other school of social work in the United States," he declared, "has had the good fortune to be associated with an agency as progressive and as aware of the need for adequate social work training as the Community Service Society."

The fiftieth anniversary celebration of the Community Service Society in April 1948 was a dramatic projection of many of the basic ideas and issues in social work that were inherent in Dean Pettit's summary. The theme of the symposium was Professional Social Work: Its Substance and World Significance. In addition to the many faculty members who took part in the program, there was a distinguished roster of outside speakers: James B. Conant, president of Harvard University; Frank B. Fackenthal, acting president of Columbia University; Sir Raphael Cilento, director of the Division of Social Activities of the United Nations; Brooke Claxton, minister of national defense of the Dominion of Canada; Brock Chisholm, executive secretary of the World Health Organization, and nearly a score more. "The mood of the symposium audience," a reporter noted, "was one of sober promise. The profession of social work had reached a definite state of maturity and this fact was made manifest in the very candor with which both its theoreticians and practitioners inspected its methods and its goals. But what seemed more important was the patent recognition that maturity brings new duties and responsibilities."

With Dean Pettit's resignation, Margaret Leal, who had joined the School in 1916 and been assistant director since 1933, became acting dean, a post she held throughout the anniversary year.

If 1948 was an eventful year, 1949 suggested that the second half-century of the School's history would be no less dramatic. In its fifty-first year, the School acquired, practically simultaneously, a new home, a new professional library, and a new dean.

The forces that brought the New York School of Social Work into being were both dynamic and self-renewing. The School remained strong and dynamic because it never hesitated to meet the challenges of changing times. Each test brought to light qualities of leadership and integrity which have, in their turn, attracted new strength.

1950: THE NEW YORK SCHOOL AT MID-CENTURY

If persons like Robert V. deForest, Edward T. Devine, John S. Kennedy, and the others who pioneered the development of the New York School of Philanthropy so many years ago could have returned in 1950 to see how their great vision had been realized, it is likely that they would have been impressed but not surprised. Much of the practical progress that had been made in professional training for social work had been derived directly from the fundamental principles established in the formative years of the School's existence.

There had also, however, been important shifts of emphasis in concepts of social work since the turn of the century. At the turn of the century, social work was a passionate crusade. The social worker was an unpopular and misunderstood reformer. He or she often did not work *with* people as much as *on* people; the elimination of social wrongs was the primary concern. Later the tide changed. Emphasis shifted to the individual, his or her motivations, reactions, and rights. At mid-century, largely due to the leadership of the New York School, there was an increasingly successful attempt to develop a more balanced approach to welfare problems. Understanding of the *interaction* between the individual and the social forces that constitute one's environment was the important basic objective. Emphasis on practice fieldwork, on the avoidance of specialization for specialization's sake, and on the development of well-rounded professional workers was never sacrificed. The result was a curriculum that served as a model for more than sixty similar professional schools established between 1900 and 1950. Within the framework of these principles, the School's faculty was able to work out distinctive educational and research procedures that made it a mecca for thousands of aspiring social workers each year.

The New York School in 1950 required a baccalaureate degree from an "approved" institution from all applicants for full-time or part-time work. At least two of the four years of college work had to be devoted to "strictly liberal arts studies." Eighteen months of continuous work, divided into six quarters, constituted the School's basic educational program. Students could aim for a master of science degree or, if their academic background did not qualify them for an M.S., for a professional certificate. In 1949, after many years of study of all factors involved, the School was authorized by Columbia University to grant a doctorate in social welfare.

The basic curriculum of the School embraced more than sixty courses designed to cover the field of social work in four main groups:

1. Methods and procedures common to all forms of social work;

2. Special problems of the different fields of social work;

3. Subject matter essential to social work which was especially adapted from the social and biological sciences and from the practice of other professional fields;

4. Technical, philosophical, and scientific phases of social work as a basis for effective correlation in practice.

In addition to the basic curriculum, there was an expanding "advanced curriculum" for workers who had already earned a master's degree in an accredited school of social work. Two-week institutes for persons with professional or volunteer experience in social work were offered by the School each summer, and special extension courses were frequently organized by request.

The burden of sustaining a professional educational program of this magnitude was carried by a full-time faculty of thirty-three men and women, a third of whom had been associated with the School for more than fifteen years. The full-time faculty was assisted by more than fifty part-time instructors and more than a dozen supervisors in fieldwork units.

After occupying seven floors in its building on Twenty-second Street for eighteen years, the School, in the fall of 1949, moved into a spectacular new location at 2 East Ninety-first Street. The School's striking home was the famous sixty-six-room house and garden (with an adjoining twenty-nine-room residence) from which the great financier and philanthropist, Andrew Carnegie, had given away nearly $350 million for the education and improvement of humanity during the last eighteen years of his life. The property was transferred to the School by the Carnegie Corporation on a no-rent basis for a period of twenty-one years, with an option for renewal.

Aside from the fact that it was admirably adaptable for use by an educational institution, the great mansion was a particularly appropriate setting for the New York School. More important than the physical structure was the fundamental faith in humankind and in American institutions which were associated so irrevocably with the tiny Scotsman who rose from poverty to become an industrial titan and who preached and practiced the gospel that the acquisition of great wealth involved responsibility to help improve the general welfare.

Much of the charm of the mansion, built in 1900, remained. Left intact were most of the hand-carved paneling on walls and ceiling, the teakwood room which the Carnegies used as their upstairs library, the parquet floors, and the Carrara marble fireplaces—elements that made the building the showplace of its era.

The library facilities of the School were enhanced considerably when the School moved into its new home. This unexpected development came about when the board of the Russell Sage Foundation decided to discontinue maintenance of its own valuable library. The New York School was given priority of selection, and an intensive study of the School's needs was made by a faculty committee with the help of a Foundation library staff member. The result was the acquisition of fourteen thousand bound volumes and thirty-two thousand pamphlets, which together were believed to make the School's library the equal of any specializing in the field of social welfare.

When it got under way in 1898, the old School of Philanthropy was distinguished by few physical or material appurtenances. It started with an idea, an ideal for improving practices in the social service field. And it started with men and women who believed in that idea and who were willing to forego many of the comforts of living and learning to make the idea a practical reality.

1950–1998: EXPANSION AND CONSOLIDATION

As noted in chapter 1, the School of Social Work has metamorphosed further in the second half-century of its existence. In the latter part of the 1950s, with renewed financial assistance from the Russell Sage Foundation, social science concepts once again were reintroduced into the social work curriculum, but in greater depth and with a more systematic approach toward their actual application in social work practice. In the 1960s, social activism was resurgent at CUSSW in conjunction with the societal movements concerning civil rights, the War on Poverty, Mobilization for Youth, welfare rights organization, and protests against the Vietnam War. As a result, the School's curriculum introduced sequences in community organization and group work. Research became increasingly important to the School. Its doctoral program entered a golden era during which it produced graduates who became among the most prominent social work educators, deans, and directors of the next generation. In the same era, and largely as a result of these movements, the School's governance system was modified so as to enable students to have one-third voting membership on all bodies responsible for educational policy, including the School's Committee on Instruction, the School Council (the ultimate arbiter of major educational decisions), and the full range of fieldwork committees. Enrollments at schools of social work nationwide grew considerably due in large part to the proliferation of training funds for graduate social work education that occurred under the aegis of the National Institute of Mental Health. The director of social work training at NIMH who spearheaded the expansion of such training programs was an alumnus of CUSSW, Dr. Milton Wittman.

In the early 1980s, however, the School of Social Work entered a phase of marked contraction and retrenchment. Shortly after Ronald Reagan became president of the United States, federal scholarship monies for social work students were slashed dramatically. Applications for nearly all schools of social work plummeted. In 1981, they declined by nearly two-thirds at Columbia. To balance the School budget that year, it was necessary to raise tuition by 17 percent and for the School to borrow $1 million from the central administration of Columbia University. Each year thereafter, applications rose slowly by about 5 percent per year. In the early 1990s, however, after the inauguration of President Bill Clinton, applications skyrocketed by 60 percent to 50 percent per year for each of three successive years, resulting in an extraordinarily strong applicant pool which has been sustained through the present day. The student body is both large—nearly one thousand M.S. and Ph.D. students (of whom approximately 750 are full-time enrollees)—and extremely diverse. Nearly 35 percent of the School's students are persons of color; about half of these are African American, a quarter are Hispanic American, and a quarter are Asian American. About 10 percent of the student body comes from a wide range of foreign nations. As in previous decades, the overwhelming proportion of students (85 percent) are women.

In 1970, the option of renewing the School's lease at the Andrew Carnegie Mansion could not be exercised. The School moved for one year into a temporary location near the main Columbia University campus on Morningside Heights. A year later it relocated to McVickar Hall, formerly a single-room occupancy hotel and for a brief period the home of the School of International and Public Affairs while it awaited the construction of a new fifteen-story facility. Located at 622 West 113th Street, McVickar Hall was to be merely a "temporary" facility for the School of Social Work. Offering only seven classrooms no larger than conventional odd-shaped living rooms, and unable to bear the weight of a library, McVickar Hall was an inhospitable setting for modern professional education. At the time of the School's centennial celebration, it was still the home of the School of Social Work.

In the early 1980s, casework, group work, and community organization lost their distinct identities as components of the School's curriculum. They were replaced by Concentration I, Concentration II, and Concentration III — descriptors that were so bereft of identifiable referents that it was not long before the major practice methods were renamed again. Today, the School's master's degree curriculum is arrayed along two basic axes. Each student enrolls for one of five methods of social work practice: Clinical Social Work Practice, Advanced Generalist Practice and Programming (which previously had been defined as PPS, or Practice, Programming, and Supervision), Social Administration, Social Research, and Policy Practice. Concurrently, each student also enrolls in one of eight fields of practice which offer specialized training within the context of the student's practice method. Respectively, these are Health, Mental Health, and Disabilities; Family and Children's Services; Aging and Adult Human Development; the World of Work; International Social Welfare and Services for Immigrants and Refugees; School-Based and School-Linked Social Services; Contemporary Social Problems; and Personal Social Services. All but the lattermost, which has few student enrollees, are discussed in detail in parts 2 and 3 of this volume.

In its second half-century, CUSSW has emerged as a leader in the establishment of innovative dual degree programs with other professional schools and disciplines. These programs provide in-depth training in allied fields, create new and productive career pathways for CUSSW-trained social workers, and, most importantly, generate new strategies, venues, and methods for attacking social problems that have resisted traditional interventions. They include

1. a dual degree program with the Columbia University School of Business resulting in a master of science in social work and a master of business administration.

2. a dual degree program with the Columbia University School of Public Health that yields a master of science in social work and the master of public health.

3. a dual degree program with the Columbia University School of Law in which the student earns both the master of science in social work and the juris doctor degree.

4. a dual degree program with the Graduate School of Jewish Theological Seminary whereby students earn the master of science in social work and the master of arts in Jewish Studies.

5. a dual degree program with the Union Theological Seminary in which students earn both the master of science in social work and the master of divinity.

6. a dual degree program with the Columbia University Graduate School of Architecture, Planning, and Preservation that yields the master of science in social work and a master of science in urban planning.

7. a dual degree program with the Columbia University School of International and Public Affairs in which the student earns the master of science in social work and the master of public administration.

8. a dual degree program with the Bank Street College of Education which yields the master of science in social work and the master of science in education, with specialization in special education.

In addition, within the School of Social Work, several "minors" have been established for students who are interested in business administration, international social welfare, law, and public policy and administration.

In 1998, at the School's centennial anniversary, the faculty consisted of forty-five full-time tenured or tenure-track faculty members. Unlike a mere decade earlier, all of the full-time faculty members had a doctoral degree. In addition, there were about fifty part-time or adjunct faculty members. More than two hundred course sections were taught every year.

THE CENTENNIAL CELEBRATION

Like the milestone celebrations held in conjunction with the School's twenty-fifth and fiftieth anniversaries, the centennial anniversary offered another opportune occasion to contemplate past, present, and possible future developments at the School of Social Work. A three-day celebration was held June 11–13, 1998, at the elegant Low Memorial Library on the Columbia University campus and at the Holiday Inn-Crowne Plaza Hotel in midtown Manhattan. The theme of the centennial celebration, which was attended by some nine hundred participants, was Celebrating the Past, Confronting the

Present, and Visioning the Future. Attendees at the "kick-off reception" at Low Memorial Library were welcomed by Columbia University's President George Rupp, Dean Ronald A. Feldman, and the co-chairpersons of the Centennial Celebration Planning Committee, Professors Sheila B. Kamerman and Donna Rosenthal. Under their leadership, more than 120 alumni/ae and friends of the School had a unique opportunity to contribute to the planning of the centennial celebration. In addition, a fifty-person honorary committee co-chaired by Columbia University trustees and CUSSW alumni/ae Maureen Cogan, Marylin Levitt, and Maurice V. Russell worked to bring the centennial celebration to fruition.

The keynote speaker at the celebration was Tipper Gore, the wife of U.S. Vice President Albert Gore. Hillary Rodham Clinton, the nation's First Lady, addressed the assemblage by videotape. Another keynote speaker, Marion Wright Edelman, president of the Children's Defense Fund, was unable to attend because air traffic from Washington D.C. to New York City had been halted by a severe thunderstorm.

Theme 1 of the celebration, Lessons from the Past, was spearheaded by a plenary session at which Professor Emeritus Alfred J. Kahn '46 M.S., '52 D.S.W., spoke about CUSSW and Social Work: the First Century. His speech appears as chapter 1 of this volume. The discussants for this presentation were Betty Broadhurst '71 D.S.W., David Rothman, and Herman Stein '41 M.S., '58 D.S.W. This plenary session was followed by seventeen workshops focusing on such topics as clinical social work, child welfare, social advocacy, social policy, health and mental health, aging, social work in the workplace, doctoral education, settlement houses, urban problems and community interventions, and social group work. In addition, round table discussions were held for graduates of CUSSW's dual degree programs with the Bank Street College of Education, the Jewish Theological Seminary, the Union Theological Seminary, the Columbia University School of Public Health, and the Columbia University School of International and Public Affairs.

A second plenary session addressed theme 2: Current Issues and Controversies in Social Work Education and Practice. The speakers were the key elected officers or administrative officials of the five leading organizations in social work education and practice: the Council on Social Work Education, the National Association of Social Workers, the National Association of Deans and Directors of Schools of Social Work, the Baccalaureate Program

Directors, and the Group for the Advancement of Doctoral Education in Social Work. This workshop was followed by a series of twenty-one workshops that addressed such topics as Transforming Social Work Agencies in an Era of Crisis and Change; Private Practice and Social Work; Practice and Research: New Models of Intervention; Confronting the New Ethical Dilemmas in Social Work; Social Work and Social Reform; Meeting the New Demands of Social Work Administration; Is Social Work Losing Child Welfare? Making the Media Work for Social Work; Doing Social Work with Private Philanthropy; What Social Workers Need to Know When They Are Expert Witnesses; Malpractice in Social Work: Do's and Don'ts; New Models for Community Practice; Welfare, Workfare, and Jobs: Emerging Roles for Social Workers; Advocacy Through Electronic Communications; Persons with Disabilities: Recent Issues and New Practices; International Immigration: Recent Issues and New Practices; The Changing Face of Volunteers and Voluntarism; The New Audio-Visual Technologies in Social Work; and CUSSW Abroad: Effecting Change Around the Globe. The speakers and discussants at these workshops were predominantly alumni/ae of the School who represented a wide range of practice areas, personal backgrounds, and geographic areas.

The third plenary session was a panel discussion that addressed the theme Visioning the Twenty-first Century: Where Do We Go from Here? The participants were Joseph T. Coyle of Harvard University Medical School; Rebecca Rimel, president of the Pew Charitable Trusts; and Paul Goldberger, architectural and urban critic of *The New York Times* and the *New Yorker Magazine*. The topics considered in conjunction with this theme included CUSSW: The Second Century; Social Service Delivery: For-Profit, Non-Profit, and Governmental Agencies—What Can We Expect?; How the New Information Technologies Will Affect Social Work Practice; The Effects of Emerging Sociodemographic Trends on Social Work Education and Practice; Social Work in Tomorrow's Cities: Visioning the Next Century; Future Challenges and Opportunities in International Social Welfare; Biomedical Dilemmas and Social Work Practice in the Next Century; Practicing Social Policy in the Next Century; Visioning Field Instruction for a New Millennium; The Shredded Social Safety Net: What Policies Next?; Visioning the Future of Child and Family Services; Community Practice in the Next Century; Visioning the Future of Clinical Social Work; Centenarians in the New Millennium; Is There a Safety Net in Our Future?; Visioning the Virtual Social Work Agency; The Future of Social Work in Health Care; Breaking Human Services Boundaries in the Next Century; Visioning the Future of Social Work in Mental Health; and Breaking Issues: An Open Forum for the Discussion of Emerging Issues in Social Work.

A special session called "The Deans Remember" offered an opportunity for more than a score of CUSSW alumni/ae who were present or former deans or directors of schools of social work to reminisce publicly before the assembled gathering. To celebrate the School's centennial anniversary, four endowed centennial professorships were funded. A CUSSW Hall of Fame was newly established in conjunction with the School's centennial celebration, and its first inductees were Ada E. Deer '61; Sister Mary Paul Janchill '75; Alfred J. Kahn '46, 52 D.S.W.; Helen Rehr '45, '58 D.S.W.; and Herman Stein '41, '58 D.S.W. In addition, seven special Centennial Leadership Awards were presented at a luncheon on June 13. The recipients were Susan Matorin '66 and Barbara Silverstone '73 D.S.W. (Leadership in Social Work Practice); Megan McLaughlin '81 D.S.W. and Alan Siskind '61 (Leadership in Advancing the Mission of Social Work); Francis Akukwe '79 D.S.W., Karen Olsen de Figueres, and Tomi Itabashi '53 (International Leadership in Social Work Practice); Robert Morris '59 and Ben Orcutt '58, '62 D.S.W. (Leadership in Social Work Education); Samuel Cotton '95 and Garnethia Pettiford '90 (Young Leadership Award); Sidney Berengarten '43, Maureen Cogan '77, and Marylin Levitt '73, '82 D.S.W. (Significant Contributions to the School of Social Work); and Beatrix Hamburg and C. Virginia Fields (Centennial Leadership Awards). In addition, a special dinner was held for graduates of the School's doctoral program.

The centennial celebration represents a historic landmark in the development of the Columbia University School of Social Work. It is hardly coincidental that certain of the themes, issues, and discussions from the School's earliest days are still evident a century later. Yet, even as continuities and trends are observed in the School's development, at each phase there also have been historic advances, breakthroughs, and cutting-edge innovations. In 1998, the School of Social Work was still attending to the synergies that had emerged from the interrelationships between theoretical advances and practical applications. To the present day, curriculum development is still characterized by continuous attention to the sequencing of required courses, the harmonizing of substantive content within differing sections of the same course, and superior faculty instruction. New fields of practice and new practice methods have been introduced to the curriculum while longstanding and highly distinguished fields of practice and practice methods have been revitalized and updated. The quality of field instruction at more than four hundred social work agencies in the New York City metropolitan area is assured by a Field Instruction Department consisting of seven full-time social work professionals. New electronic, information, and computing technologies are introduced through the Office of Computing and Information Technology. And, the School's fiscal well-being is strengthened inestimably through continuing support from a large and dedicated body of twelve thousand living alumni /ae and the activities of four professionals in its Office of Development and Alumni Relations.

It may be beyond our present capacity, but not our hopes, to envision the nature of social work education at the time of CUSSW's next hundred-year anniversary. The world has been transformed dramatically in a single century and is likely to change even far more rapidly in the next one hundred years. But, if the past is truly the best predictor of the future, in 2098 many of the same challenges, issues, and controversies will confront social work education. However, more likely than not, the profession's means of addressing them will vary in ways that are beyond our imagination. We can only hope that peoples and societies worldwide will have learned to build upon the strengths of their prior achievements and of their best educational institutions so as to avoid the pitfalls that have befallen humankind thus far in the unsteady journey toward a better world.

Part Two

METHODS OF PRACTICE

TODAY THE Columbia University School of Social Work educates M.S. students in one of five different methods of social work practice. Respectively, these are clinical social work, advanced generalist practice and programming, social administration, social policy, and social research. The essays in part 2 examine each of these five practice methods from the perspectives of "yesterday, today, and tomorrow."

The clinical social work method educates students who are interested in working directly with individuals, families, and groups. The courses in this method train students from an ecological perspective that entails the assessment of individuals, families, and groups in relation to their environments and, subsequently, the conceptualization and implementation of appropriate interventions for these populations. Among the specific topics studied are differential assessment, intervention, and evaluation within a selected field of practice; utilization of individual, family, group, and case management modalities; the clinical application of risk and resiliency theories and research to at-risk populations; and relevant clinical issues regarding specific client populations. Chapter 3, "Clinical Practice," is authored by Martha Dore. As with all of the other essays in part 2, Dore considers clinical practice education at CUSSW from past, present, and future perspectives. She examines the landmark Milford Conference and its now-classic report, social casework in the 1930s and 1940s, efforts to connect diagnosis and treatment from the post–World War II years through the mid-1960s, and key challenges to the casework paradigm in the late 1990s.

Advanced generalist practice and programming builds upon the direct practice skills learned by M.S. students in the first year of their graduate studies. Students who major in this method during their second year learn to intervene at the program delivery, organizational, and community levels.

This practice method seeks to develop social work professionals who are skilled in direct practice and who are astute in their assessment of ways in which their own organizational settings and the contexts in which clients live and work both facilitate and hinder their welfare. Attention is paid to the development of a wide range of skills, including those of direct practice, community and population-focused needs assessment, program planning and evaluation, the supervision of volunteers and paid staff, community outreach, and group leadership. Among the specific topics studied are community practice, movement from case to cause, development of innovative and responsive social programs and resources, and staffing and funding. In chapter 4, "Advanced Generalist Practice and Programming," Donald McVinney traces the development of this practice method at CUSSW. He attends in particular to the specific skills and curriculum issues pertinent to this practice method.

The social administration method trains M.S. students who are especially interested in acquiring administrative and planning skills. This method prepares professionals who can administer agencies or programs and work as planners in the development of social services. The requisite course work emphasizes organizational behavior, social planning, fiscal and personnel management, and evaluation strategies. Specific topics that are studied in this method include the administration of social service programs, program evaluation, financial management, staff development and training, human resource management, and management information systems. Chapter 5, "Social Administration," is co-authored by Lawrence L. Martin and Karla Toruño Aguirre Choudhury. The authors examine education for social administration from the perspective of the philanthropic years at CUSSW (1898–1929), the New Deal years (1929–1941), the Great Society years (1965–1972), and the devolution years (1976 through the present).

The social policy method is the most recent addition to the M.S. curriculum at CUSSW. Established in 1995, this method trains students to become policy analysts, policy planners, and policy advocates in a wide range of social work settings, including public and private agencies at the local, national, and international levels. The curriculum teaches students the knowledge, values, and skills needed to define policy issues from a social work perspective, collect and analyze relevant data, develop policy options, prepare testimony, and formulate recommendations. Authored by Sheila B. Kamerman, chapter 6 is entitled "Social Policy." Respectively, the sections of this essay address social policy education at CUSSW in the first fifty years of the School's development; from the end of World War II to the 1960s; from 1960 to the end of the 1980s; and the 1990s. In a final section, Kamerman discusses key issues pertaining to the future of social policy education at the School of Social Work.

The social research method trains M.S. students who are interested in learning the methods and practices of social work research and in pursuing careers in this field. It encompasses expanded studies of research technology and methods and their application to the problems of social work and the needs of a wide range of at-risk constituencies. Required courses in this method include statistics, computer technologies, and advanced research methods as well as independent research projects that take place at students' field instruction placements. The social research method is linked with students' assignments in one of the four above-cited practice methods. In chapter 7, "Social Research," Steven Schinke and Tony Tripodi examine highlights of social research education and projects at the School. They review the historical context of social research at CUSSW, professionalization and education (including national research groups and research centers, research journals, the teaching of research methods, training at the M.S. level, and training at the Ph.D. level), and the development of substantive and methodological knowledge about social research (including social science and social work, the empirical practice movement in social work, practice theory research, agency-based research, and research in selected substantive areas). A final section examines the future of social research at CUSSW.

Taken together, the five essays in part 2 provide a comprehensive overview of past and present aspects of each of the five major methods of social work practice that are taught in the M.S. degree program at the Columbia University School of Social Work. In addition, they highlight critical issues and anticipated future developments pertaining to these practice methods. While focusing specifically upon the curriculum of CUSSW, many of these issues are of general concern to social work education nationwide and, indeed, worldwide.

Chapter 3

CLINICAL PRACTICE

Martha Morrison Dore

An oft-cited exchange between Mary Richmond, general secretary of the Baltimore Charity Organization Society (COS), and Jane Addams, a founder of the Hull House Settlement in Chicago, has Addams excoriating the charity organization movement for relying on a retail method of philanthropy, while upholding the superiority of the wholesale method of the settlement movement.[1] Addams complained that COS workers obsessively gathered limitless details about a client's problem, while doing little or nothing to address the source of the client's difficulties. Richmond, on the other hand, believed that the settlement methods romanticized clients' problems and failed to consider the uniqueness of the client in his or her situation. Further, according to Richmond, every response to need on the retail level has the potential for generating wholesale change.[2]

This paper examines the retail approach to social work, the method of practice that in Richmond's day evolved from "friendly visiting among the poor," the title of her first book, to become social casework, and, much later, clinical social work.[3] It also examines how that development was influenced by faculty and alumni of the New York School of Philanthropy, which evolved in its title and form into the New York School of Social Work in the early 1920s, and into the Columbia University School of Social Work in the

I wish to thank colleagues Alfred Kahn and Brenda McGowan as well as two very knowledgeable anonymous reviewers for their helpful comments on this work. I would also like to acknowledge the intellectual curiosity and enthusiasm of several cohorts of doctoral students at Columbia University and at the University of Pennsylvania who have stimulated my interest in the development of social casework theory and practice.

late 1950s.[4] While those scholars and clinicians who influenced the development of the retail approach to social work came to appreciate and even adopt some ideas from the wholesale method, casework has its own unique history in social work that is worth examining for what we can learn about the profession's heritage and about its current state.

It is safe to say that for much of its first hundred-year history the New York School was the preeminent casework school. That is not to say that faculty affiliated with other schools of social work did not make important, lasting contributions to casework theory and method. Jessie Taft, Virginia Robinson, Mary Jarrett, Bertha Reynolds, Harriet Bartlett, and many others come immediately to mind. However, nowhere else was such collective intellect and energetic inquiry devoted over so many years to developing this method of practice. Casework texts authored by New York School faculty members Mary Richmond, Gordon Hamilton, Florence Hollis, Carel Germain, and Carol Meyer have trained many generations of social work students in schools throughout the country. This paper describes the evolution of casework practice that took place at the New York School and identifies some of the factors that played a role in making this school the center for development of this social work method.

THE EARLY YEARS

In 1912 Mary Richmond, who until that year regularly taught courses in Family Rehabilitation at the New York School, wrote a memo to the newly reinstalled director of the school, Edward Devine, registering her dismay that the school was proposing to appoint "three young university men" as full-time instructors in the program.[5] She questioned whether course work in such topics as "the economic basis of social work," "social reformers," and "race problems" would provide "practical workers" with the technique necessary to tackle the intransigent social problems of the day. Her vision was of a school for social workers in which "in the classroom, the seminar, the field training and the assigning of fellowships there shall be unity of method and aim."[6] She recognized that the newly emerging field of social work was still far from having a well-conceptualized method of practice, and she suggested that, rather than devoting the greatest portion of their time to studying theory, aspiring social workers should be attending "practical courses" that would more closely reflect actual social work in the field. Faculty members, she believed, should reflect this practical experience and should devote their time to "the painstaking working out of the more important social work processes . . . [which] in turn might become our unique contribution to social reform in this country."

In these earnest comments to her colleague Devine, Richmond articulated a central tension in the development of social work as a profession and in the training of its practitioners, one that is with us still.[7] How is training in the practical work of responding appropriately and with skill to the needs of clients to be integrated with building the more abstract, foundation knowledge necessary to inform that practical work? As we examine the development of clinical social work practice in the ensuing years, we must acknowledge what Mary Richmond recognized in the profession's founding years: that social work, unlike nearly any other profession, is shaped largely by its environment in all its dimensions. It is not a profession that can be solely learned in the classroom through a process of didactic instruction. Its principles and techniques must be tested and honed in the laboratory of human interaction. Clinical social work practice is an organic process, shaping and shaped by this interaction. Those who practice it know and understand that the enterprise is not a static entity, but, like clients in interaction with the environment, it influences and is influenced by the context in which it is carried out.

From the beginning the direction of casework practice was determined at the New York School through its affiliation with the Charity Organization Society of New York City, an affiliation that continued for over fifty years. Other early schools of social work, such as the Boston School for Social Workers, a cooperative venture between Harvard University and Simmons College, were begun under university auspices, growing out of undergraduate courses in social economics and philanthropy; they were staffed by university faculty members with doctorates in the social sciences.[8] Other programs, such as the Chicago School of Civics and Philanthropy, were started as a series of lectures offered by a particular settlement house; these programs quickly affiliated with an educational institution because of the stability of the resources found there.[9]

By retaining its status as an independent school of social work under the auspices of the COS, the New York School maintained a firm identity as a training school for practitioners, most particularly caseworkers. This affiliation also helped to institutionalize field training in social work education; for many years students at the New York school completed the first two months of their field training in a COS district office learning about "practical work with families."

During the New York School's formative years, casework was nearly synonymous with family work as practiced in charity organization societies. The limited practice literature available prior to World War I was written by and for COS workers. Edward Devine, who was general secretary of the Charity Organization Society of New York City prior to appointment to his first tenure as director of the New York School in 1904, wrote several volumes of advice for charity workers, including *The Practice of Charity* (1904), *Efficiency and Relief: A Programme of Social Work* (1906), and *The Principles of Relief* (1907). The last work formed the basis of a lecture series for students in the New York School led by Devine under the title, The Care of Families in their Homes.[10]

In *The Practice of Charity* Devine described the emerging profession of social work thus:

> We may ask the most searching and the most sweeping of questions without impertinence and without offense. "You are in trouble. Well, what is the difficulty? Just tell me all about it." Family relationships and family tragedies, it is our province and our duty to investigate. Weaknesses of human character and heroic human qualities are alike laid bare before us . . . The psychologist studies the mind, the physiologist the body, the sociologist social relations; but to us it is given to know on the one hand the woes and failures of men, and on the other the regenerating and curative forces at work in the community — all of them, religious, educational, industrial, social, personal. We may not directly wield all or many of them, but we must know them and summon them in individual instances to their task.[11]

In the 1905–06 *Handbook* for students in the New York School a requirement for admission to the school, in addition to "one year of actual service in social work, membership in some board of directors, or a college degree," was to have read Devine's *The Principles of Relief* as well as the latest annual report of the New York Charity Organization Society.[12] It was suggested but not required that entering students read Mary Richmond's *Friendly Visiting Among the Poor* as well. Students in the New York School were clearly exposed to a vision of social work practice that drew heavily on the COS model, for while the prevailing theories of how people came to grief were social and economic in their focus, the model for intervening in these problems was on the individual and family level.

This approach may be contrasted with the approach to social work practice being taught during the same period at the Chicago School of Civics and Philanthropy, which had its start under the aegis of the settlement movement. Its first director was Graham Taylor, also director of the Chicago Commons Settlement, and its curriculum, while including fieldwork (voluntary) at local charitable and relief societies, emphasized methods of social change addressing neighborhood and community problems.[13] This was particularly true after 1907, when a grant from the Russell Sage Foundation enabled Taylor to hire Julia Lathrop to head a department of social research.[14] In 1905–06 students at the Chicago School included eighteen YWCA workers and seventeen settlement workers as opposed to eleven "workers in charity."[15]

In the 1912–13 *Bulletin* of the New York School, Director Edward Devine announced a reorganization of the curriculum into a two-year course of study.[16] The first year would be a foundation year in which all courses were required, and the second would be a year of specialization, or "vocational" year, as it was termed. Students who successfully completed the first year could be admitted into the vocational program. Specialization areas proposed for the vocational program included Public Service, Organized Charity, Delinquents, Housing and Town Planning, Medical Social Service, Children's Agencies, Recreation, Institutions, and Settlements. Illustrated here is the beginning of a lengthy struggle in social work education over whether to train students in a specific field of practice or in a universal practice approach that could be applied in any setting. For those who advocated a universal approach, the next decade would be occupied with identifying the generic elements in all of casework practice. Leadership in this effort was provided in large part by the New York School, particularly by Porter Lee, who joined the faculty in 1912.

Lee was former director of the Philadelphia Society for Organizing Charity, the agency Mary Richmond had once headed; thus he was the "practical type" espoused by Richmond. Succeeding Edward Devine as the school's third director in 1917, Lee would move the New York School further away from academia and further into the world of casework practice in the years to come. In his first year on the faculty, Lee, together with Henry Thurston, an experienced practitioner in the area of child welfare, taught the two-semester foundation course Principles and Technique of Social Work. The course description in the School's bulletin reads very much like a contemporary generalist practice course. The other required foundation courses in 1912 were History and Development of Social Work, whose content was comparable to our contemporary introductory social policy sequence; The Scientific Basis of Social Work, a course which, like our courses on human behavior in the social environment, surveyed the social science contributions to social work practice; and Social Statistics, which was designed "to acquaint the student with the extent, uses, and limitations of the collected quantitative information on social subjects."[17]

By 1912 Mary Richmond was no longer listed among the staff of the New York School, although she was chosen to deliver the prestigious Kennedy Lectures at the school in 1914. Her topic was First Steps in Social Case Work. A brochure describing these lectures, which took place Wednesday afternoons at 4 o'clock from mid-March to mid-April, suggests they were a preview of *Social Diagnosis,* Richmond's book on casework practice published by the Russell Sage Foundation in 1917. *Social Diagnosis* described for the first time elements of the casework process for practitioners. It was widely used as the primary text in the training of caseworkers in schools of social work for the next twenty years. It also formed the conceptual basis — study, diagnosis, and treatment — for the casework method, which, while refined over time, has remained remarkably consistent and relevant to this day.

Porter Lee Becomes Director, 1917

Porter Lee's ascendancy to the directorship of the New York School in 1917 was propitious for social casework. As the former director of a charity organization society, he was familiar firsthand with the training needs of practitioners. He also understood the intellectual demand on casework faculty to integrate theory and practice and to develop accessible materials for student training. In his first report as director of the New York School, Lee noted the lack of "scientific teaching material on technical aspects of social work."[18] He acknowledges formation of the Association of Training Schools for Professional Social Work, whose object was "to develop standards of training for professional social work."[19] These standards, according to Lee, required a universally accessible body of knowledge regarding the "processes of social work." Lee voiced hope that eventually the new Association of Training

Schools would undertake research to develop materials for teaching. In the meantime, however, he believed it was also incumbent on the individual schools of social work to carry out their own research studies on elements of effective practice.

Throughout the 1920s the New York School continued to analyze and refine its approach to casework, even as it trained scores of students in its application. A noteworthy event in relation to the future development of social casework was the addition of Gordon Hamilton to the school's faculty in 1923. A New Jersey native and Bryn Mawr College graduate, Hamilton was one of the group of social workers trained by the American Red Cross Home Service during World War I. As a Red Cross Home Service Worker in Denver, Colorado, her path crossed that of Mary Richmond, who recognized the potential of the younger social worker and who urged her to go to New York to work for the Charity Organization Society there. From 1920 until she joined the New York School faculty in 1923, Hamilton worked as caseworker and research secretary for the New York COS.

Hamilton was greatly influenced by Richmond's work. In her first published paper, "Progress in Social Case Work," which appeared in the July 1923 issue of *The Family*, the journal of the American Association for Organizing Family Social Work, Hamilton began her discussion by quoting Richmond's now familiar definition of social casework: "Social case work consists of those processes which develop personality through adjustments consciously effected, individual by individual, between men and their social environment."[20]

In her article Hamilton looked at the evolution of family casework concepts. She observed that despite differences in the language used, many early ideas regarding family work had withstood the test of time. She noted, for example, that COS workers were admonished in the 1890s to gather facts, rather than rely on personal judgments, in developing plans for alleviating family suffering. Hamilton then traced the influence of knowledge gained from the social and behavioral sciences on caseworkers' understanding and interpretation of the facts they had gathered. She noted that this knowledge had increased significantly over the previous thirty years, giving caseworkers a very different lens—a psychodynamic one rather than an idiosyncratic one—through which to view families in trouble. Hamilton noted also the growing emphasis on evaluation of "accomplishment": "What do we actually succeed in doing for the individual, for the family, for society?" She suggested that evaluation of method and outcome would hasten the development of social casework, a recognition that presaged later efforts by New York School faculty to develop ways of doing just that. In closing Hamilton remarked on the current state of casework, which reflected disparate fields of practice rather than a unified method of treatment. She cautioned caseworkers in the various fields not to become complacent about the current state of practice and made projections about the influence of the scientific method in shaping casework in the future.

Mary Antoinette Cannon, a nationally known medical social worker, and Marion E. Kenworthy, a psychiatrist who was to be influential in developing psychiatric casework at the New York School, also joined the faculty in the early 1920s. Around that same time, as the result of a proposal developed by faculty member and child welfare scholar Henry Thurston for training social workers to work with children, the Commonwealth Fund established eight child guidance clinics in major cities across the country, including one affiliated with the New York School.[21] The Bureau for Children's Guidance, of which Marion Kenworthy became medical director, was described in the New York School *Bulletin* for 1926–27 as "a behavior clinic for the study and treatment of maladjusted children and for the training of the School students majoring in mental hygiene through participation in this program."[22] Several alumni/ae of the New York School, such as Charlotte Towle and Helen Harris Perlman, who were later to influence the development of social casework through their own writing and teaching, were involved as fieldwork students or supervisors with the Bureau of Children's Guidance.

Despite organized efforts to identify similarities in casework activities across fields of practice, including a major study by the newly formed American Association of Social Workers in the early 1920s, social work educators continued to worry publicly throughout the 1920s that the field was becoming fragmented, that no attention was being paid to developing a uniform body of knowledge and technique applicable to all forms of casework practice. In his 1925–26 report as director of the New York School, Porter Lee remarked that "in so far as the development of specialized programs of instruction contribute to this separatist tendency, they contribute to the weakness of social work despite their unmistakable contributions also to the achievement of higher standards."[23] He called for schools of social work to collaborate in formulating "the requirements which social work makes of its practitioners" and to "define the scope and content of the equipment which our best experience in training suggests as practicable for those who try to meet these requirements." [24]

This preoccupation with finding common elements in all of casework practice was again reflected in a speech given by Mary Antoinette Cannon in 1928 at the National Conference of Social Work in Memphis. It was reprinted in *The Family* as "Underlying Principles and Common Practices in Social Work." [25] In this speech Cannon reflected social work's ongoing preoccupation with its status as a profession, a continued reaction to Abraham Flexner's speech at the National Conference of Charities and Corrections some thirteen years before. Flexner had questioned whether social work could call itself a profession, stating that, among other failings, it lacked a unified body of knowledge it could call its own, as well as an "educationally communicable technique." [26]

Cannon responded by identifying eight principles underlying all methods of social work practice, including casework and community organization. She suggested that social work is primarily educational in nature: "the subject taught being the social life of the client (individual or group) past, present, and future." [27] She refuted the notion that caseworkers are concerned primarily with personality adjustment. What sets social work apart from other professions that aim to restore social functioning is social work's concern with "the personality in interaction with the environment." [28] "Other professions have social concepts and social objectives, but I think that only social work *never* has a purely individual objective" (emphasis added). [29] Cannon thus reflected the continuing theme found in the writings of educators associated with the New York School: casework is focused on the interaction between the individual and the environment. Psychodynamic principles and concepts may be important in understanding the individual's response to, and actions upon, the environment—as are other sources of social and behavioral knowledge—but treatment clearly targets both sides of the person–environment equation.

The Milford Conference and Its Report

Cannon's paper noted the contribution of the recently released preliminary report of the Milford Conference, which offered a paradigm for generic social work practice. The Milford Conference, led by Porter Lee, was composed of representatives of six national social work organizations who had begun meeting together in 1923 in Milford, Pennsylvania, to identify training needs for the field.[30] As a first step in specifying the necessary components of social work training, the group wrestled with answering the question, "What is social case work?" Unable to come to a mutually agreeable definition, the group continued to meet annually to study this question, as well as training concerns.

In 1929 the Milford Conference issued a report titled "Social Case Work: Generic and Specific," based on the findings of a subcommittee assigned the task of defining social casework. The report echoed Mary Richmond's lament to Edward Devine in 1912 regarding the absence of specific formulations of philosophy, methods, and experience in the practice of social casework. What had changed in the ensuing seventeen years was casework practice itself, according to the Milford study. The committee members had studied the subject intensively and found that there was, indeed, a well-defined entity called casework, that it demonstrated beginning adherence to scientific principles in its application, and that its practitioners ascribed to conscientious professional standards.[31]

The Milford Conference report defined social casework generically as dealing with "the human being whose capacity to organize his own normal social activities may be impaired by one or more deviations from accepted standards of normal social life . . ."[32] It listed about fifty such deviations, including alcoholism, bad housing, child labor, communicable disease, delinquency, mental ill health, and others, some located in the individual and others in the environment. These deviations are ideally managed by the individual within his or her natural helping network. The need for casework services is indicated "only when their presence or persistence implies impairment of the capacity for self-maintenance."[33]

The Milford Conference report also addressed the norms by which caseworkers assess the individual's capacity for self-maintenance. It admonished the field to recognize the existence of these norms and to seek to more clearly define them. In addition, it identified a structure for collecting case data that could enable caseworkers to more accurately assess whether an individual is functioning at a normative level: "Treatment is possible only when generalizations regarding human personality and its capacities, and regarding deviations from accepted standards of normal social life, have been particularized for the individual concerned . . . This particularization is achieved by the social case worker in large measure through the social case history."[34]

The committee's list of methods by which the caseworker assists the individual "to develop his own capacity to organize his own normal social activities" revealed the conceptual and methodological limitations that concerned Mary Richmond and, later, Gordon Hamilton and Porter Lee. This methods list was a hodgepodge of activities; some were process oriented, such as "interviewing" and "observation," and others were interventive in nature, such as "commitment" and "adoption." It reflected more than any other aspect of the Milford report casework's difficulties in defining its procedures for bringing about change in the person–environment dynamic. The need to more clearly identify and define such procedures was to become a preoccupation of casework scholars at the New York School and elsewhere in the years to come.

The Milford Conference report appeared just on the threshold of enormous changes in the context of social work as well as in the philosophy of practice itself. In 1929, when the report was released, the country was on the verge of the Great Depression, years of economic turmoil that would bring with them a reawakening of the old struggles in social work over mission and methods. Many questioned how casework would — or whether it even could — respond to the economic deprivations of the Depression era. Quick on the heels of the depression came the political turmoil in Europe and the Pacific that culminated in World War II. Again, social work was called upon to respond to the needs of a country at war, as it had been in World War I.

Also in the early 1930s, a new model of casework practice, the functional approach, entered onto the scene, challenging the fundamental structure of the diagnostic paradigm. This practice approach, whose primary authors were Jessie Taft and Virginia Robinson at the Pennsylvania School of Social Work, was based on the psychodynamic theory of Otto Rank, a former disciple of Sigmund Freud. Rank's theory emphasized human agency in the form of the Will. The functional approach sought to engage the client's Will in a dynamic process toward change bounded by the realities imposed by the host agency's function and purpose.[35] With its focus on agency setting and its ready adaptation to relief giving, functional practice was eager to establish a niche in the newly formed public assistance programs and other public institutions developed in response to the effects of the depression.[36] Had these social changes rendered obsolete the diagnostic model so carefully honed at the New York School?

To practitioners and educators struggling to respond to the social upheaval of the 1930s and 1940s, the Milford Conference report must have seemed an anachronism, reflecting as it did absorption with the development of the profession rather than concern over the crumbling social order. Yet in retrospect, as a summation of the state of casework just a quarter-century after the need for training in "applied philanthropy" had been recognized by Mary Richmond and others,[37] it is a worthy reminder of how early the groundwork for the enduring foundation of clinical social work practice had been laid. By 1929 the principle of gathering data to formulate an understanding of the unique person–environment interaction was firmly established, as was the need to intervene in both spheres. The importance of the worker–client relationship as the foundation of the casework process was well recognized, as was the need to engage the client in the process of change. Both the importance of drawing on knowledge from the social and behavioral sciences and the need to develop methods of research and evaluation of casework practice were widely discussed in the literature. Finally, through the efforts of those involved in the Milford Conference, a recognized foundation of generic casework practice applicable across fields of practice had been laid.

Social Case Work Comes of Age: The New York School in the 1930s and 1940s

If the development of a new profession is an evolutionary process, it is possible to see in the 1930s and 1940s the beginning of a new maturity in social casework. In the early 1930s there was for the first time a significant number of casework faculty at the New York School; this provided an intellectual community of scholars who thought, taught, and wrote about the casework method. Leading this group was, of course, Gordon Hamilton, who had joined the faculty in the early 1920s along with Mary Antoinette Cannon. These two were joined by Grace Marcus in 1929, Lucille Nickel Austin in 1930, and Fern Lowry in 1931, as well as others who came and went along the way.

All of these women were active in developing aspects of casework theory and practice throughout the 1930s and 1940s. As Jessie Taft and other proponents of the functional approach began writing about this emerging alternative to traditional casework theory,[38] a flurry of speeches and articles by New York School faculty members appeared in social work journals defending the diagnostic model.[39]

It is perhaps unfortunate that the model of social casework developed at the New York School came to be known as the diagnostic approach. This shorthand label, although well understood by the approach's adherents to include a progression of activities in the casework process, allowed critics, particularly those looking back at this era, to claim that members of the diagnostic school were preoccupied with diagnosing the individual's intrapsychic functions in accordance with Freudian theory and using psychoanalytic techniques to attempt personality change.[40] These critics often cite Virginia Robinson's *A Changing Psychology in Social Case Work*, published in 1930, as evidence that casework training was replete with references to psychoanalytic principles and that psychiatric social work was the centerpiece of the curriculum in schools of social work. For example, Specht and Courtney state, "Most of the seminal figures in psychiatric social work during the 1920s were heavily influenced by the psychoanalytic view and communicated this to the field through written word as well as through their teaching at various schools of social work."[41] In support of this statement they cited Robinson's work.

Yet course offerings at the New York School in the 1920s through the 1940s suggest otherwise. Although Marion Kenworthy, a psychiatrist, did join the New York School faculty in 1921 and throughout her long tenure there taught courses in psychopathology and Clinical Psychiatry,[42] for those students majoring in social casework during the 1926–27 academic year, required courses included The Method of Social Case Work and Content of Family Case Work, both taught by Gordon Hamilton; Social Work and Social Philosophy, taught by Eduard Lindeman; and Seminar in Family Case Work, taught by Porter Lee. Kenworthy's psychopathology course was just one among fourteen suggested electives for students in the casework concentration. Ten years later, Introduction to Social Case Work, a required casework course, was taught by Hamilton, Fern Lowry, and Lucille Austin. Mary Antoinette Cannon taught Analysis of Social Case Method, a second required course in the casework sequence. Dr. Kenworthy, the only faculty member teaching in the psychiatric (*Mental Hygiene* was the term used at the New York School) concentration, taught Psychiatric Social Work—Its Theory and Practice in the fall quarter (the School was then on the quarter system) and Psychopathology and Advanced Psychiatric Social Work in the winter quarter. All three of these courses were repeated spring quarter.

The list of faculty specialties contained in the School's 1937–38 *General Announcement* gives some indication of the relative importance of psychiatric social work in the curriculum. Three faculty members' specialties were listed as Social Case Work (Hamilton, Lowry, Austin), one as Medical Social Work (Cannon), one as Child Welfare (Ethel Taylor), and one as Mental Hygiene (Kenworthy). Ten years later, in the 1946–47 academic year, there were four specialists in Social Case Work; Kenworthy was still the only faculty member listed as specializing in Mental Hygiene. It would seem, then, that at the New York School, at least, psychiatric social work was not accorded the primacy that some historians of the profession have claimed.

Although psychiatric social work was clearly not the centerpiece of the curriculum at the New York School, there is no doubt that members of its casework faculty were influenced by contemporary ideas regarding human psychological development, including psychoanalytic theory. In a speech before the National Conference of Social Work in 1937 titled "Basic Concepts Upon Which Case-Work Practice Is Formulated," Gordon Hamilton reiterated the long-standing New York School philosophy that "problems are both individual and social; that a case for us is always a complex of inner and outer factors." [43] She went on to say that "the typical case situation is that of a person in conflict with environmental factors, or with a deficiency which must be compensated for by community resources; or, again, the case-work situation is one in which the conflict has to some degree been internalized so that the client is in some conflict with himself as well as with society." [44] She noted that casework's understanding of social and individual conflicts had changed rapidly in recent times, influenced by ideas from anthropology and psychology which had "recently thrown much light on the factors in adequate personal adjustment." The contribution of psychiatry, according to Hamilton, was its knowledge of social and cultural pressures on the individual.

Hamilton responded to critics of social casework who decried its "interest in personal as well as environmental causes of distress" by suggesting that dichotomous thinking is limiting, that caseworkers must be able to move back and forth between the individual and the environment to effect change. Hamilton also addressed client self-determination and the need for caseworkers to engage clients in solving their own problems. She focused on the caseworker's use of authority and cautioned that its use must be related not only to the capacities of the client and the realities of the situation but also to the worker's own awareness of self and his or her internal processes. Hamilton harkened back to Mary Richmond, citing her emphasis on helping the client to tell his or her own story, and noted that the importance of this aspect of casework was being reemphasized by present-day psychiatry. Finally, not unlike social work scholars currently, Hamilton called for "testing and sift-ing" casework knowledge toward the end of better integrated concepts and methods, which in turn would allow for differential approaches to treatment.

While it is clear that by the 1930s and 1940s New York School faculty had incorporated many ideas from Freudian psychology and, eventually, from ego psychology, a close reading of their published work makes it abundantly clear that they still held closely to the person-in-environment focus estab-lished by Mary Richmond many years before. Newly developed theories in the social and behavioral sciences were used to further refine and generate greater understanding of this basic, enduring principle of social casework. It was this "scientific attitude," this belief that further understanding of the person–environment interaction and how to influence it could be achieved through incorporating knowledge from other fields, as well as by generat-ing original understanding of the casework process, that marked the work of faculty at the New York School in its second quarter-century. In 1939 Lucille Austin wrote in "The Evolution of Our Social Case Work Concepts":

> From the beginning of the social case work movement in this country there has been a general line of development which has had its roots in the scientific attitude. Intuition has been recognized as a positive force but we have on the whole measured progress in the development of our profession by the growing body of knowledge adapted from the sciences and made available for conscious application. Mary E. Rich-mond's efforts were all in this direction of developing a scientific way of looking at case work practice.[45]

Casework scholars at the New York School such as Austin and Hamilton saw the study/diagnosis/treatment paradigm as a scientific process of gather-ing data, formulating a hypothesis, and testing this hypothesis in the treat-ment process. Indeed, their major objection to the functional approach was that it was not scientific, that the treatment process itself was not planned on the basis of a clear hypothesis regarding the source of the client's difficulties.[46] The functional principle that all that could be known about a client was con-tained in the interaction between worker and client negated the carefully con-structed investigation first proposed by Mary Richmond in an effort to move charity workers away from reliance on personal prejudices and beliefs as the basis for their work. In a profession that had been stung by Abraham Flex-ner's critique that social work lacked a basis in science and learning, an approach to casework based in mysticism, as Austin saw functional practice, generated great anxiety indeed.

If Mary Richmond's *Social Diagnosis,* published in 1917, could be said to summarize the development of casework practice over its first quarter-century, then Gordon Hamilton's *Theory and Practice of Social Case Work,* published in 1940, summarized the second. Richmond taught the first generations of caseworkers how to gather the facts of a case rather than rely on personal, moralistic interpretations of behavior. Hamilton and her colleagues at the New York School taught the next generations how to interpret those facts to develop a better understanding of the client in his or her presenting situation, in other words, how to formulate a "social diagnosis." It would fall to the next half-century of casework scholars to develop the methods of treatment or models of intervention designed to respond to these diagnoses.

Connecting Diagnosis and Treatment: Casework at the New York School from the Post–World War II Years to the Mid-1960s

At mid-century the hegemony of social casework at the New York School appeared secure. Out of thirty-one full-time teaching faculty listed on the school's roster in the 1955–56 General Announcement, fourteen were identified as Casework faculty—many more than in any other practice method. By comparison, there were five Group Work faculty, four Research faculty, and one faculty member specializing in Community Organization. A notable addition to the roster of casework faculty around this time was Florence Hollis, who came to the New York School in 1947 after receiving her Ph.D. from the Bryn Mawr School of Social Work and Social Research that same year. She had earned her master's degree in social work at Smith College and afterward had served on the faculty at the School of Applied Social Sciences at Western Reserve University in Cleveland for six years. Over the next two decades, as one of the few casework faculty members with an earned doctorate, Hollis was to become a primary force in the effort to make casework a more scientific endeavor.

Beginning in 1951 students at the New York School could specialize in social casework, social group work, community organization, and, a few years later, social administration. In the three required social casework courses, students learned application of the "technical processes of social study, diagnosis, and treatment, and an understanding of the individual and his psychosocial problems . . ."[47] In an integrative casework seminar, methods of treatment were emphasized. Students studied the management of the casework relationship as well as principles of interviewing and the use of social resources.

Elsewhere alumni of the New York School were emerging as prominent casework scholars on the faculties of other schools of social work. In 1945, while a faculty member at the University of Chicago, Charlotte Towle published *Common Human Needs*,[48] a slim volume of instruction for public assistance workers written at the request of Jane Hoey, head of the U.S. Bureau of Public Assistance. Hoey recognized the difficulties faced by public assistance workers who, when determining whether applicants met eligibility requirements for aid, struggled to protect the entitlement rights of applicants for public assistance, while at the same time responding to the interests of the taxpaying public. Hoey turned to Towle for training materials to help public assistance workers with this formidable task. Towle had studied with Gordon Hamilton, Porter Lee, and others at the New York School in the 1920s and had returned there in the early thirties as supervisor of a field unit at the Bureau for Children's Guidance, where she was influenced by Fern Lowry. At the time, Lowry was working on a model of practice that focused on client need as the central consideration in casework practice.[49]

Towle became interested in the caseworker's task of integrating casework concepts regarding individual functioning with principles of social reform.[50] She saw clearly the impact of insufficient social resources on the adequate functioning of the individual, the philosophy underpinning her discussion of public assistance in *Common Human Needs*. As obvious as this insight might sound today, in a climate of postwar preoccupation with Russian communism, the concept was close to heresy. By 1951 the furor over the "socialistic" ideas promulgated in *Common Human Needs*, fanned by conservative politicians and the American Medical Association, which feared "socialized" medicine, resulted in the head of the Federal Security Administration ordering the destruction of all copies of the book in stock as well as the printing plates so that it could not be reprinted. However, because Towle retained copyright to the manuscript, she was able to grant permission to the American Association of Social Workers to keep the book in print.

Another New York School alumna who made her mark at the University of Chicago at about the same time as Charlotte Towle was Helen Harris Perlman, who had completed the master's program at the New York School in

1938 and, like Towle, spent several years afterward as field instructor at the Child Guidance Bureau. Also like Towle before her, Perlman was recruited to the School of Social Service Administration (SSA) faculty to strengthen the faculty's expertise in social casework.

During her years at the Chicago school, Helen Harris Perlman was a prolific and gifted scholar of the casework process. She was also an able integrator whose first book, *Social Case Work: A Problem-Solving Process,* drew directly from both diagnostic and functional concepts and methods to develop an integrated theory of practice based on current principles of ego psychology. Perlman's book had been presaged a few years earlier by an article she wrote for the *Social Service Review,* "The Basic Structure of the Casework Process."[51] In this article Perlman laid out the elements of the problem-solving process, which clearly parallel those of the study/diagnosis/treatment formulation of social casework: (1) facts constituting the problem must be made clear; (2) these facts must be analyzed and a conclusion about their meaning formed; and (3) an action must be consciously chosen based on this conclusion, and then the conclusion must be tested for its validity by "experimentation or reconsideration."

Perlman suggested that this problem-solving process is used constantly, often without our conscious awareness, as we go about our daily lives. However, there are occasions when this process breaks down. Either the facts of a situation are not known or our perception of the facts is limited in some way. Or, the facts are known but not clearly understood in a way that can lead to the formulation of a plan of action. Or, perhaps, the necessary action based on analysis of the facts is unavailable. It is the role of the caseworker to work through these problem-solving steps with the client to identify where the obstacles to effective problem resolution lie. The caseworker's understanding of these obstacles is informed by knowledge drawn from the social and behavioral sciences. In carrying out this problem-solving process, the caseworker makes informed use of the helping relationship (diagnostic) as well as the agency and its resources (functional).

While in retrospect the notion of the helping process as a problem-solving one may seem obvious, Perlman's formulation was a watershed in the development of social casework in that it made use of seminal ideas from both the diagnostic and functional paradigms and showed the aspiring practitioner how to apply this model in practice. It enabled the field to move past its focus on the diagnostic–functional dichotomy and to draw on each school of thought to develop new ideas and methods of clinical practice. As has been discussed in more depth elsewhere,[52] current clinical practice makes use of concepts from both functional (use of time; beginning, middle, and end phases of treatment; partialization of client's problems; client participation in the therapeutic process) and diagnostic (separation of fact from inference; goal setting; selection of intervention strategies based on assessment of client-in-situation; evaluation of client progress and treatment outcome).

While Perlman was formulating her problem-solving approach at Chicago, Florence Hollis was studying the procedural elements of casework treatment assisted by a group of New York School doctoral students. She hoped to develop a typology of casework practice that would enable clinicians to select more rationally among the variety of casework techniques.

Efforts to analyze the process of social casework treatment and to develop typologies of casework procedures were not new in the 1950s. As early as 1921 Virginia Robinson had reviewed the case records of caseworkers in family agencies in the hope of better understanding just what they did with their clients. Others, including Porter Lee and Gordon Hamilton, had differentiated among caseworker activities, using categories such as "direct methods" and "indirect methods."[53] However, Hollis was the first to try to specify categories of procedures with scientific rigor. She obtained a sample of twenty-five case records from six voluntary family and children's agencies. Careful analysis of the content of these records led her to identify six categories of procedures. She described each category and how it was to be used in the treatment process in her book, *Casework: A Psychosocial Therapy*. This work was a stunning contribution to social casework. For the first time there was a mechanism whereby students could be taught specific casework techniques, as well as how and when to apply them in practice situations. Practitioners could use the schema to analyze their own work with clients and identify places in the interaction where they might have responded with a different procedure to better effect. Having access to a typology of procedures could also enable clinicians to make more rational connections between assessment, treatment, and client outcome goals.

Hollis's work influenced other studies of the casework process, including those carried out by doctoral students William Reid and Helen Pinkus. One such study was the dissertation research of Edward Mullen, also a student of Hollis's at the New York School. Findings from his doctoral dissertation, based on case analyses using the Hollis typology, were published as three separate papers in *Social Casework*,[54] and together in 1968 as *Communication in Casework Counseling*.[55] His study confirmed what other researchers, including Hollis, had found: the focus in casework treatment was on helping the client to tell his or her story, to ventilate feelings about his or her situation, and to reflect on his or her role and functioning within the problem situation. The findings of Mullen, Hollis, and others regarding casework procedures seem to belie the widespread belief that casework in the 1950s and 1960s focused exclusively on personality change and relied heavily on such psychoanalytic techniques as exploration of early life experiences.

In the early 1960s, just as Florence Hollis's book furthering the development of the diagnostic—now psychosocial—model of casework appeared, the social context for casework again erupted in a spasm of social change. If Richmond's *Social Diagnosis* could be said to have marked the end of the first quarter-century of casework development, and Hamilton's *Theory and Practice of Social Case Work* to have marked the second, then publication of the first edition of *Casework: A Psychosocial Therapy* in 1964 symbolized casework's evolution in the third. The process of social casework had been subjected to intense scrutiny and its elements further refined. Historical calls for the scientific study of casework procedures and techniques had been heeded. A burgeoning body of casework literature was available, much of it emanating from Columbia faculty and graduates.

Challenges to the Casework Paradigm

In the 1950s and early 1960s casework seemed solidly ensconced in the social work firmament. Yet along with the social upheaval of the following decade came a barrage of questions about the effectiveness, the usefulness, and even the ethics of this core social work method.[56] Several outcome studies of programs that purported to use the casework method found few positive results for clients; some programs were even found to have negative effects on clients' well-being.[57]

Among those who questioned the prevailing casework paradigm were many of Columbia's own graduates. According to Reid, a number of social work scholars and educators who had become interested in research on casework practice while doctoral students at Columbia in the 1950s and 1960s went on to play influential roles in advocating for empirically based practice models.[58] Reid, along with his colleague Laura Epstein at the University of

Chicago, developed the empirically based task-centered model.[59] Other Columbia doctoral graduates who advocated and developed empirically based practice approaches include Scott Briar, Irwin Epstein, Arthur Schwartz, and Tony Tripodi.[60]

In 1972 Florence Hollis, the last of the "casework ladies," retired from the Columbia faculty, and Carol Meyer assumed her role as doyenne of clinical social work practice. Meyer, one of the first to graduate with a specialization in direct practice from Columbia's newly established doctoral program in 1957, had studied with Hollis, Austin, and the other prominent casework theorists of the New York School. A generation younger, however, Meyer was attuned to the social changes of the 1960s and recognized that psychodynamically informed models of clinical practice had only limited application to the myriad social problems with which social workers of the era were grappling.[61] She also understood the criticisms of those seeking a more scientific basis for social work practice. For Meyer, the concepts offered by general systems theory and ecological theory provided the framework for clinical practice she was seeking. The systemic perspective made it more possible to "see" the complexity in cases, because it allowed the "viewer" to place a figurative or literal circle around the case phenomena, to note the interrelatedness of case variables, and to understand the real-life context of each client's situation.[62]

"Systems Concepts in Casework Theory and Practice," a seminal article by Sr. Mary Paul Janchill, then a Columbia doctoral student, demonstrated the applicability of systems theory to clinical social work practice in ways that moved traditional practice away from its dependence on linear processes and enabled it to integrate more fully the multiple environmental forces that impact on individual functioning.[63] The following year Ann Hartman, also then a Columbia doctoral student, published "To Think About the Unthinkable," which further developed the application of systems theory to social work practice.[64] In subsequent publications[65] Hartman helped clinical social workers "translate concepts from this middle-range theory into specific and testable prescriptions for practice."[66] Her eco-mapping procedure, first introduced in 1978, has become a staple in the armamentarium of clinical social workers seeking to understand the vital complexity of the person – environment gestalt.

Carel Germain, another former Columbia doctoral student and then a faculty member, was instrumental in introducing concepts from ecological theory into social work practice.[67] In a groundbreaking article entitled "General Systems Theory and Ego Psychology: An Ecological Perspective," Germain proposed ecological concepts of organism–environment relations to bridge ego psychology and general systems theories. Perhaps the greatest contribution of ecological theory to social work's person–environment understanding was its emphasis on the reciprocal nature of this interaction; the individual is not a passive but an active player in the process of determining "goodness-of-fit" with her or his ecological niche. Ego psychology suggests ways that this proactivity is generated and actualized. Along with her Columbia colleague Alex Gitterman, Germain integrated these concepts into the Life Model,[68] an approach to practice that focuses on enhancing the client's capacities to positively influence this ongoing, ever-evolving process of interaction with the social environment.

Carol Meyer's work incorporating general systems theory and ecological theory in clinical practice was reflected in her edited book, *Clinical Social Work in the Eco-Systems Perspective*, as well as in two book chapters, "The Eco-Systems Perspective" and "The Eco-Systems Perspective: Implications for Practice."[69] She also drew on these theories to inform the process of client assessment in *Assessment in Social Work Practice*.[70] According to Meyer, assessment from an ecosystems perspective allows for "encompassing people's multiple, interactive, simultaneous, and historical experiences."[71] In this way Meyer embraced the complexity that social workers have come to recognize as the hallmark of understanding the client in her or his social context.

Other contemporary scholars of clinical practice associated with Columbia have found in ego psychology, object relations theory, and other current psychodynamic theories keys to understanding environmental influences on individual functioning and to enhancing the person–environment interaction. Eda Goldstein, a faculty member at New York University and a Columbia doctoral graduate, has written extensively on ego psychology as providing a theoretical foundation for clinical practice.[72] In ego psychology, with its emphasis on the essential quest for personal and social competence, Goldstein found the concepts needed to inform clinical practice in a range of social work settings. Harkening back to the work of Lowry and Towle, Goldstein demonstrated the critical importance in clinical practice of developing environments that support the individual's quest for competence.

As Mattaini noted of clinical social work in 1990: "Emerging conceptual frameworks are more contextual, incorporating a rigorous examination of the complex interactions and interdependencies inherent in person-in-environment configurations. Within a contextual framework, available data can be organized in multiple ways, offering alternative potential approaches to effective change."[73]

Clinical practice currently embraces an eclectic blend of interventions derived from a variety of theories of human development and change. As empirical studies of treatment effectiveness increasingly guide intervention selection, clinical social workers, like their peers in the other helping professions, must be knowledgeable about effectiveness studies and able to apply their findings in a range of practice situations. Guiding this intervention selection, however, is social work's particular understanding of the person–environment gestalt.

While the actual clinical process of study/diagnosis/treatment, or, more recently, exploration/assessment/intervention/evaluation,[74] may not be unique to social work, our historical effort to include in this process an understanding of the individual in interaction with the environment, including family, group, community, organizations, and institutions, as well as culture and society, makes it social work's own. As this brief and somewhat cursory review of the development of clinical social work practice as influenced by the New York School has shown, at times we have emphasized understanding the individual factors in the person–situation dynamic and at other times the contributions of environmental factors. Whichever emphasis the social context has encouraged and supported, scholars of clinical practice at the New York School and its successor, Columbia, have always honored the person–situation dynamic as the subject of our professional focus. Ideas about how to intervene successfully to change that dynamic have altered over the years in response to new knowledge emanating from the social and behavioral sciences, as well as our evolving understanding of intervention techniques and procedures.

As Mary Richmond showed us in her now-famous 1903 diagram, clinical social work attends to multiple factors in understanding the particular individual in his or her situation. As Edward Devine, an early leader of the New York School and formulator of social casework, presciently informed us in 1904, only to social work is it given to know the "woes and failures" of people in trouble on the one hand and to draw on, on the other, the "regenerative and curative forces at work in the community—all of them, religious, educational, industrial, social, and personal . . ."[75]

NOTES

1. Mary E. Richmond, "The Retail Method of Reform," in *The Long View,* ed. Joanna C. Colcord and Ruth Z. S. Mann (New York: Russell Sage Foundation: 1930), 214–221.

2. Richmond, "The Retail Method of Reform."

3. The term *case work* was spelled as two words until the late 1940s or early fifties, when it became *casework.* At the New York School, for the first decade or so, it was the only method of direct practice taught; administration was added in 1914. Community organization appeared in the curriculum in the 1920s. Clara Kaiser arrived from Western Reserve University to offer the School's first group work course in 1935.

For many years casework in the New York School curriculum included specialties in family casework, child welfare, medical social work, and psychiatric social work. After 1915, when the second year of study was added, students took basic or foundation casework courses in the first year, then specialized in one of the areas of casework practice in the second. After changes to the curriculum in the early 1950s elevated methods of practice to concentrations, students elected to study casework, group work, community organization, or administration.

4. Henceforth, I shall refer to the School in all its permutations as the New York School, the name by which it was known throughout the country for many years.

5. Mary E. Richmond, Memorandum to Edward T. Devine, March 12, 1912. Microfilm, Mary E. Richmond Archives, Columbia University, New York.

6. Richmond, Memorandum to Edward T. Devine.

7. See Carol H. Meyer, *Assessment in Social Work Practice* (New York: Columbia University Press, 1993), for a contemporary articulation of this dilemma.

8. Jeffrey R. Brackett, "Training of Social Workers: Report of the Committee," in *Proceedings of the 33rd National Conference on Charities and Corrections* (Chicago: Hildmann, 1906), 445–451.

9. Graham Taylor, "Report on the Committee on Training for Social Workers, in *Proceedings of the 32nd National Conference on Charities and Corrections* (Chicago: Hildmann, 1905), 436–442.

10. New York School of Philanthropy, *Handbook for 1905-1906* (New York: Charity Organization Society of New York, 1905).

11. Edward T. Devine, *The Practice of Charity* (New York: Lentilhon, 1901), 118.

12. New York School of Philanthropy, *Handbook for 1905-1906.*

13. L. C. Wade, *Graham Taylor: Pioneer for Social Justice* (Chicago: University of Chicago Press, 1964).

14. Lela B. Costin, *Two Sisters for Social Justice: A Biography of Grace and Edith Abbott* (Urbana: University of Illinois Press, 1983).

15. Brackett, "Training of Social Workers."

16. New York School of Philanthropy, *Bulletin for 1912-1913* (New York: The Charity Organization Society of the City of New York, 1912).

17. New York School of Philanthropy, *Bulletin for 1912-1913,* 8.

18. Porter R. Lee, *Annual Report of the Director, 1918-1919* (New York: New York School of Social Work, 1918), 3.

19. Lee, *Annual Report of the Director, 1918-1919.*

20. This quote is taken from Mary Richmond's *What Is Social Case Work?* (New York: Russell Sage Foundation, 1923), 98.

21. David Levy, "Beginning of the Child Guidance Clinic Movement," *American Journal of Orthopsychiatry* 38 (1968):447-459.

22. New York School of Social Work, *General Announcement, 1926-1927* (New York: Charity Organization Society of the City of New York, 1926).

23. Porter R. Lee, *Annual Report of the Director, 1925-1926* (New York: New York School of Social Work, 1925), 2.

24. Lee, *Annual Report of the Director, 1925-1926.*

25. Mary Antoinette Cannon, "Underlying Principles and Common Practices in Social Work," *The Family* (July 1928):163-166.

26. Abraham Flexner, "Is Social Work a Profession?" In *Proceedings of the National Conference of Charities and Correction, 1915* (Chicago: Hildmann, 1915), 576-590.

27. Cannon, "Underlying Principles."

28. Cannon, "Underlying Principles," 165.

29. Cannon, "Underlying Principles," 165.

30. Milford Conference, *Social Casework: Generic and Specific* (New York: American Association of Social Workers, 1929).

31. Milford Conference, *Social Casework*, 11.

32. Milford Conference, *Social Casework*, 13.

33. Milford Conference, *Social Casework*, 14.

34. Milford Conference, *Social Casework*, 17.

35. Martha Morrison Dore, "Functional Theory: Its History and Influence on Contemporary Social Work Practice," *Social Service Review* 64 (1990):358–374.

36. Ann Hartman, "Casework in Crisis: 1932–1941" (D.S.W. diss., Columbia University School of Social Work, 1972).

37. Mary E. Richmond, "The Need of a Training School in Applied Philanthropy," in *Proceedings of the National Conference of Charities and Corrections* (New York: Hildmann, 1897), 181–186.

38. See the following for elements of functional practice: Jessie Taft, *The Dynamics of Therapy in a Controlled Relationship* (New York: Macmillan, 1933); Jessie Taft, "The Relation of Function to Process in a Controlled Relationship," *Journal of Social Work Process* 1 (1937):1–18; Robert Gomberg, "Function as a Psychological Concept in Case Work Theory," *The Family* (1943):58–64.

39. The following are representative diagnostic responses to functional ideas: Lucille N. Austin, "The Evolution of Our Social Case Work Concepts," *The Family* (April 1939):42–49; Gordon Hamilton, "Basic Concepts Upon Which Case-Work Practice Is Formulated," in *Proceedings of the National Conference of Social Work* (1937), 138–149; Gordon Hamilton, "The Underlying Philosophy of Social Case Work," *The Family* 22 (1941):139–147.

40. See, for example, John Erenreich, *The Altruistic Imagination* (Ithaca, N.Y.: Cornell University Press, 1985); Harry Specht and Mark Courtney, *Unfaithful Angels* (New York: Free Press, 1994); Katherine Woodroofe, *From Charity to Social Work* (Toronto: University of Toronto Press, 1962).

41. Specht and Courtney, *The Altruistic Imagination*, 235.

42. New York School of Social Work, *General Announcement, 1926–1927*.

43. Hamilton, "Basic Concepts."

44. Hamilton, "Basic Concepts," 140.

45. Austin, "Evolution," 42.

46. Austin, "Evolution," 42.

47. New York School of Social Work, *General Announcement, 1951–1952* (New York: 1951), 17.

48. Charlotte Towle, *Common Human Needs,* rev. ed. (Silver Spring, Md.: National Association of Social Workers, 1987).

49. Fern Lowry, "The Client's Needs as a Basis for Differential Approach in Case Work Treatment," *Differential Approach in Case Work Treatment* (New York: Family Service Association of America, 1936), 75–89.

50. Charlotte Towle, "Social Casework in Modern Society," *Social Service Review* 20 (1946):165–179; Charlotte Towle, "Casework Methods of Helping the Client to Make Maximum Use of His Capacities and Resources," *Social Service Review* 22 (1948):469–480.

51. Helen Harris Perlman, "The Basic Structure of the Casework Process," *Social Service Review* (1953):51–64.

52. See Dore, "Functional Theory."

53. Florence Hollis, *Casework: A Psychosocial Therapy* (New York: Random House, 1964).

54. Edward J. Mullen, "Casework Communication," *Social Casework* (November 1968):546–551; Edward J. Mullen, "The Relation Between Diagnosis and Treatment in Casework," *Social Casework* (April 1969):218–226; Edward J. Mullen, "Differences in Worker Style in Casework," *Social Casework* (June 1969):345–352.

55. Edward J. Mullen, *Communication in Casework Counseling* (New York: Family Service Association of America, 1968).

56. Scott Briar and Henry Miller, "The Scientific Method in Casework Practice," in *Problems and Issues in Social Casework* (New York: Columbia University Press, 1971), 79–88.

57. Joel Fischer, "Is Casework Effective? A Review," *Social Work* 18 (1973):5–20; Joel Fischer, *The Effectiveness of Social Casework* (Springfield, Ill.: Charles C. Thomas, 1976); Edward J. Mullen and James R. Dumpson, *Evaluation of Social Intervention* (San Francisco: Jossey-Bass, 1972).

58. William J. Reid, "The Empirical Practice Movement," *Social Service Review* (1994):165–184.

59. William J. Reid and Laura Epstein, *Task-Centered Casework* (New York: Columbia University Press, 1972).

60. Reid and Epstein, *Task-Centered Casework*.

61. Carol H. Meyer, *Social Work Practice: The Changing Landscape* (New York: Free Press, 1976).

62. Carol H. Meyer, *Assessment in Social Work Practice* (New York: Columbia University Press, 1993).

63. Sr. Mary Paul Janchill, "Systems Concepts in Casework Theory and Practice," *Social Casework* 50 (1969):74–82.

64. Ann Hartman, "To Think About the Unthinkable," *Social Casework* (1970): 467–474.

65. Ann Hartman, "The Generic Stance in Family Agencies," *Social Casework* (1974):199–208; Ann Hartman, "Diagrammatic Assessment of Family Relationships," *Families in Society* 76 (1978, reprinted 1995):111–122; Ann Hartman and Joan Laird, *Family-Centered Social Work Practice* (New York: Free Press, 1983).

66. Hartman, "Diagrammatic Assessment," 112.

67. Carel B. Germain, "An Ecological Perspective in Casework Practice," *Social Casework* 54 (1973):323–330; Carel B. Germain, "General Systems Theory and Ego Psychology: An Ecological Perspective," *Social Service Review* (1978):535–550; Carel B. Germain, *The Ecological Perspective in Social Work Practice: People and Environments* (New York: Columbia University Press, 1978).

68. Carel B. Germain and Alex Gitterman, *The Life Model of Social Work Practice* (New York: Columbia University Press, 1980); Carel B. Germain and Alex Gitterman, *The Life Model of Social Work Practice*, 2d ed. (New York: Columbia University Press, 1996).

69. Carol H. Meyer, ed., *Clinical Social Work in the Eco-Systems Perspective* (New York: Columbia University Press, 1983); Carol H. Meyer, "The Eco-Systems Perspective," in Rachel Dorfman, ed., *Paradigms of Clinical Social Work* (New York: Brunner/Mazel, 1988), 275–294; Carol H. Meyer, "The Eco-Systems Perspective: Implications for Practice," in Carol H. Meyer and Mark Mattaini, eds., *The Foundations of Social Work Practice* (Washington, D.C.: National Association of Social Workers, 1995), 16–27.

70. Meyer, *Assessment.*

71. Meyer, *Assessment,* 103.

72. Eda G. Goldstein, *Ego Psychology and Social Work Practice* (New York: Free Press, 1984); Eda G. Goldstein, *Ego Psychology and Social Work Practice,* 2d ed. (New York: Free Press, 1995).

73. Mark Mattaini, "Contextual Behavior Analysis in the Assessment Process," *Families in Society* 71 (1990):236–245.

74. Meyer, *Assessment.*

75. Devine, *The Practice of Charity,* 118.

Chapter 4

ADVANCED GENERALIST PRACTICE AND PROGRAMMING

L. Donald McVinney

In the mid to late 1960s, during a period of tumultuous social upheaval and change in American history, there was an increasing perception that social workers were not adequately addressing social concerns and assisting people in need. A consensus began to emerge among social workers to address the perceived inadequacies of the profession and of professional education in response to social problems. In much of the social work literature of this time there was an emphasis on the importance of reform and relevance, both socially and within the profession, as a way to address social problems. The professional focus at this time was on the contemporary issues of social injustice, inequality, and neglect of the poor and minorities. There was also particular attention devoted to the manner in which social welfare agencies were failing to meet the needs of clients in general, but particularly the recipients of public services (Titmuss 1968). The allegations that the profession had failed society were blamed on the nature of social work education. New practice approaches needed to be envisioned (Hearn 1969).

During this era, the magnitude of tension and debate between "micro" and "macro" practice and on the roles and goals of social work education is reflected in the literature. The perception that social workers were meeting the needs of bureaucratic institutions (agents of social control) rather than acting as agents of social change or serving the needs of clients was pervasive (Piven and Cloward 1993). The tension seemed to be one of approach and mission. On one hand, much emphasis was placed on social action. For many practicing social workers and educators, there was a belief that institutional change should focus on interpersonal transactions. For another group of social work practitioners and educators, emphasis was placed on the immediate relief of suffering through direct practice and the assistance of clients in accessing resources that existed in the community (Brager and Holloway 1978). This tension began to subside, leading to a paradigm shift. The demand for social workers to become more socially responsive led to a proposal by the National Association of Social Workers (NASW) in 1971 in which this sentiment is overtly expressed:

> Social work must move away from such centralized agencies that are downtown, impersonal, and non-functional in relation to the constituencies that they are to serve. As long as social workers are located away from those they serve, the participation in policy of the organization by those who are served is effectively minimized. To be successful in the future, social work must be community based. (NASW Delegate Assembly 1971)

To begin addressing the profession's mission of meeting human needs and simultaneously resolving social injustices, a movement began to take place in the 1970s away from discrete modes of practice, such as casework, group work, and community organizing, toward attending to the needs of categories of people (A. J. Kahn 1973). In 1970, Meyer had begun to conceptualize the need for what was called "developmental services" (Meyer 1970). This call for a developmental model of social work practice to be integrated with systems theory (Hearn 1969; Janchill 1969), ecological theory, and life model practice (Germain 1973; Germain and Gitterman 1980; 1996; Gitterman and Germain 1976) can be regarded as the beginnings of advanced generalist practice, as it would become known, at the Columbia University School of Social Work. Meyer described the need for social work services to become more responsive to the needs of the community and to exist as "generalist" organizations for clients to access services as needed, rather than having services imposed upon them. The concept of a developmental range of services based on client need was eventually broadened to include an understanding of the need for attention to systems, or systemic levels (Meyer 1976). Meyer articulated the frustration around professional identity in the 1970s and the need for solidifying the profession's purpose by stating that "if social workers are to move into the life of the community and be available at the potential developmental stress points where people are, there will have to be a major revamping of the use of social work manpower" (Meyer 1976: 203). Meyer further elaborated that the need "to reconceptualize the purposes of social work practice comes out of the conviction that the time is overdue and that urban populations are in danger of becoming lost in the bureaucratic maze . . ." (Meyer 1976:217).

This was the start of the elaboration of the responsibility of social work education to (1) expand the understanding of the role of social work practitioners, (2) teach students ways to consider methods or approaches that would insure effective intervention, and (3) emphasize problem resolution. Bartlett (1970) articulated the need for common knowledge, values, and skills for social work practice at various levels. Because most graduate schools had been organized by method, the focus began to move more toward agency- and community-based practice and toward expanding the functions of social workers toward client advocacy. Accountability, as a basis for practice, was a concept that had become either diluted or absent from social work practice and theory. It was this concept that Meyer (1976) began to reinforce and institutionalize in her writing and teaching.

The search for a proper balance between social action and direct services in a generalist framework began to take place and was paralleled by the development of new curricula in social work education. A new conceptual framework was developing as social workers articulated the need for a solution-seeking approach to client problems that was balanced with thinking about, and doing something about, specific cases. A need was also expressed for social workers to address ways of changing agencies and organizations so that they might become more responsive to client needs (Brager and Holloway 1978).

The need for generalist intervention based on the notion of social disorganization emerged, as distinct from the concept of social intervention. The concept that humans have basic needs that must be met became a major focus in considering generalist practice. Therefore, integrating the work of Maslow (1954) was essential to the development of advanced generalist practice and programming. Maslow wrote that attending to basic survival needs must come before meeting other needs along a hierarchy toward self-actualization. For generalist practice this means focusing on an assessment of needs, beginning with basic survival needs and then moving toward community problem identification. That generalist practice should focus on the interrelationships between individuals and their environment simultaneously was an important supposition of this emerging method. As Meyer wrote, "Despite the shared concern among professions for people in trouble, there is no profession other than social work that encompasses the people to be helped within their social context. It is this focus that is served by our thrust toward developmental services, the concomitant ecosystems perspective, a life model of practice, and a clear sense of social accountability" (1976:202).

Thus the concept of generalist practice began to solidify. Garvin delivered a paper at the annual program meeting of the Council on Social Work Education (CSWE) in 1973 entitled "Education for Generalist Practice in Social Work: A Comparative Analysis of Current Modalities," in which he proposed an integrated model of social systems practice that targeted various client systems (Garvin 1973). Interest in the concept of generalist practice, distinct from "specialist" practice, can be noted in the convening of a CSWE task force and the report it issued (Ripple 1974, cited in Meyer 1976).

Within this historical context, the concept of generalist practice blossomed and a distinct generalist method of practice was conceptualized at CUSSW. According to internal documents at CUSSW and interviews with faculty, the impetus for development of an advanced generalist practice method at Columbia University was initially student driven. As noted, most schools of social work had been organized around method, CUSSW included. Learning the methods of organizing communities had been in high demand among social work students in the 1960s and early 1970s. However, increasingly during the 1970s there was less community organizing taking place in communities as well as diminishing interest in learning the principles of this method by students. An initiative to reconsider the community organizing method took place at CUSSW that led to the merger of community organizing with social administration and social planning. This approach reflected a trend across the country. As Charles Grosser noted in 1976:

> A number of issues in social work education and practice, which emerged in the mid-1970's directly reflect experience in the antipoverty programs. The division of social work into three separate practice entities — casework, group work, and community organization — has been replaced in most social work schools by some sort of generic or integrated practice model. Such models reflect the comprehensive approach, which disallows the division of human problems to conform to a trimethod practice model. Comprehensive programs called forth the use of all practice modalities and required that practitioners be trained broadly enough to use whatever skills were necessary to deliver ser-

vices. This could involve mobilizing an individual's personal resources, changing an agency policy, or locating and using scarce community resources. (243)

In considering a new practice model that would emphasize an integrated approach, the role of advocating for the needs of clients emerged as crucial. From a contemporary perspective, the notion that advocacy was a "new" idea for social work education and practice may come as a surprise; yet, one must consider the historical context, wherein most social workers were employed in public agencies, and there was the perception that professionals should not rock the boat (Grosser 1976). The insights and writing of Paolo Freire (1970/2000) on social change have been seen as integral to the conceptualization and development of this new method in the 1970s.

Also at this time, McGowan (1973, 1975) developed a model of case advocacy practice that was integrated into the curriculum. This new practice model of integrated case advocacy, along with advocacy for the needs of classes of clients, was expanded in 1977, when the concept of case management was added. The model of integrated practice stresses understanding of (1) recognizing that human needs exist along a hierarchy, (2) providing direct intervention, (3) managing a case, (4) advocating for a client, and (5) conceptualizing the needs of classes of clients. This model led inductively to the realization that new programs had to be designed and new methods taught for their development.

In 1980 the new method, or concentration, as it was known, was adopted at CUSSW. "Concentration III," as it was termed, included for the first time program development as part of the curriculum. For the first three years of this new concentration, team teaching was adopted. The team-teaching approach had also been piloted at other schools of social work around the country, notably the School of Social Service Administration at the University of Chicago, which was also developing a generalist paradigm. In the team teaching approach adopted at CUSSW, the participation and utilization of all of the faculty who had been previously involved in teaching community organizing were encouraged. This, in turn, led to a developing conviction on the part of the faculty for a need to teach new ways of conceptualizing client-centered and problem-solving practice.

The new concentration of generalist and integrated practice was useful for marketing the relevance of social work to prospective students and to increase slumping enrollment in social work in the early 1980s, when the literature was citing a shortage of professionally educated and trained social workers. The increasing public need for workers and the smaller number of graduates had already been observed by the end of the 1970s (Meyer 1976). The impact of this shortage was circuitous: with limited staff, agencies were reluctant to reach out to the communities they were supposed to be serving. To assure students that they would be able to find jobs in agencies upon graduation, the concentration was again expanded to include methods of supervision in the curriculum. The name Practice, Programming, and Supervision was thus adopted at CUSSW during the tenure of Dean George Brager (1981 to 1986).

In the first year of study, emphasis was placed on educating social work students about (1) the history and mission of the profession; (2) the foundations of social work practice, including a focus on human behavior; (3) interactions with the social environment; (4) problem identification; and (5) the correspondence of problem identification to intervention. Systems theory was now solidly part of the canon of social work practice as taught at CUSSW and nationally. In the second year, two methods of practice were now taught: (1) Direct Practice with Individuals, Families, and Groups; and (2) Practice, Programming, and Supervision, which emphasized agency-based practice, including advanced case management services. The need for this new method of generalist practice, one that was initially student driven, was formally recognized in the profession when, by 1987, the Council on Social Work Education, the accrediting body for schools of social work nationally, required that a generalist method be offered (Sheafor and Landon 1987).

ADVANCED GENERALIST PRACTICE
AND PROGRAMMING TODAY

As currently taught at Columbia University School of Social Work, Advanced Generalist Practice and Programming (AGPP) is a distinct method of practice with courses taught over two semesters in the final year of the graduate program. The goal of this method is to prepare students for agency-based practice as advanced generalist social work practitioners and for students to understand how advanced generalist practice and programming fits into the social work profession's mission and purpose.

Beyond focusing on the needs of individuals with intrapsychic problems amenable to direct clinical intervention, students in the AGPP method are taught to consider more broadly the role of the social environment and the impact of social injustices in shaping and constructing an individual's problems. Students acquire skills in identifying systemic barriers that inhibit problem resolution and searching for programmatic solutions. Advanced generalist practitioners learn to conceptualize "problems" through multiple identifications, to think systemically, and to design intervention strategies at each level with clients. Students then consider other clients who may have similar needs through a formal needs assessment process in a "case to class" model. Programs may then be designed to meet these clients' needs. Advanced generalist practitioners then advocate, "case to cause," for the creation of new services or for the changing and expanding of existing services.

The advanced generalist practice method has multiple aims. First, students gain an understanding of the holistic needs of their clients, agencies, and society, with an emphasis on needs assessment. Second, students learn to conceptualize their agency-based practice from an integrative perspective in order to function competently in multiple roles simultaneously. This is in contrast to an additive model, in which their roles or tasks are considered as discrete and discontinuous. Third, students are taught to design effective interventions across systems and to create or expand programs to meet the needs of classes of clients.

Several tasks are involved in advanced generalist practice and programming with client and community groups. Students are taught to consider them throughout the curriculum. Using a problem-solving approach, students identify and analyze "the problem" at whatever systemic level is relevant. At this stage, the role of an advanced generalist practitioner is to interview the client or clients, listen to presenting issues that are self-reported or reported by collaterals, and consider the overt reasons for help seeking, including the referral source. At this point, identification of gaps in services or the lack of services should not be considered as primary. What is taught as essential is an ability to focus on the primary problems for which services are sought, and to consider the ways in which these problems impair or interfere with the client's social functioning. An essential question considered by the advanced generalist practitioner is, Who is the client? For example, a single mother with two small children may present to an agency because she is experiencing stress overload. There are many options for intervening which flow from conceptualizing "the client." In some agencies, the three-unit family would be the client, while in another agency it would be the adult mother, and in another agency it may be the children who become the focus of intervention. An advanced generalist practitioner would view "the client" from all of these systemic levels and begin to identify and analyze problems accordingly.

At this initial stage of advanced generalist practice, an assessment of a client, defined broadly, is undertaken (Berlin and Marsh 1993; Mattaini 1995; Mattaini and Kirk 1991; Meyer 1993). The client may be an individual, a couple, a group, a family, a neighborhood or community group, or an organization experiencing problems. An advanced generalist practice method of assessment broadly considers the environmental, interpersonal, intrapsychic, and life transitional needs of clients (Long and Holle 1997) as well as their perceived meanings, or hermeneutics, which will then be utilized to develop intervention strategies and service goals and plans. Attention to issues regarding the diversity of client backgrounds and the multiple modes of oppression that impact clients is essential. Students become familiar with the organizational context as well as the sociocultural landscape as these affect practice. The interactive processes by which community and agency contexts shape the practice goals of clients and workers are clarified. Monitoring and evaluating empirically grounded interventions that are pertinent to the case are taught as an ongoing process.

Following a thorough initial assessment of problem identification, which should remain an ongoing feature of the case within the agency, the advanced generalist practitioner begins to conceptualize interventions by using a social work practice knowledge base that includes an understanding of the complexity of the ecosystems involved. For the actual intervention, the advanced generalist practitioner may select to work with an individual, a couple, a group, a family, or a neighborhood. These levels of intervention are conceptualized differently for the advanced generalist practitioner, who engages in these interventions flexibly, rather than through a professional "role" of individual, couples, group, or family therapist. Specific points of intervention are identified and selected, and the rationale as to why these interventions were selected is explicated along with instruction as to how they are prioritized. Familiarity with the theoretical frameworks for various models of intervention and their applications and efficacy with at-risk client populations is paramount in advanced generalist practice. The costs of seeking simple solutions to complex social problems as they affect vulnerable clients are discussed. Therefore, it is expected that advanced generalist practitioners will be able to intervene on different levels simultaneously. Students begin to conceptualize and work in a culturally competent manner through various theoretical frameworks previously acquired in a foundations-of-practice course that allows for progressively larger units of attention. Integrating knowledge from a variety of practice philosophies, perspectives, and theories of intervention takes place as they are applicable to the dynamics of the case. These practice models may include psychosocial (Hollis 1972), task-centered (Reid and Epstein 1972), ecosystemic (Meyer 1983), behavioral (Mattaini 1996), constructivist, and social constructionist (Davis 1993; Franklin and Nurius 1998; Sexton and Griffin 1997); they may also include planned short-term treatment (Wells 1994) as well as life model (Germain and Gitterman 1996) or strengths perspectives (Saleebey 1997), as these are deemed relevant to the case.

Simultaneously, the advanced generalist practitioner begins to consider the client as representative of a potential class of clients. This larger system, or class of clients, may also have similar unmet needs. During this process, students become aware of the potential dilemmas as well as opportunities associated with integrating direct practice and program planning. The generalist practitioner is constantly mindful of the question of whose interests and needs are being met, i.e., the needs of the client, the worker, the agency, the insurer, or the community, and is attentive to these systemic complexities, as well as the ethical implications involved.

After the initial problem identification, analysis, and intervention, problems are reconceptualized as needs. After selecting the intervention to meet the presenting problems of the client, the advanced generalist practitioner (1) begins to assess how often this problem occurs among other clients who present for services, (2) questions if there are additional clients already being served who could benefit from expanded services, and (3) evaluates whether there is a community concern that is emerging that was not previously recognized. One example of the latter might be when an agency that provides substance abuse services begins to see clients from the community who initiate substance use in problematic ways not previously observed, such as new designer drugs (Kuhn, Swartzwelder, and Wilson 1998). Another example might be an agency that primarily has served alcohol-dependent clients which then begins to experience an influx of clients who smoke crack cocaine (McNeece and DiNitto 1998; Reinarman and Levine 1997). An agency that has traditionally served mostly men may begin to see an influx of women who seek services and whose needs differ from the traditional client population. The substance use patterns and gender demographics of the clients served in these examples have changed and, therefore, the clients, the agency, and the community require that these needs be addressed in new programmatic ways. At this stage, needs assessment techniques are employed.

Client- and community-based needs assessment techniques are taught in order for advanced generalist practice students to learn formal methods of identifying unmet needs and then to develop programs that are responsive to these diverse needs. Maslow's (1954) hierarchical model of human needs is reviewed, which postulates that individuals become aware of and identify their needs in a recognizable order; first with basic survival needs, then security needs, needs for a sense of belonging, needs for self-esteem, and finally the need for self-actualization. Bradshaw's (1972) four typologies of need are also reviewed in the course. The first, *normative* need, is based on an expert definition of adequate levels of services. The second type of need, *felt* need, is based on how the members of a group define their own needs. The third need is *expressed* need, which is indicated by how services are accessed and utilized. And fourth is *comparative* need, which is reached through an analysis of the performances of groups other than the targeted population. All of these are essential to consider in any needs assessment.

The model of need analysis developed by McKillip (1987) is introduced in the AGPP curriculum as well. McKillip described five steps in an analysis of need beginning with the identification of users, specifically, those who will be using the information gathered. Second, the target population is described with demographic characteristics, eligibility criteria and restrictions, and the existing services capacity. Third, a need identification is outlined; this includes a description of the problems and possible solutions to the problems. The fourth step is a needs assessment, in which needs are evaluated, including prioritizing the needs of the target population and determining the degree to which they are compatible with the agency's mission. Finally, the results of the needs analysis are written up and communicated to the users of the information so that appropriate actions can be taken.

Students also learn the community-oriented needs assessment (CONA) model, developed by Neuber and associates (1990) to enhance communication between service providers and the community. The model employs data collected from three sources: (1) Demographic statistical profiles are obtained from available public records or published professional literature. (2) With random sampling techniques, key informant data may be obtained from individuals who have direct experience or knowledge of those who are experiencing problems. Key informants include referral sources and other service providers. (3) Data may be obtained from consumers or the public. These data are gathered through random interviews in the geographic area served by the agency. This model is useful for collecting and comparing related data to be utilized in program design.

Although presented only briefly in this essay, the various approaches to needs assessment are covered extensively in the classroom and in written assignments. In one of the written assignments, for example, students identify an unmet service need in their agency. They then learn and apply the various needs assessment techniques, such as a key informant approach (Neuber et al. 1990), community planning forums (Neuber et al. 1990), a survey approach (McKillip 1987), and focus group techniques (Fatout and Rose 1995; Krueger 1988; Steward and Shamdasani 1995). Students select one or more of these approaches and undertake a needs assessment. Familiarity with these techniques is obtained from the assigned readings and class discussions. Students explain why a particular needs assessment technique was chosen and indicate the kind of data they expect to obtain. Because of the increasing emphasis placed on focus groups in agencies, focus group exercises are practiced in the classroom and focus groups are conducted by students in their agencies or in a community setting.

The etiology of historically chronic as well as contemporary social problems is understood to be multifactorial. Some programs will be less effective than others in addressing social problems. Therefore, the next step is for students to begin designing effective programs, which is an hypothesis-generating process. Program hypotheses, as outlined by Kettner, Moroney, and Martin (1990), are essentially a series of "if–then" statements. The program hypothesis is linked to identified objectives that can be measured. The following example, using harm reduction principles with substance-using clients (Erickson et al. 1997; Heather et al. 1993; Inciardi and Harrison 1999; Marlatt 1998; Marlatt and Tapert 1993; O'Hare et al. 1992), is offered as a simple example of this:

> *If* binge-drinking college students can be identified, and
>
> *if* binge-drinking college students will participate in a program to reduce or eliminate bingeing-related harm,
>
> *then* binge drinking will be reduced in the social environment (on and off campus), and
>
> *then* harmful consequences to college students of binge-drinking behaviors will be reduced or eliminated.

The program hypothesis also provides the rationale for designing the new program or for expanding existing programs based on need. The hypothesis is focused as much as possible on the causality or associated causal factors of the social problem (Kettner, Moroney, and Martin 1990). The goals and objectives of the program, which will be tied to program evaluation, are then considered. Goals are statements of long-range ideal outcomes. They provide a rationale as to why a program should be considered and funded, and are intended to help generate support for the program. Objectives are realistic and explicit statements that name the expected results and the ways in which these results will be achieved, in what time frame, and who would be defined as accountable for monitoring the program. Objectives also specify the target population (Kettner, Moroney, and Martin 1990). It is suggested that outcome measurement is increasingly important for effective program designs and should be considered at the beginning of the process, rather than at the end (Hudson 1997; Rossi 1997).

Once the program rationale is clear and the hypotheses are written, with goals and objectives (who? will do what? in what time frame? and who will monitor this?), organizational cooperation for implementation of the program or redesign of an existing program must take place. This process, referred to as the "buy-in," is essential for an effective program. The support of administrators, supervisors, professional colleagues, line workers, and support staff must be in place, and organizational resistance should be anticipated. Human services organizations often resist changes, including the creation of new programs, the delivery of new services, or the shifting demographics of clients served (Brager and Holloway 1978; Hanson 1995; Hasenfeld 1992). In preparing the agency for change, an effective way of ensuring or maximizing the effectiveness of the program within the organization is by providing inservice training for staff in order to build consensus for the new programs (Craig 1987). Staff training is often considered an administrative function, but as taught from an advanced generalist practice perspective at Columbia University, the function of the advanced generalist practitioner is to negotiate the differential needs of the administration and the needs of the participants in training, that is, the staff who will be involved in or affected by implementation of the program. The function of training for an advanced generalist practitioner is considered from a needs assessment perspective as well as a program implementation perspective. Students are introduced to the skills, methods, and agency structures involved in supervision and staff development functions, which includes inservice training models that are incorporated into the AGPP curriculum.

In addition to gaining acceptance within the agency, acceptance within the community is also essential for a new program. Community input will assure successful and effective programs that are responsive to the needs of the community (Gutierrez and Lord 1998; Saleebey 1998). Problems in not anticipating this crucial step have been cited in the literature (Scott and Delgado 1979). The important function of task groups in community practice to minimize some of the problems of program implementation and to maximize program effectiveness is explored in depth in the advanced generalist practice method. Students begin to explore task-centered work (Parihar 1984) and are taught the principles of task group formation and leadership roles (Fatout and Rose 1995). Students learn the skills of convening, facilitating, developing, and evaluating the effectiveness of task groups, as well as other organizational groups and committees, such as planning and action groups (Brown 1991). Leadership styles and group member roles, decision making in groups, and task attainment are all explored in the AGPP curriculum.

As programs are implemented, there must be a formal mechanism for evaluation and feedback. Increasingly, this is a requirement from agency administrators or from government and foundation funders. Therefore, the Columbia University School of Social Work emphasizes the important role of program evaluation in advanced generalist practice and programming. Program evaluation has been defined as a systematic method of assessing the impact that a program has had on the problem it was designed to address. Program evaluation produces necessary information about the success or failure of the program used to improve operations and to benefit the clients served. Program evaluation is intended to assess the success of the designed programs in attaining the objectives set forth in the program hypothesis and to identify the ways in which the program can be improved (Berk and Rossi 1990; Chen 1993; Grasso and Epstein 1992; Kettner, Moroney, and Martin 1990; Rossi and Freeman 1993). In order for a program to be effective, evaluation must be integrated from the initial hypotheses and design and throughout its implementation.

Proposal writing is a skill that is required in order to attain funding for new programs or to implement pilot programs, and is therefore incorporated into the curriculum of the AGPP method as well. Writing proposals is often a function of the development department of large social services organizations in which generalist practitioners may be employed. Small community-

based agencies often do not have adequate staffing patterns for such specialized functions. Therefore, generalist practitioners often integrate this role
into their community-based agencies. Advanced generalist practitioners who
function in the role of proposal writers learn to identify funding streams from
government agencies and private foundations, integrate program hypotheses
with goals and objectives, and identify how the program will be monitored
(Coley and Scheinberg 1990; Lauffer 1997). Learning the skills of proposal
writing in the AGPP curriculum is another example of the manner in which
Columbia University students in the AGPP method integrate complex roles
in agency-based practice.

Understanding the role of community practice is another hallmark of the
AGPP method, at the center of which is teaching students to practice across
systems and in a holistic, integrated way. The emphasis placed on learning
the skills to negotiate various roles simultaneously includes exposing students to the methods, uses, and limits of advanced case management. Students learn to move from case advocacy to cause advocacy on behalf of clients
while using advanced case management theory to manage client care and locate appropriate services (Raiff and Shore 1993). The AGPP curriculum also
entails teaching students the tools and strategies for helping community
groups gain power and influence (empowerment practice) and to provide the
knowledge of grass-roots and community organizing (Cox et al. 1987; Gutierrez 1990; Gutierrez and Nurius 1994; S. Kahn 1991; Kemp 1995; Rivera
and Erlich 1992.)

A new offering within the AGPP method is a course that critically examines the professional use of self in advanced generalist practice. This course
provides an in-depth learning of the integrated practice approach and ex-
plores the student's experiences, values, culture, and beliefs as they influence
interactions within multiple systems. The content of this course enables students to identify and analyze the ethical and value dilemmas associated with
advanced generalist practice when the competing interests of individuals,
groups, organizations, and communities may diverge.

ADVANCED GENERALIST PRACTICE
AND PROGRAMMING TOMORROW

Predicting the future is a dubious task, as most forecasters of negative events
at the advent of this millennium must now grudgingly acknowledge. Ponder-
ing the future of the advanced generalist practice and programming method

at Columbia University School of Social Work is a challenge on many levels. As the first professional school of social work in America enters the twenty-first century, a historical lens can be applied to a consideration of the near future of the profession. At the beginning of the new century, a bright future is hoped for Americans during a time of great prosperity. Recent trends suggest, however, that advanced generalist social worker practitioners will continue to play a vital and dynamic role in the profession and in society. While the stock market's rise and the expanding economy have resulted in unprecedented wealth and employment for many Americans, the widest disparity in U.S. history between wealthy and poor citizens existed at the end of the twentieth century. In 1999 the first surgeon general's study of mental health in U.S. history was published, indicating that an alarming number of Americans suffer from mental illness and yet do not seek help because of stigma, lack of education or information, and lack of affordable or existing programs in their communities (Satcher 1999). The Office of the Secretary of Housing and Urban Development has published a study of homelessness that, while taking into consideration recurring methodological issues in "counting" the homeless (Jencks 1994; O'Flaherty 1996), indicates that enormous numbers of Americans are homeless and do not have access to adequate housing, jobs, or food (Housing and Urban Development 1999). Hate crimes against gay men and lesbians are increasing across the nation and in branches of the military while overall crime has been waning in the last decade for most Americans (National Gay and Lesbian Task Force 1999). The frequency, intensity, and pervasiveness of intimate partner violence against women is of national concern (Begun 1999; Crowell and Burgess 1996; Dutton 1995). As reported in *The New York Times* (Wren, December 9, 1999), General Barry McCaffrey, President Clinton's director of the Office of National Drug Control Policy, has acknowledged that the war on drugs has been a failure. McCaffrey noted that 50 to 85 percent of the 1.8 million inmates in prisons and jails were incarcerated for drug use, and they rarely receive treatment.

Increasingly, the prevailing trend of responses to these social problems has been the criminalization and incarceration of individuals and groups experiencing these social problems, rather than expanded community-based social services. Recent reports indicate that more African American male youths are incarcerated than are in college. Untreated mentally ill Americans are being incarcerated and then released back into the community with inadequate or nonexistent aftercare plans. Substance users in New York City who are recipients of public assistance may now be denied their public assistance benefits for failure to comply with drug treatment referrals (The City of New York 1999). Additional sanctions indicate that for the first time, this class of clients could potentially lose Medicaid insurance, which is essential for access to health care.

So as not to perpetuate media stereotypes about substance users as poor or unemployed, a federal study reports that 70 percent of illicit drug users and 77 percent of heavy alcohol users are employed full time (Beaucar 2000). These employed substance users are often in need of planned interventions that social workers are trained to provide. The economic cost to American society in 1992 from alcohol and other drug abuse was estimated by the National Institute on Drug Abuse at $246 billion (National Institute on Drug Abuse 2000). As reported in *The New York Times,* homeless women with children in New York City who are not employed will be thrown out of the shelter system, originally developed as a solution to homelessness, and will have their children taken from them and placed in foster care. This may happen despite the possibility that many women who seek shelter are fleeing domestic violence and cannot maintain employment because of stalking or threatening behaviors on the part of their partners. The "problem" of homelessness has been redefined politically as "not employed" or "laziness," for which the solution would be to deny shelter to adults and place their children in foster care. A New York State court temporarily halted a punitive plan that would have gone into effect on December 22, 1999, three days before Christmas and again halted it in January 2000. Five thousand homeless families, including nine thousand children, would be affected by the policy (Bernstein 1999).

These identified social issues and problems are persistent and numerous. Given the chronicity of some of these social problems, and the array of additional and emerging contemporary social problems that could be measured in the United States at the end of the twentieth century, advanced generalist social work practitioners will be ideally situated to meet the demands of the social work profession in the future.

Graduates of Columbia University's School of Social Work in the Advanced Generalist Practice and Programming method have been taught to function flexibly in an integrated manner. The emphasis that is placed on integrated practice and flexible roles, along with acquired skills concerning multiple systems interventions and formal needs assessment techniques, will make social work students who are educated in the generalist practice method sought after providers in the social work professional workforce of the future.

Students who are prepared for professional practice in the AGPP method will be able to respond effectively to emerging social problems within community-based agencies by understanding community needs assessment techniques and by having the knowledge and capability to design programs that meet their communities' needs. Using the range of acquired formal needs assessment techniques, advanced generalist practitioners not only can create new programs but also can anticipate emerging trends and needs within communities and begin to prevent social problems from becoming worse. With regard to prevention, the concept of hysteresis is an important one, requiring us to consider historical and contemporary conditions in the development and resolution of social problems.

Particularly with the knowledge and skills of proposal writing that are emphasized in the AGPP method, advanced generalist practitioners will be able to meet the mandates of community-based nonprofit agencies to identify and increase funding. This is already an important function for advanced generalist practitioners in agency-based work that will only increase in importance if current trends in the workplace are maintained.

As new programs are implemented, there must be formal mechanisms for evaluation and feedback. Increasingly, this is a requirement of agency administrators and is often stipulated as mandatory for government and foundation grants. Advanced generalist practitioners will be ideally situated in the future to develop, monitor, and evaluate programs.

As professional social workers, we benefit from learning and caring about our history and our traditions. Following a time of social upheaval in the 1960s, the National Association of Social Workers challenged graduate social work schools to teach students to become more responsive to the needs of clients, to work for organizational change, and to develop community-based programs. This challenge was made in response to the bureaucratic model that had become the dominant service delivery vehicle at the time. Bureaucracies were rarely responsive to clients' or communities' needs, according to NASW. Given the current trend in some fields of practice (such as hospital-based, psychiatric, and substance abuse services) for large organizations to merge and form enormous conglomerates of services, students who are educated and trained in the AGPP method will be able to apply this historical knowledge and become advocates for organizational change that addresses clients' needs. With this historical perspective in mind, concern should be expressed about health care delivery in this country when managed care agencies monitor health care costs for industries. Social workers should not function as bureaucrats who deny health care benefits or services to employees and their family members merely in order to cut costs. The historical "bind" between employment practices and the goals of the profession is highlighted by this trend. As Simon has written, "Social workers who desire to serve clients to the best of their ability must become astute assessors of the culture, dynamics, and structures of the institutions in which they work" (Simon 1995). In looking forward to the future of advanced generalist practice and programming, we must be diligent in remembering our rich professional past.

REFERENCES

Bartlett, H. M. (1970). *The common base of social work practice.* Washington, DC: National Association of Social Workers.

Beaucar, K. O. (2000, January). Federal study profiles substance abuse. *NASW News, 45*(1), 10.

Begun, A. L. (1999). Intimate partner violence: An HBSE perspective. *Journal of Social Work Education, 35,* 239–252.

Berk, R. A. and Rossi, P. H. (1990). *Thinking about program evaluation.* Newbury Park, CA: Sage.

Berlin, S. B. and March, J. C. (1993). *Informing practice decisions.* New York: Macmillan.

Bernstein, N. (1999, December 9). *State court halts Guiliani plan to make homeless families work for shelter* [WWW document]. URL http://www.nytimes.com/ yr/mo/day/news/national/regional/ny-homeless.html

Bradshaw, J. (1972). The concept of social need. *New Society, 30,* 640–643.

Brager, G. and Holloway, S. (1978). *Changing human service organizations. Politics and practice.* New York: Free Press.

Brown, L. M. (1991). *Groups for growth and change.* New York: Longman.

Chen, H. (1993). Emerging perspectives in program evaluation. *Journal of Social Service Research, 17*(1/2), 1–17.

The City of New York. (1999, September). *Clinical practice guidelines for moving individuals with substance abuse disorders from welfare to work.* New York: The City of New York Human Resources Administration, Office of Health and Mental Health Services.

Coley, S. M. and Scheinberg, C. A. (1990). *Proposal writing.* Newbury Park, CA: Sage.

Cox, F. M., Erlich, J. L., Rothman, J., and Tropman, J. E. (Eds.). (1987). *Strategies of community organization* (4th ed.). Itasca, IL: Peacock.

Craig, R. L. (1987). *Training and development handbook. A guide to human resource development* (3rd ed.). New York: McGraw-Hill.

Crowell, N. A. and Burgess, A. W. (Eds.). (1996). *Understanding violence against women.* Washington, DC: National Academy Press.

Davis, L. V. (1993). Feminism and constructivism: Teaching social work practice with women. In J. Laird (Ed.), *Revisioning social work education: A social constructionist approach* (pp. 147–163). Binghamton, NY: Haworth.

Dutton, D. G. (1995). *The domestic assault of women* (rev. ed.). Vancouver, BC: UBC Press.

Erickson, P. G., Riley, D. M., Cheung, Y. W., and O'Hare, P. A. (Eds.). (1997). *Harm reduction: A new direction for drug policies and programs.* Toronto: University of Toronto Press.

Fatout, M. and Rose, S. (1995). *Task groups in the social services.* Newbury Park, CA: Sage.

Franklin, C. and Nurius, P. S. (Eds.). (1998). *Constructivism in practice. Methods and challenges.* Milwaukee, WI: Families International.

Freire, P. (2000). *Pedagogy of the oppressed* (rev. ed.). New York: Continuum. (Original work published 1970.)

Garvin, C. (1973). *Education for generalist practice in social work: A comparative analysis of current modalities.* Paper presented at the annual meeting of the Council on Social Work Education, San Francisco. (Internal CUSSW document.)

Germain, C. (June, 1973). An ecological perspective in casework practice. *Social Casework.*

Germain, C. B. and Gitterman, A. (1980). *The life model of social work practice.* New York: Columbia University Press.

Germain, C. B. and Gitterman, A. (1996). *The life model of social work practice. Advances in theory and practice* (2nd ed.). New York: Columbia University Press.

Gitterman, A. and Germain, C. B. (1976). Social work practice: A life model. *Social Service Review, 50,* 601–610.

Grasso, A. J. and Epstein, I. (1992). Toward a developmental approach to program evaluation. *Administration in Social Work, 16*(3/4), 187–203.

Grosser, C. F. (1976). *New directions in community organizing. From enabling to advocacy* (expanded ed.). New York: Praeger.

Gutierrez, L. M. (1990). Working with women of color: An empowerment perspective. *Social Work, 35,* 149–153.

Gutierrez, L. M. and Lord, C. (1998). Toward a social constructivist model for community practice. In C. Franklin and P. S. Nurius (Eds.), *Constructivism in practice: Methods and challenges* (pp. 279–290). Milwaukee: Families International.

Gutierrez, L. and Nurius, P. (Eds.). (1994). *Education and research for empowerment practice.* Seattle: Center for Policy and Practice Research.

Hanson, M. (1995). Practice in organizations. In C. H. Meyer and M. A. Mattaini (Eds.), *The foundations of social work practice. A graduate text* (pp. 205–224). Washington, DC: National Association of Social Workers Press.

Hasenfeld, Y. (Ed.). (1992). *Human services as complex organizations.* Newbury Park, CA: Sage.

Hearn, G. A. (Ed.). (1969). *The general systems approach: Contributions toward an holistic conception of social work.* New York: Council on Social Work Education.

Heather, N., Wodak, A., Nadelmann, E., and O'Hare, P. (Eds.). (1993). *Psychoactive drugs and harm reduction: From faith to science.* London: Whurr.

Hollis, F. (1972). *Casework: A psychosocial therapy.* New York: Random House.

Housing and Urban Development. (1999). *Homelessness: Programs and the people they serve.* [WWW document]. URL http://www.huduser.org/publications/homeless/homelessnessgov.html

Hudson, W. W. (1997). Assessment tools as outcomes measures in social work. In E. J. Mullen and J. L. Magnabosco (Eds.), *Outcomes measurement in the human services* (pp. 68–80). Washington, DC: National Association of Social Workers Press.

Inciardi, J. A. and Harrison, L. D. (1999). *Harm reduction: National and international perspectives.* Newbury Park, CA: Sage.

Janchill, M. P. (February, 1969). Systems concepts in casework theory and practice. *Social Casework* 50(2):74–82.

Jencks, C. (1994). *The homeless.* Cambridge, MA: Harvard University Press.

Kahn, A. J. (Ed.). (1973). *Shaping the new social work.* New York: Columbia University Press.

Kahn, S. (1991). *Organizing: A guide for grass roots leaders.* Washington, DC: National Association of Social Workers Press.

Kemp, S. P. (1995). Practice with communities. In C. H. Meyer and M. A. Mattaini (Eds.), *The foundations of social work practice. A graduate text* (pp. 176–204). Washington, DC: National Association of Social Workers Press.

Kettner, P. M., Moroney, R. M., and Martin, L. L. (1990). *Designing and managing programs: An effectiveness-based approach.* Newbury Park, CA: Sage.

Krueger, R. A. (1988). *Focus groups: A practice guide for applied research.* Newbury Park, CA: Sage.

Kuhn, C., Swartzwelder, S., and Wilson, W. (1998). *Buzzed. The straight facts about the most used and abused drugs from alcohol to ecstasy.* New York: W. W. Norton.

Lauffer, A. (1997). *Grantsmanship* (3rd ed.). Newbury Park, CA: Sage.

Long, D. D. and Holle, M. C. (1997). *Macro systems in the social environment.* Itasca, IL: Peacock.

Marlatt, G. A. (Ed.). (1998). *Harm reduction: Pragmatic strategies for managing high risk behaviors.* New York: Guilford.

Marlatt, G. A. and Tapert, S. F. (1993). Harm reduction: Reducing the risks of addictive behaviors. In J. S. Baer, G. A. Marlatt, and R. J. McMahon (Eds.), *Addictive behaviors across the life span. Prevention, treatment, and policy issues* (pp. 243–273). Newbury Park, CA: Sage.

Maslow, A. (1954). *Motivation and personality.* New York: Harper and Row.

Mattaini, M. A. (1995). Generalist practice: People and programs. In C. H. Meyer and M. A. Mattaini (Eds.), *The foundations of social work practice. A graduate text* (pp. 225–245). Washington, DC: National Association of Social Workers Press.

——(1996). "Acting to save the world": Elements of action. In M. A. Mattaini and B. A. Thyer (Eds.), *Finding solutions to social problems: Behavioral strategies for change* (pp. 397–414). Washington, DC: American Psychological Association.

Mattaini, M. and Kirk, S. A. (1991). Assessing assessment in social work. *Social Work, 36,* 260–266.

McGowan, B. G. (1973). *Case advocacy: a study of the interventive process in child advocacy.* New York: Columbia University School of Social Work.

——(1975, May). *Case advocacy practice.* Paper presented at the National Conference on Social Welfare, San Francisco.

McKillip, J. (1987). *Need analysis. Tools for the human services and education.* Newbury Park, CA; Sage.

McNeece, C. A. and DiNitto, D. M. (Eds.). (1998). *Chemical dependency: A systems approach* (2nd ed.). Boston: Allyn and Bacon.

Meyer, C. H. (1970). *Social work practice: A response to the urban crisis.* New York: Free Press.

——(1976). *Social work practice. The changing landscape* (2nd ed.). New York: Free Press.

——(Ed.). (1983). *Clinical social work in the eco-systems perspective.* New York: Columbia University Press.

——(1993). *Assessment in social work practice.* New York: Columbia University Press.

National Association of Social Workers Delegate Assembly. (1971). *Proposal for the future delivery of social services: Position of the western coalition.* Unpublished paper, Columbia University School of Social Work collection.

National Gay and Lesbian Task Force. (1999). [Website]. URL http://www.ngltf.org/downloads/hatemap1299.pdf

National Institute on Drug Abuse. (2000). *The economic costs of alcohol and drug abuse in the United States—1992* [WWW document]. URL http://www.nida.nih.gov/economic costs.html

Neuber, K. A., Atkins, W. T., Jacobson, J. A., and Reuterman, N. A. (1990). *Needs assessment: A model for community planning.* Newbury Park, CA: Sage.

O'Flaherty, B. (1996). *Making room. The economics of homelessness.* Cambridge, MA: Harvard University Press.

O'Hare, P. A., Newcombe, R., Matthews, A., Buning, E. C., and Drucker, E. (Eds.). (1992). *The reduction of drug-related harm.* New York: Routledge.

Parihar, B. (1984). *Task-centered management in human services.* Springfield, IL: Charles C. Thomas.

Piven, F. F. and Cloward, R. A. (1993). *Regulating the poor: The functions of public welfare* (rev. ed.). New York: Vintage.

Raiff, N. and Shore, B. (1993). *Advanced case management: New strategies for the nineties.* Newbury Park, CA: Sage.

Reid, W. and Epstein, L. (1972). *Task-centered casework.* New York: Columbia University Press.

Reinarman, C. and Levine, H. G. (Eds.). (1997). *Crack in America: Demon drugs and social justice.* Berkeley: University of California Press.

Rivera, F. G. and Erlich, J. L. (Eds.). (1992). *Community organizing in a diverse society.* Boston: Allyn and Bacon.

Rossi, P. H. (1997). Program outcomes: Conceptual and measurement issues. In E. J. Mullen and J. L. Magnabosco (Eds.), *Outcomes measurement in the human services* (pp. 20–34). Washington, DC: National Association of Social Workers Press.

Rossi, P. H. and Freeman, H. E. (1993). *Evaluation: A systematic approach.* Newbury Park, CA: Sage.

Saleebey, D. (Ed.). (1997). *The strengths perspective in social work practice* (2nd ed.). New York: Longman.

——(1998). Constructing the community: The emergent uses of social constructionism in economically distressed communities. In C. Franklin and P. S. Nurius (Eds.), *Constructivism in practice: Methods and challenges* (pp. 291–310). Milwaukee: Families International.

Satcher, D. (1999). *Mental Health. A Report of the Surgeon General* [WWW document]. URL http://www.surgeongeneral.gov/library/mentalhealth/index.html

Schwartz, W. (1969). *Social welfare forum.* New York: Columbia University Press.

Scott, F. and Delgado, J. (1979, October). Planning mental health programs for Hispanic communities. *Social Casework,* pp. 451–456.

Sexton, T. L. and Griffin, B. L. (Eds.). (1997). *Constructivist thinking in counseling practice, research, and training.* New York: Teachers College Press.

Sheafor, B. W. and Landon, P. S. (1987). Generalist perspective. In A. Minahan et al. (Eds.), *Encyclopedia of social work.* (18th ed., pp. 660–669). Silver Spring, MD: National Association of Social Work.

Simon, B. L. (1995). The profession of social work. In C. H. Meyer and M. A. Mattaini (Eds.), *The foundations of social work practice: A graduate text* (pp. 260–273). Washington, DC: National Association of Social Workers Press.

Steward, D. W. and Shamdasani, P. N. (1995). *Focus groups.* Newbury Park, CA: Sage.

Titmuss, R. (1968). *Commitment to welfare.* New York: Random House.

Wells, R. A. (1994). *Planned short-term treatment* (2nd ed.). New York: Free Press.

Wren, C. S. (1999, December 9). *Top U.S. drug official proposes shift in criminal justice policy* [WWW document]. URL http://www.nytimes.com/yr/mo/day/news/washpol/drug-policy.html

Chapter 5

SOCIAL ADMINISTRATION

Lawrence L. Martin and Karla Toruño Aguirre Choudhury

The Columbia University School of Social Work (CUSSW) is to a great extent a reflection of the history of social work and social work education in general. From its earliest beginnings, social work education has grappled with the question: to what extent should administration be taught as part of a larger social work curriculum? The answer to this question has changed and evolved over the last century as the role of social work and social work education has changed and evolved. When one looks back over the last century at the relative importance of social administration within the larger social work curriculum at CUSSW, two observations come readily to mind. First, social administration topics have been part of the CUSSW curriculum from the earliest days of the school. Second, the relative importance of social administration within the CUSSW curriculum has increased in importance over time, particularly in the last two decades of the twentieth century.

This essay takes a look back at the history and evolution of social administration at CUSSW over the last hundred years. As part of this review, major milestones in the history of social administration at CUSSW are noted and commented upon (see table 5.1). In addition, changes in the "social work context"—including larger societal changes and developments as well as changes and developments in social work practice and social work education in general—are identified and their implications for social administration at CUSSW noted.

In tracing the history of social administration at CUSSW, we divide the last one hundred years into four major time periods:

1. The Philanthropic Years (1898–1930)
2. The New Deal Years (1930–1940)
3. The Great Society Years (1965–1972)
4. The Devolution Years (1976–Present)

TABLE 5.1

Major Milestones in the Social Administration Program

YEAR	
1898	The Charity Organization Society of the City of New York establishes a summer school for volunteers and others involved in philanthropy. The Society names the program the New York School of Philanthropy (NYSP), which eventually becomes the Columbia University School of Social Work.
1904	The basic series of introductory lectures of the NYSP includes several with a social administration focus.
1927	Major fields of study are identified, including personnel administration.
1934–1940	Several new social administration courses with a government focus are added to the CUSSW curriculum to help with implementation of President Roosevelt's New Deal programs.
1950	All CUSSW students are required to complete two courses, Community Organizing 1 and 2, which include social administration concepts and principles.
1970–1980	Social administration attempts to develop an identity separate from community organization.
1982	Social administration is designated as a social work method.
1998	The current social administration curriculum is formulated.

Any attempt to impose structure on history — and to assign descriptive names to specific historical periods — must always be somewhat arbitrary and consequently subject to criticism. Nevertheless, attempting to discuss a century of social administration history at CUSSW requires some sort of classification schema in order to bring perspective to the subject matter. In selecting our time periods, we generally follow the guidance suggested by Alfred Kahn in his keynote address at the Centennial Celebration of the Columbia University School of Social Work.[1]

THE PHILANTHROPIC YEARS (1898–1930)

In the beginning, the focus of social work, and consequently social work education, was on private philanthropy. The early years of this era were characterized by rapid industrialization, record immigration, and the social reforms of the Progressive Era. The CUSSW curriculum was a mirror reflection of its times (table 5.2). For example, the curriculum of the New York School of Philanthropy for the academic year 1904–05 had a decidedly private philanthropic focus and included lectures under such major topic headings as The State and Its Relation to Charity, The Care of Needy Families in Their Homes, and Child Helping Agencies.

An interesting feature of the 1904–05 curriculum is the inclusion of social administration topics, but with a private philanthropic perspective. For example, the basic set of introductory lectures that surveyed the field of social work included five lectures dealing with the administration and management of charitable organizations (table 5.2). The topics covered included financial statements, bookkeeping, bequests and endowments, and office economy (defined as the study of efficient administration).[2] The emphasis on financial management practices in the overall CUSSW social work curriculum is of particular interest. The notion that all social workers should be grounded in at least some of the tools of social administration, with an emphasis on financial management tools, was an operating assumption of the CUSSW curriculum from its earliest days.

Two observations can be made about the initial relationship of social administration to larger issues of social work education at CUSSW. First, social administration topics were seen as a legitimate part of the educational preparation of professional social workers. Second, social administration topics appear to have been somewhat randomly distributed throughout the curriculum. Thus, from CUSSW's earliest days, social administration topics were accepted as an important component of the larger social work curriculum. However, uncertainty existed in terms of just how social administration topics should relate to larger issues of social work education.

In looking back at the CUSSW curriculum in the 1920s and 1930s, Saul Bernstein commented on what he called the "social administration dilemma."[3] Should CUSSW teach students to administer in specific fields of practice (e.g., child welfare, immigration resettlement, etc.)? Or, should a generic approach to social administration be adopted, with the idea that

TABLE 5.2

New York School of Philanthropy Curriculum, Academic Year 1904–5

GROUP A — SURVEY OF THE WORLD

1. General Survey and Analysis of Social Work
2. The Literature on Charity
3. Social Reform in the Nineteenth Century
4. Some Industrial Causes of Distress
5. Financial Administration of Charitable Agencies*
6. Office Economy*
7. The Value of Annual Reports and the Art of Writing Them*
8. Bequests and Endowments*

GROUP B — THE STATE AND ITS RELATION TO CHARITY

1. Public Charitable Institutions in New York State
2. The New York State Board of Charities
3. Boards, Institutions and Methods in Various States
4. Public Aid and the Right of Relief

GROUP C — RACIAL TRAITS IN THE POPULATION: A STUDY IN SOCIOLOGY

1. Immigration
2. The Social Meaning of Immigration
3. Italian Characteristics
4. The Characteristics of Jews Coming from Eastern Europe
5. The American Negro
6. The Negro in the City: Health and Morality
7. The Negro in the City: Economic Conditions
8. The Characteristics of Slaves
9. Special Course: The New Basics of Civilization: A Study in Economics

GROUP D — CONSTRUCTIVE SOCIAL WORK

1. Social Work in Large Cities
2. Social Aspects of Sanitary Work
3. The Tuberculosis Problem
4. The Scope and Function of the Board of Health
5. Welfare Work in Factories and Stores
6. Social Tendencies of Modern Industrialism
7. The Boys Club
8. The Modern Church as a Factor in Social Progress
9. The Visiting Nurse as a Social Factor

TABLE 5.2

Continued

GROUP E — THE CARE OF NEEDY FAMILIES IN THEIR HOMES

1. Principles of Relief
2. History of the Development of the Scientific in Charity
3. Systems and Methods of a Charity Organization Society
4. Investigation and Treatment: Illustrated by a Study of Actual Case Records
5. A Modern Mendicancy Department
6. The Homeless Man
7. Hospitals, Dispensaries and Diet Kitchens

GROUP F — CHILD HELPING AGENCIES

1. Care of Destitute, Neglected and Delinquent Children
2. Problems of the Institutions
3. The Organization and Management of a Society for Helping Children*
4. The Practical Work of the Committees and Agents of a Child Helping Society*
5. Placing Out and Probation
6. The State and the Defective Child
7. The Feeble-Minded Child: Psychical and Physiological Problems
8. Methods of Education of Feeble-Minded and Backward Children
9. Defective and Backward Children in the Public Schools

GROUP G — TREATMENT OF THE CRIMINAL: REFORMATORY METHODS OF PROBATION

1. The New Penology: Its Principles and Problems
2. Prison Labor
3. Minor Correctional Institutions
4. Principles and Methods of Reformatory Work
5. Probation: Work for Girls and Women
6. The Practical Art of Dealing with Wayward Girls

Source: Saul Bernstein et al. (1942). *The New York School of Social Work: 1898–1941.* New York: Institute of Welfare Research, Community Service Society of New York.

*Lecture with a social administration focus.

students would then apply general administrative principles to various fields of practice? Review of the 1927–28 *General Announcement* of the then New York School of Social Work suggests that the "social administration dilemma" was resolved in favor of the generalist approach. The 1927–28 *General Announcement* lists a two-quarter generic administration course, Administration of Social Agencies, which is described as follows:

> Elements of administrative organization in social agencies; functions and interrelationships, for boards of directors, executives, and staff; principles involved in formulation and administration of finance policy, budgeting, accounting, office management; principles of executive efficiency.[4]

The recognition of the importance of administration concepts and tools as a component part of social work education, as well as the adoption of a generic approach to administration, is a characteristic of CUSSW's approach to social administration that continues to the present day. Over the years, the relative importance of social administration within the larger CUSSW curriculum has waxed and waned with the times. But social administration topics have always been an important component of the school's curriculum.

THE NEW DEAL YEARS (1930–1940)

With the stock market crash of 1929, the resulting depression, and eventually the advent of President Roosevelt's "New Deal," the nature of social work and social work education began to change. While social workers with administrative skills were still needed in the private philanthropic sector, they were now also needed by the federal government and the forty-eight states to assist in the implementation of the New Deal programs. Social work education in general, at CUSSW and at other social work schools, now needed a government focus. In addition to understanding private philanthropy, social work education, and in particular social administration, needed to also educate social workers on how to plan, establish, implement, and manage large-scale government programs.

Review of the CUSSW curriculum during this period indicates a shift toward more concern with the following areas: government, political forces, public welfare, and the administration and management of public welfare agencies. For example, in the *General Announcement* for 1934–35, new government and administration courses were offered bearing such titles as Public Welfare Problems, Problems of Unemployment Relief Administration, and Government and Social Work.[5] The latter two courses had a decidedly social administration focus. The Government and Social Work course is described in the *General Announcement* as dealing with

> those phases of government structure and public administration which affect any form of social work conducted under government auspices. Consideration is given to the advantages and disadvantages of social work under public auspices; the influence of political forces on public administration; the merit system; supervision by the state government over local functions; grants in aid from the federal government, etc.[6]

In 1937–38 another new government-oriented administration course, Problems and Techniques of Administration in Public Welfare Agencies, appears. The 1937–38 *General Announcement* described this new course offering as follows:

> This course covers the origin and functional correlation of policies, methods, and procedures; supervision of the operations of the agency; integration of the social service, business and other departments; analysis of types of administrative controls and practices; formulation of personnel standards; training programs, staff relations, committees and organizations; case load trends, accounting and assignments; budgets and administrative costs.[7]

Still another administration course, Personnel Problems in Operating Agencies, was added during the 1939–40 academic year.[8] One could argue that by the end of the decade of the 1930s, the number and types of administration courses offered by CUSSW resembled a minicurriculum in public administration with an emphasis on public welfare and social services delivery.

In summing up the New Deal years and their effects on CUSSW and on social administration, three major observations can be made. First, CUSSW responded quickly to the new educational demands associated with social work practice in government agencies. Second, CUSSW's response included several new courses with a decidedly government focus. Third, social administration, while important during this period, was still not considered a major CUSSW program.

THE GREAT SOCIETY YEARS (1965–1972)

The Great Society years saw a virtual explosion of new federal programs designed to wage an all-out war on poverty. The Office of Economic Opportunity (OEO) was created, the Medicaid and Medicare programs were started, the Model Cities program was initiated, and a plethora of other federal grant programs came into being. Examples of social administration courses offered at CUSSW during this period include Aspects of Social Agency Administration, Financing of Social Work, Social Work Administration, and Administration of Social Agencies.

During the 1960s, social administration at CUSSW was considered a part of community organization. Because many of the Great Society programs had a grass-roots and community organization focus (e.g., community action and Model Cities) and because of CUSSW's nationally prominent community organization faculty, social administration went into a period of hibernation. Toward the end of the Great Society years, however, prominent social work educators began to speak out about the complexity of social administration practice and the need for schools of social work to place more emphasis on management and administrative issues.[9] In a major social administration text of the times, Harleigh Trecker noted that the American social welfare system had attained a "scope and complexity which would strain the credulity of bygone humanitarians."[10]

By the early years of the decade of the 1970s, the argument could be made that the community organization and grass-roots movements of the 1960s had succeeded in creating institutionalized social welfare. Public welfare and social services were now major components of the activities of federal, state, and local governments. Social welfare, social services, and social work now needed to change from an advocacy approach (attempting to get social issues on the government agenda) to more of an institutional approach (successfully administering, managing, and consolidating the gains of the 1960s).

Despite recognizing the need to focus more on social administration topics, most schools of social work were slow to respond. A 1971 study conducted by the Council on Social Work Education found that only twenty-two schools of social work, out of sixty-six surveyed nationally, offered any type of concentration in administration or management either separately or in conjunction with social policy.[11] As late as 1977, the number of graduate students pursuing administration and management course work in schools of social work nationally totaled only 342 (4.0 percent) out of 8,500 students.[12] During this period, Burton Gummer noted that three models of social administration education tended to predominate: (1) social administration as a distinct two-year concentration; (2) social administration as a subspeciality within a combined policy, planning, and administration concentration; and (3) social administration as a second-year concentration.[13] Social administration at CUSSW followed model 3, a second-year concentration.

CUSSW was among those schools of social work that attempted to revisit, revise, and strengthen the social administration components of their curriculums during the 1970s. CUSSW's attempt to focus more on social administration was to become a protracted process of separating social administration from community organization. Review of the Columbia University *Bulletins* for the decade of the 1970s yields an interesting picture of "one step forward, two steps backward." The 1971–72 *Bulletin* refers to a Community Organizing and Planning and Administration sequence within CUSSW.[14] However, the 1972–73 *Bulletin* refers to only a Community Organization and Planning sequence which included social administration.[15] The 1975–76 *Bulletin* identifies something called "Concentration II," which contained a series of four courses with *no names*.[16] The uneasy and undifferentiated relationship between social administration and community organization (Concentration II) continued throughout the 1970s.

THE DEVOLUTION YEARS (1976–PRESENT)

Beginning with the administration of President Carter in the late 1970s and continuing under the subsequent administrations of Presidents Reagan, Bush, and Clinton, political power and decision making moved away from Washington and to the states and local governments. During this period, the number of categorical federal grants decreased, while the number of block grants to states increased significantly.

In a devolved social welfare system with only limited guidance being provided by Washington, the nature of social policy, social service delivery, and social administration began to change. The nature of the change can be described as movement away from a centralized policy/decentralized administration system and movement toward a decentralized policy and entrepreneurial administrative system.[17] The tools of social administration practice also began to change. Direct government service delivery became less prominent and private sector (both nonprofit and for-profit) service delivery more prominent. Less use of grants was made by the federal government and by state human service agencies and more reliance on contracting became the norm. Cooperation between private sector human service agencies was replaced by competition with a new emphasis on cost efficiency and cost effectiveness. The application of information technologies to better manage caseloads and agency finances became increasingly important. Many government and nonprofit human service agencies began adopting tools from the business world, including strategic planning, marketing, sophisticated budgeting techniques, and cost analysis, among others.

To keep pace with the changing nature of social administration practice, the social administration curriculum at CUSSW also changed. In 1982, social administration and community organization were formally separated. Social administration was designated by CUSSW as a social work "method." This designation meant that social administration was given equal status with other CUSSW methods such as clinical practice. The social administration curriculum was also changed from being exclusively a second-year program of instruction to becoming a full-fledged two-year program. This change enabled CUSSW to offer more social administration courses and also enabled social administration students to begin integrating administration principles into their learning at the outset of their CUSSW education.

In terms of course offerings and content, more emphasis in the social administration curriculum began to be placed on understanding the new roles of the states, local governments, nonprofits, and for-profits in the delivery of publicly financed social services. Returning to its roots of nearly a century ago, financial management became more important within the social administration curriculum, as did information management. A 1987 CUSSW publication identified six major content areas that comprised the new social administration program:

1. Constituency Development
2. Program Development
3. Human Resource Management and Supervision
4. Financial Management

5. Information Management
6. Program Evaluation[18]

In addition to these six major content areas, social administration students were also required to take a one-semester course in Computer Usage and Application.[19]

SOCIAL ADMINISTRATION IN THE TWENTY-FIRST CENTURY

As the Columbia University School of Social Work prepares to enter its second century, the social administration program is stronger than it perhaps has ever been. In addition to a cadre of full-time faculty conducting state-of-the-art research, the social administration program also makes judicious use of adjunct faculty, who are respected practitioners. The numbers, as well as the quality, of students applying to and being accepted into the social administration program continue to increase from year to year.

The social administration curriculum was significantly revised in 1998. With the advent of the Advanced Generalist Practice and Programming (AGPP) concentration, a need existed to more clearly define and distinguish social administration from AGPP. The social administration concentration was reconceptualized as educational preparation and training for social workers aspiring to middle and top management positions in government and private, nonprofit human service organizations as well as in less traditional social work organizations such as for-profit businesses. The revised social administration curriculum consists of six courses; five core courses and one elective (see table 5.3). The increasing importance of information technology is recognized in the curriculum by the presence of a required core course devoted exclusively to this topic. In addition to the CUSSW course offerings, an increasing number of social administration students are also choosing to pursue either minor or dual degree programs in such other specializations as public administration, public health, and business administration.

Field education has always been an important part of any social work curriculum, and so it is in the social administration concentration. In their first year of fieldwork, social administration students are provided with a mixture of direct client work and administrative assignments. By the end of their first year at CUSSW, social administration students have completed two courses,

TABLE 5.3

Social Administration Curriculum, Academic Year 1998–99

CORE COURSES

Integrating Seminar in Social Administration—a foundation course designed to expose students to the broad spectrum of issues that confront social administrators today, including organizational and management theories, strategic and operational planning, leadership, employment law, different modes of service delivery (e.g., contracts, grants, and vouchers), and budgeting and current management trends (quality management, government reinvention, and process reengineering).

Program Planning and Development—this advanced course provides an in-depth treatment of the tasks and processes involved in initiating, modifying, and improving human service programs, defining social issues and problems, assessing community needs, formulating alternative courses of action, developing goals and objectives, and carrying out implementation and monitoring.

Macro Community Practice—this advanced course covers the concept of change in organizations, groups, and communities. In addition to change and community organization theories, the course also deals with coalitions, coalition building, collaboratives, networks, social marketing, and other change and leadership strategies.

Information Management—this advanced course is designed to develop a working knowledge of management information systems and their application in human service agencies, including knowledge of relational databases, common office software applications, and the use of management information in decision making.

Program Evaluation—this advanced course is designed to enable students to conceptualize and carry out quantitative and qualitative assessments of human service programs; develop output, quality, and outcome performance measures for human service programs; conduct cost–benefit studies; and present study findings using descriptive and inferential statistics.

ELECTIVE COURSES

Human Resources Management and Supervision—an advanced course that covers the legal context of human resources management, theories of leadership, supervision and motivation, and such other topics as recruitment, selection, job descriptions, promotion, training, performance appraisal, termination, and other topics.

TABLE 5.3
Continued

Staff Development and Training—an advanced course that covers such topics as assessing staff training needs; developing, implementing, and monitoring a staff training and development plan; selecting outside training vendors, and evaluating the results of staff training and development plans.

Financial Management—an advanced course dealing with performance and program budgeting, service costing and pricing, differential cost analysis, government grants and contracts, foundation funding, auditing, risk management, and other topics.

Source: CUSSW Social Administration course syllabi.

Integrating Seminar in Social Administration and Program Planning and Development, in addition to their first-year field experience. The combination of first-year course work and field experience provides social administration students with a solid foundation for their second year of fieldwork, which is exclusively administrative in nature. Table 5.4 identifies some of the second-year field assignments available to social administration students. As table 5.4 illustrates, the field placements represent a mixture of traditional government (New York City Administration for Children and Families) and private, nonprofit (Korean Community Center) human service agencies, as well as international organizations (United Nations Council on Aging), and nontraditional field placements such as Harris-Rothenberg International, Colgate Palmolive, and Mutual of New York (MONY) Foundation.

Graduates of CUSSW's social administration program are going on to work in a variety of interesting, challenging, and rewarding positions in government and the private sector. They include legislative analysts, management analysts, program planners, evaluators, contract administrators, financial administrators, executive directors of private nonprofit organizations, grant writers, staff developers, trainers, Office of Equal Opportunity officials, employee assistance program specialists, outreach workers, management information specialists, and others. Additionally, during the 1990s, several social administration graduates were selected for the prestigious Presidential Management Intern (PMI) program. CUSSW PMIs have gone on to work for

TABLE 5.4

Second-Year Social Administration Field Placements (Partial Listing)

Actors Fund	Fountain House
Administration for Children and Families (City of New York)	Hamilton-Madison House
	Harris Rothenberg International
Banana Kelly Community Improvement Association	Hoffman-LaRoche, Inc. (Employee Assistance Program)
The Bridge	Human Resources Administration (City of New York)
Bronx Borough President's Office	
Bronx Jewish Community Council	Korean Community Center
Center for Health Care Initiatives	Lutheran Immigration and Refugee Service
Center for Social Policy and Practice in the Workplace	Montefiore Medical Center
Center for Urban Community Services	Mutual of New York (MONY) Foundation
Central Employee Assistance Program	
Colgate Palmolive, International Human Resources	New York Department of Aging (New York City)
Community Counseling and Mediation	Project Return Foundation
Court Dispute Referral Service	Union Settlement
Cypress Hills, Local Development Corporation	United Jewish Appeal/Federation of Jewish Philanthropies
Daughters of Israel	United Nations (National Council on Aging)
Episcopal Center	
Families and Work Institute	United Nations (UNICEF Program Division)
Federation of Protestant Welfare Agencies	

Source: CUSSW Placement Planning Book 1996–97.

such federal departments and organizations as the Department of Health and Human Services, the Department of Justice, the Office of Management and Budget in the Executive Office of the President, and the U.S. Senate.

In sum, today's CUSSW social administration graduates are prepared better than ever before to usher in a new century of excellence in the administration of social work services.

NOTES

1. Alfred Kahn, "Themes for a History: The First Hundred Years of the Columbia University School of Social Work." Keynote address at the Centennial Celebration of the Columbia University School of Social Work, New York City, June 1998.

2. Saul Bernstein et al., *The New York School of Social Work: 1898–1941* (New York: Institute of Welfare Research, Community Service Society of New York, 1942).

3. Bernstein et al., *The New York School of Social Work.*

4. The Charity Organization Society of the City of New York, *The New York School of Social Work General Announcement 1927–1928* (New York: Author, 1927).

5. The Charity Organization Society of the City of New York, *The New York School of Social Work General Announcement 1934–1935* (New York: Author, 1934).

6. The Charity Organization of the City of New York, *General Announcement 1934–1935,* 28.

7. The Charity Organization Society of the City of New York, *The New York School of Social Work General Announcement 1937–1938* (New York: Author, 1937).

8. The Community Service Society of New York, *The New York School of Social Work General Announcement 1939–1940* (New York: Author, 1939).

9. Rosemary Sari, "Updating Education for Administration." Paper presented at the annual meeting of the Council on Social Work Education, Cleveland, January 21–24, 1969.

10. Harleigh B. Trecker, *Social Work Administration: Principles and Practices* (New York: Association Press, 1971).

11. Council on Social Work Education (CSWE), *Concentrations and Special Learning Opportunities in the Master of Social Work Curricula of Graduate Schools of Social Work 1971–1972* (New York: Author, 1971).

12. Allen Rubin and G. Robert Whitcomb, *Statistics on Social Work Education in the United States: 1977* (New York: Council on Social Work Education, 1977), 53–54.

13. Burton Gummer, (1975) "Social Planning and Social Administration: Implications for Curriculum Development," *Journal of Education for Social Work* 11 (Winter): 66–73.

14. *Columbia University Bulletin 1971–1972,* 25.

15. *Columbia University Bulletin 1972–1973,* 24–25.

16. *Columbia University Bulletin 1975–1976,* 17.

17. Lawrence L. Martin, "The Environmental Context of Social Welfare Administration," in Rino Patti, ed., *Handbook of Social Welfare Administration* (Thousand Oaks, CA: Sage, 2001), 55–67.

18. Columbia University School of Social Work, *The Social Administration Sequence* (New York: Author, 1987).

19. Columbia University School of Social Work, *The Social Administration Sequence.*

Chapter 6

SOCIAL POLICY

Sheila B. Kamerman

Social policy—and its antecedent and correlate social reform—has been an integral part of the Columbia University School of Social Work (CUSSW) since its inception, but it has vacillated over the years between being a highly visible and co-equal component of direct practice and being a part of the context in which social work practice was carried out. The School was launched as an institution for the training of practitioners of scientific philanthropy working with individuals and families. But its establishment by both leading practitioners and leading academic social scientists in the early years of what later came to be known as the Progressive Era sustained its place in the broader movement of social reform. During its first two decades, social problems and social reform were a core concern; Meier's (1954) history of the School's first half-century, Bernstein et al.'s (1942) 1898–1941 history of the School, and the School's *Studies in Social Work* (New York School of Philanthropy 1915), as well as early faculty and curriculum reports, confirm this. Subsequently, however, "social policy" (whether social reform, public welfare, or other related topics) gradually became contextual in the curriculum, or was viewed as a device for advancing the development of services for individuals having problems of social adjustment. The doctoral program, established in 1950 under the leadership of the economist Eveline Burns, who then chaired the program until her retirement in 1967, took the lead in reviving interest in social policy. The 1960s constituted a second period in which social policy became more visible at the School, largely in the form of social action, with Richard Cloward, George Brager, and Mitchell Ginsberg in leadership positions at the School and in the City. At the same time, the doctoral program confirmed its role in training social policy educators and scholars under the leadership of Alfred J. Kahn, who chaired the program for ten of the next twenty years, followed by Sheila B. Kamerman for eight years.

Only in the last two decades has social policy practice reemerged as a method as well as substantive content, first in the doctoral program and second, recently, in the M.S. program.

Individual faculty members have always played important roles in developing, modifying, implementing, or assessing social policies, but the curriculum did not always reflect a similar commitment. For example, during the Great Depression of the 1930s, there was still no *required* course on public welfare, although there were several new elective courses dealing with some of the major social policy developments, and faculty members did go on leave to consult on the training of public welfare workers as well as holding special evening workshops for relief workers. Meier (1954) makes little reference to these courses or their content. No social workers (other than Harry Hopkins, and perhaps, depending on definition, Frances Perkins) were directly involved in the New Deal social policy initiatives.

Only with the advent of the economist Eveline Burns as a member of the faculty in 1946 did the curriculum begin to reflect renewed attention to social policy, first in the doctoral program and then, to a lesser extent, as the result of a curriculum review, in the master's degree program. Austin (1986), in his history of social work education, refers to the development of social policy as derived from the public welfare content included in "the basic eight" (see below). He states that social policy courses from 1950 to 1980 focused on descriptions of policy issues, laws, and service structures related to poverty and income transfer programs. It would seem that the policy "content," as defined by Austin, was in the curriculum from 1940, a decade before the Council on Social Work Education (CSWE) was recommending it.

Faculty have often expressed their frustration with what they believed was inadequate attention and curriculum space devoted to policy content. After World War I, the curriculum was increasingly devoted to direct practice, including community organization and later social administration. Even when an additional "policy" (public welfare) course was required in the 1940s, it was still viewed largely as contextual. No attention was paid to policy as a "method"—to policy formation, advocacy, or analysis—until the late 1960s (still well before the profession generally acknowledged the development, according to Austin [1986]).[1] Where the School was concerned, it was the doctoral program that played the leadership role in social work education in social policy. In recent years the School has moved to make a significant commitment to social policy as a form of social work practice for training master's degree students. What the implications of this may be for the future remains to be seen.

In this paper, I will trace the history of the role of social policy at the School, from the Summer School of Philanthropy (1898), to the New York School of Philanthropy (1904), to the New York School of Social Work (1919), to the CUSSW School of Social Work (1940 and 1962), paying attention along the way to the curriculum and the research and scholarship of individual faculty members and alumni. I will highlight those periods when the School has been particularly invested in social policy and those aspects of social policy where the School has been especially influential, noting the work of several individuals who played important roles in social policy developments in the School, the country, and elsewhere. I will conclude with some brief comments on the implications for the future. Two themes are dominant: (1) the vacillating and sometimes lagging institutional role of the School in responding to significant external developments, as reflected in the curriculum; and (2) the influential role of individual faculty members' research and scholarship and its impact on social policy initiatives in the School and developments outside the School, both in the profession and in the broader society.

THE DAY BEFORE YESTERDAY: THE FIRST FIFTY YEARS

The School was launched under the aegis of the Charity Organization Society (COS) to provide training (practical experience) and education (knowledge) for what we would now call "direct service practitioners." Regardless of the terms used, social policy was an integral part of the curriculum from the onset; and the focus was national and international in scope, by design. The Summer School offerings included lectures (there were no "courses" as such) on the following (Bernstein et al. 1942; Meier 1954):

Private Charitable Agencies
Child Saving (placement; kindergartens)
Public Charities
Medical Charities
Public Activities Affecting the Poor
Treatment of Needy Families in Their Homes
Neighborhood Improvement

Immigrants (the history and location of foreign populations in Manhattan
and the Bronx)
Child Labor

By 1904 the School was operating a one-year program, but the plan
for classroom teaching remained groups of lectures rather than integrated
courses. In the curriculum for 1906–07, Meier (1954) notes that there were
eight groups, four of which were required (including one on the demographic
and racial characteristics of the New York population, with particular attention to "Negroes" and immigrants) one on child welfare, and two from another group of four. The latter four included Administration of Charitable
and Educational Institutions and the State in Its Relation to Charity (with
particular attention to the work of the New York State Board of Charities).
Meier (1954:25–26) points out,

> As in the case of the Summer School curriculum of the first seven years,
> the course of study reflects the problems with which the field of social
> work was concerned . . . The social worker took an active role in the
> movement to eradicate specific evils through control of disease, tene-
> ment regulations and child labor laws. In this period, however, there is
> deeper probing into social and economic causes of individual distress
> and the economic structure itself is questioned. Social and economic
> inequities rather than the supposedly inferior "moral fibre" of the indi-
> vidual are more clearly postulated as the cause of distress.

Between 1904 and World War I the School's curriculum reflected these major concerns. The causes and consequences of slums, industrial accidents,
and unemployment were all addressed in the curriculum, along with child
labor and other child-related problems, and the problems of immigrants. Required readings for these courses included Amos Warner's (1894) *American
Charities* and the latest report of the COS.

The 1906–07 curriculum included several series of lectures, including one
on economic changes in the nineteenth century, a second on economic problems and social reform, and a third on Social Tendencies of Modern Industrialism. The content of these three courses constituted about one sixth of
the offerings in the one-year program. Fieldwork experiences included a wide
range of "policy" placements such as state boards of charities and social
agencies.

In 1907 the COS, the administrative aegis of the School, launched the first Pittsburgh Survey, a study of workers in the steel industry. A series of independent studies of selected community problems were carried out, with a major emphasis on social and industrial problems (industrial accidents, working hours and wages, workers' living conditions, women-employing trades), and a little attention to "child-helping" institutions (Zimbalist 1977). The objective was social reform rather than the individualistic and moralistic focus that was more usual for the COS. The study was subsequently taken over by the Russell Sage Foundation and became the catalyst and forerunner of more than one hundred such studies around the country of living conditions and other economic and social conditions in large cities. The final six-volume report was edited by Paul Kellog, the director of the survey and an alumnus of the School, and published by Russell Sage. The report was an important factor in generating a movement to establish Workmen's Compensation laws (Leiby 1978). The impact of the study can be seen in the enactment of federal legislation to protect federal employees in 1908. Between 1910 and 1913, twenty-two states enacted some compensation legislation, and by 1920, forty-three. Kellog and his fourteen fieldworkers included eight people who had given lectures at the School, were alumni, or later became faculty members. These included Kellog himself; John Fitch, who joined the faculty in 1919 and remained until his retirement in 1946, teaching about industrial problems; and Florence Kelly, an expert on child labor issues. The Pittsburgh Survey and its effects and spin-offs could be viewed as the School's first major policy impact, albeit an indirect one, through the work of a graduate, and faculty.

Another major component of the curriculum was concern with the situation of children, the juvenile court movement, child labor laws, and the whole cluster of developments related to "child saving." The first White House Conference on Children (1909), with its strong recommendation that children should not be removed from their parents for reasons of poverty alone, was established and organized in part as a result of the School's efforts. Florence Kelly, of Hull House; Lillian Wald from Henry Street; and Edward Devine (the school's director from 1904 to 1917 and the first Professor of Social Economy at Columbia), are described as playing a catalytic role in the development of the Conference, urging then President Theodore Roosevelt to hold such a conference.

By 1911–12, when the School began its two-year program, half the curriculum was on economic and social problems and approaches to reform. One of the four required core courses was now Modern Industrial Conditions, taught first by Mary Van Kleek, who later went to Russell Sage, and then by John Fitch, who had been a major contributor to the Pittsburgh study and who was to become a long-time faculty member at the School.

In 1912–13, I. M. Rubinow, the well-known expert and scholar of social insurance, taught a fifteen-week series of lectures in the spring semester, on social insurance. This was the first such course taught at a major U.S. university and was followed by similar courses taught at other leading universities. Rubinow had been responsible for the U.S. commissioner of labor's massive (3,000-page) report on *Workmen's Insurance and Compensation Systems in Europe,* covering eleven countries and the following topics:

- the concept of social insurance and social risks
- the development of social insurance in Europe
- the need for social insurance in the United States
- insurance against industrial accidents
- insurance against sickness
- insurance against old age, disability, and death
- insurance against unemployment

In 1913, Rubinow published a pioneering book based on these lectures (*Social Insurance*). He strongly recommended that the United States adopt a similar package of social insurance benefits, a goal that took another two decades to be achieved, and even then, only in part.

In 1916–17, among the courses that second-year students were required to take was a course taught by Edward Devine in Problems in Social Work and, for the first time, a course on Social Policies, taught by Sidney D. M. Hudson. The latter course is not mentioned again, but its content included "a concrete study of principles and tendencies" reflected in legislation and problems such as social insurance, wage and price regulation, public assistance to the dependent, public sanitation, labor exchange, and widows' pensions (New York School of Philanthropy, *General Announcement,* 1916–17).

Illustrative of the kinds of scholarly work carried out during the first two decades by faculty at the School is the collection of reports published under the title of *Studies in Social Work* (1915). In addition to the influential lecture by Abraham Flexner ("Is Social Work a Profession?"), this collection included a translation of the powerful eighteenth-century essay by Juan-Luis Vives ("Concerning the Relief of the Poor," a letter published in Valencia, Spain, in 1783 and a major influence throughout Europe in the late eighteenth and early nineteenth centuries), as well as a section of the Shulhan Arukh on charity (translated by Louis Feinberg of the Jewish Theological Seminary) and a report by Devine entitled "Organized Charity and Industry." In this report, Devine stresses the theme that America was among "the first and foremost countries to realize that poverty is largely due to industrial maladjustment and that charity in and of itself is no cure and never can be for industrial evils" (17). Devine's personal ambivalence—and the ambivalence of the day—was reflected in another of his contributions to this collection, "Pauperism." Distinguishing pauperism from poverty as a condition consisting of "the habitual receipt of official public relief" (4), he views pauperism as poverty plus an attitude in which discouragement, lack of ambition, profligacy, irresponsibility, and a parasitic relationship to society are all intermingled (an early twentieth-century version of the underclass and in stark contrast with his earlier essay). Devine, like some others at that time, vacillated between a concept of poverty as resulting from external factors and a concept of poverty as resulting from psychological problems of the individual (in current terms, "blaming the victim"). *Studies in Social Work* also included a report on industrial conditions, another on wages and wage earners, a report about death rates, and a discussion of "the war on tuberculosis."

By 1917, according to Meier (1954:55), it was clear that there were two large divisions in social work: "working with individuals and families and working toward social betterment through mass programs of legislation and social action." As she and others argue, however, the impact of Flexner was such that the School, like the profession, focused subsequently largely on the "method" of working with individuals and families (and later, groups). Social policy was not yet viewed as a social work practice method, not even when linked with social reform or social action. Individual faculty members like John Fitch might remain convinced that "social work must remain focused upon the economic conditions under which men lived for in economic well-being, individual felicity and community improvement [are] rooted" (Meier 1954:70). But this is not where most faculty or students were grounded.

Meier's (1954) account suggests that the Great Depression did not have a significant impact on the School. The School's resources were constrained, and by deliberate policy in the early 1930s, fewer applicants were accepted, though more applied. Even though the numbers increased later, the ratio of rejections to acceptances rose. A "quota" was placed on New York City admissions, limiting them to no more than one-third of the student body. Despite the growth in public welfare, more graduates were employed in voluntary agencies in the middle of the decade than in 1930. A course was added (an elective) on Emergency Relief, and material on social security was incorporated into existing courses, but no special course was taught. A second Pittsburgh Survey, directed by faculty member Philip Klein, was carried out between 1934 and 1936, but in contrast to the earlier study, this was more of a community/social services needs assessment rather than a study leading toward recommendations for major social and economic reform. In general, there was only a limited "institutional" response to the Depression by the School.

A review of the School bulletins suggests a more responsive picture; there were significant additions to the curriculum, albeit still no change in what students were "required" to take. Among the courses listed in the bulletins for the years 1930–1933 are a course on public welfare, two courses on labor problems, and one on immigrants. Clarence King, a leading community organizer, taught the public welfare course throughout the 1930s. Fitch taught the courses on labor problems. Jane Hoey, who later directed the first federal public assistance agency in 1936, taught a course on public welfare. Philip Klein, a leading social researcher who became a long-time faculty member and who was director of research for the 1930 White House Conference on Children, taught research methods and a course on delinquency. Dorothy Hutchinson, a child welfare expert, also was a member of the faculty during these years.

In 1933, the School added two courses on unemployment relief administration (taught by another leading community organizer on the faculty and later dean, Walter Pettit), a third on unemployment remedies, and a course on social legislation covering "protective or welfare legislation considered from the standpoint of social policy," which was open to second-year students (*Bulletin* 1933–34). About 20 percent of the course offerings were social policy–related courses. In addition, the *Bulletin* lists fieldwork placements in "public welfare" for the first time.

In 1937, the above course offerings were supplemented by a course on Public Relief Administration and a second on Public Assistance and Child

Welfare Aspects of the Social Security Program, taught by Walter Pettit; a course on Government and Social Work; and another on Economic Insecurity and the State. In the 1938–39 *Bulletin,* King is listed for the first time as "Professor of Community Organization and Public Welfare," and a new faculty member, Robert Lansdale, who had prior experience in the field, is newly listed as "Professor of Public Welfare." While at the School, Lansdale also headed the Community Service Society's (CSS) Institute for Welfare Research.[2] After leaving the School in 1943, he became the New York State commissioner of welfare. The 1935 dean's report contains the first mention of faculty going on leave to train relief workers for federal, state, and local public welfare agencies.

As late as 1938, requirements for the two-year diploma included

- two courses in casework
- four courses in community organization
- two courses in mental hygiene
- three courses in social research
- two courses in a final social work integrating seminar
- fieldwork

Despite the several electives, no course on public welfare was required. Not until 1941 was the curriculum changed to require that newly entering students take such a course, and all students were so required by 1944. This change was made largely in response to alumni/ae pressures. An alumni/ae panel at the 1939 Annual Alumni Conference expressed concerns regarding the lack of attention to the growing role of government in social welfare and the inadequacy of the School's offerings in public welfare. The School's 1941–42 *Bulletin* reveals its response. Of the fifty-seven courses listed, ten could be viewed as related to social policy. These included Industrial Relations, Labor Problems, Social Legislation, Public Welfare (three courses), Government and Social Work, and Economic Insecurity and the State. And a minimum of one course in public welfare was now to be required of all students in the two-year program. The American Association of Schools of Social Work, the precursor of CSWE, adopted a curriculum of eight basic areas of study for professional social work practice. The eight areas that were recommended included casework, group work, community organization, administration, research, medical information, psychiatry—and, for the first time, public welfare.

The experience of World War II clearly affected the School.[3] More students were admitted, and the bulletins explicitly noted the need for courses and fieldwork to include material relevant to the war. Both during and after the war, several faculty members became actively involved in international relief operations, in various international social welfare activities, and in the development of new schools of social work in other countries.

In some sense, 1948 constituted not only the fiftieth anniversary of the School but also a turning point with regard to its commitment to social policy. In 1947–48 the first course on Social Security was listed in the *Bulletin,* as were the first courses on The Negro in American Society and on international social welfare—Inter-Country Family Services. Plans began for a doctoral program, and two new faculty members arrived at the School (Eveline Burns and Alfred J. Kahn), both of whom were to have significant impacts on social policy at the School and in the field in general.

Meier (1954) ends her history of the School at this point, having paid little attention to social policy—a reflection, perhaps, of attitudes at the School at that time. Social policy appears to have been central to the School only in its first two decades, during a period of intense and extensive social reform, when the leadership was deeply invested in social reform as well as direct practice. Social policy was certainly integral to what students had to deal with in the 1930s, but it was not central to the curriculum. In the 1950s, Meier notes, social workers were again being urged to become "formulators of social policy"; but she also stresses that social policy must be seen as inseparable from the needs of individuals, groups, and communities. She argues that social work should not be criticized for being too preoccupied with the psychological needs of individuals and that social policy should facilitate the development of services for individuals having problems of social adjustment.

YESTERDAY: FROM THE END
OF WORLD WAR II TO THE 1960s

Renewed interest in social policy emerged at the School with the appointment of Eveline Burns to the faculty in 1946, as Professor of Social Security.[4] An economist trained at the London School of Economics, Burns had been appointed to the economics department of the Graduate Faculties at Columbia in 1928.[5] She was a consultant to the Committee on Economic Security—the committee that developed the Social Security legislation—from 1934 to

1935. Subsequently, she left Columbia, first to become a senior staff member of the Committee on Economic Security in 1936, and then to become a member of the Social Security Board when it was first established in 1936, where she served until 1939, when she left to become director of research at the National Resources Planning Board, remaining there until 1945, when the war ended. Once at the School, Burns rapidly embarked on a campaign to raise the consciousness of the profession regarding social policy and to increase curriculum space and attention to policy at the School. At the fiftieth anniversary of the School and the hundredth anniversary of the Community Service Society, Burns's (1949b) paper, entitled "Economic Factors in Social Life," stressed the need for more attention to economic and social measures to aid the family in caring for its aged members or sharing the economic costs of children with their parents.

Burns set the stage for the School to become a leader in the training and education of policy scholars and practitioners. In 1947–48, in addition to teaching the first course on U.S. and comparative Social Security at the School, she taught three courses in the new "advanced curriculum": Foreign Social Security Systems, Advanced Seminar on Social Security Problems, and International Social Welfare Organizations and Administration (heralding the School's growing awareness of the importance of international social welfare at that time). Later, this last course was replaced by a course on Financing of Social Welfare, which she taught for many years. By 1949, at the onset of the doctoral program, "Social Security" (by which was meant social policy in current terms) was an explicit option for students to specialize in.

In an essay written in honor of Burns, Vera Shlakman (1969), an economist who was brought on to the faculty when Burns retired, highlighted major themes in Burns's work: the need for a society to define a floor or minimum standard of living below which individuals and families would not be permitted to fall (Burns 1949a and 1956), a rejection of policies that stigmatized beneficiaries and a preference for universal eligibility criteria (Burns 1949a and 1956), a high priority on meeting the needs of children (Burns 1965), accountability, and (a lesser priority) protection of the social and economic position of women.

When the doctoral program was established at the School in 1950, Eveline Burns became its first chair, and remained as chair until 1967, when she retired. She was listed in the *Bulletin* as "Professor of Social Security" from the time of her appointment until 1964–65, when she was listed for the first time as "Professor of Social Security and Social Policy" and then as "Professor of Social Policy" the following year. The doctoral program provided the platform for the School to assume a leadership role in training social policy scholars and analysts, and several of her students became leading social policy scholars, including Samuel Mencher, Robert Morris, and Winifred Bell. A few comments about these scholars here and elsewhere in this paper suggest the scope of Burns's influence.

Mencher had a master's degree in sociology from Columbia and received the M.S. in social work from the School in 1947. After a brief stint as a child welfare practitioner and an instructor in sociology at Bowdoin College, he returned to Columbia to work on a doctorate under the tutelage of Eveline Burns. While working on his doctorate, he received a Fulbright fellowship at the London School of Economics, thus working under both Burns and Richard Titmuss. His dissertation was on public/voluntary relationships in the child welfare field. He received his D.S.W. in 1957 and soon after left the faculty of the School of Social Work at New York University to join the faculty of social work at Pittsburgh. He was a popular teacher and taught a full teaching load despite extensive research and writing. His splendid history of social policy in Britain and the United States (1967) was published shortly after his untimely death at the age of forty-nine. Burns wrote the foreword to the book and clearly viewed Mencher as both a student of whom she was proud and a colleague and friend. He carried her message forward and was a productive and influential social policy scholar whose potential was limited only by his early demise.

Robert Morris (D.S.W. 1959) was another of Burns's students who became a leading social policy scholar. Morris has written extensively about U.S. and British social policy, as well as developing a concept of "personal care" as the organizing principle around which social work social policy could be organized. He was on the editorial board of the first *Encyclopedia of Social Work* (Lurie 1965) and the editor of the second (Morris, 1971).[6] Morris has had a long career at the Heller School at Brandeis University.

Shlakman (1969:9), commenting on the task of the social policy practitioner, notes the following:

> In the Burns tradition, the first task of the social policy analyst is to define the problem in its socio-economic context. He must go on to invent and assess alternative means of intervention, formulate questions for research, and scrutinize programs as they evolve.

She continues:

> What Burns was talking about was more than recognizing and securing
> a place for social policy in the curriculum, more than placing practice
> in a social policy context, more than emphasizing the significance of
> social policy solutions for practice problems. These are all highly de-
> sirable objectives and social work education is undoubtedly closer to
> them because of her work. Her central concern, however, had been
> with the need to produce social policy experts and analysts who are
> recognized as professional social work practitioners. The curriculum
> for such specialists, in addition to some elements that would be shared
> with the clinical curriculums, would include study of economics, gov-
> ernment, policy research, administration, and probably some field
> work experiences. (20)

Burns challenged the profession as well as the School. At the 1949 National Conference of Social Work, she criticized the School for its lack of
attention to social policy content and the profession for not accepting its responsibilities. She argued that social workers have been remiss in not learning from the social policies of other countries, especially about child and family allowances, national health insurance, and the other components of a
social protection system that were missing in the United States. Social workers were not grappling with the problems facing the country and with the policy issues that should be addressed, Burns asserted. Social workers should
be working at convincing Americans that social welfare is worth paying for
and should help set the priorities with regard to how public monies should
be distributed and how social expenditures should be allocated.

At a 1961 CSWE Annual Program Meeting, Burns delivered a paper entitled "Social Policy: The Stepchild of the Curriculum," in which she argued
for more attention and space in the curriculum for social policy. Nonetheless,
despite her conviction of its importance, she was not convinced that social
work schools could train social policy analysts. The major obstacle, for her,
was social work's "excessive preoccupation with training for the provision
of individualized services which followed from the profession's treatment-
oriented, clinical model" (Shlakman 1969:17).

Burns left her mark on the field, on the School, and on social work education more broadly through her students. One of her major contributions,
apart from her work on social security, was the development of a model for

social policy analysis that was widely used subsequently (Kahn 1969; Congress of the United States 1972; Gilbert and Specht 1974, 1986). She was both a social policy scholar whose primary focus was on social security in the broadest sense, and a social policy educator, interested not only in conveying the substance of social policies but also in training policy analysts. She was eminently successful in the former, less so in the latter, but she did set the stage for social policy scholars in social work who taught, subsequently, what Austin (1986) referred to as the "technical-analytic and research processes of policy analysis" and "policy advocacy" skills as a social work practice method. Austin did not see this content in social work schools around the country in the mid-1980s when he was writing; but it was being incorporated into doctoral education at CUSSW well before that time, and more recently in master's degree education as well.

Burns's major accomplishment at the School was the establishment of the doctoral program in 1950; its first degree was awarded to Alfred J. Kahn in 1952. It was in the curriculum of that program, which she chaired, shaped, and partly taught, that social policy content and practice finally assumed its rightful place at the School, as a social work method co-equal with clinical practice. And it is here that the School produced the social work deans, faculty members, and leading social policy scholars.

YESTERDAY: 1960 TO THE END OF THE 1980s

The 1960s was a decade of major social change and social reform, the third such decade in this century. It was reflected in a variety of social policy, research, and curriculum developments at the School and constitutes a kind of watershed with regard to social policy. The School played an important role in the social reform and social action arena, but was less visible in the social policy formation arena. This difference may say something about the profession as well as the School.

The project on Public Services for Families and Children was organized in November 1960 to focus attention on a particular area of public social policy: government services for children and their families, public assistance, child welfare, juvenile delinquency, and the interrelationship of the three. Elizabeth Wickendon was the project director; Winifred Bell, a doctoral student, was the primary staff member, and Eveline Burns and Alfred Kahn were the main consultants. The incident that led to the development of the project was the Louisiana law that resulted in the dropping of those families on assistance who had children born out of wedlock while receiving assistance. By definition, the homes of such families could not meet the law's definition of a "suitable home." At one fell swoop, children were denied aid because they were deserted by a parent and then, as a consequence, they were denied protection by the state. An earlier development that also raised serious concern was the decision in Newburgh, New York, to require that those receiving assistance carry out work for the community.

The report (Wickendon and Bell 1961) highlighted the problems of Aid to Dependent Children (ADC) and child welfare, and proposed a series of reforms. It played an important role in the subsequent enactment of a Health, Education, and Welfare (HEW) policy and two important amendments to the Social Security Act. The HEW regulation, issued in 1961 in response to the Louisiana case, stated that no home could be found "unsuitable" and children nonetheless left in it. If the home was unsuitable, the children would have to be removed. The relevant Social Security amendments were (1) the 1961 amendment stating that the federal government would pay for foster care for a child in an ADC-eligible family who was viewed by the court as endangered and needing placement outside of his or her family—thus assuring states that ADC status could be a channel to subsidized foster care; and (2) the 1962 amendment stating that the federal government would be responsible for reimbursing state governments for $.75 of every dollar spent for child and family social services for children receiving ADC. Bell, another of Burns's students, carried out her doctoral research on ADC. Her dissertation was published by Columbia University Press in 1965, as *Aid to Dependent Children,* and was the definitive work on ADC for some years to come.

Paralleling the growing interest in social policy was the explosion of interest in social action and advocacy. Mobilization for Youth (MFY) was the prototypical program, designed to combat delinquency through intervention involving an entire community (a significant part of New York City's Lower East Side). The source of many subsequent community-based programs of the War on Poverty, MFY's program was based on an opportunity theory of delinquency developed by Richard Cloward and Lloyd Ohlin (1961), both faculty members at the School. According to this theory, delinquency represented "not a lack of motivation to conform but quite the opposite; the desire to meet social expectations itself becomes the source of delinquent behavior if the possibility of doing so is limited or nonexistent" (Brager and Purcell

1967:18). Cloward and his colleague Frances Fox Piven, who was also a faculty member in the 1960s, have continued their influential role in social action up to the present, through their scholarship and professional practice.

Other faculty members also played active roles in social reform initiatives. For example, Mitchell Ginsberg, a faculty member, associate dean, and later CUSSW dean, was involved in the training of VISTA and Peace Corps workers at the School. In 1966, he left the School to become welfare commissioner of New York City, and then, after returning to the School as dean, became an active figure in several welfare reform efforts.

Despite the importance and influence of MFY as a social action initiative, neither the School nor the faculty was actively involved in the creation of the federal War on Poverty initiatives. Economists took the lead in the equal opportunity legislation. Child development psychologists were at the forefront of the Head Start developments. Relevant courses on poverty or the new federal initiatives were not added to the curriculum until the early 1970s.

Later in the 1960s, however, social workers were involved in the community action movement, in the movement to separate the delivery of social services from cash assistance, in the efforts taken to expand federal funding for social services and extend the criteria for receipt of social services, and in the efforts to expand and integrate these services. This concentration on social services was to have more significant implications for the School in later years.

Fred Delliquadri stated in his final dean's report (1965–67) that the curriculum needed more attention to social policy and social action, especially methods courses. He stressed the need to train social workers for social policy positions, and a curriculum review carried out in those years resulted in adding a third required course in social policy in addition to the required history course.

Alfred J. Kahn succeeded Burns as doctoral chair when she retired in 1967. He joined the faculty as a research instructor in 1947 and received the first doctorate from the School in 1952. His dissertation, "The Children's Court," was sponsored by Philip Klein and was published as a book by Columbia University Press in 1953. In a sense, Kahn responded to the Delliquadri call. His influence was apparent when the doctoral specialization in social security was renamed Social Policy, Planning, and Administration in 1963–64, reflecting his special interest in social planning.[7] Kahn was to chair the program for ten of the next twenty years, and for all twenty of those years, he taught three of the required courses taken by students specializing in social

policy and planning. He taught History and Philosophy of Social Welfare, required of all doctoral students, as well as the courses on social planning and
social policy analysis required of all policy students. He also taught a field
of practice course on what was later called Personal Social Services. Doctoral
students who were interested in social policy came to the School to study
with Kahn. His students became faculty members throughout the country,
carrying his message widely.

Like Burns, Kahn made his mark in social policy at the School through his
impact on the doctoral program, his teaching, his policy "practice" (in particular, his long-term role as a consultant to the Citizen's Committee for the
Children of New York), his links with governmental and nongovernmental
agencies, and his scholarship. A popular teacher and effective lecturer, Kahn
made an impact on both master's degree and doctoral students. An anecdote
that has been reported dozens of times over the years illustrates his command
of content and his authority as a teacher. Lecturing to the 125 master's degree
students in the required social policy course when the power failed throughout the city, Kahn continued to lecture for another hour in a room without
any lights, completing the class as scheduled, without any student leaving the
room. His doctoral students later became faculty members, directors of doctoral programs, and deans at metropolitan area schools as well as schools
around the world, including Rose Dobrof, Francis Akukwe, Norman Wyers,
Ron Dear, Joel Blau, Gary Cameron, Anne Westhuis, Agnes Ng, Ralph Dolgoff, and myself.

In his own work, Kahn developed the concept of social planning, writing
the first textbook on that topic. He also developed the concept of "social util-
ities" to describe those social services—such as childcare, information and
referral, and senior centers—that should be available to all, not just to the
poor or those with severe problems. He identified the individualized, helping
services as central to social work practice and a special social work domain,
employing the British concept of the "personal social services" to describe
this central social work domain. His monograph *Social Policy and Social Services* (1972/1979) underscored the centrality of social service policies and
programs to social work education and practice.

Bridging yesterday and today, Kahn has continued to have a major impact
on the field through the Cross-National Studies Research program, which he
established in 1973 with the support of HEW and several foundations. Sheila
B. Kamerman, his former doctoral student and colleague, joined initially as

staff and associate director, and then as co-director from 1975. Together, they developed an internationally known research program for which both received numerous awards, including an honorary doctorate from the University of York in England, awarded in 1998. Jointly, they carried out studies of social service delivery in the United States and internationally, of income transfer policies, and comparative welfare state developments. These studies were supplemented by U.S. and comparative research, which Kamerman took primary responsibility for initiating, and focused on social policies affecting children, women, and families such as childcare services, maternity and parental leaves, child allowances, and child support.

Kamerman, who chaired the doctoral program for eight years and played a major role in transforming the School's doctoral degree from the D.S.W. to the Ph.D., introduced a doctoral seminar in social policy to the program and a field of practice course (or tutorial) on U.S. and comparative child and family policy. She also developed an elective course on women and social policy. Later, she helped design and launch the policy practice method concentration for master's degree students at the School.

TODAY: THE 1990s AND BEYOND

The School is well positioned today to play a leadership role in training social policy practitioners and scholars. With five full-time faculty members teaching social policy, all of whom have active policy practice roles and research programs, the School seems ready for the first time since World War I to teach policy not as social work's "step-child" but as an equal (or perhaps junior sibling). Clinical practice still dominates the curriculum, the faculty, and the student body, but the policy practice students are increasing in number. With the expansion of public policy schools since the early 1970s, such a development has been essential if social work is not to relinquish its role in social policy developments other than that of advocate.

The School now offers its master's degree students a method concentration in social policy practice and the option of a dual degree with the School of International and Public Affairs (SIPA) leading to a master's in public affairs (M.P.A.) as well as an M.S. in social work. Appropriate fieldwork placements are available to those students. The doctoral program continues to reflect a strong commitment to social policy. Irwin Garfinkel joined the faculty in 1990, when Kahn retired from his faculty position, to teach social policy analysis and to train policy researchers. He brings expertise in child poverty and, in particular, in child support policy, where his research has constituted the definitive work in the field. Younger faculty members (Marcia Meyers and Jane Waldfogel) are also active and important contributors to social policy developments, both in the School and outside, through their teaching and their research.

The University has recognized the School's role in social policy as well, with the School represented by Professors Garfinkel and Kamerman on the Steering Committee of the University's Public Policy Consortium.[8] The establishment by the University of the University-wide Child and Family Policy Institute, with Kamerman as its first director, is another illustration.[9]

The School is well positioned to assume a leadership role in training social policy practitioners as well as social policy scholars. However, it has yet to provide adequate curriculum space for social policy courses or content in the master's degree program. There is no required course on the history of American social policy. Such a course was in the curriculum from the early years until the mid 1970s, exists in most other graduate social work schools, and is still taught at the doctoral level by Kahn. The required fields of practice foundation courses, established initially as policy and program focused, only occasionally have systematic policy content, and even less often are taught by policy faculty. Except for the students concentrating in social policy practice, students are required to take only one course in social policy and obtain their master's degree, with little in the way of policy knowledge.

CONCLUSION

The term *social policy* appeared in the curriculum as early as 1916, when a course on social policy was first given at the School, and again briefly in the early 1930s. Social policy content played a significant role in the first two decades of the School, but then not until the doctoral program was established, with its strong commitment to training policy scholars along with scholars of practice theory. The 1960s constituted the second wave of interest in social policy, largely in the form of social action. In the 1970s, when the skills of policy analysis began to be taught at the new public policy schools, the doctoral program refined its training accordingly. From the late 1960s on, when funding for social services expanded dramatically, social services policy became a more important focus at the School. Under the leadership of faculty scholars, the School became a leader in child and family policy from the 1970s to the present, especially comparative social policies directed at children and their families. Only with the establishment of a special method concentration in 1995 did the M.S. curriculum reflect a commitment to social policy as a social work practice method. Individual faculty members played influential roles in social policy, often even when the School's response lagged.

The School and the profession are at a critical point now with regard to social policy. This is a period of major social policy churning, when there are many opportunities for new actors to emerge. The faculty is strong and there is renewed interest in policy. But social work is competing for recognition with public policy schools, too. To sustain its institutional role, there must be commitment both to curriculum space and to student training and education at both the master's and doctoral program levels; and to sustain its influence, there must be commitment by the School to the policy research and scholarship of its faculty.

NOTES

1. Reference to "social policy practice" can be found in the early years of the School's development, but "policy analysis" as a method grew out of the Ford Foundation's initiative in establishing seven special schools of public policy analysis in the early 1970s.

2. CSS was the result of a merger between the COS and the Association for Improving the Conditions of the Poor.

3. In 1940, the School became formally affiliated with Columbia University, with a Master of Science (M.S.) degree granted after six quarters.

4. That same year, Clarence King was listed as Professor of Community Organization and Administration and relinquished his primary responsibility at the School for the teaching of public welfare.

5. It appears from several School bulletins that Burns held this appointment from 1928 to 1942, and was on leave while at the Social Security Board.

6. Also on that Board were two other CUSSW alumni, Bess Dana and Martin Rein (M.S. 1956).

7. In 1986, Administration was dropped as a required course for doctoral policy students, just as Community Organization had been earlier.

8. The Public Policy Consortium is a University-wide, third-year program for doctoral students interested in working on public policy – related dissertations. Students chosen for the program are awarded a fellowship, take a special advanced policy seminar, and have opportunities to work with faculty throughout the University.

9. Professors J. Lawrence Aber of the Mailman School of Public Health and Jeanne Brooks-Gunn of Teachers College are co-directors, with Kamerman as the first executive director.

REFERENCES

Austin, David M. *A History of Social Work Education.* Austin: University of Texas School of Social Work, 1986.

Bell, Winifred. *Aid to Dependent Children.* New York: Columbia University Press, 1965.

Bernstein, Saul, et al. *The New York School of Social Work: 1898–1941.* New York: Community Service Society, 1942.

Brager, George A. and Francis Purcell, eds. *Community Action Against Poverty.* New Haven, Conn.: College and University Press, 1967.

Burns, Eveline. *The American Social Security System.* Boston: Houghton Mifflin, 1949a.

——*Economic Factors in Social Life.* Paper presented at the Conference on the Family in a Democratic Society, New York School of Social Work. New York: Community Service Society, 1949b.

——*Social Security and Public Policy.* New York: McGraw-Hill, 1956.

—— ed. *Children's Allowances and the Economic Welfare of Children.* New York: Citizens Committee for Children, 1965.

Cloward, Richard and Lloyd Ohlin. *Delinquency and Opportunity.* Glencoe, Ill: Free Press, 1961.

Congress of the United States, Joint Economic Committee (the "Griffith Committee"), *Studies in Public Welfare.* Washington, D.C.: Government Printing Office, 1972.

Gilbert, N. and Specht, H. *Dimensions of Social Welfare Policy.* Needham Heights, Mass: Allyn and Bacon, 1974, 1986.

Kahn, Alfred J. *Theory and Practice of Social Planning.* New York: Russell Sage Foundation, 1969.

——*Social Policy and Social Services.* New York: Random House, 1972. (Reprinted in 1979.)

Leiby, James. *A History of Social Welfare and Social Work in the United States.* New York: Columbia University Press, 1978.

Meier, Elizabeth G. *A History of the New York School of Social Work.* New York: Columbia University Press, 1954.

Mencher, S. *Poor Law to Poverty Program: Economic Security Policy in Britain and the United States.* Pittsburgh: University of Pittsburgh Press, 1967.

New York School of Philanthropy. *Studies in Social Work.* 11 vols. New York: New York School of Philanthropy, 1915.

Rubinow, I. M. *Social Insurance: With Special Reference to American Conditions.* New York: Henry Holt, 1913.

Shlakman, Vera. "Eveline Burns: Social Economist." In Shirley Jenkins, ed., *Social Security in International Perspective: Essays in Honor of Eveline Burns.* New York: Columbia University Press, 1969.

Warner, Amos. *American Charities.* New York: Thomas Crowell, 1894.

Wickendon, Elizabeth and Winifred Bell. *Public Welfare: Time for a Change.* New York: New York School of Social Work, 1961.

Zimbalist, E. Sidney, ed. *Historic Themes and Landmarks in Social Welfare Research.* New York: Harper and Row, 1977.

Chapter 7

SOCIAL RESEARCH

Steven Schinke and Tony Tripodi

Columbia University School of Social Work (CUSSW) enjoys a long history of teaching and engaging in social research. Since its founding, CUSSW has trained leading scholars and practitioners of social research and has witnessed original and influential research studies conducted by its faculty and graduates. Continuing its tradition of social research excellence today, CUSSW is among the top schools of social work in the country in the breadth and depth of external sponsorship for its studies. In its hundredth year alone, CUSSW accounted for nearly $20 million in sponsored research projects — with much of that work funded by the National Institutes of Health and other United States Public Health Service agencies.

This paper offers an overview of the contribution of CUSSW to advancing the research agenda of not only social work and social welfare, but also of allied disciplines and of social policy at the national and international levels. In so doing, the paper highlights the value of a CUSSW education and of a faculty position at the School toward enhancing the social research productivity of those involved professionals. As important, the paper sets forth an agenda for future social research, based upon work undertaken over the years at CUSSW.

HISTORICAL CONTEXT

Columbians (faculty, students, and alumni/ae of the Columbia University School of Social Work) have been an integral part of the development of social work research during the past century. Prior to joining the faculty, Mary Richmond analyzed case records to understand the social conditions that impinged on individuals in a study of deserted wives that she reported in 1895 (Austin et al., 1991). Richmond further developed the case study method by calling for the comparative study of client records to identify factors related to social problems (Dunlap 1993), and she incorporated the scientific method in the formulation of social diagnoses (Reid 1994; Richmond 1917).

The survey movement in the United States was evident in the early 1900s; and this was incorporated into the training provided by the New York School of Philanthropy, which focused on the analysis of social conditions. The social survey was emphasized in the Social Research Bureau, established by the school in 1906 (Austin et al., 1991). Phil Klein (1938) was the principal investigator of an analysis of social and health agencies in Pittsburgh. The study was a forerunner of many community needs and resources studies that took place in the 1940s to 1960s. Martin Wolins (1954) described how one might conduct community studies, providing a guide for future community analysts. The development of the doctoral program in the late 1950s and early 1960s produced a number of research scholars who have made important research contributions over the past forty years.

Columbians have made significant contributions that have been nationally recognized. That this is so can be discerned by referring to two very influential publications in social work research: *Five Fields of Social Service Research* (Maas 1965) and *Building Social Work Knowledge for Effective Services and Policies: A Plan for Social Development* (Austin et al., 1991).

Maas's book has the purpose of presenting research reviews in five areas of social work, indicating what was learned and what research needs to be done. Of the five chapters in that book, three were by Columbians. Scott Briar wrote on family services; David Fanshel, child welfare; and William Schwartz on neighborhood centers. In Austin's report of the work of a task force on social work research sponsored by the National Institute of Mental Health (NIMH), eleven examples were cited of work that made significant contributions to services and policies in the United States. Of these examples three represented the work of Columbians:

> In the area of child welfare, the foster care studies over many years by David Fanshel, Columbia University School of Social Work, have contributed to changes in child welfare practice throughout the United States. (Austin et al., 1991:5)

> In the area of income supports, research on child support payments carried out by Irwin Garfinkel [now with Columbia University School

of Social Work; formerly] at the School of Social Work, University of Wisconsin at Madison, has led to public policy changes at both state and federal levels, resulting in increased income for thousands of single parent households. (Austin et al., 1991:5)

In the area of psychosocial counseling, the development and testing for task-centered casework by William Reid, who received his D.S.W. from Columbia University School of Social Work and who taught at the School of Social Service Administration, University of Chicago, and the School of Social Welfare, State University of New York at Albany, have resulted in major changes in the practice of social casework over the past twenty years. (Austin et al., 1991:5-6)

Columbians have made enormous contributions in all aspects of social work research. Although it is impossible to specify all of the work conducted by Columbians, we can illustrate highlights of some important activities. For purposes of this paper, we will limit discussion to two major areas that impinge on social work research: professionalization and education, and the development of substantive and methodological knowledge.

PROFESSIONALIZATION AND EDUCATION

This area includes organizations that affect the development of a research infrastructure by means of professional groups and research centers, the production of research journals that are specific to the profession of social work, and those activities and publications that influence the teaching of research methods to social work students.

National Research Groups and Research Centers

Columbia in its early history established a social research bureau to conduct surveys of needs and social conditions. Moreover, it was among the first schools of social work to establish research centers in the 1950s (Austin et al., 1991). The research center hosted a number of important studies, including "Mobilization for Youth," by Richard Cloward and Lloyd Ohlin; "Clinical Judgment," by James Bieri; and other studies by Herman Stein, Irving Lukoff, Martin Whiteman, Sam Finestone, and others. Research centers have been a locus of research activities within schools of social work, serving as structures for communication among researchers and as sources of support for doctoral students.

The NIMH Task Force on Social Work Research (Austin et al., 1991) has been a chief stimulus for the development of NIMH-sponsored research centers, the creation of the Institute for the Advancement of Social Work Research, and the call for professional social work organizations to devote more time, energy, and resources to social work research. Three Columbians were on that task force: Dean Ronald Feldman (vice-chair), Scott Briar, and Tony Tripodi.

The first formal structure for social work research, the Social Work Research Group (SWRG), was developed in 1949 (Dunlap 1993). Alfred Kahn was among the early members of this group, which merged with the National Association of Social Workers (NASW) in 1956. Columbians David Fanshel and Herman Stein were also involved, and they contributed to the planning of a four-day institute on social science theory and social work research. SWRG, according to Al Kahn (personal communication), was disbanded due to its low priority within NASW at a time of budget restructuring.

Columbian Janet Williams founded another research group in 1994, the Society for Social Work and Research (SSWR). She was the first president. Tony Tripodi became the second president, and Columbians Mark Mattaini and Ellen Lukens have served on its board of directors. Dan Herman, a CUSSW doctoral graduate, edits the Society's newsletter. The membership of SSWR has grown to approximately six hundred to seven hundred social work researchers. Each year at its conference, SSWR hosts approximately three hundred papers and posters, all dealing with substantive or methodological results of social work research.

In 1986, in conjunction with the Jewish Board of Family and Children's Services, the School of Social Work established the Center for the Study of Social Work Practice. Its founding director was Shirley Jenkins. Currently, Edward J. Mullen serves as its director. Focusing entirely on practice-based research, the Center for the Study of Social Work Practice is the only endowed research center linked with both a leading school of social work and a leading social work agency. It sponsors a wide range of research projects and international conferences aimed at linking the activities of social work researchers and practitioners. In addition, it publishes a widely disseminated newsletter.

Research Journals

Social work researchers publish research results in a variety of journals, not just social work journals. This is because much of the research carried out by social workers is interdisciplinary and has implications for social, economic, and health problems and issues. Nevertheless, one indicator of growth is the publication of scientific journals within the profession. Currently, there are four journals devoted exclusively to social work research.

The first journal, *Social Work Research and Abstracts,* was established by the National Association of Social Workers in 1977. Its first two editors were Bill Reid and Tony Tripodi. The second journal, the *Journal of Social Service Research,* was also launched in 1977, and *Research on Social Work Practice* was initiated in 1991. Columbians sat on the editorial boards of both of these journals. And, the fourth journal, founded and co-edited by Tony Tripodi, published its first issue in the winter of 1999–2000: *The Journal of Social Work Research and Evaluation: An International Publication.* Four Columbians serve on its board.

The Teaching of Research Methods

The teaching of research methods to social work students is influenced by research textbooks, journal articles, and policies of the Council on Social Work Education and the Group for the Advancement of Doctoral Education. The first textbook on social work research was edited by Polansky (1960); it included seminal chapters on research methods. Al Kahn wrote about research design and Martin Wolins discussed ways to measure the effects of social work intervention.

Influenced by teachings of Sam Finestone, Irving Lukoff, Dave Fanshel, and Al Kahn, Tripodi, Fellin, and Meyer (1969) wrote the first book devoted to the critical analysis and utilization of social research in social work. Other Columbians were involved in writing textbooks on research methods, social program evaluation, and the incorporation of research methods in administration and direct practice (Blythe, Tripodi, and Briar 1994; Mullen, Dumpson, and Associates 1972; Epstein and Tripodi 1979; Grasso and Epstein 1992; Reid 1994; Tripodi and Epstein 1980).

Columbians have contributed significantly to the policies of the Council on Social Work Education. A history of research in social work education is provided by Dunlap (1993), who points to the increased interest in social work research and the trend toward empirical research in the last two decades (see also Tripodi 1984). Further, there was an important curriculum policy statement in 1982 which emphasized the integration of research and practice, as well as a major development in 1984 when the board of the Council on Social Work Education required social work undergraduate and M.S. programs to prepare students to evaluate their practice. Today, students evaluate their practice in the field, and they learn about methodologies of practice evaluation. These requirements for integrating research methods in practice were largely initiated by Scott Briar, who was the chair of the Accreditation Committee of the Council on Social Work Education.

Advances in doctoral education have contributed to the teaching of doctoral students, who comprise the bulk of social work researchers. As president of the Group for the Advancement of Doctoral Education, Columbian Sheila Kamerman helped to set an agenda for higher standards and greater rigor in doctoral dissertations and in research requirements. The Columbia School of Social Work has produced a large number of doctoral students who have been leaders in the development of social work research. For example, Bill Reid (1994) cites a group of Columbia doctoral graduates who helped develop and stimulate the empirical practice movement: Scott Briar, Irwin Epstein, Harvey Gochros, Henry Miller, Edward Mullen, Arthur Schwartz, Richard Stuart, Tony Tripodi, and, of course, Bill Reid. These are only a few of the names of Columbians who are teaching or have taught research methods in schools of social work throughout the United States. The research specialization spurred and developed by Shirley Jenkins and other Columbians has led to the development of many research specialists who conduct research and teach its methodology.

Social Research Training: M.S. Level

At CUSSW, social research is one of five social work practice concentrations offered students in the two-year master's degree program. Social research at the School is pursued in combination with another practice method. The emphasis is on advanced social work research technologies and methods, data analysis and statistics, application of research methods to social work problems and constituencies, and completion of a research study in the student's practicum agency. This concentration is open to students who are interested in learning the methods and practices of social work research and in pursuing careers in this area. The course work includes the expanded study of research technology and methods and their applications to the problems of social work. Required courses in the second year of study include statistics, advanced research methods, and courses in another practice method. Students conduct independent research projects at their field placement settings.

The second-year research project for social research majors is offered as an elective and fulfills the requirement of an advanced research course. In this year-long course, students conduct a practice-related research project, usually in their field placement. During the first semester, they formulate a research question, review relevant literature, and select appropriate methodologies for the project. The final product for the autumn semester is a research proposal. In the spring, students collect and analyze data using SPSS or SAS. Finally, they combine their findings with the literature review and methodology from the autumn proposal in a "journal article." Students present their projects in a "poster session" at the school.

Social Research Training: Ph.D. Level

The doctoral program at Columbia University School of Social Work enables students with professional degrees and experience to broaden their knowledge and develop increased competence in social welfare. The program prepares students for careers as researchers, teachers, policy analysts, and administrators. Most graduates seek positions in academia, or as researchers, clinical instructors, or senior administrators in government or nonprofit agencies.

Students may choose from one of three areas of concentration: advanced practice; social policy, planning, and policy analysis; or social policy, planning, and administration. They also select a field of practice specialization from among a wide range of available options and elect an area of social science. Intensive course work in research methods and statistics is required.

DEVELOPMENT OF SUBSTANTIVE
AND METHODOLOGICAL KNOWLEDGE

Substantive knowledge is that which is generated from the results of social work research, while methodological knowledge refers to the development and use of research methods for the generation of substantive knowledge. All of this knowledge cannot be easily specified; however, to show the contributions of Columbians, we illustrate some of the activities that are important nationally. These are social science and research, the empirical practice movement, and research in selected substantive areas.

Social Science and Social Work

In 1959 the Social Work Research Group sponsored a four-day institute on social science theory and social work research (Kogan 1960). There was much discussion about the use of social science theories in social work as well as the relationship of social science and social work research. What was not discussed in detail were the methodological contributions derived from various social sciences. Perhaps, as much as social science theory, research methodologies have been utilized by social work researchers: the survey, experimental methods, laboratory experiments, ethnographic studies, statistical developments, econometrics, demographic analyses, statistical sampling, social epidemiologic methods, and so forth. Doctoral students and faculty have been influenced by social scientists teaching in the School of Social Work as well as by social scientists teaching in their own disciplines at Columbia.

In the late 1950s and early 1960s many Columbians were stimulated by the theories of Robert Merton and the methodological innovations of Paul Lazarsfeld, Herbert Hyman, and others associated with the Bureau of Applied Social Research. Herbert Hyman, who wrote texts on survey design and analysis, secondary data analysis, and program evaluation, stimulated textbooks by Columbians on those same topics (Epstein and Tripodi 1979; Mullen, Dumpson, and Associates 1972). Sophia Robison studied juvenile delinquency, and she was concerned about measuring the results of delinquency prevention programs (Polansky 1960). Richard Cloward and Lloyd Ohlin (1960) pursued theoretical notions of anomie and alienation and devised typologies of delinquency, as well as running a large research project, Mobilization for Youth, which was a forerunner of antipoverty programs developed under Lyndon B. Johnson's presidency. They developed social action strategies with other colleagues such as Francis Fox Piven, and they trained doctoral students in sociology, including Irwin Epstein and others, to examine social work and its politicization. Howard Polsky (1962), using the sociological research methods of participant and nonparticipant observation, studied the structure and dynamics of delinquent boys in residential treatment.

James Bieri, a clinical psychologist, was also a social scientist teaching at the Columbia School of Social Work in the 1950s and 1960s. His NIMH-funded projects on clinical judgment supported doctoral dissertations by Harold Plotnick, Scott Briar, Henry Miller, Ben Avis Orcutt, and Tony Tripodi. A series of interrelated dissertations were published in a book on clinical and social judgment (Bieri et al. 1966) which was designated as a citation classic in the 1970s. Psychological notions of anchoring phenomena, information theory, signal detection theory, information processing, and personality structures were used in studying clinical and social judgment that social workers make.

Columbia faculty and students continue to be at the cutting edge in the use of social science concepts, as well as contributing to social science and theories from other disciplines. For example, Dean Ronald Feldman has contributed to child development and child psychiatry. Other faculty have engaged in extensive research in substance abuse and psychological interventions.

Empirical Practice Movement

Bill Reid (1994) distinguished three facets of the empirical practice movement:

> One is the use of research methods in practice to facilitate assessment, to guide intervention planning, and to evaluate results in work with individuals, families, and groups. The second is the application, whenever possible, of interventions of demonstrated effectiveness, that is, interventions whose efficacy has received research support. The third is knowledge building through disseminated studies carried out by practitioner-researchers. (165)

Columbians have been among the key persons involved in the empirical practice movement, which blossomed in the 1950s and 1960s and is manifest in contemporary social work. For purposes of discussion, we will look at the influence of Columbians in two interrelated parts of the empirical practice movement: practice theory research and agency-based research.

Practice Theory Research

Mary Richmond (1917), according to Bill Reid (1994), used the scientific method in that she advocated for the gathering of facts, the forming of hypotheses to understand them, and the testing of hypotheses by available evidence. Florence Hollis (1964) developed a psychosocial theory of social casework, and she was devoted to devising categories of treatment and testing for their reliability. Her students, discontented with the lack of knowledge about the effectiveness of social work interventions, developed their own theories about social work treatment.

Scott Briar and Henry Miller (1972) wrote about problems and issues in social casework, and called for a scientific approach to the study of practice. This was further clarified by Scott Briar (1979), who wrote about the need for clinical scientists in social work. Bill Reid (1992) developed his own theory of social work intervention, and he has tested task-centered casework and task-centered group work in social agencies throughout the world. Moreover, he has trained colleagues and students in his approach, both theoretically and methodologically. Richard Stuart was trained in Hollis's psychosocial theories, which were heavily influenced by psychoanalysis. He turned to the use of learning theories and behavioral therapy. He was joined at the University of Michigan by another Columbian, Tony Tripodi, who assisted him in conducting field experiments to evaluate the effectiveness of contracting with families and predelinquents in middle school settings. Stuart (Stuart, Jayaratne, and Tripodi 1976) was one of the first social workers to advocate for the use of single-subject designs, and the first book in social work on those procedures was written by his students (Jayaratne and Levy 1979).

Agency-Based Research

Sam Finestone (1963), in his discussion of the requirements for agency-based research, emphasized the social agency as a laboratory where research could be conducted. The purpose was to develop knowledge for the social researcher, irrespective of whether it would be useful in agency practice. Contrary to that notion, Scott Briar, Ed Mullen, and Bill Reid indicated that knowledge should be generated in social agencies for direct use. They subsequently directed their students in exploring such knowledge development.

Scott Briar and his colleagues wrote a research methods book illustrating how social work practitioners could carry out research themselves in social agencies (Blythe, Tripodi and Briar 1994). David Fanshel and his colleagues (Fanshel, Marsters, Finch, and Grundy 1992) specified ways in which modern technology could be employed to analyze data in social service information systems. Perhaps the best illustration of practitioner research is that

of BOMIS, the Boysville Management Information System, developed by
A. J. Grasso and Irwin Epstein (1992). Researchers worked with practitioners to develop information about practice and to generate and test hypotheses. Irwin Epstein continues his pursuit of incorporating research that can be
carried out and used by practitioners. He has identified facilitators and barriers related to agency-based research, and he is developing new strategies
and procedures in that regard.

Research in Selected Substantive Areas

Throughout CUSSW's history, as we have shown, Columbians have been at
the threshold of innovations in research. We close this paper by pointing to
some of the significant contributions made in other substantive research areas. David Fanshel has produced important follow-up studies on adoption
and foster care. His students, Eugene Shinn and Trudy Festinger, for example, have contributed in that tradition. Sheila Kamerman and Al Kahn
have engaged in national and cross-national studies on social policies, and
their results have been used by researchers and policy developers worldwide.
André Ivanoff has studied the effects of prisons and jails on inmates, and she
has increased our understanding about suicide. She has also incorporated
notions of empirical practice in writing about a research-based approach to
working with involuntary clients (Ivanoff, Blythe, and Tripodi 1994). Irving
Piliavin is studying income maintenance and welfare reform issues, and Irwin
Garfinkel is producing and analyzing social indicators about New York City.

FUTURE OF SOCIAL RESEARCH: A COLUMBIA PERSPECTIVE

What has gone on in the past is of unquestioned value for laying a solid foundation of social research, not only for Columbia, but also for the country and
the larger world we serve. Still, resting on laurels has never been a tradition
of CUSSW, and it certainly does not pertain to those in the forefront of social research at the School today. That research understandably focuses on
urban problems and on problems of poor and minority people. But work at
the School also has currency for setting the future research agenda nationally
and globally.

CUSSW has much to do in its second century. The problems and at-risk
populations that concern our profession have not abated in the last hundred
years. In the next hundred years, we can expect continued inequities as so-

ciety only grows more complex, high tech, and demanding. The field and CUSSW alumni and faculty can therefore take comfort that the School will stay its course of remaining ahead of trends as they consume social services resources. Doubtless, the future will witness new and aggressive programs of research undertaken by CUSSW faculty. At the M.S.W. and Ph.D. levels, our graduates must shape the agenda of services, policies, programs, and scientific inquiry as they move out into the world of practice, teaching, and research. And, CUSSW's constituencies that stay current with the School by reading the literature produced therefrom will be pleased to note that social research will remain the leading priority of the nation's premier and oldest school of social work.

REFERENCES

Austin, D., et al. (1991). *Building social knowledge for effective services and policies: A plan for research development.* Austin, TX: Task Force on Social Work Research.

Bieri, J., Atkins, A. L., Briar, B., Leaman, R. L., Miller, H., and Tripodi, T. (1966). *Clinical and social judgment: The discrimination of behavioral information.* New York: Wiley.

Blythe, B., Tripodi, T., and Briar, S. (1994). *Direct practice research in human service agencies.* New York: Columbia University Press.

Briar, S. (1979). Incorporating research into education for clinical practice in social work: Toward a clinical science in social work. In A. Rubin and A. Rosenblatt (Eds.), *Sourcebook on research utilization,* 132–140. New York: Council on Social Work Education.

Briar, S. and Miller, H. (1972). *Problems and issues in social casework.* New York: Columbia University Press.

Cloward, R. A. and Ohlin, L. E. (1960). *Delinquency and opportunity: A theory of delinquent gangs.* Glencoe, IL: Free Press.

Dunlap, K. M. (1993). A history of research in social work education: 1915–1991. *Journal of Social Work Education, 29,* 293–301.

Epstein, I. and Tripodi, T. (1979). Incorporating research into macro social work practice and education. In A. Rubin and A. Rosenblatt (Eds.), *Sourcebook on research utilization,* 121–131. New York: Council on Social Work Education.

Fanshel, D., Marsters, P. A., Finch, S. J., and Grundy, J. F. (1992). Strategies for the analysis of data bases in social service systems. In A. J. Grasso and I. Epstein (Eds.), *Research utilization in the social services.* Binghamton, NY: Haworth.

Finestone, S. (1963). Some requirements for agency based research. *Social Casework, 44,* 132–136.

Grasso, A. J. and Epstein, I. (1992). *Research utilization in the social services.* Binghamton, NY: Haworth.

Hollis, F. (1964). *Casework: A psychosocial therapy.* New York: Random House.

Ivanoff, A., Blythe, B. J., and Tripodi, T. (1994). *Involuntary clients in social work practice: A research-based approach.* New York: Aldine De Gruyter.

Jayaratne, S. and Levy, R. (1979). *Empirical clinical practice.* New York: Columbia University Press.

Klein, P., et al. (1938). *A social study of Pittsburgh community problems and social services in Allegheny County.* New York: Columbia University Press.

Kogan, L. S. (Ed.). (1960). *Social science theory and social work research.* New York: National Association of Social Workers.

Maas, H. S. (1965). *Five fields of social service research.* New York: National Association of Social Workers.

Mullen, E. J., Dumpson, J. R., and Associates. (Eds.). (1972). *Evaluation of social intervention.* San Francisco: Jossey Bass.

Polansky, N. A. (Ed.). (1960). *Social work research.* Chicago: University of Chicago Press.

Polsky, H. W. (1962). *Cottage six: The social system of delinquent boys in residential treatment.* New York: Russell Sage Foundation.

Reid, W. J. (1992). *Task strategies: An empirical approach to social work practice.* New York: Columbia University Press.

——(1994). The empirical practice movement. *Social Service Review, 68,* 165–184.

Richmond, M. (1917). *Social diagnosis.* New York: Russell Sage Foundation.

Stuart, R. B., Jayaratne, S., and Tripodi, T. (1976). Changing adolescent deviant behavior through reprogramming the behavior of parents and teachers: An experimental evaluation. *Canadian Journal of Behavioral Science, 8,* 132–144.

Tripodi, T. (1984). Trends by research publication: A study of social work journals from 1956 to 1989. *Social Work, 29,* 353–359.

Tripodi, T. and Epstein, I. (1980). *Research techniques for clinical social workers.* New York: Columbia University Press.

Tripodi, T., Fellin, P., and Meyer, H. J. (1969). *The assessment of social research: Guidelines for use of research in social work and social science.* Itasca, IL: Peacock.

Wolins, M. (1954). A base for community welfare studies. *The social welfare forum,* 316–233. New York: Columbia University Press.

Part Three

FIELDS OF PRACTICE

I N ADDITION TO enrolling for one of five different *methods* of social work practice, each M.S. student at the Columbia University School of Social Work (CUSSW) also enrolls in one of seven special *fields of practice*. This specialized feature of the educational program provides students with an intensive learning experience in a particular problem area or with a particular population at risk. The field instruction placements in each field of practice are cross-listed with the other fields of practice, allowing students flexibility in choosing courses and field instruction sites. Respectively, these seven fields of practice are Family and Children's Services; Health, Mental Health, and Disabilities; Aging; World of Work; International Social Welfare and Services to Immigrants and Refugees; School-Based and School-Linked Services; and Contemporary Social Problems.

In the second year of the M.S. program, each student enrolls in a field of practice "platform" course in which she or he learns to apply an analytic framework that includes the following components: the target or focal point (a population group, problem, or setting); historical responses; relevant legislation, policies, and funding; program models, delivery systems, and administrative auspices; models of practice interventions and staffing patterns; research, evaluation, and outcomes; and issues, trends, and current debates. The student applies her or his chosen practice method in the context of the special field of practice examined in the platform course.

The Family and Children's Services field of practice specifically addresses the needs of families and children. The required platform course in this field focuses on changing family composition, special needs related to ethnicity, the legislative and regulatory framework for service delivery, and implications for research and family policy. Students are introduced to the agencies primarily concerned with the social problems of this population: family services (e.g., family counseling, advocacy, and education); child guidance and childcare services (e.g., day care and homemaker programs); services for single parents; protective services; schools; and substitute care or placement services (e.g., foster care, group homes, residential treatment, and adoption centers). In chapter 8, "Family and Children's Services," Brenda G. McGowan examines this field of practice from the perspective of past, present, and anticipated future developments. She focuses upon the early days of this field of practice (1898–1930), the middle years (1930–1960), and the more recent years (1960–1990). Particular attention is paid to the unique contributions made by faculty and alumnae/i. McGowan concludes the paper with a discussion of the 1990s and beyond.

In chapter 9, Barbara Berkman and Peter Maramaldi discuss Health, Mental Health, and Disabilities. This field of practice offers M.S. students an overview of the health delivery system in the United States. The required platform course focuses on the organizational structures, legislation, and health policies that determine how health services are delivered and that affect social work practice. Students examine the health practices and social stressors that affect clients; identified risk factors and their application to program development and evaluation; fiscal, legal, and organizational sanctions and influences, including managed care; and the assessment of system entry points for client care and advocacy. Students who select clinical social work or advanced generalist practice and programming as their method of practice typically take their field instruction in placements such as hospitals, nursing homes, ambulatory settings, neighborhood health centers, public health departments, and primary care practices or psychiatric settings, including mental hospitals, psychiatric clinics, day hospitals, day school programs, residential treatment centers, community mental health centers, and child guidance clinics. Those who select social administration as their practice method typically are placed in municipal and federal settings, state health planning agencies, or hospitals. In focusing on past and present developments, chapter 9 attends especially to such topics as health care for the vulnerable, health promotion and disease prevention, multidisciplinary practices, and the biopsychosocial approach to health care. The paper concludes by viewing these developments as a prologue to the future.

Aging, another major field of practice at CUSSW, is open to students who are interested in the developmental, social, physical health, mental health, and service needs of the aging population and its families. The emerging service delivery system of this field of practice includes services for middle-aged adults (e.g., preretirement planning, family treatment, and lifelong learning), healthy senior citizens (e.g., resocialization, crisis intervention, advocacy, functional assessment, and postretirement planning), the frail elderly (e.g., specialized housing, congregate care, long-term care, community outreach, and information and referral), and dying patients and their families. The required platform course in the aging field of practice covers such topics as demographic trends, developmental perspectives, national policies and trends, family and intergenerational relations, and pertinent service systems. Entitled "Aging," chapter 10 is authored by Abraham Monk. Employing the perspectives of "yesterday, today, and tomorrow," Monk traces the history of this field of practice at CUSSW, which, for the most part, parallels the development of his own career at the School.

Work, workers, and work organizations are the focus of attention of the World of Work field of practice. The required platform course in this field addresses key aspects of social work in the workplace, including the needs and help-seeking behaviors of workers and their implications for social service practice and the design of delivery systems. A wide variety of settings provide field placements for students who seek to carry out clinical service delivery, research, program development, and training or administrative roles. They include trade unions, corporate headquarters, employee health programs, mental health centers, and family and rehabilitation agencies. Among the subjects addressed by this field of practice are the links between work and physical health, mental health, family well-being, and aging. Problems examined include developmental crises, alcohol and drug abuse, marital and family problems, job jeopardy, retirement adjustment, credit, and related legal matters. Students learn how work organizations and their policies affect individuals and families. They are prepared to engage in preventive, therapeutic, and rehabilitative interventions. In chapter 11, entitled "World of Work," Sheila H. Akabas examines this field of practice from the perspectives of past, present, and anticipated future developments.

The field of practice in International Social Welfare and Services to Immigrants and Refugees is open only to M.S. students whose method of practice is policy practice, social administration, research, or advanced generalist practice and programming. It covers the activities of intergovernmental organizations and voluntary nongovernmental organizations that operate cross-nationally, as well as national governments and their interactions with other governments regarding social policies, programs, and practices. Relevant activities include standard setting, technical assistance, cross-national research, and the exchange of ideas, personnel, and information. The direct service element of this field of practice focuses on immigration and refugee programs, intercountry adoptions, and programs that occur in response to natural and human-made disasters. The required platform course introduces students to this field of practice and exposes them to the workings of the major international organizations, the programs of voluntary agencies that work internationally, and the major international trends in social policies and programs, as well as the nature of social work practice and training in other countries. In chapter 12, entitled "International Social Welfare," Sheila B. Kamerman explicates the dimensions and definition of this field of practice and then examines its various forms at CUSSW in the first fifty years of the School's history, the second fifty years, and from the perspectives of present and anticipated future developments.

School-Based and School-Linked Services comprise another field of practice at CUSSW. Focusing on the delivery of social work services to school-age children, adolescents, and their families, students in this field gain the knowledge and skills needed for practice in a wide range of educational settings, such as preschool, elementary, middle, and high school; regular education and special education settings; and alternative educational systems. The required platform course in this field of practice examines social service and educational systems in terms of their interrelationships and combined potential for improving the lives of at-risk children and their families. Chapter 13, authored by Mary McKernan McKay and Ernst O. VanBergeijk, discusses the distinguishing features of school social work practice. School-linked and school-based social work services are described in detail. The essay examines the historical precedents for school social work practice, contemporary issues resulting in the establishment of a school-based field of practice at CUSSW, and core features of the school social work curriculum. It concludes with a discussion of the challenges regarding preparation of school social workers for the twenty-first century.

Contemporary Social Problems was introduced to CUSSW's curriculum as a special field of practice so that the School can be responsive to new or significantly shifting societal problems as social work education and the social work profession undergo further development. This field of practice is designed to address new issues as they emerge. Currently, the core topics are homelessness, violence, and substance abuse, as well as issues related to the criminal justice system. It focuses on the most vulnerable and marginalized populations served by social workers. While problems such as homelessness, violence, and substance abuse are discrete social problems, there is substantial confluence among them. The required platform course focuses on particular issues and practices concerning each of these problems as well as their convergence. Chapter 14, entitled "Contemporary Social Problems," is authored by Nabila El-Bassel, Marianne Yoshioka, and Clarener Moultrie. It discusses the epidemiology and co-morbidity of social problems, addressing, in particular, partner violence, homelessness, substance abuse, and the criminal justice system. Specific attention is paid to the platform course, the clinical course, and field instruction placements for this field of practice.

Taken together, the seven essays in part 3 provide an extensive overview of past and present developments in each of the seven major fields of social work practice taught in the M.S. degree program at CUSSW. They also highlight critical issues and anticipated future developments regarding these fields of practice. Like the essays in part 2 of this volume, many of the papers discuss issues that are of overarching concern not only to the Columbia University School of Social Work but also to social work education nationwide and, indeed, worldwide.

Chapter 8

FAMILY AND CHILDREN'S SERVICES

Brenda G. McGowan

Since child welfare services were initiated long before the development of social work as a profession, it is not surprising that child welfare leaders were among the founders of what is now the Columbia University School of Social Work (CUSSW). What is not as well known is the key role that many of the School's faculty and graduates have played in the evolution of child welfare services over the years. Although I have spent most of my professional life working in different aspects of family and children's services and have been affiliated with the School in various capacities for almost thirty years, I was still somewhat surprised when I began the research for this paper to discover how intimate the relationship has been between Columbia and the child welfare field. Not only have our graduates been administrators and practitioners in many of the country's leading family and children's service agencies, but many of our faculty and alumni/ae have been recognized as leading theoreticians, researchers, advocates, teachers, and policy analysts, contributing to most of the significant developments in this field of practice.

In this paper I will trace the role child welfare has occupied in the curriculum at the School, from its establishment as the Summer School of Philanthropy in 1898 to the present. In this context, I shall highlight the scholarly and practice contributions made by individual faculty and alumni/ae to the evolution of this field of practice. The paper will conclude with a brief assessment of where we are now and implications for the future.

---

*The author is indebted to Marilyn Lewis, CUSSW doctoral candidate,
who provided assistance with the initial research for this paper.*

THE EARLY DAYS: 1898–1930

The School's establishment in 1898 under the aegis of the Charity Organization Society occurred in the midst of the rapid expansion of social services that accompanied the Progressive Era. It also essentially foreshadowed the steady bureaucratization and professionalization of services and the increased state intervention in family life that would characterize development of child welfare services during the twentieth century. Thus, the early lectures and courses at the Summer School of Philanthropy inevitably emphasized content on family and children services.

The general topic of study during the first three weeks of this six-week program was Treatment of Needy Children in Their Own Homes; the fourth week focused on study of the Care of Dependent, Neglected, and Delinquent Children. A number of the early students and lecturers were current or emerging leaders in this field of practice. For example, C. C. Carstens, who was a student in 1900, became director of the Massachusetts Society for the Prevention of Cruelty to Children and later served as director of the Child Welfare League of America. Florence Kelley, a veteran of Hull House in Chicago and Henry Street Settlement on the Lower East Side, lectured at the School while serving as executive secretary of the National Consumer's League; she was the first to educate students about the problems of child labor.

A similar pattern persisted after the School was reorganized in 1904 as an eight-month full-time course of study. One of the four required lecture series was The Care of Families in Their Homes, and one of the four additional elective lecture series focused on Child-Helping Agencies. The School also retained its early emphasis on social reform after the reorganization, giving increased emphasis to work on behalf of children.

Elizabeth Meier (1954), author of the history of the School's first fifty years, tells a story about the School's role in the initiation of the first White House Conference on Children in 1909. Apparently, Lillian Wald and Florence Kelley were breakfasting together at Henry Street Settlement, became angry upon reading in the newspaper that the president was calling a special cabinet meeting to consider the menace of the boll weevil, and began to consider the possibility of creating a federal agency as concerned about the welfare of children as other federal agencies were concerned about agricultural issues. Mrs. Kelley talked with Edward T. Devine, the director of the School, who wired and later went to meet with President Theodore Roosevelt. As a consequence of this meeting and subsequent hearings around the country, the president called the first White House Conference on Children, which later led to the creation of the U.S. Children's Bureau in 1912.

In the 1911–12 academic year, the School began to require two years of study for the diploma and hired its first full-time faculty. The core curriculum plan introduced at that time offered first-year students a general introduction to social work knowledge and processes and second-year students a choice of an area of specialization that integrated fieldwork with a field of practice seminar and preparation of a master's thesis.

Two of the full-time faculty hired in 1912 were Henry Thurston and Porter Lee, two major figures in the development of the profession. Together they assumed responsibility for teaching the Individuals and Families course for first-year students and two specialized seminars for second-year students in Family Welfare and Child Welfare.

By the end of the decade, the profession began to experience increased pressures toward specialization, and the School responded by becoming more departmentalized in the 1920s than at any other time in its history. To illustrate, in the 1923–24 academic year, the School had eight separate departments, including one in Family Case Work and another in Child Welfare. Each of these departments issued its own bulletin and had its own prerequisites, courses, and fieldwork. Students were even graduated from particular departments!

In the latter part of the 1920s the School began to shift back to increased emphasis on the common content among different fields of practice and the generic base of social work as a profession. A new curriculum was adopted in 1928–29 that closely reflected the recommendations of the Milford Conference of 1925 regarding the generic base of casework.

Several developments related to child welfare in this era of specialization during the 1920s essentially foreshadowed later developments in family and children's services. First, although social workers in hospitals, schools, and psychiatric settings formed specialized national associations, no parallel association of social workers in child or family welfare was formed. Second, although the Bureau of Child Guidance, established in the School in 1922, was designed to provide psychiatric treatment for children with behavioral difficulties and served as an impetus for the introduction of extensive psychiatric content within the School's curriculum, there was little exchange between this bureau and the Child Welfare Department. Third, as Meier (1954) noted, the studies undertaken in the School's Child Welfare Department during the 1920s emphasized the historical development of programs and current problems in the field rather than the methods and techniques of casework.

Finally, the first major evaluation of child welfare services was published in 1924 by the State Charities Aid Association (SCAA). This study, which was the first in a long history of child welfare research, examined the known capability of former foster children aged eighteen or older who had been placed by SCAA and had been in foster care one year or longer (Van Senden Theis 1924). Over three-quarters (77 percent) of the subjects who could be located ($N = 897$) were judged to be "capable"; that is, they were law-abiding, able to manage their affairs with good common sense, and were living in accord with good moral standards of the community. Collectively, these developments suggest that the leading educators and administrators of the time in the child welfare field were less interested in helping practitioners develop specialized professional practice skills than were some of their counterparts in the health, education, and mental health fields. They seemed more concerned about developing specialized service programs for high-risk families and dependent children than in developing the knowledge and skills required to "treat" the problems these clients presented.

A book published in 1930 by Henry Thurston, *The Dependent Child: A Story of Changing Aims and Methods in the Care of Dependent Children,* conveys what seems to have been the view of the field by child welfare faculty at that time and set the stage for developments in the field over the next three decades. This book, which was apparently designed as a textbook, provides a wonderful picture of different historical methods of caring for dependent children from the days of slavery and feudalism through indenture, almshouses, and orphan asylums, to the free foster homes of Charles Loring Brace. He compared these single approach solutions to the "scientific process" of Charles W. Birtwell, director of the Boston Children's Aid Society, who sought to provide diversified services that would meet the range of needs of each individual child in care. Highlighting the concept of viewing every child as "a total personality in a total situation," Thurston (1930) argued that there were two tasks that must be accomplished in every state and community: (1) extension and improvement of intake processes to insure individualized assessment of the service and placement needs of each child as an individual and a family member, and (2) development of the variety of placement resources required to meet the needs of each child as soon as he or she has to enter care. (These, of course, continue to be major challenges confronting the child welfare system, in the New York City area at least.)

THE MIDDLE YEARS: 1930–1960

During the 1930s the School attempted to help deal with the effects of the depression and introduced new courses on public welfare, but its primary focus was on developing the curriculum with a strong emphasis on the social work methods of casework, group work, community organization, and research. Similarly, during and after World War II, the School remained preoccupied with developing its methods-oriented curriculum. However, individual faculty members were still very engaged with issues and problems in the larger community.

For example, in the child and family service arena, Gordon Hamilton conducted a job study at the request of the Children's Bureau and the Social Security Administration for an analysis of training programs for public welfare in schools of social work. In 1939 Mary Hurlbutt and others assisted with the organization and administration of the U.S. Committee for the Care of European Children. Phillip Klein served as director of research for the 1940 White House Conference on Children. Dorothy Hutchinson served as consultant to the New York State Department of Welfare from 1943 to 1945 and provided extensive inservice training to child welfare workers in other parts of the country. Leontine Young gave institutes on child welfare in South America. The leading child welfare scholar at the School during this period was Dorothy Hutchinson, who joined the faculty in 1935 and remained until her death in 1956. Her many writings on child welfare services contributed significantly to developments in the field, including the need for collaboration between family and child welfare agencies and the importance of generic casework in both fields of practice. In her early days Hutchinson focused primarily on issues in foster home care and later wrote a book, *In Quest of Foster Parents* (1943), that became a standard reference for home finders. She also wrote repeatedly about the need for self-awareness among social workers engaged in child placing and was an early advocate of practice with biological families.

In the *Encyclopedia of Social Work* ("Dorothy Hutchinson" 1977), it is noted that Hutchinson was an especially gifted teacher who generated interest in child welfare services and had a close relationship with many of her students, such as Leontine Young and Elizabeth Meier, who later went on to assume leadership roles in the School and were viewed as scholars of child welfare practice in the postwar period.

What is most striking in reading some of the publications of these two women today is the strong emphasis placed on psychodynamic understanding of children and their parents and how this knowledge must be used to guide casework interventions. To illustrate, in a paper titled "The Separated Child," Young (1948) comments:

> In a very real sense, we are the link between [the child's] unhappy past and the unknown future. We are also the person who actually makes the physical change in his life situation, and inevitably we incorporate for him a maze of feelings. We know that his own family has failed him, a fact which causes him bitter shame as well as pain and grief. Do we also know the anger he has felt against his parents, his secret wish to hurt, perhaps destroy them for they have disappointed and hurt him, and his growing fear that separation from them is punishment for these angry wishes? We are the weapon which inflicts that punishment as we are the witnesses of his shame and grief. Yet we are also the all-powerful adult who may place him where we will, expose him to new dangers which because they are unknown, leave him prey to his own fantasies already given shape by previous hurts. Even the older child has few defenses against a combination like this. (106–107)

(One can only wish that foster care workers today were given such an understanding of what their clients are facing rather than being asked to focus first on accountability demands and second on concurrent planning!)

Although Young wrote extensively on foster care and child abuse issues, she is best known for her work on unmarried mothers and basically created a specialization within the child welfare field on services to unmarried parents. Although some of her concepts about the unconscious, purposeful nature of out-of-wedlock pregnancy and the "mother-ridden" and "father-ridden" unmarried mother seem almost laughable today, I remember taking her book *Out of Wedlock* (1954) as my bible when I started out in this field in 1963!

Elizabeth Meier, who, like Young, resigned from her faculty post to complete her doctorate at the School, also made many contributions to child welfare practice theory. However, she is best remembered today for her history of the school and her dissertation, "Former Foster Children as Adult Citizens" (1962). Although this was a much more sophisticated study than the one conducted by Sophie Van Senden Theis in 1924, it yielded similar results regarding the social effectiveness and general well-being of these former foster children.

In much the same way that Thurston's *The Dependent Child* essentially foreshadowed developments in child welfare for the succeeding three decades, a book written by Henry Maas (1942) and Richard Engler (1959), *Children in Need of Parents,* set the stage for child welfare developments for the next three decades. This book was based on a massive study of children in foster care and sixty child welfare agencies in nine communities around the country. The authors concluded that there were many children in "foster care limbo" who were likely to remain in care until they reached adulthood and that more than half of the youths studied were likely to spend the major part of their childhood in care. Arguing that every child has a right to his or her own parents, Maas and Engler emphasized the need to provide permanent substitute parents if a child's own parents were inadequate. The fact that this book has been cited in almost every single publication since that time about the importance of permanency planning testifies to the seminal impact of this research.

It is also important to acknowledge the initial contributions of Alfred Kahn, who started writing on children's issues in the early 1950s and who continues to be a vibrant force in the profession today. As research consultant for Citizen's Committee for Children of New York for many years, he authored and/or edited a series of research reports on the status of different children's service systems that had significant impact on various City institutions. His doctoral dissertation, "A Court for Children: A Study of the New York City's Children's Court" (1952), was published as a book by Columbia University Press in 1953.

RECENT YEARS: 1960–1990

In the years since 1960, there has been marked fluctuation in the curriculum in the amount of attention devoted to specialized fields of practice. In the 1960s and early 1970s, selected electives were available to students relating to practice in child welfare, as in other fields of practice, but there was no requirement that students specialize. This picture changed in the mid-1970s when still another curriculum study determined that students should select a field of practice specialization that would integrate class and fieldwork and take a required course on policies and programs in their selected fields of practice. This same curriculum pattern remains in effect today, although an additional requirement was added in 1995 specifying that clinical practice students also take a required clinical course in their chosen field of practice.

Despite the relative lack of attention in the curriculum to child welfare issues during the 1960s and early 1970s, a significant number of faculty and alumni/ae have continued to make important contributions to this field of practice. The report of a project organized at the School in 1960 on Public Services for Families and Children highlighted issues in the relationship between Aid to Families with Dependent Children (AFDC) and Child Welfare Services and contributed significantly to the enactment of the 1961 and 1962 Amendments to the Social Security Act (Wickenden and Bell 1961). These amendments provided federal payment for foster care for AFDC-eligible children requiring court-ordered placement outside their own homes and 75 percent federal cost sharing for social services to children receiving AFDC.

Faculty Contributions

Alfred Kahn maintained his active research consultation role with the Citizen's Committee for Children during the 1960s and wrote a number of papers and monographs that had a direct impact on children's services in the City. One later resulted in a book titled *Planning Community Services for Children in Trouble* (1963) with a foreword written by Eleanor Roosevelt. This book called for a community network of services for children with proper mechanisms for service coordination, case integration, and accountability. Although it seems hard to believe so now, it was the first to focus across the needs of children with different labels such as "neglected" or "delinquent" and to envision a community system of services for children rather than a collection of discrete children's service programs. Another important monograph by Kahn (1971), *A Dream Deferred,* documented long-standing problems in children's services that the City was still failing to address. Unfortunately, many of the issues he documented almost thirty years ago still persist today.

Although Kahn expanded his interests to broader issues of social policy and planning in a cross-national context and wrote little about child welfare for many years after the early 1970s (Kahn, Kamerman, and McGowan 1973), in recent years he has again focused some of his research on issues in child welfare services. The publications based on the study he completed in 1990 with his long-time collaborator Sheila Kamerman on social services for children, youth, and families in the United States drew widespread attention because the research highlighted the ways in which child protective services had started to drive the entire child welfare field (Kamerman and Kahn 1990a, 1990b). More recently, Kamerman and Kahn have issued several monographs that address issues related to service reform strategies for children and their families in big cities and the potential impact of the "welfare reform" legislation of 1996 on child welfare and other children's service fields (Kahn and Kamerman 1996, 1998; Kamerman and Kahn 1997).

Perhaps the most important child welfare researcher of our time, David Fanshel, who received both his M.S. and doctorate from the School, joined the Columbia faculty in 1962. His most significant contributions seem to fall in four areas. First, he directed the Child Welfare Research Program at the School from 1964 to 1975. In that context he was responsible for directing the first major longitudinal study of children in foster care ($N = 624$) and writing with Eugene Shinn a number of articles as well as a widely cited book on this research (Fanshel and Shinn 1978). One of the most influential conclusions of this study was the importance of parental visiting of children in care, a finding that resulted in many subsequent policy changes at the federal and state levels. Another important finding of this study was the fact that children who remained in care did as well or better than children who returned home. This finding has not had as much impact on public policy, perhaps because of the widespread impact of the monograph he wrote, also with Eugene Shinn, called *Dollars and Sense in the Foster Care of Children: A Look at Cost Factors* (1972). This monograph, which provided detailed projections of the costs of maintaining children in care for an extended period, was used extensively by advocates pushing for permanency planning and tighter time limits on the amount of time children are allowed to remain in foster care.

A second major contribution of Fanshel's relates to his work in developing computerized information systems regarding children in foster care. Although it seems hard to believe now, at the time he began this work, neither the city nor the state had an automated information system for tracking the progress of children in care (Fanshel and Grundy 1975; Fanshel 1979).

Fanshel's third important contribution derived from his role as director of a retrospective study of 585 children in five Western states who were provided foster care by the Casey Family Program from 1966 to 1984. By tracking the placement histories of these youngsters and relating them to children's adjustment at various times in care and at discharge, he was able to demonstrate the negative effects of multiple replacements and the value of the agency maintaining its involvement with multiply traumatized children who may have to be moved repeatedly (Fanshel, Finch, and Grundy 1989a, 1989b, 1990).

Finally, it is important to note the contribution Fanshel made to current understanding of preventive services for children at risk of placement through his work as director of a major evaluation of the Lower East Side Family Union (Fanshel, Finch, and Grundy 1992a, 1992b). The study findings indicated that children with high behavioral adjustment problems were most likely to be members of families experiencing a high degree of stress and that relief of even *some* of the family problems could result in a higher degree of parental and child functioning.

David Fanshel is clearly the School's child welfare luminary and was awarded a commemorative award on the seventy-fifth anniversary of the Children's Bureau by the Secretary of the U.S. Department of Health and Human Services for "significant contribution in promoting the well-being, growth and development of America's children." However, it is also important to identify the contributions of the other recent faculty members who have made significant contributions to this field of practice.

The late Carol Meyer, who was also a graduate of our M.S. and doctoral programs, joined the faculty in 1962 after serving for three years as director of training for the New York City Department of Welfare. On the basis of this experience, she wrote a book that is still referenced today on staff development for public child welfare and family service workers (1966). She also did extensive staff training in voluntary child welfare agencies and was closely identified with the development of Family and Children's Services as a field of practice at the School. Ultimately, her major contribution was to apply her insights about the ecosystems perspective on practice to the child welfare field and to legitimize this as a significant arena for clinical practice (Meyer 1970, 1983).

The late Shirley Jenkins, who served as co-director of the Child Welfare Research Project, directed a study of the parents of the 684 New York City children in foster care that Fanshel followed in his longitudinal study. This research contributed significantly to current understanding of what Jenkins termed "filial deprivation," meaning the deprivation that mothers feel when separated from their children. The study demonstrated that once parents have resolved this sense of deprivation by separating psychologically from their children, they are less likely to be reunited (Jenkins and Norman 1972). Jenkins also directed an important study on Ethnic Factors in Child Welfare that led to increased understanding of issues of concern to members of ethnic minority groups, the relationship between ethnic minority status and child placement, and variables that characterize ethnic-sensitive child welfare agencies (Jenkins and Morrison 1976; Jenkins and Diamond 1985).

Finally, I should probably add that *I* have conducted a number of studies on the organization and delivery of child welfare services, focusing primarily on New York City. This has included research on kinship foster care, school-based early intervention services, the relationship between preventive and protective services, and the distinguishing characteristics of some of the "exemplary" preventive service programs (Botsko, McGowan, and Pardee 1998; McGowan, Bertrand, and Kohn 1986; McGowan with Kahn and Kamerman 1990). Also, Associate Dean Peg Hess and I recently completed a three-year study of the Center for Family Life in Sunset Park (Hess, McGowan, and Botsko in press).

Although academics usually make their primary mark through publication, I also want to mention two former faculty members who made significant contributions to child welfare through leadership in the field. The late Mitchell Ginsberg, former dean and professor emeritus, took a leave from the School in the late 1960s to serve as Commissioner of the New York City Department of Social Services and was later named Administrator of the Human Resources Administration. In these roles he had a direct impact on delivery of child welfare services in the City. After he returned to the School, he maintained an active involvement in policy and programming issues related to the delivery of family and children's services at the federal, state, and local levels and was an unfailing advocate on behalf of parents and children at risk. (In fact, shortly before his death, he agreed to serve as the "best friend" and spokesman for one of the child plaintiffs in the *Marisol* case currently pending before the federal court. In this case, Children's Rights Inc. has sued to put the New York City Administration for Children's Services into receivership because of its long-standing and repeated failures to meet the needs of children requiring child welfare services. Ginsberg was not happy about turning to legal remedies for administrative failures, but said he could not in conscience sit silently while hearing about the terrible abuses children in the child welfare system were suffering.)

Another strong advocate for the rights of poor children and families was the late Mary Funnye Goldson, who was a beloved teacher on the faculty for many years. Like Carol Meyer, she was a superb teacher about practice in family and children's services, encouraging many Columbia graduates to enter this field of practice. Goldson also took a very active role in the community, serving on the boards of several child welfare agencies, advocating persistently for improved services, helping to design the Lower East Side Family Union, and directing the Region II Adoption Resource and Child Welfare Training Centers for five years in the early 1980s. In what seemed a fitting tribute to her memory, the School established the Mary Funnye Goldson Memorial Program about six years ago to provide alternating annual lectures and staff development seminars for practitioners in child welfare.

Alumni Contributions

Although it is easiest to recall faculty contributions, the story of CUSSW and child welfare would not be complete without some acknowledgment of the many contributions made by a number of the School's illustrious graduates. A brief review of the list of our doctoral graduates indicates that just over fifty have written dissertations on problems related to child welfare. Many of them have, of course, gone on to pursue further research in this arena. In addition, countless numbers of our master's level graduates have served as practitioners, administrators, staff development specialists, advocates, and policy analysts in family and children's services. Therefore, it is only possible to identify a few of the many alumni/ae contributions here.

Henry Maas '42, whose important work on identifying the needs of children caught in foster care limbo was described earlier, later went on to make many other contributions to the child welfare literature. Perhaps the most important of these was his study, "The Young Adult Adjustment of Twenty Wartime Residential Nursery Children" (1963), which documented the potential value of group care at a time when it was being widely criticized.

One name that is familiar to almost everyone who has studied child welfare anytime in the last thirty years is that of Alfred Kadushin, a 1947 graduate of the School whose classic text *Child Welfare Services* was first published in 1967 and is now in its fourth edition (Kadushin and Martin 1988).

Some of the other significant alumni/ae contributors to child welfare research include Trudy Bradley Festinger, Ann Hartman, Sr. Mary Paul Janchill, Mary Ann Jones, Tony Maluccio, and Bill Meezan, all graduates of our doctoral program. Festinger has not only conducted important research in the areas of adoption and court review of children in foster care (1975, 1976), but she also completed an exciting, widely reviewed study of the impressions of former foster children about their foster care experience (Festinger 1986). Hartman is perhaps best known for her articles on family-centered practice (1978, 1981) and her superb editorials in *Social Work,* but she and her long-time collaborator Joan Laird (CUSSW '71) also wrote an important text on family practice and edited the widely used *Handbook of Child Welfare.* She also served as director of the National Child Welfare Training Center at the University of Michigan in the 1980s.

Sr. Mary Paul Janchill is one of the originators and co-director of the Center for Family Life in Sunset Park, a nationally recognized, exemplary preventive service program that has been highlighted repeatedly in national studies as well as in the popular press. What is most exciting about this cutting-edge program is that it actually demonstrates the ecosystemic perspective of practice in action in a family and child welfare setting. In other words, while most of the academics have been writing about these concepts, Sr. Mary Paul has been doing it!

Mary Ann Jones, now a faculty member at New York University, conducted a number of important studies when she served as director of research at the Child Welfare League. Perhaps best known is her research on the sealed record adoption controversy (1976) and the effectiveness of the first preventive service programs in New York (Jones, Magura, and Shyne 1981).

Maluccio is well known for his many influential publications over the last twenty years on issues related to practice with parents of children in foster care and issues in permanency planning (Maluccio et al. 1980; Maluccio and Sinanoglu 1981; Maluccio and Fein 1983). He is also co-editor of a text currently used in many child welfare courses (Pecora, Whittaker, and Maluccio 1992).

Meezan has done extensive research over the years on issues in adoption (Meezan, Katz, and Russo 1978; Meezan 1980). He and I also collaborated in editing a widely used child welfare text in the 1980s (McGowan and Meezan 1983). Most recently, Meezan has focused on the impact of family preservation services on abusive and neglectful families, and he just published a book on this research that examines the important question of changes in family functioning, not simply the number of placements averted (McCrosky and Meezan 1997).

Martin Wolins, the first director of research at the Child Welfare League of America, has made many important contributions to professional knowledge of foster care (1963), group care for children, and the ways in which good programs can be beneficial for certain groups of youth in need of placement (1970a, 1970b, 1974).

Before leaving the topic of alumni/ae contributions, I also want to acknowledge the significant child welfare leadership demonstrated by two centennial celebration respondents from the practice community, Paul Gitelson and Gail Nayowith, and the scholarly and practice contributions to family support services made by Anita Lightburn.

THE 1990s AND BEYOND

In recent years the School of Social Work has experienced a number of retirements and unfortunate deaths among its senior faculty, which have left large gaps in our ranks. However, we have recruited a number of talented faculty and administrators, many of whom have a strong interest in child welfare policy, research, and practice. These include Kathryn Conroy (our director of field instruction), Martha Dore, Neil Guterman, Peg Hess (our associate dean), Helene Jackson, and Jane Waldfogel. Also, a couple of the old-timers like Sheila Kamerman and myself are still around. Collectively, we have conducted research on a wide range of topics related to child welfare, including the co-occurrence of child maltreatment and spouse abuse, practice designed to address mental health and substance abuse problems in high-risk families, exposure to violence by children in residential treatment, early intervention with families at risk for child maltreatment, issues of visiting and family reunification, child sexual abuse, privatization of publicly funded child and family services, and the future of child protective services.

To reflect this wide range of interests and encourage increased collaborative work, we are in the process of creating a Child Welfare Research Center at the School. Therefore, I am confident that the School will be able to retain its role as one of the country's leading centers of research on family and children's services.

I am also rather confident about our capacity to retain a focus on family and children's services as a critical component of our curriculum. We have strong courses and faculty in place, and approximately one hundred M.S.

students a year elect to specialize in this field of practice. Each year we also have doctoral students eager to study this field and to contribute to its impressive research tradition.

Unfortunately, I am less sanguine about the role of professional social work in the larger child welfare arena and the potential for increased collaboration between class and field. Child welfare workers today are suffering from severe funding cutbacks, increased bureaucratization, low salaries, lack of respect for professional social work training, and unprecedented attacks on their agencies and their clients. This does not create an enticing picture for our students and recent graduates, increasing numbers of whom are now considering alternative fields of practice.

The growing movement toward criminalization of parents in need of services, combined with the lack of systematic data collection by federal and state officials and the current reluctance of City officials to share data openly and to listen to research-based critiques of the child welfare system, also has the effect of discouraging young researchers about the potentials for change in this field of practice. It is difficult to feel optimistic about the benefits of one's research when policies are driven solely by political considerations and data seem to have little relevance to decision making.

Despite these considerations, poor families and children are still suffering. Therefore, it seems clear that as a profession and a School, we have no right to abandon the field because of its difficulties. Instead, I hope we can revisit our history and turn more attention to increased collaboration between the academy and the community. Porter Lee, one of the towering figures in the School's history, has been quoted as saying, "The participation of faculty in community affairs and field activities is indispensable to the vitality of professional education." Unless we find ways to move together politically and press for the changes in the child welfare field dictated by our research findings and practice wisdom, I fear we shall become increasingly irrelevant.

REFERENCES

Berengarten, S. (Ed.). (1991). *A history of social pioneering, Monograph 3*. Proceedings of the Fifth Oral History Day for Students, April 2, 1991. New York: Columbia University School of Social Work.

Bernstein, S., et al. (1942). *The New York School of Social Work: 1898 –1941*. New York: Institute for Welfare Reform, Community Service Society of New York.

Botsko, M., McGowan, B. G., and Pardee, E. G. (1998). *All in the family, a mixed blessing: Research on kinship care in New York City.* New York: Court Appointed Special Advocates.

Bradley, T. (1967). *An exploration of caseworker perceptions of adoptive applicants.* New York: Child Welfare League of America.

Dorothy Hutchinson. (1977). In J. Turner (Ed.), *Encyclopedia of social work* (Vol. 1, pp. 696–697). New York: National Association of Social Workers,

Fanshel, D. (1979). *Computerized information for child welfare: Foster children and their foster parents.* New York: Columbia University School of Social Work.

——(1980). *Computerized information for child welfare.* New York: Columbia University School of Social Work.

Fanshel, D., Finch, S. J., and Grundy, J. F. (1989a, July/August). Modes of departure from foster family care and adjustment at time of departure of children with unstable life histories. *Child Welfare, 68*(4), 391–402.

——(1989b, September/October). Foster children in life course perspective: The Casey Family Program experience. *Child Welfare, 68*(5), 467–478.

——(1990). *Foster children in life course perspective: The Casey family experience.* New York: Columbia University Press.

——(1992a, May/June). Serving the urban poor: A study of child welfare preventive services. *Child Welfare, 71*(3), 197–211.

——(1992b). *Serving the urban poor.* Westport, CT: Praeger.

Fanshel, D. and Grundy, J. F. (1975). *CWIS Report.* New York: Child Welfare Information System.

Fanshel, D. and Shinn, E. B. (1972). *Dollars and sense in the foster care of children: A look at cost factors.* New York: Child Welfare League of America.

——(1978). *Children in foster care.* New York: Columbia University Press.

Fein, E. and Maluccio, A. N. (1992, September). Permanency planning: Problem remedy in jeopardy? *Social Service Review, 66*(3), 335–348.

Festinger, T. (1975, April). The New York court review of children in foster care. *Child Welfare, 54,* 211–245.

——(1976, September/October). The impact of the New York court review of children in foster care. *Child Welfare, 55,* 516–544.

——(1983). *No one ever asked us: A postscript to foster care.* New York: Columbia University Press.

——(1986). *A study of adoptions and disrupted adoptive placements.* New York: Child Welfare League of America.

Hartman, A. (1978, October). Diagrammatic assessment of family relationships. *Social Casework, 59*(8), 465–476.

——(1981, January). The family: A critical focus for practice. *Social Work, 26*(1), 7–13.

Hess, P., McGowan, B. G., and Botsko, M. (in press). *Nurturing the one, supporting the many: The Center for Family Life in Sunset Park.* New York: Columbia University Press.

Hess, P., McGowan, B. G., and Meyer, C. H. (1996). Practitioners' perspectives on family and child services. In A. J. Kahn and S. B. Kamerman (Eds.), *Children and their families in big cities.* New York: Cross-National Research Studies Program, Columbia University School of Social Work.

Hutchinson, D. (1943). *In quest of foster parents.* New York: Columbia University Press.

Jenkins, S. and Diamond, B. (1985, April). Ethnicity and foster care: Census data as predictors of placement variables. *American Journal of Orthopsychiatry, 55*(2), 267–276.

Jenkins, S. and Morrison, B. (1976). *Identification of ethnic issues in child welfare: A review of the literature.* New York: Columbia University School of Social Work.

Jenkins, S. and Norman, E. (1972). *Filial deprivation and foster care.* New York: Columbia University Press.

Jones, M. A. (1976). *The sealed adoption record controversy: report of a survey of agency policy, practice, and opinions.* New York: Child Welfare League of America.

Jones, M. A., Magura, S., and Shyne, A. (1981, February). Effective practice with families in protective and preventive services: What works? *Child Welfare, 60,* 67–80.

Jones, M. A., Neuman, R., and Shyne, A. (1976). *A second chance for families.* New York: Child Welfare League of America.

Kadushin, A. (1967). *Child welfare services* (1st ed.). New York: Macmillan.

Kadushin, A. and Martin J. A. (1988). *Child welfare services* (4th ed.). New York: Macmillan.

Kahn, A. J. (1953). *A court for children.* New York: Columbia University Press.

——(1963). *Planning community services for children in trouble.* New York: Columbia University Press.

——(1971). *A dream deferred.* New York: Citizen's Committee for Children of New York.

Kahn, A. J. and Kamerman, S. B. (Eds.). (1996). *Children and their families in big cities.* New York: Cross-National Research Studies Program, Columbia University School of Social Work.

——(1998). *Big cities in the welfare transition.* New York: Cross-National Research Studies Program, Columbia University School of Social Work.

Kahn, A. J., Kamerman, S. B., and McGowan, B. G. (1973). *Child advocacy: Report of a national baseline study.* Washington, DC: U.S. Government Printing Office.

Kamerman, S. B., and Kahn, A. J. (1990a). If CPS is driving child welfare, where do we go from here? *Public Welfare, 48*(1), 9–13.

——(1990b). Social services for children, youth, and families in the United States [Special issue]. *Children and Youth Services Review, 12*(1–2), 1–179.

——(Eds.). (1997). *Child welfare in the context of welfare "reform."* New York: Cross-National Research Studies Program, Columbia University School of Social Work.

Laird, J. and Hartman, A. (Eds.). (1985). *A handbook of child welfare.* Englewood Cliffs, NJ: Prentice-Hall.

Lindenmeyer, K. (1997). *"A right to childhood": The U.S. Children's Bureau and child welfare, 1912–46.* Urbana: University of Illinois Press.

Maas, H. S. (1963). The young adult adjustment of twenty wartime residential nursery children. *Child Welfare, 42,* 57–72.

Maas, H. S. and Engler, R. E., Jr. (1959). *Children in need of parents.* New York: Columbia University Press.

Maluccio, A. N. and Fein, E. (1983, May/June). Permanency planning: A redefinition. *Child Welfare, 62*(3), 95–201.

Maluccio, A. N. and Sinanoglu, P. A. (1981). *The challenge of partnership: Working with the parents of children in foster care.* New York: Child Welfare League of America.

Maluccio, A. N., et al. (1980, November). Beyond permanency planning. *Child Welfare, 59*(9), 515–530.

McCrosky, J. and Meezan, W. (1997). *Family preservation and family functioning.* Washington, DC: Child Welfare League of America.

McGowan, B. G., Bertrand, J., and Kohn, A. (1986). *The continuing crisis: New York City's response to families requiring protective and preventive services.* New York: Neighborhood Family Services Coalition.

McGowan, B. G., with Kahn, A. J., and Kamerman, S. B. (1990). *Social services for children, youth, and families: The New York City study.* New York: Columbia University School of Social Work.

McGowan, B. G. and Meezan, W. (Eds.). (1983). *Child welfare: Current dilemmas, future directions.* Itasca, IL: Peacock.

McGowan, B. G. and Walsh, E. M. (1990). In C. Brecher and R. Horton (Eds.), *Setting municipal priorities, 1990* (pp. 264–306). New York: New York University Press.

Meezan, W. (1980). *Adoption services in the States.* Washington, DC: U.S. Department of Health and Human Services.

Meezan, W., Katz, S., and Russo, E. (1978). *Adoptions without agencies.* New York: Child Welfare League of America.

Meier, E. G. (1954). *A history of the New York School of Social Work.* New York: Columbia University Press.

——(1962). *Former foster children as adult citizens.* Unpublished doctoral dissertation, Columbia University, New York.

Meyer, C. H. (1966). *Staff development in public welfare agencies.* New York: Columbia University Press.

—— (1970). *Social work practice: Response to the urban crisis.* New York: Free Press.

—— (Ed.). (1983). *Clinical social work in an eco-systems perspective.* New York: Columbia University Press.

Pecora, P., Whittaker, J. H., and Maluccio, A. N. (1992). *The child welfare challenge: Policy, practice, and research.* New York: Aldine.

Stein, H. P. (1960). *Curriculum study.* New York: New York School of Social Work, Columbia University.

Thurston, H. W. (1930). *The dependent child: A story of changing aims and methods in the care of dependent children.* New York: Columbia University Press.

Van Senden Theis, S. (1924). *How foster children turn out.* New York: State Charities Aid Association.

Wickenden, E. and Bell, W. (1961). *Public welfare, time for a change.* New York: Project on Public Services for Families and Children, Columbia University School of Social Work.

Wolins, M. (1963). *Selecting foster parents: The ideal and the reality.* New York: Columbia University Press.

—— (1970a). Group care: Friend or foe? *Social Work, 14*(1), 35–53.

—— (1970b). Young children in institutions: Some additional evidence. *Developmental Psychology, 2*(1), 99–109.

—— (Ed.). (1974). *Successful group care: Explorations in the powerful environment.* Chicago: Aldine.

Young, L. (1948). The separated child. In *Proceedings of Canadian Conference on Social Work,* pp. 106–112.

—— (1954). *Out of wedlock.* New York: McGraw-Hill.

Chapter 9

HEALTH, MENTAL HEALTH, AND DISABILITIES

Barbara Berkman and Peter Maramaldi

War, economic depression, epidemics, and dramatic advances in medical technology have shaped social work in health care. The central ideas and principles of social work were born out of times of crisis and great technological change (Kerson 1982) and the Columbia University School of Social Work (CUSSW) has always been at or near the crux of the profession's transitions. In his opening remarks for an oral history program at CUSSW, Dean Ronald Feldman observed that "the highlights of Columbia's distinguished history are highlights of the social work profession's history because very often the innovations we brought forth have set the pace for the profession as a whole" (Feldman 1988:iii). History informs us about what has been tried, the conditions under which possible solutions have been explored, and then finally, what has prevailed (Rehr 1982). In addition, changes in the present always produce changes in the way the past is understood (Cronin et al. 1998). With this caveat, we will explore a few key concepts which have shaped Columbia's past, influenced its present, and will impact the future by tracing them back in time to see what we have gleaned from our past. Columbia's enduring contributions to social work's health care practice and education include (1) its commitment to health care for vulnerable populations, (2) its commitment to health promotion and disease prevention, (3) its investment in multidisciplinary practices, and (4) its biopsychosocial approach to care. Throughout the School's history, there has been a struggle around professional direction: an individualistic focus on intervention versus a population-based social reform approach to problem solving.

HEALTH CARE FOR THE VULNERABLE

Today, social work in health care has a concern for and commitment to addressing problems of vulnerable populations such as the poor, the homeless, and the chronically ill. This concern has been the underpinning of CUSSW since its inception. On June 20, 1898, under the auspices of the Charity Organization Society (COS), the first six-week Summer Training Class in Philanthropy was convened in the United Charities Building in New York City, giving rise to what is now known as the Columbia University School of Social Work. Twenty-seven students from fourteen colleges and eleven states attended the first summer session. The summer sessions continued for several years thereafter and evolved into the Summer School in Philanthropic Work. In 1904 John S. Kennedy generously endowed the School, the course of study was expanded to one full year, and the institution became known as the New York School of Philanthropy. A second year of study was added in 1911, and then in 1919 the School changed its name to the New York School of Social Work (Bernstein et al. 1942). In 1959, after transferring its endowment to Columbia University, the School became known as the New York School of Social Work of Columbia University. The final change came in 1962, when the school took its current name as the Columbia University School of Social Work (Kahn 1998). A closer look at the curriculum of the first Summer Training Classes uncovers the foundation of Columbia's hundred-year commitment to health promotion and disease prevention with vulnerable populations.

The early curriculum consisted of morning lectures by experts who were chief executives of progressive and charitable organizations, followed by field visits under the direction of the COS. The morning lectures addressed the needs of society while reflecting the ideas and philanthropic principles of the emerging profession. The lecture topics from the first summer session— Private Charitable Agencies, Child Saving, Medical Charities, Public Charities, Public Activities Affecting the Poor, Treatment of Needy Families in Homes, Neighborhood Improvements, and Institutional Care of Adults— provide insight into the School's early and enduring commitment to vulnerable populations. Medical Charities—which included work in dispensaries, hospitals, and with "sick children" living among the poor—were particularly prominent in the curriculum (Bernstein et al. 1942:10).

In the early 1900s, under the leadership of Edward Devine, the New York School of Philanthropy led significant social reform campaigns. Emphasis was given to the documentation of needs of vulnerable populations (Bernstein et al. 1942; Meier 1954), while the curriculum focused heavily on issues related to insuring patients against the costs of illness and to assuring access to care. During this "era of social reform," the School called for social action and fundamental restructuring of economic and social systems in the fight against inequalities of access to health care (Meier 1954). Social work was stressing social environmental causes as well as individual treatment. Debates were continual as to which should be the approach to solve people's problems and to improve social conditions. In 1912, Edward T. Devine supported social and health insurance proposals of the time (Mizrahi 1995). Two years later, during the 1914–15 academic year, Lee K. Frankel presented lectures on insurance and public health (*Bulletin* 1914). Three-quarters of a century later, themes of insurance and public health dominate discussions of contemporary health and mental health in social work.

In 1905, an endowed chair was established with Columbia University. The result was a unique relationship wherein the Director of the School of Philanthropy became a Professor of Social Economy at Columbia (Bernstein et al. 1942). The die was cast for both practice and academic rigor in addressing the needs of vulnerable populations. The Bureau of Social Research, established at the New York School in 1906, was tied closely to the social reform movement through research studies on poverty, malnutrition, and working conditions (Meier 1954). However, the School also focused on addressing individual patient and family issues, such as supporting compliance with medical recommendations (*Bulletin* 1923).

Throughout its history, social work debated how best to address its concerns for the vulnerable and argued the value of population-based social reform approaches versus individualist and family clinical practice models (Rehr 1982). Columbia has always been at the hub of this debate. The common thread from then until now is the commitment to, and challenge of, addressing problems of vulnerable populations such as the poor, the homeless, and the chronically ill, often through dispensaries, other medical facilities, or government and private agencies.

Physical and mental illness have been strongly represented in the School's curriculum — and concomitantly the social work profession — throughout its history. Students in the class of 1900 spent one entire week on the topic of

Medical Charities, making ten visits to medical institutions, which included Presbyterian and Bellevue Hospitals as well as prominent dispensaries of the time (Meier 1954). Medical Charities focused on both physical health and mental health, which were serious concerns of the era. At the turn of the century, large immigrant populations and the emergence of densely populated tenement neighborhoods in urban centers contributed to the importance of civil service reform as a societal goal. In the face of political chicanery, "reform was desperately needed in order that the ill, the needy, the mentally ill, and the delinquent might derive the benefits intended for them . . ." (Meier 1954:13-14).

The School's commitment to the development of professional rigor in delivering services to vulnerable populations was reflected in the celebrated Kennedy lectures, which were established in 1905 and which sought to stimulate new areas of training and inquiry (Bernstein et al. 1942). Mary Richmond's Kennedy lectures on the Beginning Steps in social work pressed for professional standards in delivering services to vulnerable populations and were later incorporated into her seminal work, *Social Diagnosis* (Meier 1954). She championed the School's drive toward accountability and practice standards in health care and in all related areas of social work practice. Professional standards were also reflected in the School's 1910 yearbook, which suggested that the New York School undertake the sponsorship of psychological clinics for children based on medical models of service delivery (Bernstein et al. 1942). In 1912, for instance, a course in hygiene and preventative disease became a requirement. Under relentless pressure from Mary Richmond, attention was heavily focused on individual and family rehabilitation (Meier 1954). In tandem with this individualistic focus, the School's commitment to population-based social reform approaches to problem solving has persisted throughout its history.

Three decades after Lee K. Frankel's early lectures on insurance and public health, social insurance and access to health care remained a haunting national issue. During the 1940s, the question of how to give the poor freedom of health brought Columbia to join in the national movement for comprehensive health insurance. The 1960s saw the issues related to inequality of access to health care at the forefront of national debates. Medicare and Medicaid stimulated the growth of social work in hospitals and in other sites, and our direct work with patients and families and group efforts increased. Social work called for universal comprehensive national health care, but with rising health care costs this social objective was stalled (Berkman 1977b). The 1960s also brought Community Mental Health Centers, for which social workers were actively recruited as service providers (Berkman 1977a, 1978). Social workers were also advocates for patients and families, with one of Columbia's esteemed graduates, Dr. Helen Rehr, creating the first Patient Service Representative Program in a hospital (Ravich, Rehr, and Goodrich 1969a, 1969b). Social work will continue in the future to advocate for our clients and to focus on the issue of access to health care services for all.

HEALTH PROMOTION AND DISEASE PREVENTION

Today, we address major public health issues and are concerned with health promotion and disease prevention. During the early 1900s, social work had a strong public health orientation. Agency-based practice was focused on the fight against the dreaded illnesses and social issues of that era: tuberculosis, syphilis, polio, and out-of-wedlock pregnancies (Ross 1995). The summer school curriculum addressed the social and economic effects of illness through practice experience and the methodical clinical study of the terrible epidemic of the day—tuberculosis. Columbia waged battles against tuberculosis, including its social causes and its economic effects. Students of the class of 1900 visited prominent medical leaders at various charities and institutions where they attended lectures on The Warfare Against Consumption, What Charity Workers Should Know of the Treatment and Prevention of Tuberculosis, and Social Factors in the Prevalence of Consumption (Meier 1954:14). The emphasis was on prevention as well as curative approaches. The Summer School was committed to mental health from the beginning. During its inaugural sessions, Frank B. Sanborn was brought into New York from Concord, Massachusetts to address the charter class on the Curability of the Insane (Bernstein et al. 1942:8).

Although social work began to emphasize services to individuals and families through casework approaches, it also invested energies in population-based public health approaches to the protection of women and children (Meier 1954). By the time the United States entered World War I, the knowledge and skills of social workers acquired in peacetime had great applicability for meeting the societal health problems evidenced in war, such as venereal disease. In the 1917 *Bulletin,* the School's response to these newly identified needs was evident. There was a recognition that the "war will make permanent changes in our social organization" (Bernstein et al. 1942: 42). The School chose not to change its entire curriculum, but offered a special Red Cross Training Course for Emergency Social Service in conjunction with a variety of local agencies under the sanction of the American Red Cross. The ten-week course consisted of two lectures and three days of fieldwork per week (Bernstein et al. 1942).

When the conflict of World War I came to a close in November 1918, content on health and disease was strong in the curriculum (Meier 1954). Venereal disease had reached epidemic proportions, and social work took a major role in tracing the illness and in establishing helping relationships with the patients. Social workers took responsibility for getting patients to inform their sexual contacts as well as to comply with the eighteen months of unpleasant treatment (Wallace, Goldberg, and Slaby 1984). The underlying premise was that all social workers needed to understand the importance of health promotion and disease prevention. The prevention of disease became a major thrust of Columbia, and both individual and community approaches were urged (Meier 1954).

The debate over individual versus population-based community approaches to social work services was fueled, in large part, by the influence of the medical profession. One of the most important examples of this influence in shaping social work's early professional identity, as well as its training pedagogy, is Abraham Flexner's 1915 keynote speech to the Conference on Charities and Corrections, entitled "Is Social Work a Profession?" (Austin 1986). Flexner was nationally recognized as an expert in education for the professions following his seminal report establishing the framework for medical education (Starr 1982), which made him an excellent choice for the keynote. Flexner urged that in order to achieve professional status, social workers should narrow their field of operations to scientifically based specific skills and intervention techniques supporting problem solving directed at individuals. By contrast, three years before Flexner's proclamation, James Alexander Miller had set Columbia on a different trajectory, which can be traced throughout its history. When Miller came to the social work faculty, he was a professor of clinical medicine at the College of Physicians and Surgeons and the director of the Tuberculosis Clinic at Bellevue Hospital. He warned social work not to make the same mistake as the profession of medicine, which he criticized for maintaining a narrow focus on "individual and immediate tasks" and widespread "social apathy." He argued that social work should be concerned with both the individual and broader programs and community approaches to disease prevention (Meier 1954:52).

In 1919, when the School became known as the New York School of Social Work, Porter R. Lee, its director, turned his attention to the problems associated with professional social work training, citing the absence of accumulated scientific teaching material as a major deficit. Although Lee accepted the increased emphasis on specialization, he warned against having too many specialists working within a single family, each with their own special solution for various social ailments. For Lee, the changing social values of the roaring twenties, women's suffrage, and new social ills following the war all served to elucidate the importance of environmental considerations (Meier 1954). While the 1920s found social work leaning toward a focus on individual client approaches to health care problems, the Great Depression beginning in 1929 brought social work back to an emphasis on addressing social issues. A major problem was that social work, like medicine and nursing, separated clinical functions from social welfare. The individual became one emphasis and health policy, research, and planning another. The remnants of this separation remain with us today (Rehr 1982).

During this period, the psychological development theories of Sigmund Freud found a receptive audience in social work, which was increasingly involved in the treatment of mental disorders. Freud's theories also provided a solution to Flexner's challenge to find scientifically based techniques that could be transferred through training. Developmental and ego psychology provided psychiatry and social work with a much-sought-after scientific base for casework practice and training (Austin 1986). The specialty of psychiatric social work sprang out of changing practice demands and professional pressures to respond to Flexner by being more "scientific."

Social work had a history of drawing upon the fields of sociology and economics in addressing client needs. Utilizing the additional knowledge of psychology and psychiatry, the new specialization—psychiatric social work—was said to have particular allure. It gave social workers a scientific means of understanding human behavior (Meier 1954). From the 1930s through the 1940s, psychiatric social work gained such stature that medical social work was seen as requiring less skill. As a demonstration of the hierarchy, many hospitals had separate medical and psychiatric social service departments (Shelvin 1983). Columbia Professor Mary Antoinette Cannon, who taught from 1921 to 1944, was considered a rebel for her efforts to integrate medical and psychiatric social work. Indeed, Professor Gordon Hamilton was also challenged for innovative efforts in eclecticism (Meier 1954).

After World War II, psychiatric social work—with its emphasis on the psychoanalytic model—began to give way to the ideas espoused by Helen Harris Perlman regarding the importance of considering the interaction between the person and society (Shelvin 1983). By 1948 there was a firm conviction that prevention is necessary, if mental illness is to be treatable, and if we wish to reduce custodial care. Gordon Hamilton wrote that social work must balance internal psychological factors *and* external social factors in both directing ourselves to individual case situations and in combating community problems in order to prevent illness (Meier 1954). Even though rehabilitative medicine and technological advances in areas such as transplant surgery presented new challenges for medical social work as early as the 1950s, psychiatric social work still prevailed (Shelvin 1983).

In the 1960s, social work again emphasized the need for social action reform and the elimination of the external causes of psychological and social dysfunction. In urban centers there was poor housing, poor schools, inadequate police, and inadequate public transportation. Emergency rooms were used as primary care physicians for the poor. Columbia became a major player in the War on Poverty, with a major initiative aimed at improving access to health care. Columbia graduates had major roles in health promotion and disease prevention in health care and in developing screening and case-finding mechanisms to identify patients and families in need of social services (Berkman and Rehr 1970; Gordon and Rehr 1969).

MULTIDISCIPLINARY PRACTICES

Today we emphasize the need for multidisciplinary practices and a more autonomous social worker on the health care team. Columbia social work was built upon multidisciplinary approaches. As noted previously, in 1911 James Alexander Miller joined the faculty (*Bulletin* 1911) to present a course on medical sociology and hospital social services. It focused on diseases and their relationship to poverty and social problems (Meier 1954). The influence of medicine on the School's development through prominent figures like Miller strongly influenced the emerging social work profession with reference to multidisciplinary and biopsychosocial thinking and curriculum development. By the time Mary Richmond formally called for "the technique of working together" in 1917 (Meier 1954), Columbia was well into its development of multidisciplinary practice.

The 1914 *Bulletin* described courses in medical social service under the joint auspices of the Bellevue Hospital Training School for Nurses and the New York School of Philanthropy. The basic nursing admission criteria were based on a clergyman's letter testifying to good moral character, good teeth, and good health. For a social work degree one needed "mental maturity and a college level education (not necessarily a degree)" (*Bulletin* 1914). The intent of the program was for women to spend two years in nursing school followed by a year of study in social work. After the completion of course work, the recipient would receive both a nursing and a social work diploma. Although this early dual degree program only lasted for two years (Meier 1954), it demonstrates the School's early recognition of the complementary relationship between social work and contemporary health and mental health services.

The *Bulletin*'s description of Bellevue Hospital reflects one of the values of the School—poor and vulnerable populations should be provided with excellent health and mental health services. Bellevue had evolved from a multipurpose almshouse in 1736 (Wallace et al. 1984) to a premier medical institution run by the City of New York. It had a capacity nearing two thousand beds and was described in the 1914 *Bulletin* as one of the "largest and best equipped hospitals in the country." The *Bulletin* went on to explain that with its

> patients largely from the congested East Side, and with its well developed Social Services Department, Bellevue offers exceptional opportunities for the study of social problems. Its services are of every variety, including medical, surgical, gynecological, obstetrical, alcoholic, tuberculosis, children's, and psychopathic wards. (*Bulletin* 1914:3)

The School—without losing sight of poor and vulnerable populations—was committed to providing training to its students in the most innovative and technologically advanced services of the day.

Psychiatric social work appeared in the School's curriculum in 1917. Columbia's readiness to take on this new and innovative challenge was reflected in the establishment of a Mental Hygiene course under the directorship of Dr. Bernard Glueck, who was associated with the Neurological Department at the Vanderbilt Clinic. For the first time, students had the opportunity to study Social Psychiatry and Psychological Measurement, with a limited number of field placements offered at Vanderbilt as well (Berengarten 1987). Innovations like this came directly from the vigilance of the School's faculty and administration in evaluating the curriculum in relation to contemporary social work practice.

In 1909–10, a faculty curriculum study revealed interest in establishing a child guidance clinic intended to provide services to external agencies while improving the internal curriculum and training offered by the School. In 1916, the faculty made a formal proposal to establish the clinic, which led to the opening of the Bureau of Children's Guidance in the early 1920s. As the first psychiatric treatment facility for children administered and staffed by a school of social work, it reflected the New York School's enduring commitment to multidisciplinary work. Dr. Glueck served as its first director until he resigned in 1924 and was replaced by the Bureau's first assistant director, Dr. Marion E. Kenworthy. Dr. Kenworthy came to Columbia with a medical degree from Tufts University and extensive training in social psychiatry at the Boston Psychopathic Hospital. Drs. Glueck and Kenworthy created an interdisciplinary team approach among psychiatry, psychology, and social work, with continuous consultation from medicine (Berengarten 1987).

In the early 1920s, social work played a major role in the discharge planning of chronic patients and homeless World War I veterans (Meier 1954). It was soon recognized that social work had a valuable contribution to make when the causes of illness were not exclusively biological, and that the onset of disease, recovery, and resumption of function are influenced by social forces. By 1963, Harriet Bartlett described social workers as integral members of the health care team who assisted in the understanding of the significance of social, economic, and emotional factors and who helped patients and family members with these issues (Ross 1995). In 1973 and again in 1981, Helen Rehr and her colleague Jeannette Regensburg (who had worked closely with Marion Kenworthy) spearheaded the exploration of innovative approaches to interdisciplinary care through national conferences. During the first conference, Regensburg (1974) called for social workers to exercise more initiative, authority, and responsibility while being members of the team.

By the 1970s there were shortages of trained social workers in health care, and the term *multidisciplinary* took on a new connotation—intradisciplinary—with Robert Barker, a Columbia graduate, studying the role of social work paraprofessionals. The United Hospital Fund, led by a committee of CUSSW faculty and alumni/ae (Doran Teague, Rosalind Miller, Maurice Russell, and Lawrence Shulman) supported the Barker/Briggs Model of the Social Service Team with the M.S.W. as leader (Barker and Briggs 1968).

Today, the School offers eight dual degree programs — including one with the School of Public Health. During the eighty-five years since the 1914 joint training program with the Bellevue School of Nursing, the training of social workers in outstanding health and mental health facilities has been one of the distinguishing hallmarks of the School. The 1998–99 *Bulletin* describes field instruction as a "central component in each student's professional education" with "medical and psychiatric hospitals [and] mental health clinics" leading the list of the types of public and voluntary agencies and organizations in which students are trained (5). It seems that the historical theme of multidisciplinary training and practice remains contemporary, as teamwork within and among the professions will be an even more important concept for health and mental health social work in the future (Berkman et al. 1996).

BIOPSYCHOSOCIAL APPROACH TO HEALTH CARE

Today CUSSW emphasizes a biopsychosocial approach to health care. Social work has contributed to the biopsychosocial model since the early 1900s. The design for taking a contemporary biopsychosocial history is reminiscent of early course lectures and clinical observations, and then more formally in the Bureau of Child Guidance, where Drs. Glueck and Kenworthy developed the Four-Fold Study Plan. It consisted of evaluations and regular case conferences regarding the physical, psychiatric, psychological, and social history of each patient (Bernstein et al. 1942). Direct treatment was then based upon this early biopsychosocial approach to assessment and service delivery.

By the 1920s Columbia had medical social work and psychiatric social work among its nine specialties. All students began to take health and mental hygiene courses, with an increasing emphasis on psychiatric information. Abnormal psychology was introduced and psychiatric concepts permeated the curriculum. As would be expected, with Dr. Marion Kenworthy's interest in the social and psychiatric needs of children with behavioral problems, knowledge in psychiatry and psychology added a new dimension to social work's understanding of human behavior (Meier 1954).

By the mid-1920s psychiatric information had taken on a glamorous aura and psychiatric social workers were viewed as specialists at the top of the social work ladder (Shelvin 1983). All of social work assumed a psychiatric identity. Social, cultural, and environmental factors were considered secondary to repressed fears and unresolved frustrations. Freudian theories of developmental psychology plus ego psychology became the "scientific basis" for social casework. However, Columbia had a few rebels who believed that there were general principles which covered all social work specialties, and Mary Antoinette Cannon, a major health care leader, and Gordon Hamilton tried to integrate these generic social work principles (the social with the psychological) into their courses. Medical social work was strong and medical information was considered necessary and a required component of social work studies (Meier 1954).

In 1925, a report titled "Social Casework: Generic and Specific," crafted by Dean Porter Lee and Professor Mary Antoinette Cannon, called for and resulted in Columbia adopting a generic base for all casework. However, what was "generic" and what was "specific" continued as a major argument (Meier 1954). During the 1930s, all social work practice was expected to include working knowledge of social psychiatry. However, physical well-being was seen as critical to emotional adjustment. The approach to mental health care was person-in-environment, where understanding of the human personality and its reaction to the environment was considered essential. Social workers trained in symptoms of mental illness worked in psychiatric clinics and assumed responsibility for carrying out the social aspects of the treatment prescribed by psychiatrists and psychologists. All social workers, regardless of site, were trained to relate to the social aspects of disease in dealing with people.

After World War II, medical doctors and social workers increased their collaboration. Veterans were wounded psychologically and physically. Medical and psychiatric clinics started to take a biopsychosocial approach. In 1946, the National Mental Health Act was enacted in response to the country's concern with the high incidence of emotional disturbances revealed by the war. Fellowships were available in advanced psychiatric casework. In 1949 the National Institute of Mental Health (NIMH) was established and offered grants for research and training of mental health professionals. Columbia's distinguished alumni/ae, including Milton Wittman, among others, received doctorates through this mechanism. Dr. Wittman subsequently became a major force for social work education at NIMH.

The expanding mental health movement of the 1950s reduced the emphasis on social work education for medical care. Columbia's specialty training in medical social work disappeared, with only a medical information course remaining. Mental hygiene was a specialty. Courses were offered in mental hygiene, human behavior and its disorders, and the science of mental testing. Upon graduation, students were expected to work in mental hygiene clinics, in aftercare of the mentally ill, and with mentally disabled soldiers. However, psychiatry in the curriculum had influence far beyond mental hygiene, with one-third of the graduates from the program going to work in psychiatric settings; the rest went to work in other fields such as medical social work, family welfare, and child welfare (Meier 1954).

By the 1980s, a call for specialization again emerged. Social work now incorporated themes from sociology, psychology, psychiatry, community mental health, and anthropology. The ecological or person-in-situation and family-centered approaches were integral parts of practice and education. Carel Germain's (1984) comprehensive theory of practice was and is applicable to a variety of roles and functions in the health field. She, along with Columbia colleagues Hy Weiner and Alex Gitterman, understood the social, psychological, and organizational dynamics affecting health care service delivery. They played major roles in the conceptualization of social work in health and mental health. Social work at Columbia will continue to emphasize a biopsychosocial approach toward understanding health care issues.

CONCLUSION: THE PRESENT AS PROLOGUE TO THE FUTURE

Today dramatic changes in patient care delivery are stimulated by advances in technology and new approaches to the financing of health care. After one hundred years of social work in health care, social workers are visible in every facet of service delivery, working as providers of new models of health and mental health care practice in addressing the needs of patients and their families. Unfortunately, many of these new models are based on a system in which health and mental health clinical services operate as separate and fragmented entities, isolated from social support services, raising increased concerns about accessibility, efficiency, and comprehensiveness. Thus, while we have had technological and scientific breakthroughs which have led to greater longevity and better health, these advances do not necessarily carry equivalent provisions for the vulnerable and the economically disadvantaged (Rogers 1986). The health care environment supportive of vulnerable clients, evident in the 1960s and 1970s, is gone. However, screening of patients at risk for physical, social, environmental, and psychological needs has become even more essential, and the timing of interventions by social workers has become paramount (Bergman et al. 1993). Our efforts in health care practice, policy, and research to inform and address the needs of vulnerable clients who depend on our advocacy and program planning are critical.

Today there is increasing recognition of the role of social workers in the collaborative process necessary to address health and mental health issues in a newly emerging health care paradigm. Multidisciplinary approaches to health and mental health—which go to the core of CUSSW's tradition—are now, more than ever, appropriate for individual and family social work practice and social reform initiatives. By focusing on health promotion and disease prevention—also at the core of CUSSW's tradition—social work moves into the public health arena, where multidisciplinary knowledge concerning risk and protective factors becomes even more important in developing approaches to intervention in the new millennium (Mrazek and Haggerty 1994).

Social work in health care today is holistic in its views of a biopsychosocial approach toward problems of the body and the mind. Recent breakthroughs in the neurosciences have contributed to the biopsychosocial understanding of mental health and illness. This approach provides a carefully balanced perspective that takes into account the entire person in his or her environment and helps social workers assess the needs of an individual and family from a multifactorial point of view. Biopsychosocial assessments play an increasingly important role in clinical practice and health planning. Social work's strength today lies in its synthesis of physical, social, cultural, and environmental variables.

Today social work education for health and mental health at Columbia offers a full menu of didactic and practicum choices among clinical practice skills, health policy analyses, program planning skills, administrative skills, and research. However, these offerings are frequently separated and fragmented entities, reflecting the fragmentation in our health care systems and social work's history of fragmenting these skill areas. The questions to be addressed are as follows: Where will social work practice and education need to be tomorrow? What will the current transitions in American health care mean for social work practice and education? What are the fundamental issues that social workers should be considering for the future?

Increasing numbers of patients will be presenting with multiple chronic health and mental health problems. Because chronic illnesses are determined by and impacted by many factors, such as an individual's social, psychological, environmental, and genetic makeup, as well as health care accessibility factors, health and mental health care is being restructured as a network of community-oriented delivery systems focused on chronic disease management (Shortell, Gillies, and Devers 1995). This has implications for our practice and for our didactic and practicum education. In this model the social worker will be expected to address patient and family needs throughout the continuum of care. Instead of thinking primarily in terms of acute inpatient care episodes, which has been the main focus of social work delivery since the advent of Medicare, social workers will move more into community-based ambulatory care services, emphasizing primary care and ongoing health care management of chronic illnesses (Berkman 1996). We will bring screening and case finding into primary care even as we continue social work efforts in hospital preadmission and admission screening for posthospital care needs, so that discharge transitions can be facilitated more effectively.

Instead of focusing primarily on the care of individual patients, social workers will be accountable for the social and health status of vulnerable at-risk populations such as the elderly, people infected with HIV, abused children and adults, victims of domestic violence, the chronically mentally ill, the poor, and the homeless. Instead of focusing primarily on curative and rehabilitative services, social workers will offer services that are oriented toward the goals of disease prevention and health promotion. Finally, for those who still will need to work with inpatient care, social workers will focus on issues where they are the primary health care professionals with skills needed to address such matters as resolving behavioral problems that impede the ability of patients and families to manage recommended treatment or discharge plans (Berkman et al. 1996).

Although Columbia's education for health care has placed greater emphasis in past years on clinical skills and, thus, on the psychological and interpersonal elements of social functioning, there is and will be a growing inclusion and integration regarding the importance of prevention, the use of standardized screening and assessment tools, skills in outcome research and data management, new models of interdisciplinary care, and the importance of policy for practice. This reflects the awareness that while there is a need to educate for specialized, diagnostically specific knowledge and skills, of both a psychodynamic and physiological nature, there still are inadequate social and economic supports, and insufficient treatment and rehabilitation services, which result in access issues as well as treatment issues. Social work didactic and practicum education at Columbia will need to integrate clinical practice skills with program planning, health policy, administrative, and research skills. It is evident to those who practice and teach in health care that the content areas conceptualized as necessary in health curricula of the future will integrate cultural, social, psychological, environmental, spiritual, and biological dimensions of social functioning.

At Columbia University School of Social Work's fiftieth anniversary in 1948, there were a number of major themes projected for the future. Among them were the importance of social workers' contributions to policy formulation through greater involvement with government, and the importance of scientific knowledge (Meier 1954). These themes are reflective of our history and are germane to where social work will be in the future. Social health policy is inseparable from the needs of individuals, groups, and communities. As health policy drives practice, what we glean from practice must direct our policy efforts. Social workers will continue to address the social, psychological, and environmental needs of individuals and families and they will study the social, psychological, cultural, environmental, and economic factors that contribute to individual growth, development, and disability. This is a significant contribution that social work at Columbia will make to health care policy and practice.

Since 1898, CUSSW has had research continuously as part of the curriculum, with greater or lesser emphases. Research now is considered an integral part of health care practice and Columbia's curriculum integrates research with practice. Health care social workers have a significant research and practice agenda. They will apply the knowledge and research methods of the social and psychological sciences to problems of concern. However, after a remarkable one hundred years of social work education and practice, it is not the technical aspects of our profession which bind us together. We have not been, we are not now, and we will not be technocrats. Research methodology does not diminish the importance of the mission of social work, or of our values, or of our caring for the vulnerable and the disenfranchised.

The bottom line is that a strong social work specialist in health or mental health care of the future will be one who is not easily overwhelmed by organizational complexities; who is knowledgeable about and comfortable with sophisticated state-of-the-art health care; who is able to be flexible, creative, and an autonomous leader in the hospital and in the community; and who can work collaboratively as that key member of a health care team who combines scientific excellence with compassion and humanism. At Columbia, as the face of health care changes dramatically, social work education in health, mental health, and disabilities will also change, expanding its foci of concern and articulating a new vision for itself.

REFERENCES

Austin, D. (1986). *A history of social work education.* Austin: University of Texas School of Social Work.

Barker, R. T., and Briggs, T. L. (1968). *The differential use of social work manpower: An analysis and demonstration-study.* New York: National Association of Social Workers.

Berengarten, S. (1987). The School's role in establishing a new field of practice: Psychiatric Social Work/Mental Health Services. In S. Berengarten (Ed.), *The Columbia University School of Social Work: A history of social pioneering. Proceedings from the First Oral History Day for Entering Students* (pp. 19–31). New York: Columbia University School of Social Work.

Bergman, A., Wells, L., Bogo, M., Abbey, S., Chandler, V., Embeton, L., Guirgis, S., Huot, A., McNeill, T., Prentice, L., Stapleton, D., Shekter-Wolfson, L., and Urman, S. (1993). High risk indicators for family involvement in social work in health care: A review of the literature. *Social Work, 38,* 281–288.

Berkman, B. (1977a). Community mental health services for the elderly. *Community Mental Health Review, 2*(3), 1–9.

——(1977b). Innovation in delivery of social services in health care. In F. Sobey (Ed.), *Changing roles in social work practice* (pp. 92–126). Philadelphia: Temple University Press.

——(1978). Mental health and the aging: A review of the literature for clinical social workers. *Clinical Social Work, 6,* 230–245.

——(1996). The emerging health care world: Implications for social work practice and education. *Social Work, 41,* 541–551.

Berkman, B., Bonander, E., Kemler, B., Rubinger, M. J., Rutchick, I., and Silverman, P. (1996). Social work in the academic medical center: Advanced training— A necessity. *Social Work in Health Care, 24*(1/2), 115–136.

Berkman, B. G., and Rehr, H. (1970). Unanticipated consequences of the case-finding system in hospital social service. *Social Work, 15,* 63–68.

Bernstein, S., et al. (1942). *The New York School of Social Work: 1898–1941.* New York: Institute of Welfare Research, Community Service Society of New York.

Bulletin of the New York School of Philanthropy. (1911). *General announcement* (Vol. 5, No. 1). New York: Charity Organization Society of the City of New York.

Bulletin of the New York School of Philanthropy. (1914). *General announcement* (Vol. 7, No. 4, Part 2). New York: Charity Organization Society of the City of New York.

Bulletin of the New York School of Social Work. (1923). *A quarter century's progress: 1898–1923*. New York: Charity Organization Society of the City of New York.

Bulletin of the Columbia University School of Social Work. (1999). *General announcement, 1998–1999*. New York: Columbia University School of Social Work.

Cronin, W., Diggins, J. P., Foner, E., Higham, J., Hollinger, D., Kerber, L. K., Lukacs, J., McDougall, W. A., Morgan, E., Ravitch, D., and Woodward, C. V. (1998, Winter). Teaching American history. *The American Scholar*, pp. 91–106.

Feldman, R. A. (1988). Foreword. In S. Berengarten (Ed.), *The Columbia University School of Social Work: A history of pioneering. Proceedings of the Second Oral History Day for Entering Students* (p. iii). New York: Columbia University School of Social Work.

Germain, C. B. (1984). *Social work practice in health care: An ecological approach.* New York: Free Press.

Gordon [-Berkman], B., and Rehr, H. (1969). Selectivity bias in delivery of hospital social services. *Social Service Review, 43*(1), 35–41.

Kahn, A. J. (1998). *Themes for history: The first hundred years of the Columbia University School of Social Work.* New York: Columbia University School of Social Work.

Kerson, T. S. (1982). *Social work in health settings: Practice in context.* New York: Longman.

Meier, E. G. (1954). *A history of the New York School of Social Work.* New York: Columbia University Press.

Mizrahi, T. (1995). Heath care: Reform initiatives. In R. L. Edwards (Ed.), *Encyclopedia of social work* (19th ed., Vol. 2, pp. 1185–1198). Washington, DC: National Association of Social Workers Press.

Mrazek, P. J., and Haggerty, R. J. (Eds.). (1994). *Reducing risk for mental disorders.* Washington, DC: National Academy Press.

Ravich, R., Rehr, H., and Goodrich, C. (1969a). Hospital ombudsman smooths flow of services and communications. *Hospitals, 43*, 56–61.

——(1969b). Ombudsman: A new concept in voluntary hospital services. In W. C. Richan (Ed.), *Human services and social work responsibility* (pp. 311–320). Silver Spring, MD: National Association of Social Workers.

Regensburg, J. (1974). The working parties. In H. Rehr (Ed.), *Medicine and social work: An exploration in interprofessionalism* (pp. 35–73). New York: Prodist.

Rehr, H. (Ed.). (1982). *Milestones in social work and medicine: Social-health care concepts.* New York: Prodist.

Rogers, D. (1986). Preface to the special issue, "America's doctors, medical services, medical care." *Daedalus, 115*(2), 5–10.

Ross, J. W. (1995). Hospital social work. In R. L. Edwards (Ed.), *Encyclopedia of social work* (19th ed., Vol. 2, pp. 1365–1376). Washington, DC: National Association of Social Workers Press.

Shelvin, K. M. (1983). Why a social service department in a hospital? In L. Hubschman (Ed.), *Hospital social work practice* (pp. 1–14). New York: Praeger.

Shortell, S. M., Gillies, R. R., and Devers, K. J. (1995). Reinventing the American hospital. *The Millbank Quarterly, 3,* 131–155.

Starr, P. (1982). *The social transformation of American medicine: The rise of a sovereign profession and the making of a vast industry.* New York: Basic Books.

Wallace, S. R., Goldberg, R. J., and Slaby, A. E. (1984). *Clinical social work in health care: New biopsychosocial approaches.* New York: Praeger.

Chapter 10

AGING

Abraham Monk

YESTERDAY

Writing almost a quarter of a century ago on the very subject that I address today, I pointed out that, notwithstanding the obvious demographic explosion of aging, and despite the fact that government officials were awakening to this reality with heightened sensitivity and even a measure of obsequiousness, the training of gerontological practitioners, in general, remained uncertain and problematic. Moreover, I indicated that social workers had not shown a decisive or pioneering commitment to this practice, even when the profession's official leadership would occasionally issue statements acknowledging its importance. Such pronouncements were nice but usually empty gestures because they were rarely followed by commensurate and sustained actions. Let us face it: geriatric practice has been, and still is, a very low priority in social work. The profession engaged in what I would characterize as "benign avoidance" but camouflaged it with ritualistic protestations of sympathy. Moreover, I believe that the reasons for this ambiguity or disvaluation of aging are the same in 1998 as those I enumerated twenty-four years ago. They include, among others:

1. The "contamination" effect of the psychodynamic theories of personality development that remain in vogue in many professional quarters. Psychoanalysis affirms that the child is the parent to the adult person, and follows the threshold at which he or she is about to reach maturity. At that point the theory comes to a sudden halt and seems to imply that whatever changes may evolve in subsequent chronological stages are mere repetitions of earlier developmental milestones. A deeper concern with later adulthood would then appear as superfluous. Symptomatic of that frame of mind was a popu-

lar text for human growth and development that swept through graduate schools of social work in the '70s and '80s. I am referring to T. Lidz's *The Person* (1983). You may recall it covered over five hundred pages, half of which were devoted to early childhood but only about ten pages were assigned at the very end to the aged. I remember students telling me that they never even read this meager chapter because the course was over once they reached young adulthood and early parenting.

2. The "generic" base of social work education sought to holistically broaden the realm of practice by making it more responsive to complex client systems. While the aged client could be individualized as part of existing networks and treatment groups, the notion of a particular focus on the oldest segment of the life cycle, to the apparent exclusion of other age stages, was viewed then as antithetical to what many perceive as the profession's universalistic scope.

3. There is the commonly held rationalization that social intervention with the aged is futile, given the limited therapeutic goals that may be pursued and their dubious chances of success. There is certainly no hope for reversing the deleterious effects of aging itself. In cost-benefit terms, and as the self-fulfilling prophecy continues, it makes more sense to allocate scarce treatment resources to younger people because they, at least, do have a future. Besides, results may be more immediate and gratifying with them, and transference far more feasible. This argument, coupled with the preceding "generic" one, underlies much of the advisement dispensed by some members of our own faculty. Rarely a year went by without having a handful of students—precisely those who came to Columbia with the explicit intent to specialize in gerontology—knock on my door, all troubled and confused, because their first-year faculty advisor had counseled them to opt instead for the "health-mental health" field of practice. With the best of all intentions these advisors argued that everything in social work is contained in the "health-mental health" field of practice. In other words, this is the most comprehensive or generic expression of practice, not really a specialization. And because it is all-encompassing, students were told, their interest in aging would also be ipso facto met. This way—the argument followed—you do not become parochial, or narrowly circumscribed. You will acquire a wider perspective, and you will ultimately increase your employability prospects. The argument was irresistible: health-mental health is the very common denomi-

nator underlying all of social work. It is therefore safer and more popular. There was an obvious gerontophobic slant in this reasoning: these students were advised to avoid making a "narrow" commitment. The same advice, however, was not given to those who selected other fields of practice, such as Families and Children. These were apparently regarded as normal, mainstream, and glamorous career paths, parenthetically related to Health and Mental Health. Practice with the aged did not seem to merit the same qualifiers.

4. There was a lack of understanding of the existential stance and its potential contribution to social work practice. The recognition of loss, grief, and suffering and some of their manifestations in the course of the growth and aging process; the stress on "interiority" and critical self-examination and their role in an individual's pursuit of authenticity, are just a couple of themes that demand the gerontological social worker's attention. They require the development of a total life perspective and a "meaning-searching" model of the person, rather than the instinct-driven or learning-conditioned models so prevalent in social work. In a related publication I pointed out that "only in gerontological practice are social workers confronted with a person's final destiny and with the true meaning of a person's life" (Monk 1981:62), but I acknowledged that for young social workers—even for those trained in gerontology—it is often difficult to attain such an understanding of life as a nearly closed or completed totality.

I do not want to create the impression that social work was totally divorced from its potential aged clients. There are many sporadic testimonies in the literature, some going back to the 1920s, of the profession's involvement with this population, but a more concerted attempt to systematize this practice and, at the same time, link it to its educational correlates did not emerge probably until the middle of the century. Lowy (1985) mentions a 1947 conference on the Treatment of Older People sponsored by no other than our own School, then called the New York School of Social Work. That was exactly fifty-one years ago, and while I am not aware whether the meeting had any lasting or radical consequences within the School itself, the stage was apparently set for a sequence of developments throughout the profession.

Surely, there were agencies and individual practitioners that single-handedly and often without coordination or mutual awareness were creating the basis for practice. It was about that time that Florence E. Vickery experimented in San Francisco with the idea of multiservice senior centers, as resocialization settings aimed at the "well" but often lonely aged. She obviously met a critical need, as evidenced today in the more than ten thousand senior centers dotting this nation. Edna Wasser headed the first project on aging, launched by the Family Society of America. She spelled out in minute detail the challenges faced when working with mentally impaired elderly and she identified what constitute successful clinical interventions with this population. Louis Lowy laid the foundations, first of group practice with the aged and then of professional training in university-based schools of social work. I wish to finally add the name of Elaine Brody, who defined and expanded the role social workers are called to play in long-term care services, in general, and in institutional care, in particular. Surely by limiting myself to these four names I am not doing justice to the myriad of practitioners and academicians who pioneered in this field. I belonged, however, to the very first cohort of doctoral students that in the mid-1960s specialized in gerontology under the aegis of Title IV-A of the Older Americans Act. Those were the names whose writings, lectures, and even personal communications most influenced my cohort. We received guidance from a rather small bunch of pioneers. Of course there were many more researchers and theoreticians outside of social work that exerted a similar influence on us: the names of Robert Havighurst, Bernice Neugarten, Ethel Shanas, Marjorie Fisk, Robert Kleemeier, Marvin Sussman, and Irving Rosow are the first that come to mind.

The period between 1958 and 1972 was probably the most creative and decisive in shaping our fledgling gerontological specialization at CUSSW. To begin, the Council on Social Work Education convened in 1958 the Aspen Conference, aimed at resolving how aging could be introduced in the curricula of the day. Next, the 1961 White House Conference on Aging, the first meeting of its kind, brought national attention to personnel deficits and affirmed the concomitant need to launch a massive training program for specialists in geriatrics-gerontology. Four years later Congress enacted the Older Americans Act. It included training as a mandated priority and it generously appropriated funds for its programmatic implementation. Many schools of social work seized the opportunity and applied for those funds, although they hardly had time to hammer out a consensus on how to do the job.

By 1970 the CSWE finally got its act together and produced a curriculum statement that mandated areas of concentration in all accredited M.S.W. programs. It became clear by then that it was difficult to teach methods without reference to specific target populations and that there was need for what Brunner (1960:17) referred to as "cognitive organization," that is, the grasping of the structure of a field or subject, or to what Bloom called "integrative threads" that connect separate experiences (1958).

There was, initially, a great deal of resistance or reluctance to identify "fields of practice" with social problems, because of the pathological quality and stigma the latter evokes, but, as Studt keenly observed (1965), what social work calls "fields of practice" are, in actuality, fields of problem management, or even better, social action systems created to handle emerging challenges in modern life. Many schools, however, could not conceive of teaching professional skills other than by emphasizing the classical methods, which were now designated "concentrations" or "fields of practice." It surely was a case of semantic opportunism, but this is how these schools succeeded in complying with the CSWE mandate. They kept doing what they always did, but they now camouflaged it with a new name.

Nancy K. Carroll aimed to overcome that polarization between classical methodological primacy in social work and the new "fields of practice" model by subsuming all forms or expressions of practice into what she called the "three-dimensional model" (1975). The first axis, or dimension, dealt in this conceptual model with actual contemporary problems, aging being one of them. The second consisted of the social systems or units of concern, varying in size and structural complexity, i.e., the individuals, families, informal support networks, social agencies, and so forth. The third were the methods of social intervention. Practice, which ultimately results from the concurrent application of these three dimensions, acquired a greater potential for variability and singularity. I was then on the faculty of the State University of New York at Buffalo, and we were already experimenting with an approach similar to the "three-dimensional model," although we were not immediately aware of Carroll's insightful conceptualization. I reported about our curriculum design at a special CSWE session that took place during the 1972 annual meeting of the Gerontological Society that was held in Puerto Rico. I then exchanged views and offered suggestions to the participants from the Columbia University School of Social Work (CUSSW), who began toying with the idea of an aging module in the M.S.W. program. A few years later this school obtained a major grant from the Brookdale Foundation aimed at launching a gerontological specialization in both the M.S.W. and the doctoral programs. The first step consisted in getting the appropriate personnel— that is, recruiting a gerontologist, and this is how I came on board. The year was 1977. I presume that those conversations in sunny Puerto Rico proved to be fateful.

The beginnings of CUSSW's concentration on aging parallel those of most of the profession's educational field. We were not unique. By 1984 half of all schools of social work had initiated such a concentration or program, but many could not sustain it (Nelson and Schneider 1984). By 1988 only 34 percent of the schools were still offering such a concentration. Four years later, in 1992, the decline was arrested and even modestly reversed as 39 percent of the schools kept developing aging concentrations (Damron-Rodriguez et al. 1997).

Overall, the outcomes of this educational enterprise are very meager. The aged constitute today over 12 percent of the population and are heading to become close to 20 percent in the first third of the twenty-first century, but only 4.2 percent of the M.S.W. membership of the National Association of Social Workers claims aging as their primary professional domain (Gibelman and Schervish 1993). Interest in aging may be even lower among M.S.W. students, as less than 50 percent of the schools of social work report that at least 5 percent of their student population registered for gerontology-specific courses (Damron-Rodriguez et al. 1997). Let us face it, we are operating in an environment of marginal interest, we are a minuscule fringe, and we continue facing severe competitive disadvantages, given the way the curriculum is structured. This is rather perplexing considering that gerontological social work is repeatedly singled out in every major forecasting study and projection of personnel needs as the wave of the future, as one of the fastest growing areas of occupational demand ("Twenty Hot Job Tracks" 1995).

TODAY

The present is here stretched over the past twenty to twenty-two years. We do not take it to be a furtive or transient episode, but it is not an arbitrary interval either. There are logical and historical justifications for selecting these chronological parameters. I am simply highlighting the time since CUSSW launched and operated its full-fledged second-year Field of Practice on Aging.

This specialization is a neat and well-articulated package consisting of two required courses: the first is an introduction, what we call a "platform" course on social gerontology, infused and saturated with all the essential social policy underpinnings, and an ambitious overview of the aging service network. The second emphasizes the clinical interventions with this population. Students are required to take these two courses, plus a full year field placement in an aging-related agency. There is ongoing synchronization with several dozen such agencies. Agencies are selected on the basis of the quality and comprehensiveness of the training opportunities they may offer. They must also collectively cover or represent the continuum of care in aging. We monitor how responsive they are to our students' educational needs, but we also listen attentively to their own concerns as well as to their instructional and operational suggestions.

Altogether, it is conceptually a straightforward and manageable model, but I find it rather succinct—a sort of minimalist sampler—for my taste. After all, we can only impart the bare bones, and yet it is better than nothing. It is also quantitatively superior to anything else offered within the immediate tri-state area. If you examine the curriculum content on aging in the eight or nine schools of social work in our vicinity, you will discover that we are the only one with an ongoing and full-fledged specialization on aging. Some of the other schools tried it early on, formulating their plans on paper and even announcing it in their official catalogs. It just did not fly. There were no takers, interest was sporadic at best, and the schools ultimately gave it up, although here and there and on intermittent occasions they will offer an elective on aging issues. Surely it was a case of lack of student interest, but my colleagues in those schools often point their fingers to the lack of persistent institutional support or to the impatience of school administrators who demanded immediate results, not realizing that it takes time to build a concentration that goes against the grain of the pervasive glamorization of youth in our culture.

All schools, including ours, have been facing a perennial marketing problem. Aging, we already mentioned, is not a glamorous topic, and it takes time to plant the seeds, nurture them, and await the eventual turnout. How did we then manage to sustain this program for over twenty years? What set us apart? There were, in my estimate, three major explanations:

The first brings us back to marketing. We were very aggressive in the way we tried to attract students. We conducted informational campaigns both among our first-year students and prospective applicants. We did it not once or twice, but repeatedly, many times each year, again and again. We made sure we were always in the limelight. We created an image of vitality and sophisticated professionalism. We also "sold" aging in a different light, by underscoring that it is "intergenerational and multigenerational" family practice. We added an emphasis on the middle-aged generation, particularly at the onset of the empty-nest syndrome, and many students could then relate to what was happening to their own parents at that precise time. The gains were limited, certainly not commensurate with the informational efforts but, on the other hand, we did not expect a tidal wave of registrations. We were realistic and consequently had to set our goals low.

Second, we slowly built a national reputation. People who were already working in geriatric agencies and felt the need to obtain an M.S.W. credential with an aging focus found their way to us, despite Columbia's high tuition and the prohibitive cost of living in New York City. We became a choice training destination. The Columbia "mystique," justified or not, was a contributing factor.

Third, the School attracted a substantial foreign student body, mostly Asian, from Japan, Taiwan, mainland China, Korea, and Hong Kong. Some also came from Latin American countries, and from India, Israel, and Australia. Many of them arrived with a career commitment linked to the aged. Overall, I estimate that between 20 and 25 percent of our gerontological trainees were or are Asians, and I venture to conclude that without them our "field of practice" may not have reached, on more than one occasion, the numerical threshold, the minimum of ten students per course that the School requires.

It has surely been an uphill and exhausting battle to continue "selling" aging. What have we accomplished?

1. Over these twenty-two years we trained some four hundred practitioners. On average, they were about 10 percent of each graduating class. This is, incidentally, twice the national average among schools of social work, and this after taking with a grain of salt how other schools have defined gerontological training. For some, passing a single elective course with aging content may suffice to formally qualify a graduate as a "specialist" in this field.

2. Our graduates have continuously expressed a higher level of satisfaction with their training, as measured in School surveys, than their classmates in all other fields of practice. The upside of teaching gerontology is that stu-

dents come with a clear identification with this field. They are like "true be-lievers," and their enthusiasm often carries and motivates the instructors, not the other way around.

3. The rate of employment among our graduates, when assessed about six months after leaving school, is the highest of their total class and the most consistent with their specialization. That is, they stay in geriatric practice and their career opportunities, as well as their potential for upward mobility, are the fastest when compared with other fields of practice.

In my opinion, we have made it against many odds. It is quite telling that we operate the only specialization in gerontology among the eight or nine M.S.W. programs in the area. But is that enough? Why can't we aim a bit higher and expand beyond the fifteen to twenty students a year we have been averaging? Why do we remain one of the smallest fields of practice? Why can't we meet more adequately the market's demand for gerontological prac-titioners? I was asked all these questions, some ten years ago, by one of our most respected and sympathetic senior colleagues. I responded, first by al-luding to the unfair competition from the most universal field of practice. Everything in social work is health or mental health related, and when stu-dents are given the option between the generic and the specific, it has been proven—I noted—that they opt for the former. But I went a bit beyond this argument and drew a comparison with medical training. Schools of medicine offer a range of options for their graduates' internships. It is known that the overwhelming majority of the graduates wish to get a residence in surgery. Only a few, however, will make it because there is a limited number of va-cancies in the most desired specialties. This is how medical schools make sure that there is a more equitable distribution among all fields, and in accor-dance with available resources and external demand. Are we willing, I asked, to put limits on our more voluminous fields of practice? Can we reduce the size of the health-mental health field of practice, which usually encompasses 60 percent of each graduating class, to, say, 25 to 30 percent, thus ensuring that the overflow would have to accept a second choice in one of the less populated but socially essential specializations? "No," was the answer; we could never get away with it in our school. We must abide by students' choices and desires, I was told. Then, I replied, there is nothing we can do, short of a miracle, to enlarge the enrollment in gerontology, and I added we should be thankful for having survived so far.

TOMORROW

Notwithstanding all these hindrances, I am convinced that there is a future for the aging field of practice in our school. I optimistically believe that Columbia will continue in the forefront of gerontological training at the M.S.W. level, but I am also a realist: we will remain quantitatively a small program, seldom exceeding our past average size, but we must strive to qualitatively rank among the top, if not the best, thus serving as a beacon to other schools. This will largely be a function of an attentive and critical curricular stance.

The social gerontological curriculum must be kept up-to-date, almost on a daily basis, in order to retain its relevance and competitive edge. It may sound like a worn-out cliche but the fact is that we live in a time of accelerated change and we have no option but to adjust to its dizzying pace, while also learning how to anticipate impending trends. Fortunately, it is not as difficult a challenge as it sounds because there are in place all sorts of sensor mechanisms such as think-tanks, research and planning agencies, academic institutions, community observers, interest groups, and investigative reporters that assess events, inventory needs, collect indicators, conduct policy analyses, and forecast possible future scenarios. The White House Conference on Aging of 1995 and many of the regional and local preconferences that anticipated it, constitute a good case in point, albeit not the only ones, of such a mobilization of energies aimed at formulating a renewed agenda on aging. And here we can also find, served on a silver platter, a blueprint of the content areas that ought to be incorporated into a curriculum for the years to come.

The 1995 White House Conference on Aging, the fourth such national meeting held since the 1960s, took place, according to Damron-Rodriguez and Lubben (1997), under the shadow of a zero deficit plan by the year 2000, thus implying that reductions in the provision of services may well become a permanent rather than a temporary reality. It is not surprising then that the Conference resolutions sought primarily to put a halt to the retreat from existing policy provisions. The language of the resolutions in question is saturated with terms such as "preserve," "ensure the availability," "reauthorize," "strengthen," and so forth. The first order of business, according to the leading resolutions, is to maintain the integrity of the great programs launched from 1935 to 1965, that is, Social Security, Medicare, Medicaid, the Older Americans Act, and Supplemental Security Income programs. The forty-one resolutions that were officially approved constitute an explicit agenda and mandate to first ensure the survival and then to fine-tune the programs in reference, so that they can better fit emerging demographic and socio-political realities. Furthermore, the text of the resolutions emphasizes the need to better coordinate and target existing services, assure their highest level of quality and effectiveness, incorporate preventive services that enable the maintenance of wellness throughout a person's lifespan, intensify advocacy functions, assure the adequate provision of long-term care services, expand opportunities for volunteerism, and demand greater public support for research concerning Alzheimer's disease and dementias. It is an ambitious, yet a predictable, agenda that hinges on the imperatives of health and financial security.

At a post–White House Conference convened in Philadelphia by the National Association of Social Workers (October 1995), attention was given to the roles and tasks that the profession at large will have to assume or perform in order to implement these resolutions. Inevitably, and because of the uniqueness of social work's mission in society, a handful of issues acquired special salience. This list of issues may well read as the challenges we will have to face in an immediate curriculum review. I will just mention the following.

First, awareness about the increasing responsibilities grandparents are taking on, not in the proverbial extended families of a nostalgic past, but simply to fill the vacuum left by their own children's overburdened, disintegrating, or dysfunctional nuclear family units. The realization that gerontological social workers do not just limit themselves to old people but attend to the full continuum of living generations is acquiring special prominence. This is associated with the more direct and primary socialization role that grandparents have been expected to assume in recent years.

Second, it will not suffice for gerontological social workers to remain proficient merely in policy entitlements and advocacy skills to secure benefits. They will also have to add versatility and familiarization with legal and ethical concerns. Gerontological social workers find themselves constantly immersed in difficult ethical dilemmas. Some relate to death and dying issues. Others deal with matters of power, control, and self-determination. A third line revolves around basic human rights, such as entitlements and access to care or treatment, without painful limitations and exclusions. A fourth domain has to do with reciprocity and mutual obligations in interpersonal relations across generational lines. The latter probe the extent to which rules of spousal or filial responsibility clash with a caregiver's own rights to fulfill his or her own life. Zena Blau stated that children are caught in an "irredeemable obligation" toward their parents because they can never make up for the initial parental gift of life (1981). Must children then extend a blank check to their parents? Are children bound by a moral imperative which requires them to put their frail parents' care ahead of all other family and personal obligations?

Social workers have to distinguish here, and more and more, between genuine and apparent ethical dilemmas. The latter often tend to be conflicts of interest, or even crude expressions of selfishness, disguised as moral conflicts. For instance, the principle of filial responsibility commands that children secure the best possible care for their older, frail parents. Children, however, are also concerned about the preservation of assets for inheritance purposes and therefore engage in all forms of rationalizations to limit the spending of their parents' resources. It is not that different in the public policy domain, where a cost containment agenda limits access—and de facto rations services—while paying lip service to a rhetoric of quality of care. The new, emerging ethics of the 1980s and 1990s questioned how much and how far society should do and give for a specific population category without infringing on the rights of other claimants. It is an ethic that affirms the legitimacy of setting limits when resources are finite.

Social workers have advocated in large numbers for a national comprehensive health system, like the one in Canada, or Great Britain, without realizing that all universal care systems practice de facto rationing and deny some benefits beyond a certain age. Services and expenditures may even be capped. Enrollees may be subject to systematic and discouraging wait-listing. The danger with such service systems lies in the inevitable arbitrariness of the limits they select. They make choices about the worthiness of each age group, for instance, and often decide that some, like the aged, are, in effect, dispensable. Gerontological practice in social work will have to assume the defense of those who are being marginalized, generally in subtle but equally cruel ways.

There are three final caveats that I regard of critical relevance for curriculum development. The first is that we tend historically to enthrone single ideas and we turn them into fashionable bandwagons. We need more than single answers: it is not just home care, or day care, or case management, or family support, or a multicultural perspective, or electronic computerized gadgetry, but the synergistic articulation of all these elements into a workable and flexible service system.

The second relates to the progressive privatization of geriatric services. Social workers will have to learn how to relate to large corporate systems and understand how they work, how they communicate, what their underlying agendas are, and how they make decisions. We have underscored in our profession the concept and the ideal of "advocacy." Now we need a new "executive" model that will enable us to insert ourselves into the private market as negotiators and facilitators.

The third caveat is the risk of abstract categorizations. Every time that we refer to the people who need our attention as clients, patients, or subjects, we run the risk of depriving them of their personal uniqueness. We may be reducing them to faceless specimens, and yet no two older persons are alike in every sense. Sure, researchers must find the common threads, or the dominant traits that characterize large population aggregates. They can seldom afford to handle so many individualized profiles. There is need for this macro or unifying perspective, but we must also train social work practitioners to gain illuminating insights from single-case designs, that is, on a case-by-case basis. We need, in sum, a curriculum that balances the universal and the particular. Ronald Blythe offered, in his now nearly forgotten book, *The View in Winter* (1979), dozens of life histories and reflections of the very old concerning their "oldness." It is a wonderful text on the uniqueness of each individual life. I would like to conclude with the musings of a then eighty-four-year-old schoolmaster, out of Blythe's pages:

> Old age does not mean that one is entirely old—all old. It is complicated by the retention of a lot of one's youth in an old body. I tend to look upon other old men as old men—and not include myself. It is not vanity, it is just that it is still natural for me to be young in some respects. I am fundamentally the same, and I know that I am still deeply engrained with my boyhood. My boyhood stays imperishable and is such a great part of me.

I do hope that our students will see in each older person a life lived in its totality, including his or her childhood and youth. Only then will they have the skill to successfully bridge the span between generation and generation. Isn't this what our mission is all about?

REFERENCES

Blau, Z. (1981). *Aging in a Changing Society* (2nd ed.). New York: F. Watts.

Bloom, B. (1958). Ideas, Problems, and Methods of Inquiry. In N. B. Henry (Ed.), *The Integration of Educational Experiences.* National Society for the Study of Education, Fifty-Seventh Yearbook. Chicago: University of Chicago Press.

Blythe, R. (1979). *The View in Winter: Reflections on Old Age.* New York: Harcourt Brace Jovanovich.

Brunner, J. (1960). *The Process of Education.* Cambridge, MA: Harvard University Press.

Carroll, N. K. (1975). Areas of Concentration in the Graduate Curriculum: A Three-Dimensional Model. *Journal of Education for Social Work,* 11(2), 3–10.

Damron-Rodriguez, J. A. and Lubben, J. E. (1997). The 1995 WHCoA: An Agenda for Social Work Education and Training. *Journal of Gerontological Social Work,* 27(3), 65–78.

Damron-Rodriguez, J. A., Villa, Tseng, H. F., and Lubben, J. E. (1997). Demographic and Organizational Influences on the Development of the Gerontological Social Work Curriculum. *Gerontology and Geriatrics Education,* 17(3), 3–8.

Gibelman, M. and Schervish, P. H. (1993). *Who We Are: The Social Labor Force as Reflected in NASW Membership.* Washington, DC: National Association of Social Workers Press.

Lidz, T. (1983). *The Person: His and Her Development Throughout the Life Cycle.* New York: Basic Books.

Lowy, L. (1985). *Social Work with the Aging: The Challenge and Promise of the Later Years* (2nd ed.). New York: Longman.

Monk, A. (1975). A Conceptual Base for Second Generation Programs in Gerontological Social Work. *Journal of Social Work Education,* 11(3), 84–88.

Monk, A. (1981). Social Work with the Aged: Principles of Practice. *Social Work,* 27(3), 65–78.

Nelson, G. M. and Schneider, R. L. (1984). *The Current Status of Gerontology in Graduate Social Work Education.* Washington, DC: Council on Social Work Education.

Studt, E. (1965). Fields of Social Work Practice: Organizing our Resources for More Effective Practice. *Social Work,* 11(2), 3–10.

Twenty Hot Job Tracks. (1995, October). *US News and World Report,* pp. 98–108.

Chapter 11

WORLD OF WORK

Sheila H. Akabas

We are gathered today to celebrate the history of social work, and it is my assignment to apply this positive orientation to social work in the workplace. This has been a difficult paper for me to write because I am troubled, as I feel sure many of you are, by the changes I see in social work. In recent years, social work has seemed to have an increasingly limited impact on setting the social welfare agenda in American society, and that agenda has certainly turned negative in the recent past. My challenge is to praise our history, accomplishments, and potential without ignoring these negative circumstances. I propose to consider the interconnections between the world of work and social welfare—what has happened, what is happening, and what can happen in the future to improve our world—in short, how occupational social work has and can contribute to a positive agenda for the profession and to community social welfare in the future, what is standing in the way of this accomplishment, and what are some of the ways in which we can overcome those barriers.

It seems wise to start with the context in which this is taking place. Change is a constant to which we are all accustomed. The evolution of humanity and society is a theme throughout history. But if one takes a step back and peruses the landscape, it is apparent that the pace of change has quickened. In fact, the last decade of the twentieth century can more appropriately be identified as a period of revolution rather than the outcome of an evolutionary process. Fax machines, the Internet, cyberspace, the information age, global markets, a single superpower, and vast international migrations are some of its hallmarks. Only H. G. Wells and a handful of Bill Gates's followers might have predicted all this just a decade ago.

The cusp of this revolution has been found in the world of work. Rapid transportation, new technologies, and new means of communication have brought both global competition and cross-national corporate cooperation, adding a whole new dimension to the life cycle of organizations and their leaders. Not surprising in an era of such rapid change, it is left to some aspects of society to bring up the rear. This role is often typical of the professions which are tied to their relatively more stable knowledge bases and methodologies. So even as they may be battered by a sense of change, social work as a profession, and social agencies as settings, have remained quite consistent in their culture, policies, and practices. There are still social agencies that are without computers, despite the demands for productivity, funding accountability, participation in governmental databases, and useful information that can be accessed through the Internet. There are still social agencies fighting the battle for protection of long-term psychological counseling despite the combined pressures of managed care insurers and research findings concerning the positive value of brief therapy (Corwin 1993; Orlinsky and Howard 1986; Reid and Hanrahan 1982; Reid and Shyne 1969).

But for those involved in social work in the workplace, the luxury of marking time, of "business as usual," is not available. The very connection that occupational social work has with the labor and management parties, which are themselves at the cusp of the revolution, demands a parallel action by any profession related to these sites. What this has meant in application is restrictions inherent in the high visibility that accompanies all the actions of occupational social work, and a demand that practice formulations be based on outcome measures related to productivity, containment of medical care costs, attendance, and turnover. But it has also provided an opportunity for occupational social work to lead the profession down the new paths possible in the twenty-first century. I will examine how occupational social work has made use of that opportunity. But I am getting ahead of the story.

YESTERDAY

No one can think about occupational social work without touching base with Freud's theoretical formulation of the hallmarks of adult functioning—the ability to love and to work (Freud 1930). Those in the field have long accepted that underpinning, noting, however, that Freud went on to concentrate on love, leaving to us the responsibility of mining the work side of the hallmark conditions. But not everyone would agree with Freud about the value of work. Many have viewed work as the necessary evil to be endured on the road to affording leisure and play, and this theme continues to resonate among some today (Macarov 1982; Wagner 1994). In fact, there is a long and sometimes acrimonious debate concerning the contribution of work to the well-being of humanity (Shostack 1982). The historic picture of the reclining Greek noble-man, able to enjoy the luxuries of life without work because of the slave, in bondage, exerting superhuman effort to perform impossible physical feats and falling by the wayside in the attempt, does little to enhance the image of work. A review of medieval and later Western history suggests that, in the agricultural economy, the avoidance of work was the goal that made holidays so frequent and so dearly loved. Early industrialization did little to heighten the reputation of work. For most, factory labor was dull, dirty, and dangerous. Accidents were rampant. The demands of most work were acknowledged to destroy the body and the spirit. Power was centralized in the hands of the few and poverty was widely distributed in the lives of the many.

But the realities of subsistence living have always made work necessary, and slowly work has taken on a more even keel, at least in the United States and most of the rest of the Western world. The Protestant ethic managed to elevate work to the status of insurance of a heavenly end. The rise of trade unionism in those countries has provided a measure of protection against the worst ills of industrialization. We know, however, that the theme of work as a negative continues and that the early industrial conditions are still rampant elsewhere in the world. The disaster of Bhopal, where thousands died in the aftermath of a chemical leak, and Chernobyl, were only the merest eruption of the deadly volcano that keeps children working in unbearable conditions and adults receiving less than poverty wages throughout the developing coun-tries so that we can enjoy cheap sneakers and clothing and industrial manage-ment can enhance its sometimes obscene profit levels.

Subsistence living may have made work necessary, but it seems clear, none-theless, that people wish to work. Studies on the work ethic are illuminating. Given an opportunity to retire because of the windfall of being a lottery win-ner, most report a continued expectation to work. Comparative studies of the work ethic across nations confirm that the vast majority of Americans view work as a desired and desirable activity (MOW International Research Team 1987). In fact, there has been a long struggle in the United States to pass legislation to equalize the starting line so that access to work is more available to all. Under such circumstances, those who assist people to achieve and sus-tain the goal of stable work are somehow ennobled. This has been the role and opportunity of occupational social work.

Some would date the beginnings of social work in the workplace to the house mothers who watched over the living arrangements of the farm girls who came to work in the early mills, to earn money for their dowries (Popple 1981). These women helped the young girls acclimate to the demands of the factory system, but also watched over their "morality" until they returned home to wed. They were followed by Lady Bountiful, who carried her charity to the homes of working families when illness or death occurred and wages were insufficient to cover immediate needs (Wagner, Queen, and Harper 1930). Too often, these ladies came with their own moralistic message, removing their aid from poor families who were without resources because the breadwinner chose to support a union strike against inhuman and underpaid working conditions. Neither of these beginnings represents a great history upon which to build a positive professional presence. Others, therefore, focus on origins in the 1920s when the Hawthorne experiments encouraged management to pay attention to workers and their needs, and resulted in some social work presence in the world of work (Dickson and Roethlisberger 1966). Whenever one dates the start, it seems clear that the goal of these early efforts was twofold: to help meet the basic survival needs of labor force participants and to keep workers working by ameliorating any conditions that could interfere with their ability to contribute to corporate and national productivity.

The depression of the '30s ended any employer-sponsored benevolence, but both employer and government interests converged during World War II to direct social workers and social services into the workplace as everyone understood the intimate connection between productivity and national survival and the dependence of both on employee well-being. Day care arrangements for working mothers, services to members of the armed forces, and the great contributions of Bertha Reynolds (1951), who advocated bringing services to the natural life space (including the workplace) of those in need of services, marked the war years, only to disappear from the postwar scene with the expectation that women would return to their homes.

We come, then, to the more recent incarnation of social work and the workplace — services delivered to workers, and their dependents, at work, or through the auspices of labor and management, and/or community services directed at entering the world of work or sustaining one's role in that world (Weiner et al. 1971). The great appeal of workplace-sited services includes their availability as an entitlement with eligibility universal to all employees/ members, the early intervention, and, therefore, prevention that they make possible, the resources the parties (labor and management) can bring to bear, the destigmatized setting in which they are offered, and the target as functional performance rather than long-term well-being (Akabas 1995).

In this incarnation, Columbia has played a major role. I hope you will all forgive me a personal memory digression at this point. From the early 1950s, I was privileged to be working with the late Dr. Howard Rusk on issues of rehabilitation of people with disabilities, with particular focus on employment opportunities for them. In 1960, the late Dr. Morris Brand, then medical director of the Sidney Hillman Health Center of the Amalgamated Clothing and Textile Workers Union, an early health care facility jointly sponsored by management and labor, came to Dr. Rusk and indicated his interest in establishing a rehabilitation program at the Hillman Center for workers in the men's clothing industry who were losing time from work because of disability. Dr. Rusk asked me to consult with Dr. Brand and to write a proposal for funding from the then Rehabilitation Services Administration of the U.S. Department of Health, Education, and Welfare, for a rehabilitation study of the impact of physical disability on workers in the industry. The proposal was funded, and since I was at the time a mother with a new third baby, I was available for only two days of work a week. We looked for someone who could direct the project, and were fortunate to find Hyman Weiner, then a doctoral student at Columbia University School of Social Work whose father had been a worker in the men's clothing industry. With Hy directing, I took on the role of research director, probably one of the first workers to receive a workplace accommodation to balance work and family life. I worked two days a week in New York, and at least one day from home. Together we carried out the original proposal I had written, and followed it with another to the National Institute of Mental Health which was also funded. Hy's doctoral dissertation, which was the basis of a publication from the first project (Weiner, Akabas, and Grynbaum 1964), and my dissertation from the second (Akabas 1970) were the results.

These projects were the first in the nation to look seriously at the demand for rehabilitation in a working population and to enlist the joint efforts of labor and management in return-to-work activity (Weiner, Akabas, and Sommer 1973). The reports delineated roles for the industrial parties in the rehabilitation and continuing employment of workers despite physical or emotional disability. Increasing interest, nationally, in rehabilitation resulted in 1967 in the Rehabilitation Services Administration (RSA), then a unit of the

U.S. Department of Health, Education, and Welfare (HEW), funding ten regional centers to examine the role of rehabilitation for various populations. We were invited to establish such a center, in this HEW region, for workplace issues. Hy had just received a doctorate from Columbia and been invited to join its faculty. We proposed, and the University accepted, establishing the Industrial Social Welfare Center at Columbia in November 1967, with five years of funding from RSA, and the rest is history.

With Hy as director, and with me serving as research director, we delineated the field of industrial social work in a monograph that had a significant impact on social work thinking and education thereafter (Weiner et al. 1971). In 1970, Paul Kurzman joined our staff as program director, starting a partnership between Paul and myself that has been important to each of us and, I believe, the field of social work in the workplace to this date. We have jointly authored significant scholarly work in this field (Kurzman and Akabas 1981; Akabas and Kurzman 1982; Kurzman and Akabas 1993) and are presently at work on our third textbook, for the Columbia University Press "Curriculum in Social Work" series. Dr. Weiner left the Center to accept the deanship of the New York University School of Social Work in 1973, and unfortunately died at a young age without returning to the intellectual development of the field.

The Industrial Social Welfare Center had a name change in 1975 to reflect the changes in function in American workplaces. It became the Center for Social Policy and Practice in the Workplace (the Workplace Center) and has continued to serve as a knowledge bank and major research component for the development of occupational social work throughout the three decades of its existence. Projects it has undertaken generated such memorable outcomes as the establishment of the Personal Services Unit and the Municipal Employees Legal Services at District Council 37, AFSCME, AFL-CIO, the Members Assistance Program at the International Ladies Garment Workers Union, the Employee Assistance Program at the five hospitals connected with Cornell Med/Rockefeller Institute, the training of all firefighters in New York City to accept gender integration of the fire department, quality assurance measurement of employee services in the Metropolitan Transit Authority, and numerous research projects defining the conditions under which it is possible to maintain, at work, people with social problems or physical and mental disabilities, to name just a few.

At the same time, students began to be placed at field sites that had programs that the Center had developed. When fields of practice were established at Columbia, the world of work became one of the four original fields of practice. Columbia was the first school in the country to do so, becoming a model for other schools (Akabas 1978). The first national conference on social work in the workplace was organized, in 1978, jointly by Columbia University and Hunter College, Paul Kurzman having moved to join Hunter's faculty and having established the field of practice there (Columbia University School of Social Work Industrial Social Welfare Center 1980). The conference, funded by the Silberman Foundation, provided support for bringing together one hundred practitioners in the workplace from throughout the United States along with a carefully chosen group of scholars interested in each aspect of the social work curriculum, including Martha Ozawa, Gerald Cohen, Leon Chestang, Helen Harris Perlman, Rino Patti, and Jack Rothman. Indeed, the field was so new that we had difficulty finding one hundred practitioners. Today, it is estimated that there are several thousand social workers involved exclusively in this field of practice. Subsequently, Paul Kurzman and I were asked to serve as master teachers for the Council on Social Work Education, to help spread interest and build capacity for this field of practice in other schools throughout the country. Programs at the University of Southern California, Pittsburgh University, and several others resulted from that initiative. The leading role of Columbia and the Workplace Center has continued unabated. More could be said, but now I return to the main story.

TODAY

There are at least two underlying assumptions that serve as building blocks for the rationale of occupational social work. The field assumes that work is a normative human activity in which most people would opt to participate and that service delivery systems are voluntary and in keeping with the mandates of the social work profession's code of ethics. Interpreting this means that, regardless of auspice, the social worker is the agent of the individual client when delivering direct service, with confidentiality protected, and is bound by the requirements of ethical professional behavior at all times, even when serving as organizational spokesperson and change agent.

Within this framework, all the varied methodologies of the profession are relevant, from individual treatment to community organizing and advocacy. Some of this we have done extremely well, and in other aspects of practice, we have failed our professional mandates. The remainder of this paper will examine this issue of the potential for, and actual achievement of, the social work mission in occupational settings and services. This mission can be described as attention to individual needs, human rights, and social and economic justice. For those practicing in this arena, success in direct service delivery has been notable. Starting with roots in alcohol and drug abuse initiatives, services have expanded into a broad brush model that offers individual assistance around the variety of problems adults and families encounter— marital difficulties and elder care issues, health care choices, and childcare needs, to name just a few. Innovations have included a model of short-term treatment that handles traumatic workplace events, often described as "critical incident" counseling, and interdisciplinary collaboration with an array of partners unknown in other social service settings, e.g., union shop stewards and business agents, corporate safety and benefit managers, and various human resource personnel. Many individuals have been able to remain at, or return to, work because of the availability of these services (Googins and Davidson 1993; Raber 1996; Gould and Smith 1988; Mudrick 1991; Bell 1995).

But the case can also be made that our practice in the world of work is a litany of missed opportunities. All of us, both professionals within the work setting and those outside it, have contributed to, and share in, the loss that can be identified and observed. In the world of missed opportunity, I would suggest that social workers in the workplace have played a winning game. Some years ago a survey was done by the Workplace Center of Employee Assistance Program directors who belonged to the Association of Labor-Management Administrators and Consultants in Alcoholism. The focus was on how they dealt with disability in their settings. Although many were quick to cite their contribution to working with employees with mental health problems, fewer than 10 percent regarded workers with physical disabilities as within their responsibility. This was, to us, a shocking example of the narrowness of focus of even those who are embedded in the world of work. Surely, few threats to continued employment are more evident than those resulting from limitations of functional capacity. Disability is evident in every workplace and represents a costly phenomenon. In fact, once health care costs were brought under some control as a result of managed care, the next biggest drain on corporate benefit budgets was the costs of disability, both those that are work connected, resulting in compensation claims, and those that have no connection with work, but result in lost time and costly medical care and short, or even long-term, disability payments. And here was turf that no one was claiming. Into that vacuum, social workers could so easily have stepped. We may ask, why did they remain aloof?

Or, consider the whole issue of family and work. Social workers know the cost to families of demanding and stressful work, of inflexible work schedules, of unexpected overtime, of travel connected with work, and of corporate transfers that disrupt the relationships that families have built over the years. It is social workers who hear about the difficulties in finding childcare for working families and the problems that the "sandwich generation" experiences in trying to meet the needs of the young and of older family members while trying to maintain their own work roles. Yet, social workers have been relatively voiceless in bringing these issues to the attention of businesses, unions, and government, and in seeking solutions to the fallout from inflexible work schedules and lack of community services for working families. They have not advocated as a profession for family-responsive policies in the workplace, nor have they done the research that could document the massive gap between family needs and workplace policies. Susan Lambert (1993) argues, in fact, that programs created in the workplace are directed at removing the family as a concern so that employees can concentrate on work rather than being directed at developing family-friendly programs in the hope that the workplace will benefit over the long run.

There are numerous prescriptions for how social workers in work settings should use their opportunities (Akabas and Gates 2000; Googins and Burden 1987; Iversen 1998; Jones 1992; Mor-Barak and Tynan 1993; Mudrick 1991; Vourlekis, Edinburg, and Knee 1998; Wilk 1988). In general, they lay claim to the fact that occupational social workers may be thought of as a professional group working "where the action is." Such social workers are at the site where opportunities are distributed and resources are allocated. The question arises as to what can be done with the professional role at that site. It replicates a question often heard in real estate circles concerning what makes a property so valuable. The answer is "location, location, location." Little else matters in real estate if a property is located in a pivotal position. Location accrues great value to the property, almost regardless of its condition. The same may be said for occupational social workers. Having access to the power of employers and labor unions and working with people with strength, struggling though they may be with the serious problems of life, job retention, and work opportunities, the possibilities of carrying a significant role, both in world of work settings and in the larger professional community, are great.

Ramanathan (1992) has suggested that "occupational social workers need to advocate for job enrichment and redesign activities and to offer services as consultants to personnel departments" (238). Coulton (1996) has suggested an even more activist role. She examined the issue of work activity among welfare families and found that many work in unreported jobs. She suggests that, to achieve an increase in work activity that would promote an end to welfare, new jobs need to have significantly higher wages and future opportunities that are better than the underground economy offers. Surely, occupational social workers can promote management interest in meeting that need by pointing out the ultimate impact on profits of a satisfied labor force and a fully employed economy. Further, we need to help policymakers recognize that security at work is based on support, education, and training. To accomplish work goals, intensive, long-term, individualized services across many levels are essential. Band-aids will not cover the sore of long-term unemployment. Jones (1992) offers a directive in this regard. He notes:

> Equity would mean redistributing available work to ensure that no group enjoyed more right than any other in obtaining employment . . . Equity would also demand vigorous enforcement of laws designed to end discrimination in the labor force. (362)

Examining professional role in another context, Vourlekis et al. (1998) have identified "the important reality that strengthening a profession takes place by creating turf, not just defending it" (547). We have an opportunity to legitimate and validate the voices and language of those who are unheard. In a society such as ours, where work is so vital and significant, professionals at the site of work have a special obligation to help assure work for all. The advantages of occupational social workers are their knowledge of the language of the workplace, their contact with the power brokers of the economic society, and their access to data to establish a convincing case for the need for, and value of, their services. They have the potential to influence a wide arena by using the trust, respect, and credibility that accrues to them from their position to advocate policy recommendations for the good of the many and offer their professional selves to give voice to the economically disadvantaged who seek entry into the world of work.

TOMORROW

Several observers argue that we cannot expect social work outcomes unless we assume an activist role in social policy. The advice seems applicable here. We are furthering the mission of the profession when we serve the needs of those who experience discrimination, especially in the labor market. Social workers can bring a humanist approach to work settings and to social welfare policy which involves work while helping business and labor to succeed. All research indicates that the secret to success is a productive workforce, and the secret to a productive workforce is to assure workers' understanding that they are valued and that they have an opportunity to grow and develop. We are experts in helping people understand how to make that happen.

Because none of this has happened so far, it seems clear that some fundamental changes are needed in social work. For example, social workers can

- define work, in our practice and policy approaches, as an expected option for all individuals, and give it the attention it deserves;

- expect our educational system to graduate social work professionals with the skill to understand how to evaluate clients' work experience and employment potential and their fit with labor market conditions;

- understand the nature of occupational welfare benefits and arrangements in the same way that they understand the provisions of social welfare legislation, including knowing how to advocate for their working clients within the occupational system;

- engage in political advocacy calling for a full-employment economy with a minimum wage that supports a family above the poverty level, and training programs that make the unemployed appropriate applicants for jobs with promotional potential;

- support trade unions in their struggle for full-time jobs with adequate health insurance and pension benefits;

- assure a service system that is comfortable providing vocational exploration, career planning, job counseling, and support for the temporarily unemployed;

- encourage employers to balance the demands of work with those emanating from the other dimensions of an individual's life and to create accommodation systems to meet individual needs;

- stop compulsively directing society's attention to the most needy while ignoring the opportunities to commit to prevention among working, but suffering persons;

- help business understand the high cost of not attending to the needs of its employees and those who seek entry into the world of work;

- create human resource policies in our own agencies that reflect our highest expectations of employer behavior;

- invest service delivery dollars in keeping youths in school and maintaining workers in jobs; and

- include representatives from labor and employers on our agency boards and other policy-setting bodies. (Akabas and Gates 2000)

Change is the eternal burden that the human species carries, and the eternal opportunity as well. I believe that occupational social workers have a great opportunity to create positive change in our economy and our society, and that they dare not miss that opportunity.

REFERENCES

Akabas, S. (1970). *Labor force characteristics, mental illness and earnings in the men's clothing industry of New York City.* Unpublished doctoral dissertation, New York University.

—— (1978). Fieldwork in industrial settings: Opportunities, rewards, and dilemmas. *Journal of Education for Social Work, 14*(3), 13–19.

—— (1995). Occupational social work. *Encyclopedia of social work* (19th ed., pp. 1779–1785). Washington, DC: National Association of Social Workers Press.

Akabas, S. and Gates, L. (2000). A social work role: Promoting employment equity for people with serious and persistent mental illness. *Administration in Social Work, 23*(3–4), 163–184.

Akabas, S. and Kurzman, P. (Eds.). (1982). *Work, workers and work organizations: A view from social work.* Englewood Cliffs, NJ: Prentice-Hall.

Bell, J. (1995). Traumatic even debriefing: Service delivery designs and the role of social work. *Social Work, 40,* 36–43.

Columbia University School of Social Work Industrial Social Welfare Center; Hunter College School of Social Work, City University of New York, World of Work Program; Council on Social Work Education. (1980). *Meeting human service needs in the workplace: A role for social work.* New York: Author.

Corwin, M. (1993). Solution-focused brief workplace counseling. In P. Kurzman and S. Akabas (Eds.), *Work and well-being: The occupational social work advantage* (pp. 200–238). Washington, DC: National Association of Social Workers Press.

Coulton, C. (1996). Poverty, work and community: A research agenda for an era of diminishing federal responsibility. *Social Work, 41,* 509–519.

Dickson, W. and Roethlisberger, F. (1966). *Counseling in an organization: A sequel to the Hawthorne researches.* Cambridge, MA: Harvard University Press.

Freud, S. (1930). *Civilization and its discontents.* New York: J. Cape and H. Smith.

Googins, B. and Burden, D. (1987). Vulnerability of working parents: Balancing work and home roles. *Social Work, 32,* 295–299.

Googins, B. and Davidson, B. (1993). The organization as client: Broadening the concept of employee assistance programs. *Social Work, 39,* 477–484.

Gould, G. and Smith, M. (Eds.). (1988). *Social work in the workplace.* New York: Springer.

Iversen, R. (1998). Occupational social work for the twenty-first century. *Social Work, 43,* 551–566.

Jones, L. (1992). The full employment myth: Alternative solutions to unemployment. *Social Work, 37,* 359–364.

Kurzman, P. and Akabas, S. (1981). Industrial social work as an arena for practice. *Social Work, 26,* 52–60.

Kurzman, P. and Akabas, S. (Eds.). (1993). *Work and well-being: The occupational social work advantage.* Washington, DC: National Association of Social Workers Press.

Lambert, S. (1993). Workplace policies as social policy. *Social Service Review, 67*(2), 237–260.

Macarov, D. (1982). *Worker productivity: Myths and reality.* Beverly Hills, CA: Sage.

Mor-Barak, M. and Tynan, M. (1993). Older workers and the workplace: A new challenge for occupational social work. *Social Work, 38,* 45–55.

MOW International Research Team. (1987). *The meaning of working.* London: Academic Press.

Mudrick, N. (1991). An underdeveloped role for occupational social work: Facilitating the employment of people with disabilities. *Social Work, 36,* 490–495.

Orlinsky, D. and Howard, K. (1986). Process and outcome in psychotherapy. In S. Garfield and A. Bergin (Eds.), *Handbook of psychotherapy and behavior change* (3rd ed., pp. 311–381). New York: Wiley.

Popple, P. (1981, June). Social work practice in business and industry, 1875–1930. *Social Service Review, 55,* 257–268.

Raber, M. (1996). Downsizing of the nation's labor force and a needed social work response. *Administration in Social Work, 20,* 47–58.

Ramanathan, C. (1992). EAP's response to personal stress and productivity: Implications for occupational social work. *Social Work, 37,* 234–239.

Reid, W. and Hanrahan, P. (1982). Recent evaluations of social work: Grounds for optimism. *Social Work, 27,* 328–340.

Reid, W. and Shyne, A. (1969). *Brief and extended casework.* New York: Columbia University Press.

Reynolds, B. (1951). *Social work and social living.* New York: Citadel.

Shostack, A. (1982). Work meanings through Western history: From Athens to Detroit and beyond. In S. Akabas and P. Kurzman (Eds.), *Work, workers and work organizations: A view from social work* (pp. 5–31). Englewood Cliffs, NJ: Prentice-Hall.

Vourlekis, B., Edinburg, G., and Knee, R. (1998). The rise of social work in public mental health through aftercare of people with serious mental illness. *Social Work, 43,* 567–575.

Wagner, D. (1994). Beyond the pathologizing of nonwork: Alternative activities in a street community. *Social Work, 39,* 718–727.

Wagner, Queen, and Harper. (1930).

Weiner, H., Akabas, S., and Grynbaum, B. (1964). *Demand for rehabilitation in a labor union population: Part 1. Research report.* New York: Sidney Hillman Health Center of New York.

Weiner, H., Akabas, S., and Sommer, J. (1973). *Mental health care in the world of work.* New York: Association Press.

Weiner, H., Akabas, S., Sommer, J., and Kremins, E. (1971). *The world of work and social welfare policy.* New York: Columbia University School of Social Work Industrial Social Welfare Center.

Wilk, R. (1988). Assisting in affirmative action and equal employment opportunity. In G. Gould and M. Smith (Eds.), *Social work in the workplace* (pp. 213–228). New York: Springer.

Chapter 12

INTERNATIONAL SOCIAL WELFARE

Sheila B. Kamerman

The concept of a social work "field of practice" (substantive expertise regarding particular populations, problems, or settings) in addition to a social work "method" (special interventions targeted at individuals, families, groups, communities, and the society as a whole) has a long history in social work but a more recent history at the Columbia University School of Social Work (CUSSW). Only in 1977 did the selection of a field of practice become a curriculum requirement (Kamerman 1995). However, international social welfare as a field of practice and an alternative to the "big" fields such as child and family welfare, aging, and health care, is still more recent, dating only from 1995. Nonetheless, CUSSW is the first graduate school of social work to establish such a field of practice, including both a required "foundation" or "platform" course and a year-long field practicum for students who already have completed their first year in the program and are interested in international work.

Early recognition of the importance of international social welfare, and inclusion of relevant content about it in the curriculum identified CUSSW as a "world-class" educational and training institution from its beginning. Despite the recent history of a formal field of practice and assigned curriculum space, CUSSW has had a long history—from its inception—of incorporating components of international social welfare into the School's curriculum and overall program. Thus, for example, there have been relevant courses taught at the School almost since it was first established. There have been relevant field experiences available to students. There have been significant numbers of international students enrolled at the School (or "foreign" students as they used to be called). There have been special international projects at the School. And, there has been extensive involvement of faculty in international social welfare training, research, and consultations. The pattern has not been consistent over the years, however. There was extensive interest in the first half-century, then a hiatus for almost a decade from about 1953, when the United States, too, seemed to have less interest in things international. Then, renewed interest emerged from early in the 1960s until the present, with the School having an increasingly visible international component in more recent years.

In this paper, I will trace the development of international social welfare within the School of Social Work, in the past and at present, and make some comments about possible future directions. During each period, I will pay attention to curriculum developments, the presence of international students, special projects at or linked with the School, and the activities of individual faculty members who have played especially influential roles in the field.

INTERNATIONAL SOCIAL WELFARE: THE DEFINITION [1]

International social welfare, as a field of practice, includes those activities of intergovernmental organizations and nongovernmental organizations (voluntary agencies) operating cross-nationally, and those activities of national governments in their interactions with other governments, regarding social policies, programs, and practices. These activities include (but are not limited to) technical assistance; exchange of ideas, personnel, and information; cross-national research; and direct service provision. The direct service provision includes immigration and refugee programs, programs in response to natural and human-made disasters, and intercountry adoptions. Those carrying out these activities are not necessarily social workers, but social work is clearly relevant to the work. International social work, in contrast to international social welfare, is social work practice in a setting carrying out the above activities.

In contrast to other social work fields of practice, international social welfare does not have a clearly defined or strong legislative framework. The only relevant examples of U.S. legislation are the several immigration laws beginning in the nineteenth century and continuing to the present. In particular, there is the long history of open immigration with some constraints such as the "closing of the doors" in 1924 with the Johnson-Reed Act, which set a yearly limit of 150,000 immigrants from outside the western hemisphere and then allocated those on the basis of a country's share of the total population in 1920. This "national origins" system favored the descendants of those who had been in the United States the longest, the British and Northern Europeans. The legislation prevailed for forty-one years, severely restricting immigration to the United States. Legislation enacted in 1965 (the Immigration and Nationality Act) opened the doors again, but now based on the principle of "family reunification," without imposing any numerical limit on those admitted on that basis. Legislation enacted in 1980 provided special protection for political refugees, while in 1986 legislation offered amnesty to a large number of illegal immigrants, and the 1990 law set a priority on immigrants with special skills. Over the last couple of decades, immigration to the United States has totaled about eight hundred thousand a year. Important components of international social welfare are policies, programs, and practices related to immigrants and refugees, whether in this country or elsewhere, such as the Albanians and Serbians in Kosovo or who fled Kosovo in 1999, and the displaced persons in several of the Sub-Saharan African countries.

Apart from the U.S. immigration laws, there are numerous international agreements that help frame the field. Thus, for example, the International Labor Organization (ILO), heavily dominated by developing countries, adopts conventions—international agreements concerning the safety, health, and well-being of workers—which member states are encouraged to sign and then enact in relevant national legislation. To illustrate, one relevant convention was first adopted in 1919 (No. 3), revised in 1953 (No. 103), and revised again in June 2000. This convention has to do with maternity protection at the time of childbirth, and specifies that working women should be assured of at least fourteen weeks of paid and job-protected leave at that time. Although less than half of the approximately 130 member countries have signed this convention, an additional large group have in fact enacted compatible legislation, and the convention is often touted as an example of a particularly important social policy standard for women and children. Another example of a relevant ILO activity is the intense campaign the organization has waged in recent years against child labor.

Another form of international agreement affecting the field are conventions established by the United Nations (UN). Thus, for example, the UN Convention on the Rights of the Child has been adopted by every member country except the United States and Somalia, and by more countries than any other UN convention. The United States's refusal is based on several issues, including its federal system of government, which assigns certain authority to the states rather than the federal government; the U.S. historical objection to signing agreements that it does not intend to implement (in contrast to the actions of many of the other signing countries); and the conservatives in the U.S. Congress who reject the concept of a policy that would or might "undermine" parental authority. Nonetheless, this convention has been extremely influential, with many of the European countries, in particular, enacting legislation stressing protection of children's rights. Indeed, much child policy discussion in Europe today is framed by the convention and the concept of children's rights.

Other relevant international agreements that frame certain aspects of the field include transnational agreements regarding social security, child support, and intercountry adoptions that are made by national governments with one another. Thus, setting the framework for this field of practice are U.S. laws which set immigration and refugee policy as well as international agreements which frame cross-national and national behavior. However, most of the activity in the field goes beyond these and involves significant government aid in cases of natural and human-made disasters, and extensive activities by nongovernmental organizations (NGOs).

THE PAST: THE FIRST FIFTY YEARS

From the very beginning of the School of Social Work, as Meier (1954) points out in her history, a significant part of the training and educational program involved both work with immigrants and comparative social policy. A course was taught on Immigration and Phases of Relief Work soon after the School was first established. A few years later, in 1912–13, I. M. Rubinow, the well-known scholar and advocate of social security, taught a fifteen-week series of lectures in the spring semester on social insurance. Earlier, he had been responsible for the U.S. commissioner of labor's massive report, *Workmen's Insurance and Compensation Programs in Europe,* covering eleven countries and presenting a systematic summary of European social insurance developments. Subsequently, in 1913, he published an influential book based on his lectures, with recommendations for the United States that would only begin to be implemented twenty years later.

From the early years to World War II, at least one course on immigration—and often more—was taught at the School, covering the problems of immigrants, the kinds of services and other types of help available to them regarding their adaptation to a new country (in contrast to what they needed), and direct practice with immigrants and their families. Over the years, the courses were taught by such faculty members as Kate Holladay Claghorn, a Yale Ph.D. in social research who had earlier worked for the U.S. Census Bureau, and Mary Hurlbutt, who had been an early graduate of the School (1913), was trained as an anthropologist at Columbia and Yale, and worked subsequently as the international director of the International Migration Service. She joined the faculty in 1931. Hurlbutt was one of the main contributors to the 1933–34 Pittsburgh study directed by Phillip Klein, and she carried out an influential study of recent immigrants. Her findings underscored the inadequacies of existing responses by social agencies to the needs of new immigrants, and the latter's problems in accessing social benefits and services.

Walter Pettit, who became a member of the faculty in 1915, assistant director of the School in 1917, and director in 1939, had a strong international orientation as well, derived in part from his prior experience teaching in the Philippine Islands and acting as a special assistant at the U.S. Embassy in Petrograd, Russia, in 1916–17. In reporting on faculty activities in 1924, he made a particular point of the experience of one faculty member who spent his sabbatical at the London School of Economics in London, England, citing this as an example of a good use of a sabbatical experience.

World War II clearly raised consciousness regarding international developments, but did not have as much of an impact on the School as one might have anticipated. During the war and immediately after, additional courses were taught by Hurlbutt, one on The Problems of Aliens, and a second, which was listed in the bulletin for about four years, from 1947 until 1951 and then again in 1954 and 1955, on Inter Country Family Service, dealing in part with the post–World War II problems of searching for family members lost during the war (or, perhaps, during the Holocaust).

Meier, in her history of the School's first fifty years, noted that the war years placed new demands on the profession but that "no fundamental changes were made in the curriculum" (Meier 1954:8). Some special courses were offered, such as Child Care in Wartime, Psychiatric Aspects of Veterans' Problems, and Administrative Problems in International Social Work, but no significant changes were carried out. She also pointed out that "many young men and women of the Armed Forces, who had never before considered social work as a career, were exposed to experiences which led them to choose this profession" (8).

Several faculty members became actively involved in various international social welfare activities, and in the development of new schools of social work in other countries. Before the United States entered the war, Mary Hurlbutt had gone to Europe to help arrange for refugee children to be brought to this country. Another faculty member, Clarence King, took a leave in 1944 to become executive secretary of the American Council of Voluntary Agencies for Foreign Service. A special summer training course was given in 1945 for twenty-five French women who were planning on returning to France to help in rehabilitation work. Herman Stein, Phillip Klein, and Clara Kaiser were actively involved in international relief operations in Europe and Klein played a major role in the establishment in Paris of the Paul Baerwald School of Social Work to deal with some of the consequences of World War II and the Holocaust and which subsequently became part of the Hebrew University in Jerusalem.

As to trends with regard to international students, as revealed in several School bulletins and reports: from about 1912 to the late 1930s, about 5 percent of the School's graduates were from outside the United States. In the years 1912–1925 in particular, these students came from as disparate a group of countries as the following: in Asia and the Pacific, from Hawaii, New Zealand, India, the Philippines, and Japan; and in the West, from Canada, France, Rumania, and Switzerland. Between 1920 and 1926, the School had sixty-five students in residence from twenty-five different countries. The graduating class in 1930 included seven students from Canada, five from China, and one or two each from Chile, the United Kingdom, Estonia, Germany, Ireland, India, Uruguay, and South Africa. In 1942, seven Latin American students were brought to the School for a special program, along with ten other international students.

In concluding her history of the School's first fifty years, Meier (1954:138) noted that although much had been accomplished, more needed to be done:

> Social workers have been remiss, however, in failing to urge the acceptance of some of the social inventions which other countries have already adopted, particularly in the area of aids which aim to protect family life and to increase the well-being of children. Health services for mothers and children, family allowances, parent education, and housing prerogatives for families with children are used more freely in some European countries than in our own. Social work educators have the obligation to learn as well as to teach.

THE PAST: THE SECOND FIFTY YEARS

In the immediate post-World War II period, the interest in international social welfare was sustained. However, beginning in the 1950s, interest declined.

The 1948-49 School *Bulletin* included several courses on immigrants and their problems. The course on Inter Country Family Services mentioned earlier now included attention to immigrant and refugee work and relevant policies and programs. The Bulletin also listed a doctoral course on Foreign Social Security Systems and another on International Social Welfare Organizations and Administration. The latter two courses were taught by the economist Eveline Burns.

Eveline Burns joined the faculty in 1946 and shortly thereafter helped establish the doctoral program at the School, which she directed until her retirement in 1967. She played a major role in developing comparative social policy offerings at the School and establishing the School and its doctoral program as the leading source of training in comparative social policy, with particular attention to comparative social security, her specialty. In 1947-48 she taught the first course at the School on U.S. and Comparative Social Security, as well as the two international social welfare courses mentioned above, heralding the School's growing awareness of the importance of international social welfare. Burns continued throughout her career at the School to publish on comparative social security and stressed the value of comparative research for understanding one's own country. Several of her doctoral students made their mark as scholars of comparative social policy, including Samuel Mencher, Robert Morris, and Alfred J. Kahn.

Except for the doctoral curriculum and the work of Burns, the 1950s appear to be something of a wasteland where international social welfare is concerned. No relevant master's level course was taught, and finally only one relevant course was offered in the doctoral program. Indeed, at the close of the decade, Burns's major doctoral course offering underwent a change in focus, from Comparative Social Security to Social Policy Analysis. In contrast, the 1960s was something of a watershed, not only in social welfare generally, but in the visibility of international social welfare at the School.

The School carried out a major curriculum review in the 1950s. The report of that influential study (Stein 1960) states that a group of students strongly urged Curriculum Committee members to recommend the reestablishment of a course on international social work and social welfare. The committee members noted subsequently that such a course had been given at the School several times in the past and had been viewed as very valuable for both international and U.S. students (41). The report states that such a course

> can provide a perspective for students to see the development of social welfare in various countries including the United States, in relation to political, demographic, cultural, economic, educational, and health factors. It could provide, also, a survey of agencies in the international field and the emergence of a profession crossing national boundaries. For the School with its international student body and international point of view, this course appeared highly desirable. (41)

Following the issuance of this report, the dean's report for 1960–61 defines as an "essential task" the need for the School to contribute directly to the local, national, and international community through special projects and the efforts of individual faculty members. It urged that the School provide support for this. In a special section of the report, Dean Delliquadri discussed "training the foreign student." He stated:

> The New York School of Social Work has a long tradition of training students from other countries. This program has resulted, over the years, in a worldwide spread of alumni who take leadership in already established or newly developing programs. The quality of the School's international program requires, above all, that its educational resources be used in ways which most soundly prepare foreign students for their future responsibilities. At a time when the gap between the material and the educational resources of developed and developing countries is so great, and the need for international understanding so crucial, the quality of the School's program is of particular importance. (Delliquadri 1961:5)

A subcommittee of the 1960 Curriculum Committee chaired by then Associate Dean Mitchell I. Ginsberg carried out a study of the School's program for foreign students. The report recommended—and the faculty approved—significant changes in the School's program. The changes emphasized increased individualization in programming for these students and the establishment of a special six-month block placement for them outside of New York City. These recommendations are repeated in several subsequent reports.

The dean also reported on the increased involvement of faculty in various aspects of international social welfare including Peace Corps training, his own role as U.S. representative to the Executive Board of UNICEF, and several other faculty members' activities in international organizations. He noted as well that about 6 percent of the students in residence were from other countries; the following year, almost 10 percent were.

In a subsequent dean's report (1965–67), Delliquadri described a special project linking the School with Colombia, South America, under the direction of Associate Dean Sidney Berengarten. Berengarten describes that project and its antecedent activity in his oral history report (Berengarten 1988). At the request of the Kennedy administration, in the fall of 1962, the School launched a training program for Peace Corps volunteers for service in community action and urban development. Mitchell I. Ginsberg, associate dean at the time, was named project director and Professor James Hackshaw was named associate director. Over two hundred volunteers were trained over the next few years and sent to Colombia, South America. Convinced of the value of a social work component in their training for urban development, Peace Corps administrators invited other schools of social work to participate as well.

According to Berengarten, "Because of this focused experience in Colombia, several prominent educators and social workers in that country asked for advice and help in upgrading the quality of their educational program" (17). In response, several U.S. governmental agencies combined efforts to support such a program, including the State Department's Bureau of Educational and Cultural Affairs; the Council for International Exchange of Scholars, which cooperated in the administration of the Fulbright Program; and the Department of Health, Education, and Welfare's (DHEW's) International Social Service Division. The School established a formal agreement with the Bureau to provide consultation to all the schools of social work in Colombia, to provide guidance on curriculum developments at graduate and undergraduate levels, and to recruit Fulbright lecturers.

A team of CUSSW faculty members went to Colombia in the summer of 1965 with the task of evaluating the curriculum, class and field teaching methods, administrative organization, class assignments, and library holdings. The team visited multiple sites in Colombia and interviewed a large number of high-level government and international officials. The team, which included several senior social work practice faculty from the School, found a grave scarcity of economic and social resources to deal with people's basic needs, and very limited resources for social workers, who, in turn, had very limited education, training, and skills.

Five outstanding students who had completed their first year of graduate study at the School and were fluent Spanish speakers were selected to carry out an eight-week program of observation, study, and supervised practice in Colombia in the summer of 1967. A comparable group of Colombians were at CUSSW the following winter. In the winters of 1970, 1971, and 1972, thirteen Colombian teachers spent a seven-week period of study at the School and three more students from the School spent seven weeks in Colombia. Berengarten's report of the experience is poignant.

It was a ten-year program, launched first in 1965, implemented in 1967, and closed down in 1977 when funding ended following congressional action to cut the funds for the Fulbright Program which had supported this exchange and cooperative arrangement. Certainly, the participants in the project felt they learned a great deal about educating social workers with very little formal education, in a developing country setting, with scarce resources and little in the way of basic social protection. In the same dean's report (1965–67), Delliquadri discussed further expansion of the School's international social welfare program by beginning to explore the possible establishment of a center for the training of social work educators and practitioners for leadership abroad, especially in developing countries. The hope was that DHEW would provide support, but this was not forthcoming. In 1968–69, a course on International Community Development was listed in the *Bulletin,* introducing a new master's-level course in international social welfare for the first time in about fifteen years, this time focused on community organizing skills.

In 1976, the School introduced the concept of a required field of practice into the curriculum, implementing it in the fall of 1977. Students could choose from among four options: Health and Mental Health, Family and Children's Services, Aging, and Industrial Social Welfare. (Students in the equivalent of advanced generalist practice or social administration were offered a fifth option, that of Personal Social Services.) Community organization was eliminated as a special social work method, and the course in International Community Development was dropped.

Almost a decade later, in 1985, however, at the initiative of Sheila B. Kamerman, the School established a "minor" in international social welfare with students required to take four courses — one at the School and the others from elsewhere in the University. Possible courses included courses at the School of International and Public Affairs on a particular geographic region or country, or on human rights, or on displaced persons and refugees and courses at the School of Public Health on health policies and programs internationally.

Another international project that was to have a significant impact both on its participants and on U.S. social service policies and programs was a study tour of local social services in England, Scotland, and Wales, with a reciprocal study tour by a British team of compensatory education programs in the United States. The project was funded by the Ford Foundation and organized by CUSSW in cooperation with a British planning committee. Mitchell I. Ginsberg (then dean of the School) was the U.S. study team leader; Alfred J. Kahn, professor of social policy and planning at the School, was the Ford Foundation consultant and senior consultant to the team and the Foundation; and Robert Morris, former doctoral graduate of the School and professor of social policy at the Heller School at Brandeis University, was rapporteur. The June 1973 study visit by a group of leading U.S. government officials, social welfare leaders, and social work educators to the social service departments of local government in the United Kingdom, was designed to expose U.S. social service experts to the recently reformed British local personal social services system as a possible model for an integrated, generalist social services system in the United States. Although this goal was not achieved, the experience did influence the U.S. policy regarding the separation of cash assistance and social services and did influence those who participated to advocate in favor of an integrated local social services system, a goal which has since been adopted by most scholars and advocates of social services reform, especially with regard to child and family services.

Other international activities during the 1970s and 1980s included the independent consultancies of Alfred J. Kahn and Sheila B. Kamerman in Iran. Kahn helped develop the country's social assistance system under the shah in 1977, and Kamerman was an advisor to the Aspen Institute Iran program and to the Ministry of Education in 1978 regarding the impact of modernization on families, women, and children.

A major new research initiative in international social welfare was launched at the School in the 1970s, with support from DHEW and several foundations. The Cross-National Studies Research program was established in 1973 by Kahn and has been co-directed by him and Kamerman since 1975. Together, they carried out a series of comparative studies on social services, including child welfare, child protection services, childcare, social services for the elderly, family planning services, and the organization and delivery of local social services. Subsequent studies of comparative child and family policies, childcare, maternity and parental leaves, policies and programs regarding the reconciliation of work and family life, and income transfers for families with children were also carried out by them in the 1970s, 1980s, and 1990s, as were numerous consultancies and related tasks with the UN, UNICEF, the OECD, the EU, and government ministries in Australia, Japan, Korea, Taiwan, and Hong Kong. Their comparative policy research program was viewed as the primary site for cross-national work in child and family policies, and the primary locus for obtaining information on relevant developments in the advanced industrialized world.

THE PRESENT

In 1995, the School established International Social Welfare as one of seven fields of practice. Students select a field to specialize in after completion of their first year at the School. All students except those concentrating in clinical practice for their social work method may choose this field. A further requirement for acceptance into the program is that students must have had at least one year of prior work or life experience in another country. Trips for pleasure or as a tourist do not count. Students who are fluent in another language are especially appropriate for the program if their interest is in the country or region where the language is spoken.

Students in advanced generalist practice, social administration, and social policy practice are eligible and have expressed their enthusiasm for the program in a variety of ways. An active International Social Welfare student caucus has played an important role in informing first-year students about the field. When the field was first established formally at the School, about fifteen students registered for the "platform" or foundation course. In 2000, five years later, registration was at thirty-four.

Students who choose this field are required to take the platform course, taught since first established by Sheila B. Kamerman. The concept of the course is a survey on international social welfare, with particular attention to global social problems, policies and programs, and the work of international organizations, in both developed and developing countries. The School expects to recruit a faculty member to teach a practice course in work with immigrants and refugees, work in international organizations, or relief and disaster work. Students who wish to minor in international social welfare now take the basic survey course and are helped to develop an individualized program that may include a course on displaced persons and refugees taught at the School of International and Public Affairs and a course on human rights or a course on health care in developing countries taught at the School of Public Health.

The fieldwork department has identified a series of international agencies that offer splendid learning opportunities for students in the field, including the UN, UNICEF, the International Rescue Committee, International Social Services, Lutheran Immigration Services, and New York Association of New Americans (NYANA).

Several students have had rich and unusual experiences while in the program, including one student who spent a semester in Geneva, Switzerland at the headquarters of International Social Services, another student who had a summer internship at the UN Development Program (UNDP) in Geneva, and a third who spent a couple of months in Australia on a special project working with aborigines in the Outback. Among the jobs that graduates have obtained are positions at the UN, UNICEF, Lutheran Immigration Services, and International Social Services.

The proportion of international students enrolled at CUSSW has continued to increase, with such students constituting about 15 percent of the M.S. program and about 20 percent of the Ph.D. program. Asian students are the dominant group. The School has continued to expand its efforts at providing support for these students, employing a special coordinator of international students, further individualizing their programs, deferring the beginning of fieldwork until the second semester to give them more time to adjust to a new country-city-school environment, and offering more in the way of background preparation for both class and field.

The doctoral program offers students the opportunity of specializing in comparative social policy or comparative child and family policy. Several recent dissertations have been carried out on international developments or on comparative social policies and programs, including a study of the Swedish joint custody program, a Canadian study of child support policies, a study of Korean immigrants in New York City and another of Chinese immigrants, a study of youth programs in Indonesia, a study of maternity policies in South Africa, a study of policies affecting women in Bahrain, an analysis and evaluation of social spending in Taiwan, a study of job satisfaction of Korean social workers, a study of HIV/AIDS prevention programs in South Africa, a study of the rise of single-parent families in Taiwan, a study of employee assistance programs in South Africa, and a study of national health insurance in Taiwan. Also, a special fellowship for doctoral students working in international social welfare (the Musher Fellowship) has been established through a gift to the School.

Faculty are increasingly exposed to international developments, whether through conferences, consultations, or research. The Cross-National Studies Research program mentioned earlier has been identified nationally and internationally as the leading center for the study of comparative child and family policies and programs. All five of the School's policy faculty members are actively engaged in some form of international social welfare activity. Thus, in addition to the international activities of Kamerman and Kahn, Jane Waldfogel spent 1998–99 on leave at the London School of Economics in London, England, and Irwin Garfinkel spent a recent sabbatical there as well. Marcia Meyers has carried out comparative research drawing on the Luxembourg Income Study database, as has James Kunz. Edward Mullen has played an active role in the establishment of an international organization of social work practice researchers.

Kamerman and Kahn have continued their comparative child and family policy research. Together, with Peter Flora of the University of Mannheim, they are co-directing a multicountry study of family change and family policies since World War II. Kamerman has been actively engaged in consulting for OECD on early childhood education and care and on social policy generally, with the French-American Foundation on early education in France, and on maternity and parental leaves. Both Kamerman and Kahn have been involved in work with the European Union, with the European Observatory on Family Matters, and with the OECD regarding "family-friendly" policies.

Thus, at present, the School has significantly expanded its interest in international social welfare in the curriculum—both class and field—in its recruitment of international students, in various activities at the School, and in the practice and research activities of its faculty. What, then, can one say about possible future directions?

THE FUTURE

The School of Social Work is planning to expand its international social welfare offerings and develop the field of practice further. There is strong interest on the part of students. The dean and associate dean have indicated their support, and the University president has repeatedly stressed the global role of the University and the need to expand the international aspects of the University. A high priority is the expansion of fieldwork placements, in particular, the development of appropriate placements for a semester or a year in another country, whether at an international organization or in a setting carrying out relief work. Once again, as there was in the early 1960s, there is talk of establishing some block placements to facilitate fieldwork outside of the country.

Still another priority is the need to develop more jobs in the field for graduates. The School needs to do more to link students in this field with appropriate jobs and career paths, whether in work with immigrants and refugees in the United States and around the world, in work in international organizations in the United States and elsewhere, or in on-site relief and disaster work at times of crises. Expanding job opportunities require joint initiatives with fieldwork agencies and alumni/ae to ensure that students' training and education is responsive to the ever-changing demands of this very dynamic field and to ensure that agencies working in the field understand and appreciate the expertise that social workers trained in international social welfare bring to this work.

The School is exploring the establishment of another joint degree program, this time with International Affairs, and with a specialization in human rights. Human rights is becoming an increasingly significant factor in national and global social policies and highly relevant to social work. Many CUSSW students in this field now take at least one course in human rights and would find additional course work coupled with a field placement at a human rights agency especially attractive. Agencies and organizations working in the field would find the combination of human rights expertise and social work skills very attractive as well.

The School is also exploring the possible development of relationships with schools of social work in other countries. In this context, it is interesting to look back as well as forward. At the fiftieth anniversary of the School and the one hundredth anniversary of the Community Service Society, Walter Pettit, then retiring as dean of the School, emphasized as he looked ahead the need for "a continuous interchange of thoughts and experience among schools of social work in the country and abroad." The need remains.

Finally, the School needs to launch a broader educational initiative in the field. Curricula, fieldwork, community services, and social programs and policies more broadly defined need to be informed about the rapid globalization now occurring throughout the world, and take advantage of growing faculty involvement in relevant international research. The School needs to make a concerted effort to seek opportunities for sharing with students and the broader public information about international developments which could enrich curricula at the School, the social work profession generally, and the society at large.

NOTE

1. The definition that follows draws on the several articles on international social welfare that have been published over the years in the *Encyclopedia of Social Work* (1965, 1971, 1977, 1987, and 1995).

REFERENCES

Berengarten, S. (Ed.). (1988). *A history of social pioneering.* New York: Columbia University School of Social Work.

Delliquadri, F. (1961). *Report of the dean, 1960 – 61.* New York: New York School of Social Work.

Kamerman, S. B. (1995). Fields of practice. In C. H. Meyer and M. Mattaini (Eds.), *The foundations of social work practice* (pp. 86–104). Washington, DC: National Association of Social Workers.

——(2000). From maternity to parenting policies: Women's health and child and family well-being. *Journal of the American Women's Medical Association, 5*(52), 96–99.

Meier, E. G. (1954). *A history of the New York School of Social Work.* New York: Columbia University Press.

Stein, H. (1960). *Curriculum study.* New York: New York School of Social Work, Columbia University.

Chapter 13

SCHOOL-BASED AND
SCHOOL-LINKED SERVICES

Mary McKernan McKay and Ernst O. VanBergeijk

As the twentieth century drew to a close, a new field of practice, school-based and school-linked social work services, was developed and incorporated into the curriculum of the Columbia University School of Social Work (CUSSW). However, the foundation for school social work practice had been set almost one hundred years earlier as social work reformers, both in New York City and nationally, called for increased protection of children, child labor reform, and support for compulsory education (Constable, McDonald, and Flynn 1999; Costin 1972; Allen-Meares, Washington, and Welsh 2000). This paper will highlight the distinguishing features of the school-based and school-linked field of social work practice, relevant theoretical frameworks and knowledge bases, and necessary practice skills. In addition, it will focus on contemporary events that precipitated the development of this new field of practice at CUSSW, as well as historical precedents for school social work practice. A detailed description of the Columbia University School of Social Work curriculum is provided, along with details regarding school-based and school-linked field placement experiences. Finally, challenges to educating school social work students for the next century of practice are outlined.

DISTINGUISHING FEATURES OF
SCHOOL SOCIAL WORK PRACTICE

The role of the school social work practitioner is defined by the interaction with a range of educational settings responsible for advancing the intellectual and emotional functioning of children (Constable et al. 1999; Costin 1972). School social workers can provide services within settings that offer day care for children beginning in infancy to school settings geared toward serving elementary, junior high school, and secondary students. Social workers can be located within regular education settings or within special education programs. Further, school social workers are likely to practice within an ever-expanding range of child-serving agencies, including educational programs associated with hospitals, residential treatment facilities, and the juvenile justice system. However, a common theme of all school social work practice is that "the school social workers inevitably work in the most vulnerable parts of the educational process, where education can break down" (Constable 1999:6).

The field of school social work practice has been developing for the last one hundred years. By the middle half of the century, Florence Poole (1949) made the observation that "we no longer see social work as a service appended to the schools. We see one of our most significant social institutions establishing social work as an integral part of its service, essential to the carrying out of its purpose" (in Constable et al. 1999:8).

Over time, consensus has been reached regarding the basic tasks of school social workers. Table 13.1 provides a summary of the key roles of school social work practitioners.

The tasks of the school social work practitioner are guided by ecological (Germain 1979, 1999) or person–environment (Bartlett 1970; Germain and Gitterman 1980; Pincus and Minahan 1972) theoretical perspectives that influence the field of social work more generally. The school social work practitioner has the unique opportunity to identify an individual student's strengths and needs in context, while simultaneously having an important vantage point from which to assess and interact with the two primary ecologies for children: school and home. Therefore, direct provision of services to individual students is one of many tasks for the school social worker. Of equal importance is the role of advocacy within a larger school system on behalf of an individual student or the entire student body in order to alter educational practices or policies that undermine student learning or social/emotional growth. For example, it is often necessary for school social workers to involve themselves in discussions of appropriate disciplinary practices within a school. As decisions are made within this area, the school social worker must assist school administrators and teachers to generate alternatives to school suspension, as these actions might not take into account academic or mental health difficulties contributing to a student's behavioral problems (Atkins et al. in press).

TABLE 13.1
Tasks of School Social Workers

• Provide direct social work services to students.
• Provide direct consultation to teachers and relevant school staff to create a more supportive school experience for individual students.
• Serve as a liaison between school and home setting.
• Influence school policies and practices to meet the emerging developmental, cognitive, social, and emotional needs of all students.
• Create an atmosphere within the school that supports active parent involvement.
• Coordinate relationships with other community-based institutions and resources.
• Assist the school community in responding to neighborhood and cultural needs of students.

Additionally, school social workers play a critical role in relation to the flow of information to school administrators and teaching staff. For example, social workers have knowledge about communities and cultural influences that are important to shaping a comfortable school atmosphere for students and their parents. Further, they are in a position to share information about the child (e.g., a situation that might be disturbing at home) with his or her teacher in order to collaborate on a plan that supports the child more adequately within the classroom (Costin 1972). In fact, providing consultation to teachers in a range of domains, including child management, mental health, or parent involvement, is a key responsibility for the school social work practitioner. For example, it is common for students to exhibit behavioral difficulties during less structured times within the school day (e.g., at lunch, recess, or during change of classes). School social workers might be called upon to help staff reorganize these time periods in order to prevent disruptions in learning and to increase socialization (see Atkins et al. 1998 for a description of a playground intervention; see also Fantuzzo and Atkins 1992). Specific in-service training for teachers or paraprofessionals might be provided by the school social worker to support new routines within the school building. Further, it is often appropriate for school social workers to link with community-based resources, such as mental health centers or recreational programs, to deepen the level of consultative and service-providing resources available to children and staff (Constable et al. 1999).

A final role of great importance for school-based and school-linked workers is that of liaison between home and school. School social workers have traditionally facilitated meetings with parents, either during a home visit or at the school, to gain further information about a student's functioning or to plan with a parent regarding how to support a student who is experiencing difficulties. Besides meeting with individual parents, the role of the school social worker is to support active parental involvement in the school as a whole. To that end, school social workers might hold educational meetings for parents or plan informal family events at the school. Recently, school social workers have come to recognize that although parent involvement has traditionally been defined as direct contact between school staff and parents (most frequently at school events, workshops, PTA meetings, and academic conferences), an expanded definition is needed (Chavkin 1993). Increasingly, there have been attempts to broaden the definition of parent involvement in order to encompass those activities that parents are actually engaged in with their children. For example, in a study sampling parents of low-income African American sixth and eighth graders, 61 percent of parents were not involved in school activities. Yet, 86 percent of students reported that their parents helped them with their homework (Chavkin and Williams 1993). An expanded definition of parent involvement has been proposed to include (1) ensuring that children have proper school supplies, (2) monitoring the amount of sleep that children get, and (3) ensuring that children arrive at school on time (Chavkin 1993).

Epstein and Dauber (1991) have expanded the definition of parent involvement by outlining a typology of ways in which parents are involved with their children. These include (1) performing basic parenting, (2) maintaining home setting conditions for learning, (3) communicating with schools, (4) volunteering, (5) engaging in school-supportive activities at home (e.g., reading, homework help), (6) participating in school-related decision making (e.g., being involved in leadership and advocacy organizations, such as the PTA), and (7) involvement with community agencies. Across the country, school social workers are partnering with educators and parent communities to foster a climate that supports active parental involvement in schools. Increasing parental involvement is one of the many varied roles appropriate for school social workers; however, the emphasis placed on one task over another is often determined by whether the worker is actually based at a school regularly or is affiliated with a school through a community-based agency. The next section of this paper will briefly distinguish between school-linked and school-based practice.

SCHOOL-LINKED AND SCHOOL-BASED
SOCIAL WORK SERVICES

School-based social work services are generally understood to be provided by a staff social worker who is on-site and paid by state or local educational funds. This type of social worker is considered to be part of the school staff and usually reports directly to the school administrator and a senior social worker who directs social work activities across schools. The advantage of school-based social work services is that they can have high ecological validity in that the social worker knows the culture of the school well and has formed working relationships with school staff. The availability of school-based social work services is a significant institutional acknowledgment of social workers' importance for the support of student learning and growth. However, in reality, the numbers of social workers hired to meet the needs of a student body are rarely sufficient. Rather, school-based social workers generally attend to the needs of special education students within a school building, partly due to their greater need and also to comply with federal guidelines, leaving a substantial portion of students without school-based resources.

To compensate for the lack of sufficient school-based resources, as well as to address growing concerns about youth outcomes, the field has supported school-linked services over the last two decades (Dryfoos 1994; Knitzer, Steinberg, and Fleisch 1990). School-linked services are defined by the partnerships formed between schools and community-based health, mental health, and social service resources (Center for the Future of Children 1992). "These child-focused partnerships provide services to children and their families and are generally coordinated by on-site providers at the school" (Center for the Future of Children 1992:7). School-linked services bring needed health and mental health care, as well as a variety of parental support activities, to the school building. They are provided by community-based agency staff. From this perspective, schools are viewed as a key child-serving institution, to be supported by community resources that provide access to children and families in need.

There was a dramatic increase in school-linked mental health programs in the 1980s. Adelman et al. (1993) estimated that by 1990, there were approximately 150 of these programs in operation, primarily in high schools (86 percent), and as many as an additional 50 in various planning stages. An example of a comprehensive school-linked mental health program is the Vanderbilt School Counseling Program (SBC; Catron and Weiss 1994). SBC focuses on meeting the mental health needs of children and families from socio-economically disadvantaged backgrounds. Employing a primary care model as its basis, SBC provides a wide range of services including psychotherapy, parent education, behavioral and psychiatric consultation, community liaison, and case management (Catron and Weiss 1994).

This type of school-linked program offers a new avenue for social workers to meet the needs of students. However, two challenges exist in planning and implementing school-linked services. First, coordination between community-based agencies and the schools is critical. Unless there is continual communication and feedback among parents, teachers, and agency staff, students' needs are likely to go unmet (Center for the Future of Children 1992). Second, it is critical to understand and respond to the perspective of most educators that the primary mission of the school is to increase student learning. Although teachers and school administrators would certainly endorse the importance of meeting the needs of the whole child, the day-to-day reality focuses primarily on learning and academic performance. Therefore, as often as possible, school-linked services that are directly linked to support for academic competence should be provided first in an effort to be in line with the primary mission of the school (Fantuzzo and Atkins 1992; Atkins et al. 1998).

HISTORICAL PRECEDENTS FOR
SCHOOL SOCIAL WORK PRACTICE

The foundation of school social work practice, according to Allen-Meares, Washington, and Welsh (2000), was laid in the Northeast during the early 1900s. In the settlement houses of New York City, full-time workers were assigned to link with the teachers of children coming to settlements. A decade later, the first cadre of "visiting teachers" was funded across New York State. These visiting teachers were able to provide information about a child's environment outside the school, as well as deliver primary direct service when a child was experiencing difficulty.

Early social workers also fought for compulsory education and an end to exploitation of children in the workforce (Costin 1972). Abbot and Breckinridge (1917) identified poverty as chief among the reasons for nonattendance in early research about the Chicago schools and called for school social workers to apply their knowledge and skills to address the needs of children from families newly immigrated to the United States. As the decades passed, social workers' influence within educational settings continued to grow.

By the early 1940s, the New York School of Social Work opened its first student unit in the Bureau of Child Guidance of the New York City Board of Education under the direction of Helen Harris Perlman. This student social work unit provided services within schools in the community of Harlem. The Bureau of Child Guidance was intended to provide direct services to students who were experiencing learning, behavioral, or emotional difficulties. All referrals to the unit came from teachers or school administrators. However, according to Perlman (1945), "the Bureau's more far-reaching function is seen as the education and influencing of its community (chiefly school personnel) toward understanding children, the social and emotional factors which create and influence his behavior and, growing out of this, the application of mental hygiene principles within the schools" (2). Even in this early period of school social work, there was a strong emphasis on not only intervening with individual students, but also influencing schools so that they might be more supportive of learning and also of child development and social/emotional functioning.

Perlman (1945) conceptualized the role of the school social worker as "caught in triangular situations—sometimes quadrangular—of agency, school, parent, and child." The school social worker must come to know something of schools, how and why they are as they are, and how they can best be utilized in the child's interest. Simultaneously, the worker must direct efforts toward altering the child's situation or behavior so that he or she presents no problem to the school. Further, the worker must be an ally of both school and family, though each may distrust the other. It was the work of Perlman that laid the foundation at CUSSW to support school-focused practice and to incorporate later practice innovations (see Reid and Epstein 1972;

Alderson 1972; Costin 1972) and policy initiatives (e.g., P.L. 94-142). However, even though social work practice in the schools was of historic interest to CUSSW, it took the culmination of a specific series of events to precipitate the development of a separate field of school social work practice in the 1990s.

CONTEMPORARY ISSUES RESULTING IN CUSSW'S ESTABLISHMENT OF A SCHOOL-BASED FIELD OF PRACTICE

At the beginning of the 1990s, multiple forces converged to create the foundation for the current school-based and school-linked field of practice. First, in 1990, the National Association of Social Workers in New York City convened a task force on school-linked and school-based services. That same year, funding was obtained to develop thirteen beacon schools in New York City, settings that were available to children and their families in the community six days per week with expanded programming to include mental health and social services. Nationally, these beacon schools were supported by the Full Service School movement, which called for an expanded view of schools, beyond education to the creation of a positive institution for youth that supported their health, mental health, cognitive, social, and emotional development. In addition, there was a growing recognition that schools were becoming de facto mental health providers and that the children in greatest need of mental health services were the least likely to receive them (Knitzer et al. 1990). Support from legislative and policy initiatives also intensified the need for a distinct field of practice focused on schools.

More specifically, an enduring issue for schools is the need to accommodate students with special needs. Prior to the passage of the Education for All Handicapped Children Act (EAHCA; more commonly known as P.L. 94-142) in 1975, children with a wide range of disabilities did not have the right to a free and appropriate public education. Not only did the act establish the right of disabled children to public educational opportunities, but it also introduced the concept of the least restrictive environment and procedural safeguards to protect the rights of students and their parents. Under this law each child was required to have an Individualized Education Program (IEP) outlining the services to be rendered by the school to address a handicapping condition. School social workers took an active role in assessing the needs of the student and the development of an individualized plan to meet his or her needs.

Originally, P.L. 94-142 was intended to apply to persons with disabilities from the age of three to the age of twenty-one years. The 1986 Education of the Handicapped Act Amendments (EHA; P.L. 99-457) amended the EHA of 1975 "to authorize an early intervention program for all handicapped infants and toddlers and their families and other purposes mandated by 1991" (Allen-Meares et al. 2000:158). This act recognized the importance of early intervention in the lives of children with disabilities. It repealed state exceptions to special education programs for children age three to five and mandated free public education for all handicapped children beginning at the age of three. Like P.L. 94-142, this law required a written plan for services. However, instead of the emphasis being placed on the individual, as in the IEP, the emphasis under this act is on the family. To this end, P.L. 99-457 requires that an Individualized Family Service Plan be written. Consequently, services may be rendered to the child and the family.

Further, in 1990, P.L. 94-142 was amended and renamed the Individuals with Disabilities Education Act (IDEA; P.L. 101-476). The spirit of this law was to place the emphasis on the individual, not the disabling condition. Person-first language was to be used in the writing of IEPs. For example, a child was to be referred to as a "child with a specific learning disability" rather than a "learning disabled child." This was an attempt to remove some of the stigma of labeling. The amendment also allowed states to be sued for failing to provide proper services. This large body of legislation, and the need for social workers in school settings to be well versed in these and other educationally focused initiatives, led the CUSSW faculty to consider whether a separate field of practice in school social work might be needed.

In the fall of 1992, the faculty conducted a full review of the curriculum at the School of Social Work. The knowledge base required for school social work, including practice methods and policy framework, was deemed sufficiently different to warrant the development of a separate field of practice. The faculty officially approved development of the School-Linked and School-Based field of practice in the spring of 1993. Classes began in fall 1995 under the direction of Dr. Cynthia Bailey-Dempsey.

CORE FEATURES OF THE CUSSW SCHOOL
SOCIAL WORK CURRICULUM

Two core courses were developed and brought to the classroom five years ago. These are Clinical Practice III: School-Based and School-Linked Social

Work, and School-Based and School-Linked Services: Issues, Programs, Policies, and Research. Along with a school-focused field placement, these courses are required for students who elect this field of practice.

More specifically, the clinical practice course focuses on preparing school social work practitioners to intervene at multiple levels simultaneously. Students are exposed to models of direct service provision for children. However, the course content also includes building practice knowledge and skills in the areas of family and parent involvement, engaging in teacher consultation, shaping school climate, collaborating with community-based agencies, and providing crisis intervention. The course objectives for Clinical Practice III are summarized in table 13.2.

Course assignments include written analyses of clinical issues from multiple perspectives within a school setting (e.g., student, teacher, school administrator, and parent). In addition, students in the course are asked to prepare an inservice training plan appropriate for their school-focused field placement. It must seek to impact current school practices or policies that need to be changed so that students can receive increased support within the school.

The second required course, School-Based and School-Linked Services: Issues, Programs, Policies, and Research, was designed to provide a foundation for social work practice in the field of education at the preschool, elementary, and secondary levels. The emphasis in this course is on the laws, policies, and research that shape this unique field of practice. Issues and policies that impact the delivery of educational and social service programs are analyzed from a research-based perspective.

The assignments for the course are designed to allow students to demonstrate mastery of the course objectives summarized in table 13.3.

The three major assignments for the course are all interrelated. The final paper for the course requires students to analyze a social problem or a solution to a social problem in the context of a school setting. At the midterm, students must complete an annotated bibliography that addresses a social issue which will be examined in their final paper. In addition to a final paper, they also must take part in a debate related to a societal problem and a proposed solution. In these debates, students are asked to take a stand on an issue that affects contemporary schools. They must use their knowledge of the issue to persuade the audience to adopt their position.

In their final paper, students are asked to discuss how these contemporary social problems manifest themselves in public education. They are asked to

TABLE 13.2

Clinical Practice III: School-Based and School-Linked Social Work Course Objectives

- The ability to differentially select and implement social work interventions known to be effective in working with at-risk students and their families.
- Competence in clinical practice with diverse students and their families.
- Knowledge, values, and skills needed for professional collaboration with educators.
- An understanding of the theories and research findings pertaining to parental involvement in the educational process.
- Knowledge of best practices for educating at-risk students.
- Ability to identify and confront ethical dilemmas typically encountered in school-based and school-linked social work practice.
- Understanding of the environmental context of social work practice in schools, including a beginning ability to manage organizational constraints that impinge on practice.
- Ability to systematically monitor and evaluate practice with at-risk students and their families.

TABLE 13.3

Course Objectives for School-Based and School-Linked Services: Issues, Programs, Policies, and Research

- Understanding of the school as a complex social system, including its role as a host setting for the practice of social work.
- Understanding of legal and policy issues that shape educational systems, including how the delivery of social work services is impacted.
- Understanding of current "best practices," both in education and social work for working with at-risk students and their families.
- Ability to analytically differentiate between the delivery of traditional school social work services, school-linked social work services, and social work services delivered within the context of full-service schools.
- Expanded knowledge and understanding of the emerging school-linked services paradigm, including philosophy, efficacy of existing model programs, and implications for educational and social welfare policy.
- Advanced library skills, including the identification of state and federal law, case law, and World Wide Web research skills.
- Public speaking skills.

frame their discussion in five different areas. First, they are asked to define the problem in terms of the size and scope of the problem, the impact on children's lives, and the costs of the problem in terms of human suffering and economic loss. Second, they must explicate the context of the problem. This can include the historical, political, theoretical, philosophical, and religious contexts in which the problem is manifested. The third domain that students need to address is pertinent state and federal laws as well as relevant court decisions. The fourth requires the students to explore the extant research about promising programs that attempt to ameliorate the problem. Once the students have presented the aforementioned information, they must apply what they have learned to social work practice, policy, and research. The guiding question for the fifth domain is, "What can a social worker do with this information?"

Public speaking skills are at the core of the debate and the inservice training assignment described above. A study of graduates of the Columbia University School of Social Work from 1996 to 1998 revealed that 63 percent of the respondents conducted seminars, trainings, and workshops as a part of their professional duties. This was the graduates' most frequently identified professional activity. This finding was a surprise given the fact that the graduates had been in the professional workforce only between seven months and a little over two years. It clearly established the need for students to acquire public speaking skills.

There are two general types of fieldwork opportunities within this field of practice. First, there are school-based field placements, where students are placed full time within a school setting and are supervised by a staff school social worker. The second type of placement is within a social service agency that provides school-linked services. The student typically provides services to children at their school but also has connections to other practitioners who provide services for the children and their families in related settings.

CHALLENGES TO PREPARING SCHOOL SOCIAL WORKERS FOR THE TWENTY-FIRST CENTURY

In considering the field of school-based and school-linked social work, it is critical to prepare students for host settings (namely, schools) that clearly are meant to support children but are not intended to be social service agencies. The primary mission of teachers and school administrators is education.

However, as children and their community schools increasingly are affected by community violence, gang activity, drug use, and poverty, the role of social workers becomes even more critical in supporting youths and advocating for their needs (Bell and Jenkins 1993; Tolan and Henry 1996). Schools are viewed as one of the few existing resources consistently available within inner-city communities. Therefore, they offer a unique opportunity to promote the positive mental health of children (Adelman and Taylor 1991; Saxe, Cross, and Silverman 1988; Tuma 1989). More specifically, the provision of services within schools offers opportunities to interact with a child and family in a community setting, enhance children's academic progress and their peer relations, increase social work access to underserved children and families, lessen stigma, and reduce restrictions to services. Schools also offer an opportunity to decrease the fragmentation of services by serving a coordinating function. However, for school social workers to help schools be resources for children, they must be prepared to intervene at multiple levels simultaneously.

Their ability to collaborate effectively both within a school setting and with community-based agencies is critical. School social work skills that help diverse groups to reach consensus and to plan or implement programs across sites must be well honed. As full-service schools become more of a reality across the country, school social workers are in a unique position to create innovative programs and be on the cutting edge of attempts to meet the needs of children who are overlooked.

School social work practitioners must also be prepared to be a substantial resource for their settings by providing information about changes at the national and state levels regarding services for children. In addition, they must be prepared to employ their problem-solving skills and abilities to gather information so that schools can begin to address some of the specific difficulties that they encounter. Upon graduation, school social workers should be prepared to assume a leadership role within complex institutions and to help craft agendas that support children to the greatest extent possible.

REFERENCES

Abbot, E. and Breckinridge, S. (1917). *Truancy and non-attendance in the Chicago schools: A study of the social aspects of compulsory education and child labor legislation of Illinois.* Chicago: University of Chicago Press.

Adelman, H. S. and Taylor, L. (1991). Mental health facets of the school-based health center movement: Needs and opportunity for research and development. *Journal of Mental Health Administration, 18*, 272–283.

——(1993). School-based mental health: Toward a comprehensive approach. *Journal of Mental Health Administration, 20*, 32–45.

Alderson, J. (1972). Models of school social work practice. In R. Sarri and F. Maple (Eds.), *The school in the community* (pp. 72–87). Washington, DC: National Association of Social Workers.

Allen-Meares, P., Washington, R. O., and Welsh, B. L. (2000). *Social work services in schools.* Boston: Allyn and Bacon.

Atkins, M. S., McKay, M., Arvanitis, P., and Brown, C. (in press). Disciplinary records in an urban, low income school: Rates and predictors of misbehavior and suspension. *Journal of Abnormal Child Psychology.*

Atkins, M. S., McKay, M., Arvanitis, P., London, L., Madison, S., Costigan, C., Haney, P., Zevenbergen, A., Hess, L., Bennett, D., and Webster, D. (1998). Ecological model for school-based mental health services for urban low-income aggressive children. *Journal of Behavioral Health Services and Research, 5,* 64–75.

Bell, C. C. and Jenkins, E. J. (1993). Community violence and children on Chicago's Southside. *Psychiatry: Interpersonal and Biological Processes, 56,* 46–54.

Catron, T. and Weiss, B. (1994). The Vanderbilt school-based counseling program: An interagency, primary care model of mental health services. *Journal of Emotional and Behavioral Disorders, 2,* 247–253.

Center for the Future of Children. (1992). School-linked services. *The Future of Children, 2,* 6–19.

Chavkin, N. (1993). *Families and schools in a pluralistic society.* Albany: State University of New York Press.

Chavkin, N. and Williams, D. (1993). Minority parents and the elementary school: Attitudes and practices. In N. Chavkin (Ed.), *Families and schools in a pluralistic society.* Albany: State University of New York Press.

Constable, R., McDonald, S., and Flynn, J. P. (1999). *School social work: Practice, policy and research perspectives.* Chicago: Lyceum.

Costin, L. B. (1972). *Child welfare policies and practice.* New York: McGraw-Hill.

Dryfoos, J. G. (1994). *Full-service schools.* San Francisco: Jossey-Bass.

Epstein, J. and Dauber, S. (1991). School programs and teacher practices of parent involvement in inner-city elementary and middle schools. *The Elementary School Journal, 91,* 289–305.

Fantuzzo, J. W. and Atkins, M. S. (1992). Applied behavior analysis for educators: Teacher centered and classroom based. *Journal of Applied Behavior Analysis, 25,* 35–42.

Germain, C. B. (1979). *Social work practice: People and environments.* New York: Columbia University Press.

—— (1999). An ecological perspective on social work in schools. In R. Constable, S. McDonald, and J. Flynn (Eds.), *School social work.* Chicago: Lyceum.

Germain, C. B. and Gitterman, A. (1980). *The life model of social work practice.* New York: Columbia University Press.

Knitzer, J., Steinberg, Z., and Fleisch, B. (1990). *At the schoolhouse door: An examination of programs and policies for children with behavioral and emotional problems.* New York: Bank Street College of Education.

Perlman, H. (1945). *Report on the New York School of Social Work student unit in the Bureau of Child Guidance.* New York: Columbia University.

Pincus, A. and Minahan, A. (1972). *Social work practice, model and method.* Itasca, IL: F. E. Peacock.

Poole, F. (1949). An analysis of the characteristics of the school social worker. *Social Service Review, 23,* 454–459.

Reid, W. and Epstein, L. (1972). *Task-centered casework.* New York: Columbia University Press.

Saxe, L., Cross, T., and Silverman, N. (1988). Children's mental health: The gap between what we know and what we do. *American Psychologist, 43,* 800–807.

Tolan, P. H. and Henry, D. (1996). Patterns of psychopathology among urban-poor children II: Co-morbidity and aggression effects. *Journal of Consulting and Clinical Psychology, 64,* 1094–1099.

Tuma, J. M. (1989). Mental health services for children. *American Psychologist, 46,* 188–189.

Chapter 14

CONTEMPORARY SOCIAL PROBLEMS

Nabila El-Bassel, Marianne Yoshioka, and Clarener Moultrie

Social work is an applied profession that mirrors social changes taking place in the world around us (Woods and Hollis 2000). The fundamental mission of social work is to enhance adaptations between the client (whether that may be an individual, family, community, or larger society) and the environment in which the client is embedded (Meyer 1993). The central focus on the person-in-environment is unique to social work and is the core of the profession's identity (Meyer 1993).

In tracing the history of social work education over the past century, it is evident that social work educators have been responsive to technology advancement as well as to the impact of political, demographic, social, and policy changes on client constituencies. Curricula in schools of social work are regularly modified and expanded in order to respond to emerging social problems. Curriculum developers must also rethink interventive approaches when long-standing problems are manifest in new ways as a result of social and environmental change. Through the development of new course areas and field placement opportunities for students, social work curricula have evolved to address environmental forces and trends shaping the lives of clients and the practice of social work (Reid 1977).

Social work has, perhaps, the most complicated assignment of any profession as we enter the new millennium. In a society that changes rapidly and where new policies, regulations, and technologies are introduced continuously, social workers must assist clients with multiple, complex, interrelated problems such as AIDS, violence, substance abuse, and homelessness. The aim of an evolving social work curriculum is to ensure that future social workers are well trained and equipped to work with clients using the most effective approaches and treatment modalities. For example, managed care legislation created an environment with new roles and tasks for social workers that significantly shaped and redefined their position in many settings. Adapting to such environmental changes challenges schools of social work to design curricula that prepare students to be competent and ethical professionals and that will equip them with skills and knowledge on the most effective interventive practices.

Currently, the Council on Social Work Education requires that a master's curriculum provide students with advanced social work practice training in identifiable concentration areas. These areas of concentration are not prescribed. Rather, schools may specify areas individualized to their own institution's mission and values.

Movement toward specialization within a profession is an inevitable process as knowledge and technology are amassed (Reid 1977). This process has been evident within social work. In the report from the Milford Conference, areas of specialization unique to social work include family welfare, child welfare, medical social work, psychiatric social work, and probation work. As these and other areas of specialization have emerged, the profession has responded by developing unique bodies of knowledge and associated skills (Stuart 1986; Vinton and White 1995). As with many other professions, social work has become increasingly specialized and this specialization has led to tremendous diversity in fields of practice. Consequently, faculty members have increasingly focused their research within a specialized field of practice and less on methods.

The Columbia University School of Social Work (CUSSW) curriculum provides an excellent model of how a professional school may adapt to meet the practice challenges of a rapidly changing environment and how the curriculum may play a proactive role in preparing students to respond to emerging social problems. In this paper, we describe one of the newest fields of practice offered at CUSSW, Contemporary Social Problems (CSP), which was specifically designed to respond to changing and emergent social problems. Since 1995, CUSSW has been the only school of social work in the United States to offer this field of practice.

Both social work practice methods and fields of practice organize the advanced practice curriculum of CUSSW. Selecting an area of specialization in the second year of study requires students to choose one of five practice methods and one of seven fields of practice. In each of the possible five practice methods, students develop advanced social work practice and research skills that may be utilized across diverse client systems and/or organizational and community settings.

CSP's conception grew from observations by faculty, administrators, field instructors, and students that there were several social problems warranting explicit attention because of their seriousness, their interconnectedness, and recent changes in their epidemiology. The focus of the CSP curriculum is on specific, complex, interrelated social problems, the constituencies that they affect disproportionately, and the micro and macro practice skills required to ameliorate them. Because the curriculum for this field of practice has been developed to be responsive to changing social conditions, the content is somewhat fluid but typically addresses three to four discrete but interrelated social problems.

Currently, the CSP curriculum addresses family and community violence, substance abuse, homelessness and related health and mental health problems, and HIV/AIDS issues. Because the criminal justice system cuts across each of these social problems, there is an emphasis on the role of the justice system and forensic social work practice (including juvenile justice, family and criminal court, domestic violence, child abuse and neglect, crime victim services, police social work, probation, and correctional institutions). The CSP curriculum is predicated on the assumption that these social problems are linked in their etiology and in their treatment. It is critical that students be trained to adopt an integrated approach to understanding and addressing these issues. Without a sophisticated grasp of their co-morbidity, social work interventions will be compromised.

CSP: EPIDEMIOLOGY AND CO-MORBIDITY OF SOCIAL PROBLEMS

Social problems such as poverty, homelessness, substance abuse, violence, criminality, and AIDS are deeply and inextricably linked and need to be addressed simultaneously. In the following section, we illustrate how these social problems are interrelated.

Partner Violence

Research suggests that within the last year, 3.9 million women were physically abused by an intimate partner (Family Violence Prevention Fund 1999).

The U.S. Department of Justice (1998) has estimated that 95 percent of the assaults on spouses and ex-spouses are committed by men against women. Seventy-five percent of these crimes involve an offender who has been drinking and 20 percent involve an offender who has been drinking and using illicit drugs (U.S. Department of Justice 1998). The extent to which substance abuse is a causal factor in partner violence remains a controversial issue. However, research indicates that there is likely a substantial correlation (Dunnegan 1997; Irons and Schneider 1997). Both men and women who abuse drugs are more likely to be victims of partner violence (Bergman and Brismar 1993; Brewer, Fleming, Haggery, and Catalano 1998; Kalichman, Williams, Cherry, Belcher, and Nachimson 1998) and perpetrators of partner violence (Bennett and Lawson 1994; Bergman and Brismar 1993; Schilit, Lie, and Montagne 1990) than non-drug-using individuals.

Research has identified clear links between domestic violence and other social problems such as homelessness, incarceration, and HIV risk behavior (DeSimone et al. 1998; Douglass 1995; Kalichman et al. 1998; Sargent, Marcus-Mendoza, and Yu 1993). Partner violence is one of the leading causes of homelessness among women (Bufkin and Bray 1998; U.S. Conference of Mayors 1998). Zorza (1991) reported that 50 percent of the women and children who became homeless did so in an attempt to escape from domestic violence. Research suggests that abused women are five times more likely than nonabused women to have had a sexually transmitted disease and four times more likely to engage in sex with risky partners (El-Bassel et al. 1998).

Finally, among incarcerated men and women, reports of a history of abuse and partner violence are well documented (Gilfus 1992; Hammersley, Forsyth, Morrison, and Davies 1989; Strauss, Falkin, and Janchill 1996). Studies have repeatedly shown a persistent co-occurrence between violent crimes and drug use (Brownstein, Cleary, Crimmins, Ryder, Warley, and Spunt 1999).

Homelessness

Estimates of the rate of homelessness in the United States tripled between 1981 and 1989 (Burt 1997). This dramatic increase occurred particularly among the very poor, substance addicted, mentally ill, and/or HIV-infected (Caton 1990; National Resource Center on Homelessness and Mental Illness

1999). Current estimates of the number of homeless vary from 700,000 per night to 2 million per year (National Law Center on Homelessness and Poverty 1999).

Homeless adults are overrepresented among individuals with a history of incarceration (Darnton-Hill et al. 1990; Solomon, Draine, Marcenko, and Meyerson 1992) and drug use (Des Jarlais 1992; Fullilove et al. 1993). Homelessness is strongly tied to issues of mental health and HIV infection. Current estimates suggest that approximately 20 to 25 percent (Koegel et al. 1996) to 33 percent (Torrey 1989) of the homeless single adult population has a mental illness. Approximately 15 percent of currently homeless adults are infected with HIV (National Resource Center on Homelessness and Mental Illness 1999). There is generally less information regarding HIV infection among homeless, mentally ill adults; however, available research suggests that between 10 and 19 percent of the mentally ill homeless population is living with HIV infection.

The explanations for these rates and increases are multifaceted. Certainly, changes in mental health policy that resulted in the deinstitutionalization of mentally ill adults have had a profound impact on homelessness rates. A recent study revealed that within six months of discharge from a state mental hospital, 36 percent of these mentally ill patients were living on the streets or in public shelters (Torrey 1989).

Homelessness rates have also been influenced by decreases in the availability of low-cost housing. Between 1970 and 1980 approximately 1 million single-room-occupancy dwellings were destroyed or converted into more up-scale housing in some of the largest cities in the United States (Wright and Rubin 1997). This represents a significant loss of viable living space for poor individuals, including those suffering from drug and alcohol addiction and/or mental illness (National Coalition for the Homeless 1999).

Further, homelessness rates have been affected by recent changes in eligibility criteria for Supplemental Security Income and Social Security Disability Insurance. Currently, receipt of disability benefits based on a claim of need for treatment for drug or alcohol addiction have a five-year limit, after which the individual may be found ineligible for future payments. According to the National Health Care for the Homeless Council (1997), this has resulted in increased rates of homelessness among those who abuse alcohol and drugs.

Substance Abuse

Substance abuse continues to be a difficult and pervasive problem in the United States. The prevalence of lifetime drug abuse among the U.S. population is estimated at 15.6 percent; the rate of drug abuse in the last twelve months is estimated at 5 percent (Grant 1996). Drawing on the 1996 National Household Survey on Drug Abuse, the overall number of illicit drug users did not change significantly between 1995 and 1996; however, there were important new trends in the demographic profiles of drug users and their drugs of choice. An understanding of these drug use patterns is essential to ensuring that outreach and treatment efforts are targeted accurately. Research indicates that the rate at which individuals have the opportunity to use marijuana was relatively stable in the fifteen years between 1979 and 1994 (Grant 1996; Segal 1991). However, the probability that an individual will use marijuana for the first time increased (Grant 1996). In 1995, there was an estimated 2.4 million individuals who started using marijuana (National Institute of Drug Abuse [NIDA] 1999a). The evidence also suggests that there is a trend toward the availability of higher potency marijuana and/or mixing marijuana with strong and dangerous drugs such as PCP or crack (NIDA 1999a). The years between 1993 and 1996 were witness to a dramatic increase in the number of heroin users, from 68,000 to 216,000. The National Institute on Drug Abuse (1999a) reports that the estimated number of new heroin users in 1995 was 141,000. The greatest increase was seen among individuals under the age of twenty-six.

Another important drug trend pertains to the use of inhalants. The mean age of initiation to inhalants is estimated at 9.7 years (Young, Longstaffe, and Tenenbein 1999), often preceding alcohol or tobacco use. Although inhalant usage is regarded primarily as a phenomenon among the very young (Lowenstein 1985), there is a significant number of adults who use them as well (Crider and Rouse 1988). Early age of inhalant initiation has been found to be positively associated with later heroin use (E. O. Johnson, Schuetz, Anthony, and Ensminger 1995). Finally, youth who experiment with or use inhalants are more likely to report engaging in delinquent behavior and minor criminal activity (Mackesy-Amiti and Fendrich 1999).

The impact of substance abuse on criminality, HIV infection, and violence has been well documented. Research reports indicate that 80 percent of the inmates in federal and state facilities abuse drugs or engage in the criminal activity associated with it (Belenko, Peugh, Califano, Usdansky, and Foster 1998). Drug abuse has been shown to be consistently linked to HIV transmission through the sharing of drug-related paraphernalia (J. Johnson and Williams 1993; NIDA 1999a), having sex with an intravenous drug user (Kline, Kline, and Oken 1992; Liebman, Mulia, and McIlvaine 1992; NIDA 1999b), or serving as a disinhibitory agent reducing the likelihood of engaging in safer sex practices (Forrest, Austin, Valdes, Fuentes, and Wilson 1993; Staton et al. 1999) or harm-reduction activities (such as cleaning dirty syringes before use).

Finally, there is a well-established connection between drug-related activity, levels of community violence (Bell 1997; Fick and Thomas 1995), and interpersonal violent behavior (Cuffel, Shumway, Chouljian, and Macdonald 1994). Fulwiler, Grossman, Forbes, and Ruthazer (1997) reported that the best predictor of violent behavior among individuals with a chronic mental illness was the onset of alcohol or drug abuse in late childhood or early adolescence. Other research has suggested that noncompliance with psychotropic medications plays an important role in this relationship; that is, violent behavior is predicted by both substance abuse and poor medication adherence (Swartz et al. 1998). Additionally, drug-related crimes contribute significantly to levels of community violence (Davis, Moss, Kirisci, and Tarter 1996; Skogan and Lurigio 1992). Multiple social problems such as poverty, high unemployment, lack of community resources, and high rates of drug abuse interact to elevate rates of violent crime within poor communities (Aneshensel and Sucoff 1996; Coulton 1996).

The Criminal Justice System

At the end of 1996, there were more than 1.7 million adults in the U.S. prison system (Belenko et al. 1998). Both federal and state institutions operate at over 110 percent capacity. A 1995 study of national rates of incarceration revealed that the United States ranked second out of fifty-nine countries, with a rate of incarceration of 600 per 100,000. In the decade between 1985 and 1995, this represented a 92 percent increase in the prison population (Sentencing Project 1999a). Research has also documented racial disparities in imprisonment. The Sentencing Project (1999b) reports that on any given day, 32 percent of African American males between the ages of twenty and twenty-nine are involved with the criminal justice system (e.g., awaiting trial, incarceration, probation, or parole). Rates of involvement among African American women increased 78 percent between 1989 and 1994, and rates of incarceration of Hispanic adults doubled between 1980 and 1993.

Increasingly, jails and prisons house poor, HIV-infected individuals living with mental illness as well as substance abuse problems. Approximately 70 percent of the prison population are illiterate, and it is estimated that more than 200,000 suffer from serious mental illness (Brennan, Gedrich, Jacoby, Tardy, and Tyson 1986; Solomon and Draine 1995). Teplin (1990) reported that the lifetime rates of schizophrenia, major depression, and bipolar disorders for incarcerated men were twice those of the general population.

The HIV/AIDS epidemic has had a profound effect on incarcerated men and women. It is estimated that there are 23,000 prisoners living with AIDS. Currently, the number of AIDS cases within the federal and state prison systems is seven times higher than in the general population (AIDS in Prison Project 1999). Among incarcerated women these rates are even higher. This high prevalence is a function of the drug abuse that characterizes every prison population. For example, in a study of intravenous drug users, a high-risk group for HIV infection, 68 percent reported having been imprisoned at least once (Mueller et al. 1995). Of those who injected in prison, 78 percent reported sharing needles.

Some have concluded that prison health care systems provide primary care to many people with mental disabilities (Steadman, McCarty, and Morrissey 1989). Clearly, the penal system regularly faces issues of violence, substance abuse, homelessness, and mental illness, and yet does not have the mental health and social services necessary to deal effectively with any of these problems (Sugarman and Byalin 1993).

THE CSP CURRICULUM

The interconnectedness of the social problems described above demands a field of practice curriculum that addresses integrated assessment and practice approaches. The Columbia University School of Social Work has made a commitment to train students to work effectively with clients experiencing multiple social problems from both micro and macro levels of practice. The CSP curriculum rests on the assumption that social problems are integrally connected to one another and to the larger environment (Parsons, Hernandez, and Jorgensen 1988). In addition, the curriculum is highly informed by the eco-systemic perspective. This perspective posits that social problems are influenced by reciprocal interactions between the individual, familial, community, cultural, and societal contexts in which they occur. These include macro factors (e.g., national, state, and local policy, unemployment, poverty, racism, and the responsiveness of legal, medical, and social institutions), interpersonal factors (e.g., social, sexual, and economic interactions between adversaries in domestic violence), and intrapersonal factors (e.g., acculturation, education, coping responses, history of trauma).

The development of an effective social work response requires that students have a deep understanding of the epidemiology of each individual social problem, while considering the co-occurrence and the nature of the interconnections between these complex problems. Problems do not exist in isolation but unfold within social and political contexts and in tandem with a host of other difficulties. It is essential that students develop an understanding of each problem individually, recognize its co-morbidity with other serious social problems, and comprehend the environmental factors that shape them in order to develop innovative and integrative empirically based practice approaches.

Furthermore, students need to be equipped to work within managed care environments, where new technologies and new practice models characterized by short-term approaches are employed. Increasingly, the services required by multiproblem individuals are regulated by treatment limits and accountability standards. By placing the focus on the co-occurrence and interconnections among social problems and the larger social and treatment environments within which they must be addressed, the CSP curriculum offers an integrated understanding of current urban problems.

In the specialization year (i.e., the second year of master's degree studies), CUSSW students are required to enroll in one of five advanced practice concentrations (i.e., Advanced Generalist Practice and Programming, Clinical Social Work Practice, Policy Practice, Social Administration, or Social Research) and one of seven fields of practice (Aging; Children and Families; Contemporary Social Problems; Health, Mental Health, and Disabilities; International Social Work; Social Work in Schools; or World of Work). In each area of specialization, students are required to complete a minimum of two advanced practice method courses, a field of practice, policy, research, and social issues course (the platform course), a field practicum in which the student's selected practice method may be applied within his or her chosen field of practice, and a linked advanced social work research course.

A student may select CSP for his or her field of practice in combination with any of the five practice methods. A typical course load for a clinical student includes the CSP platform course, two advanced clinical practice courses addressing contemporary social problems, a related clinical CSP field placement, an advanced research course, plus two electives. CSP students who have selected Advanced Generalist Practice and Programming (AGPP) likewise will take the CSP platform course, an advanced research course, and two electives. However, rather than clinical method courses, they will take two advanced AGPP courses and a related AGPP CSP field placement. Across student cohorts, approximately 59 percent of CSP students select AGPP as their method of concentration in the second year of study. In contrast, about 21 percent select Clinical Social Work Practice and a total of 20 percent select Social Work Administration, Social Work Policy Practice, or Social Research.

CSP Policy, Research, and Issues: The Platform Course

This mandatory course for all CSP students provides essential practice and policy knowledge and skills needed to understand and address contemporary social problems. The course also addresses how the criminal justice system encompasses all of the above-mentioned contemporary social problems. Included are the juvenile justice system, family and criminal court, domestic violence, child abuse and neglect, crime victim services, police social work, probation, and correctional facilities. In particular, the course covers (1) the epidemiology and etiology of each contemporary social problem with an emphasis on co-morbidity aspects; (2) the history of previous understandings about these social problems and their interconnectedness, and how these social problems were addressed historically from both practice and policy viewpoints; (3) current provisions of service (e.g., laws, regulations, funding streams, policy-making authorities, eligibility and coverage, drug policies, the war against drugs and its impact on substance-abusing clients); (4) the impact of managed care and welfare reform on service delivery for substance-abusing clients, homelessness, family violence, mental health, and HIV; (5) current practice models and policies that address these interrelated social problems emphasizing the best practice and policy models; (6) ethical dilemmas; (7) how the criminal justice system cuts across all these social problems; and (8) policies and ethical dilemmas facing social workers in the criminal justice system.

This platform course provides students with a deep understanding of the social policies that shape the creation and treatment of these difficult problems. Attitudes that underlie these policies are examined as well as existing research that helps to elucidate key factors that promote understanding of these problems. In their field placements, students test their developing knowledge by working with policymakers, community groups, agency administrators, treatment providers, and individual client systems. Through study and experience, they master the links that unite policy, funding streams, and services.

The CSP Clinical Course

CSP students may specialize in any of the five social work methods offered at CUSSW. The advanced clinical practice course is described here as an excellent example of how social work method content is tailored to substantive issues.

The major issues covered in the CSP clinical course are matched to the platform course content; however, the emphasis is placed on practice skills, knowledge, and theory. In the CSP platform course, students obtain a rich understanding of each social problem from practice, programming, and policy perspectives. In the CSP clinical course they learn practice skills to work with individual clients, families, groups, and communities affected by family violence, substance abuse, homelessness, and the associated difficulties of HIV infection and health and mental health problems. A basic goal of this course is the enhancement of adaptations between individuals, families, groups, communities, and their particular environments.

The focus of this course is on acquiring knowledge of empirically tested assessment and treatment models and the theories of behavior upon which they are based. Students are taught how to work within a managed care environment with an emphasis on balancing cost containment and effective service delivery. They learn how to work in multidisciplinary settings within agencies that have tremendous diversity in their client profiles with regard to ethnicity, gender, and sexual orientation. Finally, students learn evaluation strategies and how to use research findings to inform their practice. For example, the Community Reinforcement Approach (Sisson and Azrin 1993) and motivational interviewing for brief interventions (Bien, Miller, and Boroughs 1993; Handmaker, Miller, and Manicke 1999) have been demonstrated in multiple studies to be substantially superior to traditional treatment for both inpatients and outpatients with serious alcohol and substance abuse problems. Because of their demonstrated effectiveness, treatment modalities such as these are given preference in the course content over untested modalities. In their clinical field placements, students are provided ample opportunity to gain experience with assessment and intervention strategies, working cooperatively with other treatment providers, the courts, and related criminal justice settings.

CSP Field Placements

The purpose of the field practicum is to provide students with an opportunity to develop and sharpen their social work skills and to deepen their understanding about complexities of the social work profession (Livingston, Davidson, and Marshack 1989; Pease 1988). CSP students complete internships in one of four substantive program areas: criminal justice settings, substance abuse prevention and/or treatment, homeless advocacy programs and shelters, or domestic violence programs and shelters. Agencies are selected carefully to ensure that students will utilize their selected social work method. For example, an AGPP placement is one that allows students to conduct needs assessments, design programs, and apply for funding in a CSP substantive area. A clinical CSP placement is one where the student will provide clinical assessment and intervention to individuals, groups, and/or families in a CSP-related substantive area. Below we illustrate not only the breadth of CSP placements but also how clients who are served in these placements experience multiple interconnected social problems.

Veritas

Veritas is a residential treatment program serving four hundred adults and children whose lives are impacted by the abuse of alcohol and other drugs. Veritas utilizes a therapeutic community approach emphasizing the importance of community as a therapeutic agency, client empowerment, and self- and peer-led assistance (De Leon 1999). Multidisciplinary teams consisting of social workers, psychologists, substance abuse and vocational counselors, nurses, parenting coordinators, HIV counselors, drama therapists, and family counselors assist residents through twelve to fifteen months of residential therapeutic treatment and six months of aftercare services.

The majority of Veritas clients have been affected deeply by homelessness, histories of incarceration, HIV/AIDS, domestic violence, and mental illness. For example, client records show that approximately 50 percent of those served have issues of domestic violence, 75 percent have experienced homelessness, and 80 percent are involved with the criminal justice system.

As a clinical placement, it is essential that students possess a thorough knowledge of how these problems are interrelated both in their etiology and in their treatment. Students are expected to conduct individual and family assessments, master and apply the main tenets of therapeutic community models, provide individual and group counseling, and address the clinical and concrete needs in related areas such as domestic violence and HIV infection.

HELP USA

HELP USA was established in 1986 with the conviction that poor and low-income individuals and families should not be relegated to unsafe or substandard living conditions simply because they are poor and that shelter alone does not address the complex issue of homelessness. HELP USA is a transitional housing model that provides a safe and supportive living environment with on-site services tailored to meet the needs of homeless clients. Approximately 50 percent of the clients served at this agency struggle with issues of domestic violence, 30 to 60 percent have a substance abuse problem, and approximately 16 percent have criminal histories.

There are currently over 1,000 permanent housing units and 40 low-income homes located throughout New York City that are operated by HELP USA. The programs operated by this organization include domestic violence shelters, employment training, young child care services, on-site medical services, educational services, housing placement assistance, and ongoing individual and group counseling. HELP USA serves over 1,500 families annually in the New York City area and is currently in the process of expanding nationally.

As an AGPP placement, students placed at HELP USA work in both sheltering and advocacy programs. They work closely with large, broad-based housing coalitions and other organizations to monitor issues such as mental health treatment, community violence, and low-cost housing that directly impact the homeless. Students participate in public hearings and community outreach efforts to provide public education about the complex issue of homelessness. They are expected to design and implement needs assessments to determine the changing employment, education, and social service needs of the client population. They assist in grant writing to fund new or revised programs. Finally, students have ongoing direct practice responsibilities as well. Through group and individual counseling, individual and family therapy, and case management services, students placed at HELP USA are expected to address issues of substance abuse, HIV/AIDS, mental illness, and experiences of violence and incarceration as they relate to the homeless.

The Bronx Defenders

The Bronx Defenders is a recently established public defender program providing legal defense services for over 5,000 indigent residents of the New York City area who are facing prosecution within the criminal justice system. Multidisciplinary teams consisting of social workers, defense attorneys, and investigators work together with the intent of developing a sound criminal defense. In addition to the legal aspects of any given case, the team addresses client issues such as substance abuse, partner violence, child abuse, homelessness, mental illness, HIV/AIDS, and immigration difficulties. For example, 75 percent of those served have substance abuse problems, 20 percent experience problems with domestic violence, and 10 percent are homeless. In a clinical/AGPP placement, social work interns contribute to the team by conducting individual psychosocial assessments, providing long- and short-term counseling, and making referrals and recommendations designed to strengthen the legal defense of clients.

SUMMARY

The Contemporary Social Problems field of practice was designed to accommodate newly arising social problems and older problems that may require a different emphasis because of political, demographic, social, and policy changes and their impact on client constituencies. Consequently, CSP is a fluid, flexible field of practice in which current social problems and trends may be identified and incorporated into the curriculum and new field placements may be acquired to provide students with practical opportunities to work with clients who experience interrelated social problems. Our descriptions of the CUSSW curriculum and field placements illustrate a model of how the social work profession contends with a rapidly changing environment and how, through thoughtful curriculum change, schools of social work can play a proactive role in preparing future graduates to respond to the social forces and trends that will shape the lives of clients and the practice of social work in the next millennium.

REFERENCES

AIDS in Prison Project. (1999). Fact sheet [On-line]. Available: aidsinfonyc.org/aip

Aneshensel, C. S. and Sucoff, C. A. (1996). The neighborhood context of adolescent mental health. *Journal of Health and Social Behavior, 37,* 293–310.

Belenko, S., Peugh, J., Califano, J. A., Jr., Usdansky, M., and Foster, S. E. (1998). Substance abuse and the prison population. *Corrections Today, 60,* 83–154.

Bell, C. C. (1997). Community violence: Causes, prevention and intervention. *Journal of the National Medical Association, 89,* 657–662.

Bennett, L. and Lawson, M. (1994). Barriers to cooperation between domestic-violence and substance-abuse programs. *Families in Society, 75,* 277–286.

Bergman, B. and Brismar, B. (1993). Assailants and victims: A comparative study of male wife-beaters and battered males. *Journal of Addictive Diseases, 12*(4), 1–10.

Bien, T. H., Miller, W. R., and Boroughs, J. M. (1993). Motivational interviewing with alcohol outpatients. *Behavioural and Cognitive Psychotherapy, 21,* 347–356.

Brennen, T. P., Gedrich, A. E., Jacoby, S. E., Tardy, M. J., and Tyson, K. B. (1986). Forensic social work: Practice and vision. *Social Casework, 67,* 340–350.

Brewer, D. D., Fleming, C. B., Haggery, K. P., and Catalano, R. F. (1998). Drug use predictors of partner violence in opiate dependent women. *Violence and Victims, 13,* 107–115.

Brownstein, H. H., Cleary, S. D., Crimmins, S. M., Ryder, J., Warley, R., and Spunt, B. (1999, August). *The relationship between violent offending and drug use in the pre-prison experience of a sample of incarcerated young men.* Paper presented at the meeting of the American Sociological Association, Chicago.

Bufkin, J. L. and Bray, J. (1998). Domestic violence, criminal justice responses and homelessness: Finding the connection and addressing the problem. *Journal of Social Distress and the Homeless, 7,* 227–240.

Burt, M. (1997). Causes of the growth of homelessness during the 1980s. In D. P. Culhane and S. P. Hornburg (Eds.), *Understanding homelessness: New policy and research perspectives* (pp. 169–203). Washington, DC: Fannie Mae Foundation.

Caton, C. L. M. (Ed.). (1990). *Homelessness in America.* New York: Oxford University Press.

Coulton, C. J. (1996). Effects of neighborhoods on families and children: Implications for services. In A. J. Kahn and S. B. Kamerman (Eds.), *Children and their families in big cities* (pp. 87–120). New York: Columbia University School of Social Work Cross-National Studies Research Program.

Crider, R. A. and Rouse, B. A. (Eds.). (1988). *Epidemiology of inhalant abuse: An update* (NIDA Research Monograph No. 85). Rockville, MD: National Institute of Drug Abuse.

Cuffel, B. J., Shumway, M., Chouljian, T. L., and Macdonald, T. (1994). A longitudinal study of substance abuse and community violence in schizophrenia. *Journal of Nervous and Mental Disease, 182,* 704–708.

Darnton-Hill, I., Mandryk, J. A., Mock, P. A., Lewis, J., et al. (1990). Sociodemographic and health factors in the well-being of homeless men in Sydney, Australia. *Social Science and Medicine, 31,* 537–544.

Davis, N., Moss, H., Kirisci, L., and Tarter, R. (1996). Neighborhood crime rates among drug abusing and non-drug abusing families. *Journal of Child and Adolescent Substance Abuse, 5*(4), 1–14.

De Leon, G. (1999). Therapeutic communities. In P. J. Ott, R. E. Tarter, et al. (Eds.), *Sourcebook on substance abuse: Etiology, epidemiology, assessment, and treatment* (pp. 321–336). Boston: Allyn and Bacon.

Des Jarlais, D. C. (1992). The first and second decades of AIDS among injecting drug users. *British Journal of Addiction, 87,* 347–353.

DeSimone, P., et al. (1998). *Homelessness in Missouri: Eye of the storm?* Jefferson City: Missouri Association for Social Welfare.

Douglass, R. (1995). *The state of homelessness in Michigan: A research study.* Lansing: Michigan Interagency Committee on Homelessness.

Dunnegan, S. W. (1997). Violence, trauma and substance abuse. *Journal of Psychoactive Drugs, 29,* 345–351.

El-Bassel, N., Gilbert, L., Krishnan, S., Schilling, R. F., Gaeta, T., Purpura, S., and Witte, S. S. (1998). HIV-risk behaviors among women in an inner-city emergency department. *Violence and Victims, 13,* 377–393.

Family Violence Prevention Fund. (1999). Facts about domestic violence in the United States [On-line]. Available: http://feminist.org/other/dv/dvfact.html

Fick, A. C. and Thomas, S. M. (1995). Growing up in a violent environment: Relationship to health-related beliefs and behaviors. *Youth and Society, 27,* 136–147.

Forrest, K. A., Austin, D. M., Valdes, I., Fuentes, E. G., and Wilson, S. (1993). Exploring norms and beliefs related to AIDS prevention among California Hispanic men. *Family Planning Perspectives, 25,* 111–117.

Fullilove, M. T., Golden, E., Fullilove, R. E., Lennon, R., et al. (1993). Crack cocaine use and high-risk behaviors among sexually active Black adolescents. *Journal of Adolescent Health, 14,* 295–300.

Fulwiler, C., Grossman, H., Forbes, C., and Ruthazer, R. (1997). Early onset substance abuse and community violence by outpatients with chronic mental illness. *Psychiatric Services, 48,* 1181–1185.

Gilfus, M. E. (1992). From victims to survivors to offenders: Women's routes of entry and immersion into street crime. *Women and Criminal Justice, 4*(1), 63–89.

Grant, B. F. (1996). Prevalence and correlates of drug use and DSM-IV drug dependence in the United States: Results of the National Longitudinal Alcohol Epidemiologic Survey. *Journal of Substance Abuse, 8,* 195–210.

Hammersley, R., Forsyth, A., Morrison, V., and Davies, J. B. (1989). The relationship between crime and opioid use. *British Journal of Addiction, 84,* 1029–1043.

Handmaker, N. S., Miller, W. R., and Manicke, M. (1999). Findings of a pilot study of motivational interviewing with pregnant drinkers. *Journal of Studies on Alcohol, 60,* 285–287.

Irons, R. and Schneider, J. P. (1997). When is domestic violence a hidden face of addiction? *Journal of Psychoactive Drugs, 29,* 337–344.

Johnson, E. M. and Belfer, M. L. (1995). Substance abuse and violence: Cause and consequence. *Journal of Health Care for the Poor and Underserved, 6,* 113–121.

Johnson, E. O., Schuetz, C. G., Anthony, J. C., and Ensminger, M. E. (1995). Inhalants to heroin: A prospective analysis from adolescence to adulthood. *Drug and Alcohol Dependence, 40,* 159–164.

Johnson, J. and Williams, M. (1993). A preliminary ethnographic decision tree model of injection drug users' (IDU's) needle-sharing. *The International Journal of the Addictions, 28,* 997–1014.

Kalichman, S. C., Williams, E. A., Cherry, C., Belcher, L., and Nachimson, D. (1998). Sexual coercion, domestic violence, and negotiating condom use among low-income African-American women. *Journal of Women's Health, 7,* 371–378.

Kline, A., Kline, E., and Oken, E. (1992). Minority women and sexual choice in the age of AIDS. *Social Science and Medicine, 34,* 447–457.

Koegel, P., et al. (1996). The causes of homelessness. In *Homelessness in America.* Washington, DC: Onyx.

Liebman, J., Mulia, N., and McIlvaine, D. (1992). Risk behavior for HIV infection of intravenous drug users and their sexual partners recruited from street settings in Philadelphia. *Journal of Drug Issues, 22,* 867–884.

Livingston, D., Davidson, K. W., and Marshack, E. F. (1989). Education for autonomous practice: A challenge for field instructors. *Journal of Independent Social Work*, *4*(1), 69–82.

Lowenstein, L. F. (1985). Recent research into glue-sniffing: Extent of the problem, its repercussions and treatment approaches. *International Journal of Social Psychiatry*, *31*, 93–97.

Mackesy-Amiti, M. E. and Fendrich, M. (1999). Inhalant use and delinquent behavior among adolescents: A comparison of inhalant users and other drug users. *Addiction*, *94*, 555–564.

Meyer, C. H. (1993). *Assessment in social work practice*. New York: Columbia University Press.

Mueller, R., Stark, K., Guggenmoos-Holzmann, I., Wirth, D., et al. (1995). Imprisonment: A risk factor for HIV infection counteracting education and prevention programmes for intravenous drug users. *AIDS*, *9*, 183–190.

National Coalition for the Homeless [NCH]. (1999). *Addiction disorders and homelessness* (NCH Fact Sheet No. 6). Washington, DC: Author.

National Health Care for the Homeless Council. (1997). *SSI/SSDI study*. Nashville: Author.

National Institute on Drug Abuse [NIDA]. (1999a). *Nationwide trends* (NIDA Info-Fax Publication No. 041). Bethesda, MD: U.S. Department of Health and Human Services.

National Institute on Drug Abuse [NIDA]. (1999b). *Lessons from prevention research* (NIDA InfoFax Publication No. 036). Bethesda, MD: U.S. Department of Health and Human Services.

National Law Center on Homelessness and Poverty. (1999). *Out of sight — out of mind? A report on anti-homeless laws, litigation, and alternatives in 50 United States cities*. Washington, DC: Author.

National Resource Center on Homelessness and Mental Illness. (1999). Identifying a population at risk [On-line]. Available: www.prainc.com.nrc/papers/hiv

Parsons, R. J., Hernandez, S. H., and Jorgensen, J. D. (1988). Integrated practice: A framework for problem solving. *Social Work*, *33*, 417–421.

Pease, B. B. (1988). The ABCs of social work student evaluation. *Journal of Teaching in Social Work*, *2*(2), 35–50.

Reid, W. J. (1977). Social work for social problems. *Social Work*, *22*, 374–381.

Rubin, B. A., Wright, J. D., and Devine, J. A. (1992). Unhousing the urban poor: The Reagan legacy. *Journal of Sociology and Social Welfare*, *19*, 111–147.

Sargent, E., Marcus-Mendoza, S., and Yu, C. H. (1993). Abuse and the woman prisoner. In B. R. Fletcher, L. D. Shaver, and D. G. Moon (Eds.), *Women prisoners: A forgotten population* (pp. 55–64). Westport, CT: Praeger.

Schilit, R., Lie, G., and Montagne, M. (1990). Substance use as a correlate of violence in intimate lesbian relationships. *Journal of Homosexuality, 19*(3), 51–65.

Segal, B. (1991). Adolescent initiation into drug-taking behavior: Comparison over a five-year interval. *International Journal of the Addictions, 26,* 267–279.

Sentencing Project. (1999a). Americans behind bars: U.S. and international use of incarceration 1995 [Report data] [On-line]. Available: www.sproject.com

Sentencing Project. (1999b). Young Black Americans and the criminal justice system: Five years later [Report summary] [On-line]. Available: www.sproject.com

Sisson, R. W. and Azrin, N. H. (1993). Community reinforcement training for families: A method to get alcoholics into treatment. In T. J. O'Farrell (Ed.), *Treating alcohol problems: Marital and family intervention* (pp. 34–53). New York: Guilford.

Skogan, W. G. and Lurigio, A. J. (1992). The correlates of community antidrug activism. *Crime and Delinquency, 38,* 510–521.

Solomon, P. L. and Draine, J. (1995). Jail recidivism in a forensic case management program. *Health and Social Work, 20,* 167–173.

Solomon, P. L., Draine, J. N., Marcenko, M. O., and Meyerson, A. T. (1992). Homeless in a mentally ill urban jail population. *Hospital and Community Psychiatry, 43,* 169–171.

Staton, M., Leukefeld, C., Logan, T. K., Zimmerman, R., Lynam, D., Milich, R., Martin, C., McClanahan, K., and Clayton, R. (1999). Risky sex behavior and substance use among young adults. *Health and Social Work, 24,* 147–154.

Steadman, H. J., McCarty, D. W., and Morrissey, J. P. (1989). *The mentally ill in jail: Planning for essential services.* New York: Guilford.

Strauss, S. M., Falkin, G. P., and Janchill, N. (1996). Drug abuse histories of women mandated to treatment. *Sociological Abstracts, 044.*

Stuart, P. (1986). School social work as a professional segment: Continuity in transitional times. *Social Work in Education, 8,* 141–153.

Sugarman, N. and Byalin, K. (1993). Meeting the family court's need for mental health and human services: A comparison of direct service and community organization approaches. *Journal of Psychiatry and Law, 21,* 319–336.

Swartz, M. S., Swanson, J. W., Hiday, V. A., Borum, R., Wagner, R., and Burns, B. J. (1998). Taking the wrong drugs: The role of substance abuse and medication noncompliance in violence among severely mentally ill individuals. *Social Psychiatry and Psychiatric Epidemiology, 33* (Suppl. 1), S75–S80.

Teplin, L. A. (1990). Detecting disorder: The treatment of mental illness among jail detainees. *Journal of Consulting and Clinical Psychology, 58,* 233–236.

Torrey, E. F. (1989, August). Why are there so many homeless mentally ill? [On-line] Available: www.schizophreniz.com/ami/Torrey

U.S. Conference of Mayors. (1998). *A status report on hunger and homelessness in America's cities.* Washington, DC: Author.

U.S. Department of Justice. (1998). *Alcohol and crime. An analysis of national data on the prevalence of alcohol involvement in crime* (National Criminal Justice Publication No. 168632). Washington, DC: Lawrence A. Greenfeld.

Vinton, L. and White, B. (1995). The "boutique effect" in graduate social work education. *Journal of Teaching in Social Work, 11*(1/2), 3–13.

Woods, M. E. and Hollis, F. (2000). *Casework. A psychosocial therapy* (5th ed.). New York: McGraw-Hill.

Wright, J. and Rubin, B. (1997). Is homelessness a housing problem? In D. P. Culhane and S. P. Hornburg (Eds.), *Understanding homelessness: New policy and research perspectives* (pp. 205–224). Washington, DC: Fannie Mae Foundation.

Young, S. J., Longstaffe, S., and Tenenbein, M. (1999). Inhalant abuse and the abuse of other drugs. *American Journal of Drug and Alcohol Abuse, 25,* 371–375.

Zorza, J. (1991). *Woman battering: A major cause of homelessness.* Chicago: National Clearinghouse for Legal Services.

Part Four

DOCTORAL EDUCATION

THE VAST MAJORITY of graduates from the Columbia University School of Social Work (CUSSW) have pursued studies leading to the degree of master of science in social work. It was not until 1952 that the School had its first doctoral graduate, namely, Alfred J. Kahn. Hence, the history of the School of Social Work is largely, but far from entirely, a history of master's degree education in social work. To date, no comprehensive history has been written about the School of Social Work's doctoral program. This is especially regrettable given the fact that the doctoral program of the Columbia University School of Social Work probably has educated more deans, directors, and faculty members for schools of social work worldwide than any other such program.

The CUSSW doctoral program is widely considered a home of future social work leaders. Most graduates of the program assume positions in academia, or as researchers, clinical instructors, or senior administrators in government or nonprofit agencies. The doctor of philosophy in social work is offered by Columbia University's Graduate School of Arts and Sciences but is administered by the School of Social Work. Students select a method of concentration: advanced practice; social policy, planning, and policy analysis; or social policy, planning, and administration. In each sequence, students do intensive work in research methods and statistics in conjunction with their own career planning. The student's program is arranged individually from advanced courses at CUSSW and from courses available in other professional schools and graduate divisions of the University. Students must pass examinations in a social work method, a related behavioral or social science, and a substantive field of practice, and must prepare and defend a doctoral dissertation.

Part 4 of this volume constitutes a beginning effort to provide a record of doctoral education at CUSSW, but it does so from a very unique and selective standpoint. It examines certain hallmarks of doctoral education at the School, namely, the facilitative and inspirational roles played by key faculty members in helping doctoral students to complete their dissertations and, in turn, the deep appreciation of students for the expert and often unstinting assistance provided to them by faculty. Chapter 15, entitled "Doctoral Education: Looking Past the Present," is authored by Karen Staller. It was written when the author was approaching completion of her own doctoral dissertation at the School of Social Work. This essay provides an unusual, original, and therefore all the more informative and engaging view of doctoral education at CUSSW by examining systematically the Acknowledgment sections of a sample of doctoral dissertations on hand at the School of Social Work's Whitney M. Young Jr. Memorial Library. Respectively, the sections of chapter 15 are denoted as Glory Bound, Technology and the Sacred Relic, Locating Truths in Debt, and Fighting Metaphoric Clutter. Taken together, these sections yield unique insights evidenced over time regarding the nature and quality of doctoral education at the Columbia University School of Social Work.

Chapter 15

DOCTORAL EDUCATION: LOOKING PAST THE PRESENT

Karen M. Staller

INTRODUCTION: GLORY BOUND

Midway through my doctoral career (assuming a not too distant end), Professor Steven Schinke informally advised a group of anxious doctoral students on the science of picking a dissertation topic. It's not *what* you study that's important, he insisted, it's *how* you study it. He maintained it was the method, not the subject, we would reach for again when situated in a new academic home. So I suspect that Professor Schinke would not be surprised I reached for the historical case method familiar to me when confronted with today's topic: CUSSW and doctoral education: past, present, and future.

In my quest for information about doctoral education, I found myself sneezing a blessing over the 439 dusty tomes lodged in the basement of Lehman Library which stand as the ultimate monument of doctoral achievement—the bound and shelved dissertations. Although the number seemed small—which speaks to both the infancy of the program and the intimacy of its family of graduates—their contributions did not. The dissertations were bracketed on the early end by that of the program's patriarch, Alfred J. Kahn's 1952 study, *A Court for Children,* and they spilled onto the next thirty shelves revealing a lineage frequently punctuated by the names of giants in the profession.

I confess I might have looked for evidence of the raging larger debates such as the role of social science, the nature of social work practice and the-

The author wishes to thank Sheila B. Kamerman and Denise Burnette of CUSSW, Stuart A. Kirk of UCLA, and William McKinley Runyan of UC, Berkeley, for their thoughtful contributions on earlier drafts of this manuscript.

347

ory, and the changing populations of interest, but I did not. I was searching for more personal testimonials of the doctoral experience and professional influences. I found them on the pages frequently last written but first read, where accumulated debts are paid off with words of gratitude, where forgiveness is begged for sins committed, and where promises of future reform appear. These acknowledgment pages, I reasoned, would provide concluding evidence of the doctoral experience.

I analyzed 156 of them (35 percent of the total), including the entire first and last decades and a random sample of those in between. They ranged in length from a few sentences to a few pages. They registered a full spectrum of emotions from solemn to exuberant and included gratitude, relief, joy, sorrow, and pride. Many were perfunctory but some were so elegant they could stand alone as powerful pieces of writing. Some, like those of Meredith Hanson (1987), Janice Matthews (1987), and Barbara Worden (1996), included moving dedications to the memory of parents, while others, like Nancy Boyd Webb's, captured this reader's attention with a question posed by a six-year-old research subject.

I gained respect for individuals I had known only as distant shadows (like Eveline Burns, whose namesake fellowship I received my first year) and learned names I might otherwise never have known (like Mrs. Margaret Otto and Mrs. Grace Bermingham, early librarians of the New York School of Social Work). I was humbled by the esteemed composition of the program's ancestry, surprised to learn of the clusters of individuals who were classmates at given moments in time, and thrilled to discover evidence of some of the personal and professional relationships linking teacher-to-student-to-teacher in an ever impressive lineage.

The acknowledgments I reviewed were as diverse as their authors, but their collective voices revealed some universal truths that I find myself feeling uniquely, if oddly, qualified to address. A complete analysis would include discussions on funding (which appears to have been abundant in the 1960s and seems to have evaporated by the 1990s, possibly narrowing the nature and scope of the studies); the involvement of faculty university-wide who played major roles in shaping doctoral education and therefore the development of knowledge in the profession; and finally the sheer number and variety of community agencies and organizations which have been an integral part of doctoral study. However, due to time and space limitations, I will concentrate on three areas I found interesting: the role of technology, the academic community, and professional life.

TECHNOLOGY AND THE SACRED RELIC

Despite their uniform blue bindings, time and technology have altered the appearance of dissertations. Yellowed onion skin paper, buckled by the impact of typewriter key strokes, is replaced, for the moment, by pristine white bond paper fed through laser jet printers. "Errata" alerting readers to misnumbered pages are moving toward extinction thanks to computer software that automatically does the job. Typing errors carefully whited-out on originals but permanently captured on carbon copies have all but vanished with the introduction of spell-check and the easy cloning of a single page (or entire document), with the touch of a "print" command. Dissertations no longer bear the signs of physical struggle, and the final relic appears a little less sacred because of it.

Technological advances always produce a period of cultural lag. The "unsung heroes" of the dissertation process, wrote Anthony Maluccio in 1977, are "those who provided clerical and research assistance." Until relatively recently, those "unsung heroes" appeared almost universally on acknowledgment pages as members of an administrative and technical team of secretaries, typists, editors, computer programmers, and data technicians.

Secretaries were routinely thanked for both their typing *and editorial* skills. For example:

- "[this dissertation] could not have been written without the . . . editorial reading by Mrs. Louise Shoemaker and the typing service of Mrs. Gertrude Barth" (Konopka 1957);

- "special thanks to Miss Corinne Tufte for editing the text and to Mrs. Nevedith Pearman for typing it" (Shawky 1958);

- "Mrs. Mardean Ryan and Miss Ardrena Cooke have earned my respect and appreciation for . . . editing and typing this manuscript" (Herman 1959).

They are also thanked for typing *multiple* copies of manuscripts and are given special recognition for producing the final document:

- Helen Keyes is thanked for "the arduous task of typing so well the multiple drafts and final copy of this report" (Wiest 1960);

- the secretarial staff "gave unstintingly in the typing of drafts — and drafts — and more drafts" (Vigilante 1968);

- thanks are given those "who did the final retyping and correcting that produced the clean, final draft" (Seabury 1976).

Secretaries are gratefully acknowledged for organizing a "force of typists to assist in the project" (Levy 1958); "assembl[ing] the final draft of the manuscript" (Logan 1980), and arranging "the many details that accompany the production" (Abramovitz 1981). They are recognized for a whole host of personal, interpersonal, and technical skills, including their patience, intelligence, cooperation, unerring performance, perseverance, and ability to "decipher" hieroglyphics and text (Pumphrey 1956; Seabury 1976), most often under deadline pressure. Finally, secretaries also sometimes provided technical assistance with data:

- Mrs. Ida Berkowitz "sacrificed many evenings to help process the questionnaires which were employed in the study" and also "typed most of the manuscript" (Levy 1958);

- Mrs. Lily P. Silbert was not only "responsible for the typing of the final text" for Robert Morris but "did so much to compile and check the factual data" (Morris 1959).

Students also shared responsibility for computer expertise, data management, and analysis with a host of other technical specialists. They expressed "deep gratitude" for "help," "advice," "assistance," and "instruction" with "computer programming" and "in the machine records phases of data analysis" (Wittman 1956; Lotte 1969; Altman 1974; Padberg 1974; Sperr 1974). They were grateful to those who "were unstinting in their time and efforts in translating raw data into machine programs" (Wiest 1960) as well as to those who aided in the "processing and analysis of the data" (Bailey 1958; Wiest 1960), and realized that those who made "computer printout runs" and aided in "table construction" "played no small part" (Simpson 1975). In the 1960s, dozens of students, including Ben Orcutt and David Fanshel, thanked then Professor, later President, McGill, not only for his "technical help" but also for his "consultation with statistical aspects" of research (Fanshel 1960).

By the 1980s, the burden for computer expertise, data management, and statistical analysis begins to shift to the doctoral student. In 1974, Ralph Dolgoff thanked those who "served as guides through the morass of knowledge required for working with computers," but in 1988, Alma Norment received help in "conquer[ing] a technology that for me was new and formidable," while in 1996, Barbara Worden saw fit to express a "a word of gratitude" to her daughters "for sharing the computer." Advancements in technology were accompanied by innovations in software, and students came to realize "that statistics, after all, aren't really impossible" (Lynskey 1987). Students once made pilgrimages to computers that filled a room and paid homage to those experts who conversed with them, but now toss laptops—data set, SPSS, and all—into their knapsacks.

Technological innovation, of course, brings costs along with its benefits. One cost of the increasing power of the personal computer may be the loss of the team and the ritual of production. Manuscripts once represented the final work-product of a group of professionals but are now the sole responsibility of a student. This has at least four immediate ramifications. First, the student must develop expertise in areas previously delegated to others. Second, she or he must shoulder the burden for the entire production process. (I can only imagine the relief my predecessors must have felt when they placed their precious manuscript in the hands of a team of others to fuss with charts, graphs, footnotes, appendices, bibliographies, and the niceties of proper format and assemblage). Third, there is an additional, mostly hidden, cost associated with this shift in burden, since someone—either program or student—must bear the expense of the student's learning curve to master the technology. Finally, with the diminished involvement of this supporting cast, the social and cultural nature of the doctoral experience was certainly altered.

In 1959 Wolins characterized his dissertation as a "social rather than purely individual effort," and Charles S. Levy (1958) referred to his as a product of "teamwork and cooperation." The raison d'être for acknowledgments is still to pay tribute to others, but the corps of secretarial and technical staff who once appeared alongside family, friends, and faculty have all but disappeared. Perhaps coincidentally, references to the loneliness of the dissertation process begin to creep into acknowledgment pages in the 1980s. Mimi Abramovitz (1981), who did honor her typists, also observes that "writing a dissertation is a lonely and independent process"; Amy Kohn (1988) reports that others "negated all feelings of isolation," while Daniel Herman (1991) calls writing a dissertation a "uniquely solitary undertaking," and Susan Einbinder (1995) says it was an "often painful and always solitary process." I found no references to loneliness in my early sample, and I can't help but wonder if there isn't some correlation between the loss of the team and feeling of isolation in the process.[1]

Please don't misunderstand me, I cherish the good-morning "ping" of my Macintosh and appreciate the flexibility of Microsoft Word. But computers have made obsolete a social network that was an integral part of the doctoral community, doctoral experience, and the dissertation ritual of the past. Of course, at the same time that the personal computer provides a tool that diminishes the student's interaction with a secretarial community, it removes a human intermediary and creates new intimacy between the student and the substance of her or his work. With the click of a mouse, I recently created two dissertation chapters from the one I had originally planned to present. I felt relief in the process, but the act reflects a lack of discipline that my predecessors could ill afford. The technical ease of subdividing increases my direct relationship with the evolving structure and text of my work and reflects new rules governing the content and form of the product. In the long run, this increased intimacy will change not only the reporting of knowledge but its very development, substance, and structure.

Technical mastery is already a prerequisite for the academic job market. I recently attended a seminar on interviewing for faculty positions. Sympathetic junior faculty encouraged doctoral students to create Power Point presentations in order to pitch their work to hiring institutions. Multimedia productions are now the cutting edge of marketing both the candidate and the scholarship.

There are challenges here for the future of doctoral education. Doctoral education must include the training and support (technical and financial) necessary to master the skills to compete and perform in academia. But it must also teach the skepticism necessary to be sensitive to the ways in which technology alters the way we gather, interpret, construct, and peddle knowledge as well as be sensitive to how technology changes the texture and quality of our personal relationships and social communities. Technological advances are an asset as long as they don't diminish the quality of social life, dilute the substance of knowledge by valuing technical prowess over intellectual acumen, or compromise our ability to evaluate its quality and substance.

LOCATING TRUTHS IN DEBT

Although references to secretarial support have diminished, acknowledgment pages continue to reflect the need for strong academic support and guidance during the doctoral program. At first glance these clichés seemed hackneyed—polite but predictable—yet their sheer repetition demands attention. In the end, they reveal some critical features in doctoral education. There are at least three "findings" to report in this area. The first examines the kinds of words used and the concepts they embody. The second looks at the distribution of these concepts over time. The third considers the clustering of these words around individuals. Each is considered briefly.

Current definitions of the word "acknowledgment" (originally derived from Middle English *knowledgen* and *aknouen*—to recognize) include admitting a truth, expressing appreciation, conceding debt, and recognizing authority. So it is not surprising that words of "gratitude" for payment of "debts" that have "accumulated" or are "owed" by the student to others, including family and friends, are frequently used. The debts identified and gratitude offered include the following:

- Words of *difficulty* and words of *encouragement*. Students floundered when "motivation waned"; they faced "unexpected twists and turns," "encountered difficulties," and "things seemed hopeless." They faced "periods of discouragement"; the "task seemed impossible," and they had their "own doubts" and faced the "'stresses and strains' of doctoral study." But encouragement was "generously bestowed" and "continuous." They were "sustained . . . through many hurdles," "tided" over discouragement, received "help" to "keep them going," and had "perspective restored." Their spirits were "bolstered" and motivation was "re-kindled" when "all seemed lost."

- Words of *belief, faith,* and *patience*. Others' belief is described as "unwavering," faith "unshakable," and patience "endless" in the student, the doctoral process, and the dissertation project.

- Words of *inspiration*. Faculty provided "stimulation," "insight," "curiosity," and "motivation," and exhibited "enthusiasm" and helped students to "think more imaginatively."

- Words of *generosity* for sharing *time, knowledge,* and *experience.* Time is "freely," "generously," "liberally," and "unconditionally" given, and faculty are "readily" and "ever" available. Faculty generously "share" "ideas," "intellectual acumen," "insight," and provide a "wellspring of first-hand knowledge" and "immeasurable aid."

- Words of *guidance* and *direction.* Faculty are given credit for helping "develop," "identify," "clarify," and "shape," as well as "assist," "share," and bring "order" to "complexities."

- Words of *intellectual challenge* and *high expectations.* Faculty offer "criticism," "critiques," and "appraisals" that are "astute," "insightful," and "constructive."

- Words of *support, friendship,* and *mentoring.* Faculty support is "total" "indefatigable," "invaluable," and "readily available." They provided "kindness," "personal interest," "counsel," "consultation," "intellectual guidance," and "expert advice." In doing so they became "friends," went "beyond mentoring," provided a "philosophy of the academic life," and students promised they will spend their "career trying to emulate" the qualities witnessed and bestowed.

Taken together these concepts paint a fairly complete picture of the support students need. Predictably, they need guidance, direction, support, and feedback. Equally important are qualities like inspiration, motivation, and faith (in both the student and the study) and the willingness and commitment to sustain the student through the inevitable tough moments. Finally, there are the important special relationships that develop between the student and the faculty member who starts as teacher, becomes mentor then friend, and serves as a lifelong role model.

In addition to the types of support needed to ensure success, the dispersion of words is also important. This distribution has a temporal and a personal dimension to it. The temporal relates to individual stages of the process as well as to the program as a whole. The former is evident when students locate the stage of the process and describe the aid they received. For example:

- *Beginning.* At the beginning students thank those "inspiring [their] . . . initial choice," "stimulating interest," "setting them on a path," "suggesting a topic," "encouraging exploration," and "allowing them latitude";

- *Middle.* During the planning and development stages, students acknowledge help "formulating the study," "discussing the problem," "clarifying research questions and design," "identifying theory," and "assisting with methodological issues";

- *End.* Toward the end of the process, students note help "interpreting findings" and providing "critical appraisal."

The second temporal aspect of commitment speaks to faculty availability for the duration of the doctoral program. Those who stick with students are noted for remaining there "every step of the way" or "throughout" the process. When the continuity of support is broken, students acknowledge those who step forward to stabilize the project. For example:

- Bluma Swerdloff (1960) expresses "special gratitude" to Alfred Kahn, who "continued as the sole advisor after Dr. Hamilton's retirement";

- William Padberg (1974) is appreciative of "the extra burden assumed by Vera Shlakman," who "accepted responsibility" following the "untimely death" of Russell Nixon; and

- Barbara Emerson (1990) had the "good fortune to start" before James Hackshaw and Alfred Kahn retired and to "finish" with James Jones.

Finally, these words are not randomly bestowed on faculty. When you stop to consider the accumulated thanks that cluster around individual faculty members, you begin to appreciate their unique and important contributions to students and the program. The names of some, such as Carol Meyer, David Fanshel, and Alfred J. Kahn, among others, emerge as heavyweights both because of the frequency with which they are mentioned and because of their unique contributions. For example:

Inspiration and Advocate: Carol Meyer

Dr. Carol Meyer is credited with providing "early encouragement," "excitement," "excit[ing] examination," providing "inspiration" through her "vision," and acting "as mediator in the early stages" (Glassman 1991; Panzer 1990; Mattaini 1990; Seabury 1976). Rebecca Sperling (1996) says Dr. Meyer permitted her to "plan the study I really wanted to" and reports the work would have been "rudderless without her direction."

These accolades, among others, suggest a faculty member who not only inspired students early in their doctoral education but also encouraged and defended their right to follow their own passions. She seems to have combined elements of inspiration, direction, and belief in the students and their work and cultivated fledgling ideas in the process. Perhaps not surprisingly, the faculty members mentioned in Dr. Meyer's (1957) own dissertation acknowledgment page are thanked for working "long hours in helping to clarify the problem under study."

Selfless Accessibility: David Fanshel

David Fanshel "gave generously of his time and experience," "was generous with his time," made "frequent contribution[s]," was "always available . . . even during his sabbatical," and in spite of "so many demands on his time" always seemed to find "a block of several hours" (Lotte 1969; Mullen 1968; Campbell 1970; Maluccio 1977; Webb 1979; Gibson 1987; Ilian 1987). He provided "incisive comments and criticism," "nurtur[ed] interest," "provided constant steadying influence," and "was a superb teacher," providing a "model" in "countless ways."

The words that describe David Fanshel constantly refer to his generous spirit and his selfless accessibility. His dedication to students is reflected in the extra attention students take to thank him. Dr. Fanshel's (1960) own acknowledgment page thanks his mentor James Bieri (another frequently mentioned name) for having "given me generously of his time." In doing so, Dr. Fanshel, like Dr. Meyer, identifies the same feature as important in his doctoral education as those most often cited by his own students to describe his mentoring.

Omnipresent Commitment: Alfred J. Kahn

Although I can't prove it with absolute certainty, I suspect no name has appeared on dissertation acknowledgment pages more often than that of Alfred J. Kahn. In the first seven years of the program, 40 percent of its graduates mention his name in their thanks. In the 1950s words used to describe Kahn's contribution include "unstinting," "moral support and professional guidance," and a "constant and enlightening consultant" who "suffered through much manuscript reading" (Landau 1957; Levy 1958). In the 1960s they include "unstinting help," "special gratitude," "invaluable guidance," "warmth," "encouragement," "constant interest," "sound criticism," and "helpful suggestions" (Swerdloff 1960; Menon 1960; Spergel 1960; Briar 1961; Almanzor 1961; Kamal 1961). In the 1970s they include "help, criticism and encouragement," "critical diligence," and "encouragement." Students offered a "special word of thanks" because Kahn "never failed — either in the quality" or "willingness" to help (Dolgoff 1974; Dobrof 1976; Epstein 1977). Sheila Kamerman (1973), his student before she became his career-long colleague, described Dr. Kahn as her "advisor, mentor, colleague and friend." In the 1980s and 1990s he is characterized as "thoughtful, stimulating," "enabling," and a "guiding light," and he is thanked for his "intellectual and conceptual guidance" and "for his inspirational teaching" (Panitpan 1980; Cuellar 1981; Levy 1990).

References to Dr. Kahn span four decades of dissertation acknowledgment pages. The longevity of his contribution is stunning, and the constellation of his students striking (including but certainly not limited to Joseph Scott Briar, Benjamin Cuellar, William Epstein, Sheila Kamerman, Charles Levy, Carol Meyer, Elizabeth Ortiz, and Irving Spergel); and his involvement with them and their studies seems more diverse than that of most.

While I shudder to think of the number of dissertation drafts Dr. Kahn has waded through in his lifetime, I can personally attest to the fact that even forty-three years after his name first appeared on an acknowledgment page, he continues to relate to his students with warmth, patience, and extraordinary respect. This exercise has made me appreciate that he manages this in spite of the certainty that he has heard anything a neophyte could possibly say at least once or twice before.

So what is to be learned for the future from these words? Simply that some features are so basic and integral to success that they must be present in programs, available to students, and respected by doctoral faculties.

Past students address the cultural aspect of success. For example, Margaret Elbow (1993) called it "a setting conducive to exploration and learning"; Milton Lebowitz (1961) called it "providing the climate for undertaking this research" and Joseph Scott Briar (1961) described it as "creating the intellectual climate" that is necessary to both "inspire" study and "acquire the knowledge needed to conduct it." Like Dr. Briar, Carol Meyer separated the need for "tools for the writing of this dissertation" from that of having a school which provided "the stimuli." Meyer found at CUSSW "an academic atmosphere in the truest sense, for exploration of problems and pursuit of knowledge" (not surprisingly, perhaps, given her association with Florence Hollis, Nathan Ackerman, and Alfred Kahn).

What seems clear is that the optimal environment for doctoral work not only introduces students to the tools of the trade but also offers a nurturing, stimulating, and intellectually diverse atmosphere in which to master them. Ultimately the health of this environment will almost certainly correlate with the success of individual students and the program as a whole. While it may be tempting to delegate full responsibility for finding this kind of support to the doctoral student, it is equally incumbent on the faculty to provide and respect those who take the role of student mentoring seriously. Finally, it is irresponsible to take on more students than a faculty can support.

FIGHTING METAPHORIC CLUTTER

Anomalies occasionally provoke insight. I stumbled across one such snippet in Anthony Cupaiuolo's (1979) thanks to his wife, who, among other hardships, "ignored for so long the huge mess created by widely scattered questionnaires, books, notes, etc." It gave me pause, not only because a student colleague had recently commented on his partner's growing frustration with "living in a file cabinet" but also because it sadly conjured up an image of my own apartment.

My dissertation started, where it belonged, in alphabetical order in file folders restricted to a file cabinet; books were arranged by topic in bookcases and disciplined stacks of miscellaneous papers were neatly organized on my desk. However, with the ever-increasing and unanticipated growth of dissertation by-products, my living space shrank. Huge, unstable piles of books, notes, and Xeroxes began to line the bedroom wall, organized by chapter. The living room window sills provided spill-over shelving for current, possibly useful, and future reading. When my dining room table functioned as the staging ground for organizing chapters, charts, bibliographies, and appendices, I began consuming breakfast standing over the kitchen sink. I knew I had crossed a mental health line the morning I woke and realized my books lined the opposite side of the bed.

The encroachment of clutter, of course, is only the physical manifestation of the metaphoric space—emotional, intellectual, personal, and social—upon which dissertations intrude. They can rearrange social and personal relationships and priorities if you let them. Even if you fight that tide, they seep into your emotional and intellectual space as surely as they infringe on physical space. They alter your understanding of self and redefine your understanding of the world as they become part of who you are.

Acknowledgment pages are filled with hints of dissertation clutter that disrupt family and personal affairs. Families are acknowledged for "the sacrifices this project entailed" (Siska 1995), "for their understanding and forbearance" (Lebowitz 1961), and for being "often deprived of many things" (Levy 1958), as well as for putting up with "that strange phenomenon, a husband-father-student" (Wiest 1960) and enduring the sacrifice of "some part of husband and father to the completion of this work" (Wittman 1956). Irv Piliavin (1961) offers his "deep sincere apologies" to his sons for "acceptance of 'life without father,'" and Brett Seabury (1976) admits his children "waited a 'lifetime' for their daddy to finish." For Muriel Pumphrey's family, life without mother resulted in her family's "patience with meals out of the freezer and tin cans" (Pumphrey 1956), and Barbara Worden (1996) is grateful for her daughters' willingness to give Mom "quiet time to complete this work."

Importantly, these acknowledgments are usually accompanied by a promise of a different future. Bernard Wiest (1960) hoped for the "the opportunity of repaying" his family; Morton Altman (1974) "promise[d] more of my time" to his daughter; Anthony Maluccio (1977) contemplated "what we may now become," and Harry Stern (1977) observed that "it must be somewhat comforting to my daughter to know that the frantic man who went into the bedroom to work after dinner and on the weekends is indeed her father." The underlying assumption in these promises is that the doctoral program represents anomalous seismographic activity on a personal Richter's scale that climaxes with a dissertation but settles down in the aftermath.

For me, this conceptualization raises a provocative question. To what extent can the doctoral disruption be swept out the door at its conclusion, leaving life as neat—if not neater—than before? Or, to pose it differently, to what extent does the dissertation process represent the first step in the metamorphosis from student to scholar? I suspect the latter, assuming a future in an academic institution. If that's the case, how does one control the threat of encroaching metaphoric clutter, or at least keep life in some healthy balance?

It is a deceptively difficult task, in part, because all the incentives appear to be stacked in favor of being overrun. The "standards"—external and internal—that govern academic life conspire to make maintaining a healthy balance a Promethean task. I've observed the tenure process during my time as a doctoral student and feel confident that excelling in scholarship, teaching, and community service isn't always enough. The fact that the academy seems to offer little meaningful external guidelines for success leads to the question of individually defined standards.

Ultimately, academics are responsible for setting their own standards of excellence in the quality and quantity of their work as well as setting their own limits on its encroachment into their personal space. It may be a more difficult balance to strike in this trade than most, in part because scholarly pursuit engages both the heart and mind, making the professional often intensively personal. In addition, standards of excellence are an ever-moving target, elusive illusions that feed an insatiable need to know just a little more. Besides, when you are competing against yourself, the best motivation comes when you are least satisfied with what you've already done. In short, intellectual pursuit will occupy as much personal space as you let it.

All this brings me back to the doctoral education and the dissertation process. To the extent that the dissertation experience is one that begins to define the balance that will govern a student's professional afterlife, it serves as an important practicum. Implications for doctoral students, faculties, and programs follow. Institutional faculties, as a collective group, set the standard and tone, and provide role models, not just of scholarship but of the lifestyle and culture of the academic community. Their tolerance (or intolerance) for clutter may serve as a barometer of group mental health. Each faculty must make considered decisions about that community atmosphere when it fills and promotes through its ranks. So, too, must doctoral graduates consider their own tolerance for clutter when choosing an academic home and be forewarned against those ill-suited to their personal, professional, and mental health needs.

CONCLUSION

During the course of working on this paper, the latest batch of dissertations arrived from the bindery and took their spot as a temporary bookend to Alfred Kahn's study. My name, alas, was not among those on the bindings but, as fate would have it, I made my debut in the supporting role of "doctoral colleague" on Margaret Domanski's (1996) acknowledgment page. She thanked me for my "willingness to spend hours stuffing envelopes." It is a reference to an afternoon her husband and I spent around the doctoral lounge conference table affixing labels to envelopes and stuffing them with her survey instrument. The event halted abruptly when Margaret paused to wonder why she needed to make a second run to the Xerox room for additional surveys. The mystery was solved when we discovered I had opened a huge box of extra envelopes and was merrily stuffing mailings to nowhere. The group collapsed in laughter disproportionate to the episode. It was laughter which stemmed from the profound relief that another hurdle in a long process had been successfully vaulted.

Thousands of such cryptic references are woven into the text of acknowledgment pages, records of private stories, and personal memories of the doctoral experience. The stories are personal but the collective experience is part of a common bond that links Columbia family past and present and will fold in those of the future.

Carol Meyer's (1957) acknowledgment page includes the "thanks of a student who has been honored by association" with the doctoral faculty. *Honored by association.* That's what I felt seeing my name on Margaret's acknowledgment page and that's what I feel as a result of exploring the impressive history of CUSSW's doctoral program. In the process I learned something about my place in its tradition; I learned something about the qualities and skills that contribute to a sound doctoral community, and I glimpsed the usually intangible impact of the highest caliber teaching and mentorship. Honor by association, however, is only as strong as the current CUSSW community. It is an honor that must be continually earned as we move into the next century.

In the meantime, apropos for this topic, I close with my own acknowledgment to those with whom I have been "honored by association" and who provide the kind of excellence worthy of Columbia's ancestry:

- To Sheila B. Kamerman, whom I have always sensed believed in me and whose roots and lineage I am now more humbled by than ever;

- To Stuart A. Kirk, who has steadfastly encouraged my pursuit of white rabbits on the gamble the chase might feed my head, who has pulled me from despair more often than he can imagine, and who has continually reminded me that exhilaration and balance come from leaning into the dangerous curve; and

• To J. Denise Burnette, who has constantly helped me see the patterns in my pieces. I've learned that wisdom comes from observation, creativity from freedom, knowledge from outside, but power from within — and that it's only in the final stitching that the splendor of the handiwork can emerge.

I could not have found a set of more challenging or more inspirational role models. My grateful thanks.

NOTE

1. A number of alternative hypotheses can be generated to explain this apparent shift. One is that the formal rules of acknowledgment page construction (as rigidly enforced by a professional secretarial staff) were relaxed. A second is that the shift is explained by the increasing social acceptability of this kind of self-examination and confession in print. The author thanks Dr. William Runyan for both of these alternative suggestions.

CUSSW DISSERTATIONS CITED

Abramovitz, Miriam (1981). *Business and health reform: Workers' compensation and health insurance in the progressive era.*

Almanzor, Angelina (1961). *Volunteer and staff participation in a voluntary social welfare association in the United States: A study of the National Young Women's Christian Association.*

Altman, Morton (1974). *The relationship of an intensive training program and subsequent work experience to selected attitudes of non-professional staff.*

Bailey, Margaret (1958). *Community orientation toward social casework and other professional resources: A study of attitudes toward professional help for interpersonal problems and knowledge of resources in an urban community.*

Briar, Joseph Scott (1961). *The effects of client social class, social class distance, and social work experience on the judgments of social work students.*

Campbell, Margaret (1970). *Adult adjustment of former institutional children.*

Cupaiuolo, Anthony (1979). *Community interaction with V.A. family care homes for the mentally ill: A comparative study of conflict and non-conflict.*

Cuellar, Benjamin (1981). *The Chicano agency: A study of sixteen social service agencies serving the community in Santa Clara County, CA.*

Cupaiuolo, Anthony (1979). *Community interaction with V.A. family care homes for the mentally ill: A comparative study of conflict and non-conflict.*

Domanski, Margaret (1996). *Correlates of political participation among social work leaders in the health policy domain.*

Dobrof, Rose (1976). *The care of the aged: A shared function.*

Dolgoff, Ralph (1974). *Organizational structure and socialization: Educational interaction and career choices in undergraduate social work education.*

Einbinder, Susan (1995). *Toward valid measurement of poverty among families with children in the United States: Development of a consumption-based measure of relative deprivation.*

Elbow, Margaret (1993). *Attribution of blame for father–daughter incest: A study of the creation of deviance.*

Emerson, Barbara (1990). *Academic interference: A study of social welfare needs as factors in the achievement of disadvantaged students in higher education.*

Epstein, William (1977). *The domiciliary program in the Veterans Administration.*

Fanshel, David (1960). *Toward more understanding of foster parents.*

Gibson, John (1987). *Black and Hispanic teenage sexual and contraceptive attitudes and behavior: A school-based study.*

Glassman, Carol (1991). *Care partners: Gay men whose lovers have AIDS.*

Hanson, Meredith (1987). *Alcoholism treatment as an interactive phenomenon: The impact of client characteristics on treatment participation.*

Herman, Daniel (1991). *Homeless men in New York City's public shelters: A life course perspective.*

Herman, Melvin (1959). *Occupational mobility in social work: the Jewish center worker.*

Ilian, Henry (1987). *Six sessions: A study of the discourse analysis of an example of cognitive behavior therapy in a social work context.*

Kahn, Alfred (1952). *A court for children: A study of the New York City Children's Court.*

Kamal, Ahmend (1961). *Youth welfare in Egypt, United Arab Republic.*

Kamerman, Sheila (1973). *Community based child advocacy projects: A study in evaluation.*

Kohn, Amy (1988). *A study of the mother–daughter relationship among pregnant teenagers.*

Konopka, Gisela (1957). *Social work's search for a philosophy with special reference to Edward C. Lindeman.*

Landau, Claire (1957). *Interracial group work and social adjustment.*

Lebowitz, Milton (1961). *The process of planned community change: A comparative analysis of five community welfare council change projects.*

Levy, Charles (1958). *From education to practice in social group: The relevance of social work education to agency responsibilities assumed by trained social group workers upon receipt of the master's degree from accredited schools of social work in the United States in 1955.*

Levy, Paul (1990). *Supreme Court welfare reform: Has it lasted? A study of four cases between 1968–1971.*

Logan, Sadye (1980). *The Black Baptist Church: A social psychological study of survival and growth.*

Lotte, Marcus (1969). *The effect of the extra-linguistic phenomena on the judgment of anxiety.*

Lynskey, John (1987). *Puerto Rican adolescents and helpers view the helping experience: A comparison of the populations and an analysis of congruence and dissonance in their perspectives.*

Maluccio, Anthony (1977). *As client and social worker see it: An exploratory study of their perception of casework.*

Mattaini, Mark (1990). *A study of the visual representation of quantitative data for ecosystemic research and practice.*

Matthews, Janice (1987), *The effect of client's race/ethnicity status and level of acculturation and the influence of practitioner characteristics on social workers' clinical judgment.*

Meier, Elizabeth (1962). *Former foster children as adult citizens.*

Menon, Amnu (1960). *Mahatma Gandhi's contribution to social welfare in India: A study of three major programs.*

Meyer, Carol (1957). *Complementarity and marital conflicts: The development of a concept and its application to the casework method.*

Morris, Robert (1959). *Integration of social welfare resources; the dynamics of welfare planning; an analysis of processes by which integration of general hospital and long term institutional facilities was achieved in five communities.*

Mullen, Edward (1968). *Casework treatment procedures as a function of client-diagnostic variables: A study of their relationship in the case interview.*

Norment, Alma (1988). *The role of social networking in obtaining an abortion in the United States.*

Orcutt, Ben (1963). *Anchoring effects in the clinical judgments of social work students and experienced caseworkers.*

Ortiz, Elizabeth (1981). *Definition of disability: Lay opinion of factors affecting assignment of disability benefits.*

Padberg, William (1974). *The social welfare labor market attachment of the undergraduate social work major.*

Panitpan, Sritaptim (1980). *Personal (general) social services for children in Greater Bangkok, Thailand.*

Panzer, Barry (1990). *The development and testing of a practice model with families bereaved due to sudden infant death syndrome.*

Piliavin, Irving (1961). *An investigation of conflict between cottage parents and other staff in juvenile correctional institution.*

Pumphrey, Muriel W. (1956). *Mary Richmond and the rise of professional social work in Baltimore, the foundations of a creative career.*

Seabury, Brett (1976). *A systems of model of case services.*

Shawky, Abdelmonen (1958). *Urban community development in Pakistan: A study of applicability of community organization principles to urban community development in under developed countries.*

Simpson, John (1975). *The retention of participants in the public services careers (case aide) program in New York City.*

Siska, Kathylene (1995). *Social integration of the mentally retarded in the work place.*

Spergel, Irving (1960). *Types of delinquent groups.*

Sperling, Rebecca (1996). *A portrait of Marion Edwena Kenworthy.*

Sperr, Inez (1974). *On becoming a foster child: An ethnological study of the behaviors of children.*

Stern, Harry (1977). *A study of the influence of social climate on the socialization of students of social work.*

Swerdloff, Bluma (1960). *The predictive value of the admission interview: A search for the psycho-dynamic factors related to changes in the patient and his situation.*

Vigilante, Joseph (1968). *Work and training in public welfare.*

Webb, Nancy Boyd (1979). *Attachment relationships of preschoolers to parents and other familiar caretakers: Implications for day care and working mothers.*

Wiest, Bernard (1960). *The relationship of interpersonal responses to ratings and content of the interview.*

Wittman, Milton (1956). *Scholarship aid in social work education.*

Wolins, Martin (1959). *Selection of foster parents: early stages in the development of a screen.*

Worden, Barbara (1996) *Defining sexual harassment in the workplace: A factoral survey approach.*

Part Five

CUSSW AND NEW YORK CITY

A s NOTED in the preceding essays, the M.S. and Ph.D. programs at the Columbia University School of Social Work (CUSSW) are characterized by distinguished faculty, talented students, and rigorous and demanding curriculums. However, above and beyond these hallmarks, the School's educational programs also offer a particularly unique and significant advantage, namely that they are located in the best possible laboratory for social work education: the New York City metropolitan area. The educational, recreational, cultural, and, above all, social service facilities and resources in New York City offer invaluable supports to professional education. Through its location in New York, the School provides students with a rich and stimulating learning experience in urban living and the problems associated with it.

The roots of the Columbia University School of Social Work were formed in 1898 under the auspices of one of New York City's preeminent social work agencies, the Charity Organization Society. Throughout the School's history, its educational program has been nourished and strengthened by a vast array of public and private agencies. These include the public social service agencies of New York City and New York State as well as countless family and child welfare organizations, hospitals, mental health centers, and other institutions. Yet, at the same time that CUSSW benefits from its urban environs, it contributes immeasurably to them. Currently, for example, through field placements alone the School's students contribute nearly five hundred thousand hours per year of services to social work agencies and related organizations in the New York City metropolitan area. Even more important, CUSSW has played a seminal role in introducing or stimulating numerous innovations in social work service delivery both in New York City and elsewhere. The School's faculty, administrators, and alumnae/i have, for example, been leaders in establishing psychiatric social work, bureaus of child guidance, social work research programs, required fieldwork, and doctoral education. From coalitions formed with other professionals and community leaders, the School's faculty and alumnae/i also have helped to establish the White House Conferences on Children, the Urban League, the Association of Schools of Social Work, and many other institutions.

Closer to home, CUSSW alumnae/i and faculty have helped to create or revitalize a wide array of social work agencies and programs, and, even more, to spearhead major social movements in New York City and elsewhere. One limited example pertains to the School's role in promoting the growth and development of settlement houses, community centers, and related agencies throughout urban America. Perhaps the best example of such an endeavor is its relationship to settlement houses in New York City. Accordingly, chapter 16, "Settlement Houses," discusses the emergence of settlement houses in New York City and their relationship to the School of Social Work. Authored by Barbara Simon, this paper discusses only one example among many of the myriad contributions made by CUSSW faculty, alumnae/i, and students to the well-being of the city that has nourished the School's own development. It also identifies issues that remain relevant to the interfaces among professional education, social action, and institutional development.

Chapter 16

SETTLEMENT HOUSES

Barbara Levy Simon

Democracy is . . . a genuine union of true individuals.
The question before the American people today is—
How is that genuine union to be attained, how is the
True individual to be discovered? . . . The potentialities
Of the individual . . . are released by group life.

— FOLLETT 1918: 5

Democracy, community, and individuality, as settlement house leader Mary Parker Follett so ably articulated in 1918, are inextricably interdependent elements. They together served as the lodestar for the inspired women and men who began creating the settlement house universe in the United States more than one hundred years ago. The same triad of commitments led leaders of the Charity Organization Society of the City of New York, such as Edward Devine, Mary Richmond, and Robert W. deForest, to create the School whose centennial was honored in 1998. As the twenty-first century unfolds and the politics of greed, division, and exclusion continue to contort our nation, state, and city, Mary Parker Follett's answer to her own question continues to be a worthy one—sustain democracy and foster the fullest possible development of individuals through nourishing robust communities.

All entering students in 1898, upon being admitted into the Summer School in Philanthropic Work of the New York Charity Organization Society, learned that the School's founders recommended that enrollees live for at least three months in one of the many settlement houses that had sprung to life in New York City during the 1880s and 1890s. The official archival record of the Summer School notes that, in the first class of 1898, half of the entering students lived in settlement houses while they attended the six-week educational program (Community Service Society 1898–1899 : 25–61). No mention is made in subsequent reports about students' living situations. Therefore, regrettably, I am unable to know how long the School continued to recommend settlement living for its entrants. (The "School" has had several names over time, the two most recent being the New York School of Social Work, followed by the Columbia University School of Social Work.)

All entering students studied, then as now, the following subjects: methods of social work practice, social research, and theories and methods of inquiry from the humanities and social and behavioral sciences relevant to pressing problems of the day, be they economic, social, political, cultural, biological, or religious (Community Service Society 1898–1899, 1899–1900, 1900–1901). One-sixth of the overall content of the Summer School in 1898 addressed the "study of constructive social movements—Neighborhood Improvements" (Community Service Society 1898–1899 : 38–51). Topics covered in that category in 1898 included, among others, the campaigns for mandatory public schooling, tenement house reform, and a meritocratic civil service and the battles against tuberculosis and child labor.

It is worth noting that, in a school established by the most influential Charity Organization Society in the United States, settlement houses and social movements were considered pivotal to the readying of students for social work practice. The stories of tense relations between the charity organization movement and the settlement house movement in the years prior to World War I, I suggest, have been greatly exaggerated. Leaders of both initiatives served on key committees together in the Progressive Era. A significant proportion of the administrators of the New York City Charity Organization Society before 1914 had spent ample parts of their careers working in settlement houses.

Alas, after the First World War, tensions did, indeed, increase between the rapidly professionalizing world of social work education and that of the settlements. The focus of the School in the postwar period on teaching psychological treatment and child guidance had no parallel in the settlement house movement. The social settlements' embrace of group work, community development, and adult education no longer resonated with the School's priorities until the 1960s, despite the remarkable contributions of Eduard C. Lindeman, an internationally recognized professor of community work and practice.

"WITH, NOT FOR"

The settlement house movement gave to the Summer School and the emergent social work profession a core principle of practice, that of the indispensability of collaborative "give-and take" alliances between settlement workers and neighbors in the large endeavor of building enduring communities. Mary Simkhovitch's (1938) encapsulation of the settlement house movement's ethos as "With, Not For," guided her throughout her many years as head worker of the Friendly Aid House and Greenwich House in New York City. Prefiguring by eight decades that which we now term "empowerment" and "strength-based" approaches to social work practice, settlers forged partnerships with immigrants living in the neighborhoods immediately surrounding the settlement houses in which they lived. Dissatisfied with the misery of many poor people created by plutocratic imprints upon representative democracy of the late nineteenth century, settlement house workers hoped to shape what they called a "direct democracy" of neighbors, foreshadowing by six decades the movement for participatory democracy of the New Left, the women's movement, and the Black Power movement of the 1960s and 1970s.

The settlement house movement offered to the School currently known as the Columbia University School of Social Work and to the entire profession of social work a form of leadership that took its primary direction from community members themselves. Settlement house workers labored to understand neighbors' felt and expressed concerns in the light of their own experiential immersion in the neighborhood, of systematic observation and inquiry, and of the study of a broad range of scholarship from the liberal arts and applied professions. Historians who have analyzed the libraries and records of book purchases of settlement house leaders have discovered a long list of disciplines and fields represented therein, including anthropology, history, psychology, sociology, economics, political economy, political science, philosophy, literature, theology, law, education, public administration, architecture and urban planning, public health, nursing, medicine, psychiatry, and proto-social work (Crocker 1991; Carson 1990).

A DEFINITION

The settlement house movement was, from the start, a community organization sui generis. Settlement houses, also called neighborhood houses, social settlements, and neighborhood guilds, have obvious common features with YWCAs, YMCAs, YWHAs, YMHAs, and community centers, but nonetheless remain a distinctive genre. Like Ys and community centers, social settlements and neighborhood houses have focused on being a gathering place and center of community activity, recreation, and culture. Unlike Ys and community centers, settlements and neighborhood houses have insisted on maintaining nonsectarian missions and auspices (Rose 1994). An illustration, first described by Elizabeth Rose, follows.

The Young Women's Union was created as a kindergarten for the children of Eastern European Jewish immigrants in 1885 by Philadelphia women of German-Jewish extraction. It was soon expanded to become a multiservice Americanization center for Jews new to the United States and Philadelphia. Judith Solis-Cohen, a board member of the Young Women's Union, declared at a board meeting, "There is a need in Philadelphia for a Jewish Hull House. There is a need in Philadelphia for a Jewish Jane Addams" (Rose 1994:9; see also Greifer 1948:187). Soon after her recommendation, the Young Women's Union was turned over to the leadership of one Stella Rosenbaum, a worker from the College Settlement in Philadelphia. The name of the Young Women's Union was changed to that of "Neighborhood Centre," and its mission was reconfigured from "the care and improvement of Israelites" to that of offering "opportunities for social and educational activities in the neighborhood" (Rose 1994:10). Miss Rosenbaum succeeded in founding the Philadelphia Association of Settlements and in associating the newly renamed Neighborhood Centre with the National Federation of Settlements.

Five years later, in 1915, Walter Solomon, a guest speaker at the Neighborhood Centre, said that "a Jewish settlement is a contradiction in terms, an anomaly; a settlement run by a national group is a misnomer" (Rose 1994:10). The speaker's words resonated closely with those of Robert Woods and Albert Kennedy, leaders of social settlements who were authors of a now-classic directory of settlement houses written in 1911. "The typical settlement is one which provides neutral territory traversing all the lines of racial and religious cleavage. That which is wholly unsectarian . . . represents the main action of the kind of social enterprise here set forth" (Rose 1994:17; Woods and Kennedy 1911:v). To close the illustration, it is important to note that the Neighborhood Centre under discussion transformed itself yet again in the 1940s. A new director was brought in by the board to, in his words, "Judaize" the agency (Rose 1994:17). He thoroughly succeeded. The Neighborhood Centre and the settlement movement soon thereafter parted ways.

Social settlements, by contrast, continued to serve as a gathering place for all neighbors from any "classes and clans" in the immediate environs, as John Palmer Gavit wrote in 1898. Settlement and neighborhood houses were, according to Mary Kingsbury Simkhovitch, "America's committee of welcome" to the immigrant who arrives from anywhere in the world (Lindenberg and Zittel 1936:559).

A second distinction between the settlement house and the community center movements involves the centrality in settlements' mission of the pursuit of social and economic justice through social reform initiatives and social action (Trolander 1987:1–5, 21–66). An organization serving a community that does not demonstrate an ongoing commitment to environmental reform and social equity for all peoples in the polity, including its own neighbors, may be an exemplary Y, community center, or multiservice center. A settlement house, however, it is not. Frank Bruno (1948:116), a settlement movement leader and educator, wrote in 1948:

> A settlement is not only pageantry, classes, and clubhouses for those who cannot afford them. It grows out of an attitude toward the gross and unjust differences in opportunity enjoyed by different portions of people making up our communities, and an ethical drive on the part of the privileged to understand the under-privileged better and to attempt to do something about it [inequity].

SOME KEY DEBATES

I have chosen to explore a few key debates within the settlement house movement of the past 114 years, debates that have also been mirrored in the School's development, which began when the settlement movement was already twelve years old. Since the exploration of points of contention within any movement or institution usually reveals much about that entity's fundamental values, ambitions, and assumptions across time, I will analyze some tensions within the settlement house world since 1886 that have resonated with forms of internal discord at the School of Social Work at Columbia University. The first settlement in the United States was established in 1886 by Stanton Coit. First known as the New York Neighborhood Guild, it has been known since 1891 as the University Settlement. It continues to thrive in the early twenty-first century.

Why did Coit organize the Neighborhood Guild? He was a man deeply affected by his mother's dramatic turn from Episcopalianism to spiritualism and by Ralph Waldo Emerson's conceptions of transcendentalism. Coit also was influenced seriously by evangelical Christianity's urban missions, Felix Adler's philosophy of ethical culture, William James's psychology and philosophy, John Dewey's pragmatism and pedagogy, and a brief stay at Toynbee Hall, the first recognized settlement house in the world, located in the East End of London in 1884 (Carson 1990; Davis 1967). Stanton Coit, like other key settlement house founders, such as Vida Scudder, Graham Taylor, and Jane Addams, was infused with a desire to emulate the direct relationship of Jesus to serving the poor by finding a way to embed the "Social Gospel," an American version of English Christian socialism, into his everyday life and work (Carson 1990; Luker 1991).

Settlers' Crisis of Identity: Community Members or Social Work Professionals?

Almost from the beginning of settlement houses' existence, settlement leaders and other settlement workers have confronted the questions: Is it wise to professionalize? Is it necessary to professionalize? What would the settlement movement gain and lose through professionalization? Will the community remain our chief guide and commitment once we have become professional social workers? How would our relationships change with neighbors if we become graduate social workers? And is social work the best profession to choose if a settlement house is seeking a cluster of particularized skills for its staff?

At issue was the knotty question of the nature of the working alliance between settlement workers and neighbors, an alliance in which only one-half of the partnership had the chance and educational background to be part of graduate professional studies. Why not, instead, develop two major reference groups for the staff of a settlement, the neighborhood and the profession? Why would a choice between these forces be necessary when social settlement workers can employ the riches of both?

One reason why settlement leaders felt challenged by such questions was that their preferences and interests were sometimes at odds with, or at least in tension with, those of neighbors. Issues of settlement house priorities for immediate action, overall direction, budgetary decisions, fund-raising, and the role and composition of boards of directors led to debates and even verbal clashes between community residents and settlement staff (Trolander 1987:21–89). Settlement leaders and workers over successive generations have struggled internally to determine whether professional methods or community sensibilities would rule any given day or determination.

Who Calls the Tune?

The rise, during the twentieth century, of significant grants from governmental sources and foundations and, more recently, of purchase-of-service contracts has posed major opportunities for settlement houses. Such funding sources have also posed pivotal dilemmas. Has, for example, settlement house leadership put at risk its authenticity as a representative community body when it has made a social settlement reliant upon a few large grantors? Some funding agencies and foundations, of course, have labored hard to remain attuned to the intersections among local, regional, national, and global currents. Many funding streams, however, have been directed by myriad forces, convictions, and concerns distant from the community life of neighborhoods, especially neighborhoods that are poor and unfamiliar with negotiating corridors of power.

I think it fair to suggest that ignorance of and indifference to a locality's complex needs has become predictable in a time of global market imperatives, technological revolutions, polities shaped by political polling, corporate weightiness in funding election campaigns, and term limits for legislators and executives. Local community needs and preferences have also fared poorly in the face of paradoxical combinations of ideological rigidity alongside flash-in-the-pan trendiness in governmental offices, elected bodies, and some philanthropic foundations.

Settlement Houses: An Institution or Social Movement?

Another important debate in the settlement house universe that recurs in successive generations is that which surrounds the difficult questions of institutionalization. Initially, many of the founding mothers and fathers of settlements attempted to build a liberatory social movement rather than a critical mass of competing and established institutions. Their focus was fixed on the emancipatory process of involving neighbors in the building of vibrant neighborhoods and a just society.

Not surprisingly, leaders of these "nurseries of experimentation," to employ Mary Kingsbury Simkhovitch's felicitous phrase, looked to anchor their settlement houses in the neighborhoods they served. Anchors, naturally, require reliable funding. Reliable funding, in turn, comes in steadily only if a sound organizational infrastructure and set of budgetary practices remain firmly in place, year after year. Simkhovitch understood the need for longstanding and "ever-changing" nurseries. Others worried and continue to worry that institutionalization may have led or may lead settlements toward self-interested caution and away from the inevitable taking of risks that accompany social action campaigns for greater social and economic equity (Simkhovitch 1938:40–79).

Racial Segregation and Integration

Settlement houses, like most other institutions in the United States over the past century, have struggled with the vexed and vexing social problem of racism, racial segregation, and racial discrimination. Jim Crow laws and cultural boundaries made their terrible imprint on most organizations, movements, and processes created by white Americans and African Americans between, roughly, 1885 and 1935. Settlement houses and the New York School of Social Work were no exceptions.

Two settlement leaders who were nationally respected, Sidney Lindenberg and Ruth Zittel, challenged the settlement movement on matters of racism in 1936. I have included most of their extensive quotation because of its import at the time in settlement circles.

> Because of an inferior economic position and pressure from a white group, which through control of recreation, housing, and education restricts his freedom of movement, the Negro is forced into the most densely crowded, unsanitary Areas (i.e., so-called slum areas). He is going into the "Settlement areas" inhabited by the foreign born and their children, . . . This brings us to a pertinent question: "What is the Settlement, the sponsor of the underprivileged and the champion of the immigrant, doing for the Negro who has settled on its doorstep?"

We can say upon observation that comparatively few of the Settlements have even scratched the surface of this problem. Except for a scattered Settlement here and there and an occasional poorly financed, under-staffed colored Settlement, or a more rare white Settlement which in-cludes the colored in its program, the Settlement has given very little thought or attention to a problem which is growing in intensity each year, and which it will finally have to meet face to face. . . . Settlements have not been laggards in facing the demands of a new day as regards their white neighbors, the Americanized children and grandchildren of immigrants. . . . They have thrown open their buildings at all hours to these people . . . Let's face the issue! What are Settlements doing for the Negro in their neighborhoods? In most instances, absolutely noth-ing. . . . An example of a Settlement helping the Negro . . . [follows]. Henry Street Settlement in New York City handles Negro children in mixed groups, and houses several all Negro adult groups. Negroes are also represented on all house councils . . . there must be a growing de-termination among existing Settlements to do something about this problem. [Settlements] will have to find ways of eliminating the criti-cism of sectarian federations and individuals who indicate a desire for us to cater to particular groups to the exclusion of others. (562–566)

During the 1930s, a few settlement houses and schools of social work began to grapple with the discrepancy between their philosophy of inclu-sion and their practice of complete or nearly complete racial exclusion. In New York City, the "honor roll" of the 1930s on this interracial fron-tier included, among other organizations, the Union Settlement, Hamilton-Madison House, Lenox Hill Neighborhood Guild, and the New York School of Social Work.

A major barrier, aside, of course, from racism, stood in the way. Prior to the 1940s, according to historian Elizabeth Lasch-Quinn (1993), the Na-tional Federation of Settlements (NFS) was committed to remaining non-denominational.

Coupled with a northern, urban bias, this view translated into poli-cies that unintentionally, but systematically, excluded many southern settlement houses from their organization, and especially most of those conducting reform work among blacks. The NFS believed that de-

nominationalism or extreme religiosity would enhance racial and ethnic hostilities, and so contradicted the very purpose of settlement
work. (58)

Most Negro settlement houses, prior to World War II, were created by
Negro churches in the South, the region where the majority of African Americans still lived. In that section of the United States, most white southerners
interested in helping black neighbors worked through channels organized by
religious denominations or specific churches. Therefore, the National Federation of Settlements' denial of membership to denominational organizations helped keep the settlement movement racially segregated. In the early
1940s, in response to the demands of leaders of national Negro organizations
and of outraged NFS members, the NFS began extensive soul searching and
data gathering about its member houses' relationships to Negro communities. Purposeful outreach to Negro neighbors and Negro settlement houses,
denominational or not, ensued (Lasch-Quinn 1993:151–163).

CONCLUSION

Each of the internal debates discussed above informed significantly the development of the New York School. The settlement movement's ambivalent
relationship to professionalization kept relatively small the number of graduates of the School who were hired by settlement houses. Concomitantly, the
School's awareness of settlement houses' ambivalence toward creating exclusively professional staffs was one reason it has underplayed group work and
community organization in its curriculum. Nonetheless, the executive leaders
of some of New York City's most prominent settlement houses are CUSSW
alumnae/i. Examples include the Lenox Hill Neighborhood House and the
Henry Street Settlement.

The degree to which funding sources determine institutional direction
was and remains a large and problematic issue for past and present settlement
house leaders in the United Neighborhood Houses of New York City and for
the New York School, now Columbia. Both social settlements and the School
continue to seek multiple sources of funding to reduce the possibility that
any one money source becomes dominant and, therefore, determinant of
mission, methods, and personnel.

School administrators and faculty, informed by the settlement movement tradition since 1898, have necessarily been self-scrutinizing on a number of key topics, sometimes meticulously, at other times more casually. Questions that have remained over time pivotal ones in the School's self-inspection include the following:

- How shall we remain an autonomous professional school of social work, while receiving such a substantial proportion of funding from major donors, a few foundations, and government contractors, be they Robert deForest, the Russell Sage Foundation, New York State, or the National Institutes of Health?

- Does our research, advising, teaching, and institutional advocacy make a serious contribution to international, national, state, and local social welfare and social service?

- To what extent does the School balance participation in social action, community initiatives, and social movements dedicated to building greater social and economic equity and environmental reclamation with work that primarily furthers institutional and individuals' self-interests?

- Are we fighting the good fight to embrace multicultural, religious, and racial inclusiveness in the School's recruitment and retention practices regarding students, staff, and faculty; strategic planning; student financial aid; advisory boards and working groups; and curriculum development?

- Does the School continue to invest steadily and heavily in helping New York City, New York State, and the nation rebuild a public sphere?

- Does the School continue to work with other groups and organizations in addressing global conflicts, global warming, regional crises, diseases, rape as a tool of war, and poverty?

No better overture can be written for the second century of the School's work than that composed by our settlement movement predecessors of the late nineteenth century, who faced urban, suburban, and rural challenges at least as profound as those we confront as social work educators at the start of the twenty-first century. Jane Addams (1961:92), in commenting on the in-

380 Barbara Levy Simon

spirations that drove men and women to create the settlement house movement, wrote words that may well help us to carry on:

. . . that the good we secure for ourselves is precarious and uncertain,
is floating in mid-air, until it is secured for all of us and incorporated
into our common life.

REFERENCES

Simkhovitch, Mary Kingsbury. (1938). *Neighborhood: My Story of Greenwich House.* New York: W. W. Norton.

Trolander, Judith. (1987). *Professionalism and Social Change: From the Settlement House Movement to Neighborhood Centers, 1886 to the Present.* New York: Columbia University Press.

Woods, Robert and Kennedy, Albert. (1911). *Handbook of Settlements.* New York.

Part Six

THE FUTURE OF CUSSW

A T THE BEGINNING of a second century of social work education, it is timely to consider the most recent developments that have occurred at the Columbia University School of Social Work (CUSSW) and to think about the significant challenges and issues that lie ahead. Accordingly, chapter 17 of this volume reviews trends and developments in a variety of major areas including student enrollment, tuition revenues, faculty salaries and faculty workloads, faculty recruitment and development, faculty scholarship and teaching, curriculum development, administrative infrastructures, and the School's physical facility. While considerable progress has been made in each of these areas, a great deal more needs to be accomplished. The essay concludes by reviewing cross-cutting themes that appear in the preceding papers and emergent issues that must be considered as CUSSW proceeds into its second century.

Great professional schools, like great universities and great societies, are in a constant state of evolution. Emerging problems must be treated as unique challenges for, as noted by John Gardner, "Life is full of golden opportunities disguised as irresolvable problems." As the Columbia University School of Social Work embarks upon a second century of social work education, it carries the great burden of recognizing that much of what it accomplishes or fails to accomplish will have a significant impact upon social work education worldwide and, subsequently, upon the quality and effectiveness of service by future generations of professional social workers. Such are the privileges and the responsibilities of the nation's oldest program of graduate social work education.

Chapter 17

CUSSW AT THE DAWN OF ITS SECOND CENTURY

Ronald A. Feldman

INTRODUCTION AND OVERVIEW

When the Columbia University School of Social Work (CUSSW) celebrated its centennial anniversary in June 1998, that celebration was not CUSSW's alone. Rather, it also was a celebration of the entire social work profession. Throughout the first century of social work education, the histories of CUSSW and of the social work profession have been interwoven integrally and inextricably. No doubt they will continue to be interdependent in future years.

At the dawn of the second century of social work education, it is timely to take stock of recent developments at the School of Social Work and to ponder issues that loom on the horizon. While much has been accomplished, much more remains to be done. Such will always be the case for a changing school and a changing profession.

This paper briefly examines key contexts of social work education, the current state of the Columbia University School of Social Work, issues for the future, and considerations relevant to CUSSW's second century. Respectively, the specific topics to be addressed are as follows: the school in context (the profession, the University, client populations), the state of the school (tuition revenues and student enrollment, fiscal setbacks and gains, faculty salaries and workload, faculty recruitment and development, teaching and scholarship, curriculum development, administrative development, quality of life), issues for the future (finances and student enrollment, faculty workload and salaries, faculty recruitment and development, curriculum development, administrative development, quality of life), and CUSSW in the second century.

Among the significant developments described are the following. The composition of the faculty has changed extensively. Faculty appointees have come to Columbia from throughout the United States and the world. Major curriculum revisions and innovations have occurred at CUSSW. Evaluations of faculty teaching are stronger than ever before recorded. Indirect revenues from funded research have grown elevenfold. Ratings of faculty scholarship place CUSSW first nationally. Research and practice are integrated increasingly throughout the curriculum. The School's endowment has grown significantly. Faculty workloads have been reduced. And, a new physical facility for the School of Social Work is on the horizon.

THE SCHOOL IN CONTEXT

CUSSW faculty, students, and alumnae/i are well acquainted with the main sociodemographic trends that are occurring throughout the United States and the world. The future directions of social work practice and of social work education will be shaped by them. Therefore, they are central to any discussion of social work curriculums, administration, or educational planning. Among the most germane trends are pressing social problems at home and abroad; widening economic disparities between the most affluent and least affluent sectors of society; increasing public criticism of higher education; growing competition for resources within academia; blurring of disciplinary and professional boundaries; increasing size, complexity, and cultural diversity of the nation's populace; the emergence of a "global community"; accelerated explosions of information, knowledge, and technology; and corresponding strains upon the "sense of community" in today's universities. As major changes emerge in one realm, such as health care, they portend corresponding adaptations in others, such as higher education. CUSSW's future, in particular, is likely to be shaped by powerful trends occurring within the social work profession, Columbia University, and the client populations served by social workers.

The Profession

Numerous changes have occurred throughout social work practice and education in the last two decades. Most have had a determinate impact on CUSSW. Among them are the introduction in 1993 of a new Council on Social Work Education (CSWE) curriculum policy statement and, subsequently, new standards and guidelines for the accreditation of schools of social work. The latter define the basic parameters and characteristics of CUSSW's curriculum. While setting minimum standards for accreditation, they also constrain the range, the substance, and, ultimately, the quality of education that can be offered by the best schools of social work.

The 1991 Report of the National Institute of Mental Health (NIMH) Task Force on Social Work Research also has exerted a major impact on social work education. Numerous recommendations of the task force have been implemented, including establishment of the Institute for the Advancement of Social Work Research under the aegis of all five of our profession's major associations. Since 1991 the NIMH report has led to funding for nine social work research development centers throughout the country. These initiatives have substantially catalyzed and improved social work research.

Especially important, the last four decades have seen a vast proliferation of social work education programs in the United States. Master's degree programs have grown from 53 in 1953 to 130 today. Even more, the educational sector has witnessed an explosion in baccalaureate social work programs, from approximately a score or two several decades ago to 545 today. Another 49 B.S.W. programs are in candidacy. Yet, while there also has been considerable growth in the number of social work doctoral programs (from 10 in 1960 to 66 today), the total annual number of doctoral graduates has remained constant throughout the last fifteen years, viz., under 300 per year. These trends have obvious implications. Educational programs in social work are proliferating rapidly but their growth is not being accompanied by a corresponding increase in the number of doctoral graduates needed to staff them. As a result, the profession's educational sector is becoming fragmented and diffuse, few schools of social work are able to gather a critical mass of highly talented educators and scholars, and a classic "seller's market" exists in social work education.

The number of social work practitioners in the United States has increased from 20,000 members of the National Association of Social Workers (NASW) in 1965 to 155,000 today. Some observers estimate that there are as many as 600,000 professional social workers in the United States, most of whom are not members of NASW. Hence, there also is a growing gap between the number of scholars who generate knowledge for social work and the number of professionals who apply such knowledge in practice. The disparity is even more marked when one considers how these dynamics vary in accord with

388   *Ronald A. Feldman*

considerations such as race, ethnicity, and gender. For example, approximately 25 percent of the New York City population is Hispanic. Yet, even though Hispanic students at CUSSW increased in the 1999–2000 academic year to 10 percent of the entering class, this rate of growth fails to keep pace with the City's demographic and social service needs. More daunting is the fact that only one-half of 1 percent of all social work doctoral graduates each year are Hispanic. This figure—totaling about two or three graduates per year—is not even remotely sufficient to meet the needs of 675 social work education programs. Because extant demographic trends do not portend well for the recruitment of minority faculty members, unusually creative and aggressive initiatives are required on the part of CUSSW.

The University

The School of Social Work's affiliation with Columbia University has been beneficial. The intellectual, material, and administrative resources of the University are immense and they have aided CUSSW time and again. Nevertheless, CUSSW can derive even greater benefit from its affiliation with the larger University. Likewise, the University must benefit more readily and visibly from CUSSW's formidable strengths.

Relevant developments at Columbia University include a stronger emphasis upon working linkages across departments and schools, cutting-edge research programs that can compete effectively for extramural support, innovative international programs, the design and application of new digital and information technologies, and, of course, extremely high standards for achieving tenure. A particularly noteworthy development at the University is a renewed emphasis upon undergraduate education. These trends necessarily will shape the future of social work education at Columbia University.

The introduction in 1993 of the Ph.D. degree in social work, in conjunction with the Graduate School of Arts and Sciences, fostered greater mutual facilitation between the School and the larger University. Likewise, the School's leadership role in the new interdisciplinary Columbia University Institute for Child and Family Policy constitutes a major development. Yet, these are mere beginnings in the formation of strong operational linkages with other units of the University.

As noted by Harvard University's former President Derek Bok (1990), there now is a growing realization in our nation that if we are to combat such vexing problems as poverty, homelessness, drug abuse, chronic unemployment, and family dissolution, our universities must give increasing priority to schools that are directly concerned with preventing or alleviating these problems. Yet, even "wealthy" universities find it difficult to do so in view of competing demands for finite resources. In the last decade, Columbia University has undergone major fiscal challenges. Just as CUSSW's financial difficulties posed a problem for the University in 1981, so the University's fiscal exigencies in the early 1990s greatly affected the School. Faculty pension contributions were reduced, graduate tuition remissions were eliminated for new appointees, and certain expenditures were displaced from units of the central administration to schools and departments. Likewise, as the University has experienced severe constraints upon space, CUSSW has been hampered in securing University housing for faculty and students as well as classrooms for courses. In the competition for resources, the University is likely to increasingly evaluate its various schools and departments not only on the basis of their "quality" but also in terms of their relative productivity, cost-effectiveness, and ability to complement allied units and contribute to them synergistically.

Client Populations

Social work's client populations are more numerous, as well as more complex in their needs and demands and varied in terms of demographics, ethnicity, and culture than ever before. As a result, CUSSW must address continuously the diverse and complex nature of its client populations. It will need to formulate intervention theories, models, programs, and methods that are more sophisticated, multifaceted, and effective than those employed in previous years. The CUSSW curriculum has been expanded and broadened in order to address such trends. Now, however, it may be timely for the School to ponder a narrowing or refocusing of its key client populations and problem areas. Helping professions that demonstrate the most cost-effective models of education and practice for given client populations will be best able to generate resources and support in a highly competitive environment.

STATE OF THE SCHOOL

CUSSW is held in high regard by alumnae/i, University officials, and deans and social work leaders throughout the world. The resources available to the School are many. The faculty are talented, dedicated, and diverse, and, therefore, fully capable of defining the key educational issues of today and tomorrow, formulating the best ways to address them, and assuring that Columbia continues to offer the best possible social work education. Although focused particularly upon New York City and large urban areas, Columbia's historic mission necessarily entails leadership far beyond the School's immediate environs. CUSSW must develop programs and models that can inform social work education worldwide. National and international leadership in social work education is needed more than ever before on the part of Columbia.

A leading school of social work must be characterized by a number of key attributes. It must, for instance, be part of an excellent university. It must have talented students. It must have a top-flight faculty. It must have a supportive administrative environment. It must have distinguished and dedicated alumnae/i. It must have a respected doctoral program. It must have an active and mutually facilitative relationship with the community. It must have a physical facility that permits state-of-the-art professional education. And, it must have adequate financial resources. Although CUSSW already has most of these prerequisites, it cannot afford to be complacent about any of them. CUSSW must be especially concerned about its fiscal strength. With this in mind, eight main topics are addressed here: tuition revenues and student enrollment, fiscal setbacks and gains, faculty salaries and workload, faculty recruitment and development, teaching and scholarship, curriculum development, administrative developments, and quality of life. These topics are not presented in priority order; each is central to the School's health and well-being.

Tuition Revenues and Student Enrollment

Ultimately, the well-being of any school of social work depends on the strength of its fiscal resources and the extent to which they are utilized wisely. Accordingly, over the last decade or so concerted efforts have been made to improve CUSSW's financial health through a number of strategies. Among others, these have entailed giving greater attention to fund-raising; building the School's endowment; increasing indirect cost revenues from funded research; computerizing, restructuring, and streamlining of administrative activities; and introducing stringent budget-monitoring and cost-control mechanisms. These efforts have aimed not only to increase the School's resource base but also to diversify the sources of revenue upon which CUSSW depends.

While this multifold strategy has achieved considerable success, CUSSW nonetheless remains highly dependent upon tuition as its main source of revenue. Attracting substantial numbers of talented students while requiring one of the highest social work tuitions in the nation is thus a continuing challenge. Among other things, potential applicants' interest in a CUSSW education is influenced adversely by the high cost of living in New York City, undue difficulties in acquiring student housing, and fears about personal safety. Because CUSSW is excessively reliant upon tuition as its main source of revenue, it is imperative that the School develop more balanced, diversified, and stable streams of revenue while at the same time reducing unnecessary expenditures.

CUSSW can best assure a strong and talented applicant pool by delivering educational programs of superior—indeed, exceptional—quality. However, this strategy can succeed only as long as applicants are able to afford CUSSW's tuitions and realize commensurate gains from them. In short, the School's educational programs must warrant the steep financial investments required of students. Their capacity for such an investment has varied over the years. In 1976, for instance, CUSSW received 1,300 applications for admission. This number plummeted to 400 in 1982, shortly after Ronald Reagan became president of the United States. In that year tuition was raised 17 percent in order to cover the projected financial losses from declining enrollment. From 1981 through 1990, applications at CUSSW increased gradually, that is, by about 5 percent per year (see figure 17.1). Applications increased steeply each year from 1991 to 1994, however. In the same period many, but not all, schools of social work reported an increase of applications. Few if any seem to have experienced the marked four-year upsurge seen at Columbia, though.

Since 1994, applications to CUSSW have declined. However, the applicant pool remains strong due to the considerable growth experienced in the early 1990s and also due to CUSSW's introduction of new student recruitment aids such as a viewbook and a recruitment video. In 1995, CUSSW decided to enroll approximately 10 percent fewer students in order to relieve stress upon the School's overburdened physical facility and to permit better quality control in admission decisions. At the same time, the Admissions Office and faculty members Grace Christ, Neil Guterman, and others developed an evaluation instrument that made admission decisions more efficient and reliable. It also enabled CUSSW to more readily target especially talented students for speedy admission.

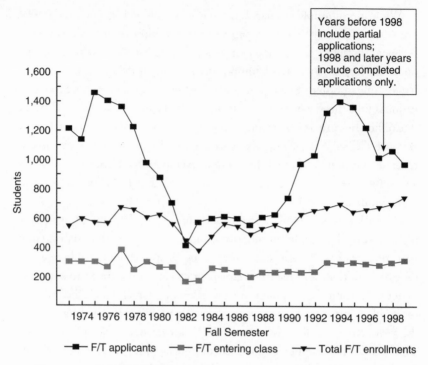

Figure 17.1. CUSSW Full-Time Applications and Enrollments, 1973 to 1999

In 1998–99, CUSSW also implemented a much more stringent method of recording "applications" than in previous years. To wit, only fully completed applications were counted. This may account partially for the modest decline in applications from 1998 to 1999. For fall 1999, CUSSW received 955 completed applications. Of these, 727 (76 percent) were accepted. Of the latter, 386 (53 percent) enrolled. Two-year M.S. program applications for fall 1999 declined by 9 percent in comparison with the preceding year—a figure that is easily sustainable in view of the skyrocketing applications in previous years. Peer schools have reported a similar decline. At least one school reported a 30 percent drop in applications for fall 1999.

A substantial portion of this one-year decline may be due, however, to the implementation in 1998–99 of a new system for recording applications. When the same system is employed for applications received through July 2000, applications for fall 2000 are ahead of those for fall 1999 by 8 percent, and paid registration fees are ahead by nearly 25 percent. This trend is all the

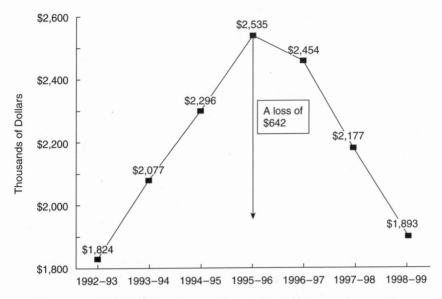

Figure 17.2. CUSSW Tuition Revenue from Purchase Site, 1992–93 to 1998–99

more remarkable in view of the fact that virtually all CUSSW's peer schools report a marked decline in total applications for fall 2000.

The most significant and serious decline in CUSSW applications has taken place at the SUNY, Purchase Educational Site. Most likely attributable to demographic and market changes in Westchester County and Connecticut, this decline has been especially steep in recent years (see figure 17.2). To offset it, CUSSW has planned a one-year program (rather than a full two years) at the Purchase site. Concurrently, enrollments at McVickar Hall necessarily have been increased, thereby placing greater strain upon the physical facility and more demand upon the limited pool of housing available to CUSSW students.

Along with these trends, CUSSW's student body has become more diverse with regard to its ethnic, racial, and cultural composition. In 1979 about 16 percent of the entering class consisted of students of color. Of these, 8.6 percent were African American and 7.1 percent were Hispanic. There were no Asian American enrollees. In 1989, 18 percent of the entering class consisted of minority students. Of these, 7.1 percent were African American, 7.5 percent were Asian American, and 3.1 percent were Hispanic. In 1999, 38 percent of the entering class consisted of minority students, of whom

11 percent were African American, 11 percent Asian American, and 10 percent Hispanic. Hence, minority enrollment has grown steadily at CUSSW.

Typically, large applicant pools ought to strengthen an institution's capacity to charge tuitions that will cover the full costs of a top-flight professional education. However, this is not necessarily the case for schools of social work, where students' indebtedness is great, earning opportunities are limited, and financial aid is scant. Therefore, CUSSW must do all that is possible to keep tuition growth at a minimum by trimming undue expenditures and securing more financial aid for students. By constraining tuition growth, CUSSW is no longer the most expensive school of social work in the nation. There is nevertheless continuing concern that future tuition increases might jeopardize CUSSW's market position, that is, that the School could reach the limits of "elasticity" in tuition growth. This could prove to be the case if either of two adverse trends should materialize. The first is unexpectedly higher central administrative charges that might be imposed upon CUSSW by the University's central administration. In recent years, the rate of growth in this area has outpaced inflation, thereby necessitating tuition increases that exceed the consumer price index. The second factor would be the failure of social work salaries to keep pace with increasing tuition charges.

Because social work graduates earn an average starting salary of only $34,000, they begin their careers with high indebtedness in relation to their earning potential. Moreover, it is evident that the gap between students' tuition costs and earning potential is growing rather than declining. For instance, in 1984 the average social work graduate would have had to expend only about ten months of her or his gross income in order to offset two years of CUSSW tuition (see figure 17.3). Today, approximately thirteen months of gross income is required to do so.

In the absence of needed financial aid, it may be impossible for many applicants to cope with the costs of graduate social work education. Since 1981, CUSSW has had to absorb steep cuts in student financial aid from federal sources. For instance, in 1979 a total of 45 CUSSW master's degree students received scholarship support from the federal government. By 1989, none did. Correspondingly, in 1979 only 142 students received some kind of grant from the School or the University. They represented about 25 percent of the full-time student body. By 1999, 223 students received such aid. This represents more than 30 percent of the full-time student body and a 57 percent increase in funded students during the last two decades. The rate of growth

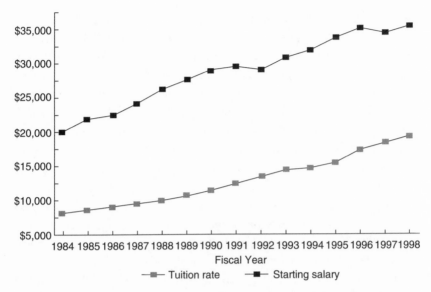

Figure 17.3. CUSSW Trends in Tuition Rate and Starting Salary of Graduates, 1984 to 1998

in student financial need and in the amount of financial aid awarded by the School has far outpaced the rate of growth of the total student body.

With specific regard to tuition growth, CUSSW is in a unique position vis-à-vis other schools at Columbia University. The School's budget is heavily tuition driven, yet it probably has less tuition elasticity than other schools. CUSSW students are likely to be among the most financially impoverished students at the University when they begin their graduate education. They arrive at CUSSW with an already high level of indebtedness. Moreover, before they can be eligible for scholarship aid, they are required to accept a minimum loan of $8,500 per year. Close to 80 percent of CUSSW students receive some form of financial assistance whether in the form of scholarships or loans. Clearly, the School's constrained financial aid budget is not adequate to meet the need.

To help defray tuition costs, since 1986 the School of Social Work has been able to generate more than $3.1 million in newly endowed scholarships for students. It also has established several endowed prizes. Among the largest are the Ruth L. Sagner Centennial Scholarship ($550,000) and the Mae L. Wien Memorial Prize ($332,000). Especially notable are scholarships for students of color and others that have been established through vigorous grass-roots fund-raising efforts initiated by former CUSSW faculty members. Examples include the Agustin Gonzalez Scholarship launched by Rita Ortiz ($224,000), the Ida and Mitchell Ginsberg Social Policy Fund ($177,000), the V. Benjamin and Agnes Louard Scholarship ($134,000), the Hyman Grossbard Scholarship ($126,000), and the newly emerging Muriel Reed Scholarship Fund and the Blanca Rosenberg Memorial Scholarship Fund. Related fund-raising endeavors of note include $414,000 in minority student fellowships from the Aaron Diamond Foundation, $60,000 from the Compton Foundation for minority child protection workers and minority doctoral students, $65,000 from the Kenworthy-Swift Foundation for a program with United Negro College Fund schools, $100,000 from the Ittleson Foundation for the now completed National Minority Leadership Project, and a gift of $125,000 to create an anonymously endowed scholarship for African American students. Additional tuition funds and stipends are available to CUSSW students through the School's programs with the New York City Board of Education, the Administration on Children's Services, and various field instruction agencies as well as from training and research grants acquired by faculty and administrators. These funds have been extraordinarily helpful, but more are needed. One promising initiative that has been established is the Lowenstein Student Loan Forgiveness Fund.

Most CUSSW enrollees hail from New York, New Jersey, or Connecticut. About one-third of the student body comes from beyond the tri-state area. Only 4 percent are from abroad. Regardless of their place of origin, however, it is evident that students enroll at CUSSW primarily due to the following considerations: the reputation and national visibility of the School and of Columbia University, encouragement from alumnae/i and students, vigorous recruitment efforts by administrators and faculty, and a desire to pursue their professional studies in New York City. More directly, they enroll at CUSSW because of the School's wide range of educational offerings, the richness of the curriculum, the quality of faculty instruction, and the readiness with which CUSSW graduates are employed as social work professionals.

Fiscal Setbacks and Gains

In seeking to overcome projected budget deficits, the fiscal growth rates for all units at Columbia University were severely constrained in the early

1990s. Correspondingly, administrative budgets were reduced. In some instances, CUSSW assumed responsibilities that had been carried previously by other units such as the University's Office of Development and Alumni Relations and its Office of Projects and Grants.

CUSSW also suffered a variety of budget setbacks. Examples include a decline in negotiated indirect cost rates for funded research projects and the loss of Urban Corps funding. Until 1991–92, for instance, the Urban Corps paid a 30 percent share of college work study funds for 60 or more CUSSW students. When the Urban Corps withdrew this support, CUSSW had to assume an additional financial burden of $76,000 per year. The School also has incurred significantly increased expenditures due to the introduction of "mini-sabbaticals" for nontenured faculty members, reductions in workloads for tenured and nontenured faculty members, debt service for renovations, and burgeoning outlays for computing and information technologies. Altogether, these expenditures and others have added hundreds of thousands of dollars to CUSSW's operating budget.

To reduce the strain on faculty resources, manage better within the confines of McVickar Hall, and improve the quality of life at CUSSW, a planned decline in student enrollment was initiated in 1995–96. The entering class was reduced by 25 students per year, or a total of 50 students for the first and second years combined. The loss of tuition revenue from this initiative totals over $5 million to date.

The above-mentioned financial stressors have been offset handily, however, by significant progress in many areas. They include major overdraft reductions, steady growth in endowment principal and annual fund revenues, and increased research revenues.

Overdraft Reductions. As noted in table 17.1, CUSSW has made dramatic progress in reducing overdrafts inherited from previous years. Nearly each year since 1988–89, CUSSW not only has achieved the goal of meeting its overdraft target at year end, but also has succeeded in lowering overdrafts significantly beyond the targeted amount. Nonetheless, these monies could have been put to better use had the overdrafts never been incurred.

Endowment Principal. Endowment growth is essential to CUSSW's continuing financial health. Accordingly, vigorous efforts have been made to

TABLE 17.1

Overdrafts, 1989–1999 (in thousands of dollars)

FISCAL YEAR	TARGET	ACTUAL
1988–89		923
1989–90	922	377
1990–91	376	308
1991–92	374	297
1992–93	296	222
1993–94	122	100
1994–95	122	121
1995–96	197	136
1996–97	158	94
1997–98	118	96
1998–99	79	79

increase the one source of revenue that can be counted on year after year, namely, endowment income. The School's record of new additions to endowment principal is depicted in table 17.2.

Work with friends of the School and prospective donors over many years has yielded significant results. In 1992–93, more additions were made to CUSSW's endowment principal than were made in the preceding five years combined. Since 1986, the book value of the School's endowment principal has nearly quintupled. In short, it rose from $8,558,176 in 1986 to $39,195,910 in 1999 (see figure 17.4). In addition, the School has benefited from roughly $9 million in gifts, endowments, or secured funds from a variety of other sources.

Through 1986, CUSSW had established only one partially endowed professorship in eighty-eight years. Today, the School has funds on hand or pledged for ten fully endowed professorships. And, with the generosity of the Jewish Board of Family and Children's Services, a sizable endowment has been established for the Center for the Study of Social Work Practice. This kind of support is increasingly essential for the continued financial health of the School. Nevertheless, despite these gains CUSSW's endowment is not yet at a level that can sustain the School in the future. CUSSW must build a considerably larger endowment.

TABLE 17.2

New Additions to Endowment Principal, 1987–
1999 (in thousands of dollars)

FISCAL YEAR	NEW ADDITIONS TO ENDOWMENT PRINCIPAL
1987–88	100
1988–89	276
1989–90	333
1990–91	324
1991–92	277
1992–93	1,459
1993–94	624
1994–95	2,039
1995–96	2,159
1996–97	1,839
1997–98	1,437
1998–99	814

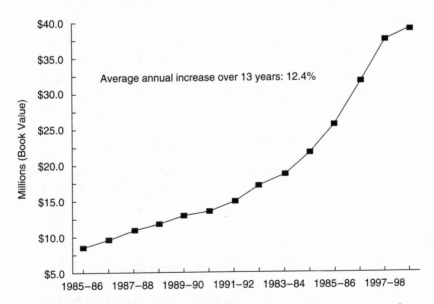

Figure 17.4. CUSSW Year-End Endowment Principal, 1985–86 to 1997–98

Annual Fund. Another factor that is crucial to any consideration of CUSSW's financial status is the annual fund. Over the years, CUSSW has fared well in this realm. Often, a higher percentage of CUSSW alumnae/i contributes to the annual fund than at other schools at Columbia. But, as might be expected, their per capita contribution is much lower than for the graduates of most other professional schools.

Research Revenues. A welcome source of income for CUSSW comes from extramural research and training awards and their accompanying indirect costs. These monies have grown markedly over the years. While funded research grew 1,047 percent between FY 1984 and FY 1998, the revenues from indirect costs grew 1,080 percent. Yet, these revenues constitute only a minor portion of the School's overall income and they are a fluctuating and undependable source of funds. Even more, the lion's share of indirect cost revenues from funded grants is attributable to a very small number of faculty members. To facilitate knowledge advancement through research and to become less financially dependent on a mere handful of faculty members, it is essential to expand the School's research funding base. Extramural funds provide the School with supplies, equipment, and jobs for students. But, above all, they offer significant learning opportunities for faculty and students, promote intellectual inquiry and innovation at the School, and constitute tangible evidence of CUSSW's commitment to discovering better ways of combating major societal ills. In short, funding from extramural sources and individual donors constitutes an area where faculty can help to improve the School's fiscal strength while advancing their own scholarly and career interests.

Faculty Salaries and Workload

Central to any discussion of CUSSW's finances are the interrelated issues of faculty salaries and faculty workload. In these domains CUSSW fares relatively well.

Faculty Salaries. In 1998–99, the median salaries for social work faculty members in the United States were, respectively, $66,800 for full professors, $51,400 for associate professors, and $42,000 for assistant professors (CSWE 1999). In region 2 (New York, New Jersey, the Virgin Islands, and Puerto Rico), they were $77,000, $57,900, and $44,200 respectively. The comparable figures at CUSSW for the same year were $93,033, $59,817, and $48,149. Paralleling national trends, mean salary increments at CUSSW have been severely constrained in the last decade. Nonetheless, every year they have significantly exceeded the rate of inflation.

Faculty Workload. The 6.5 workload units (or course equivalents) required of each CUSSW faculty member until a year ago was regarded widely as higher than at peer schools of social work and, certainly, than at other units of Columbia University. It placed CUSSW faculty members at a marked competitive disadvantage vis-à-vis peers in other schools or departments, hindered faculty recruitment, and put the School at risk of losing talented faculty. Likewise, it may have weakened nontenured faculty members' chances for favorable reviews by ad hoc tenure review committees.

A study by Locke and Patchner (1992) of faculty workloads at sixty-three schools of social work suggests that CUSSW's faculty workload has been well within traditional limits. At private schools of social work, the average full-time teaching load consisted of 5.6 courses per year plus 16.8 advisees, 14.1 field liaison students, 2.3 committees, and 3.9 dissertations. In 1999 the average workload for tenured and nontenured faculty members at CUSSW was reduced on a trial basis, respectively, by 15 percent and 23 percent. Moreover, additional workload adjustments have been made in other ways. For example, workload credit is awarded for service on the Committee on Students. Workloads also have been reduced for first-time faculty members. A workload reduction plan has been instituted for nontenured faculty members which offers some, but not all, of the benefits of the sabbatical leaves available to their tenured colleagues. In addition, a modest endowment fund has been established to support pilot research projects by nontenured faculty members. Likewise, pilot research projects are supported by the Center for the Study of Social Work Practice and by the School's Social Intervention Group. In the case of adjunct faculty members, salaries have been increased for field advising and classroom instruction. Remuneration for the latter now varies in accord with the number of years of productive service provided to the School by the instructor.

Faculty Recruitment and Development

To the greatest extent possible, CUSSW must recruit multitalented faculty members. Increasingly, they must be able to forge working linkages with educational and research programs at other units of the University. These include the Graduate School of Arts and Sciences, the School of Public Health, the School of International and Public Affairs, the School of Business, the College of Physicians and Surgeons, and the New York State Psychiatric Institute. Although noteworthy progress has been made in the last few years, social work faculty members still remain unduly isolated and insular. Ways must be found to achieve more extensive and mutually beneficial linkages.

To best attain these objectives, it is essential to recruit and retain a wide array of outstanding faculty. From 1985 through 1999 more than half of CUSSW's tenured faculty members retired or died. The relative percentage of tenured faculty members has declined from about 78 percent in 1983 to 67 percent in 1990 and to 40 percent today. As always, CUSSW must recruit and retain stellar faculty members who have the potential to become exemplary teachers and scholars. At the same time, it must be recognized that social work education and the social work profession are quite different from earlier days. Social work is larger, more diffuse, and more fragmented than before. Hence, it is unlikely that any given scholar or institution will dominate social work education as profoundly and pervasively as when the profession was younger, smaller, and more readily bounded.

As CUSSW confronts the profession's major concerns in the next decade, it must accord top priority to seeking and retaining those faculty members who can most ably address them. In particular, the School needs to appoint significantly more faculty members of color. CUSSW has been hit especially hard by deaths and retirements of minority faculty members in the senior ranks. Relative to the composition of the student body, CUSSW is especially in need of Hispanic and African American faculty members.

To strengthen CUSSW's faculty recruitment and retention efforts, the Faculty Development and Support Task Force has been established. It has spearheaded numerous initiatives at the School. Besides the above-cited workload reductions and mini-sabbaticals, faculty have been relieved from many administrative tasks by assigning these to administrators or adjunct faculty. Examples include changes in field advising and the coordination of dual degree programs. Assistance with the preparation of research proposals has been provided through in-house seminars and workshops led by faculty colleagues, establishment of a CUSSW research development office, grant proposal review teams staffed by experienced CUSSW researchers, and the creation of special research funds by the Dean's Office and the Center for the

Study of Social Work Practice. Teaching improvements have been fostered through faculty seminars and workshops. Funds for the presentation of papers at professional conferences have increased by 30 percent, and a special fund has been established to make statistical consultants available to faculty.

One variable that potently shapes faculty recruitment at CUSSW is the particular fit between specific curriculum areas and the special expertise of faculty candidates. Over the years, CUSSW has opted not to hire many talented faculty candidates because their teaching and/or research expertise did not fit neatly into the precise niches prescribed by the School's curriculum. In the future, however, the School should consider hiring at least a few exceptional candidates who may not fit squarely into traditional curriculum areas. CUSSW should seek the best possible educators and scholars, and it should encourage them to bring innovations to the curriculum that will help the School and the profession to progress even further than heretofore.

Teaching and Scholarship

CUSSW's overarching goal is to be the premier school of social work in the world. This goal can be attained only if the School is exceptional with regard to both the quality of its educational program and the quality of its research and knowledge advancement. The School's stature is linked integrally, too, with its service to the community and with the accomplishments of its faculty and alumnae/i in local, national, and international arenas.

CUSSW faculty members always have exercised leadership in social work education through their superior teaching and scholarship. By successfully melding these components of the School's mission, the faculty have brought worldwide distinction to CUSSW. Leadership in the educational realm depends especially upon the quality and consistency of teaching and upon its utility for educating skilled practitioners. At CUSSW, the mean student evaluations of faculty teaching range invariably from "above average" to "outstanding." Some observers express concern that the quality of teaching can suffer when faculty increase their research productivity. But, this does not appear to be the case at CUSSW. The mean student ratings of "teacher quality" at CUSSW have increased gradually over the years on a scale that varies from 1.0 to 5.0: 4.16 for the years 1982 through 1985, 4.20 for 1986 through 1989, 4.24 for 1990 through 1993, and 4.30 from 1995 through 1998.

Faculty leadership is expressed also in contributions to scholarship and knowledge advancement for the social work profession. Faculty can contribute to knowledge development in myriad ways, including empirical research that is either quantitative or qualitative, theoretical formulations, creative syntheses of the literature, adaptations or applications of knowledge from allied disciplines and professions, and the development of innovative teaching aids or resources. In the 1970s, several studies rated CUSSW as the nation's premier school of social work. These were primarily "reputational" studies based upon the subjective judgments of selected opinion leaders. Studies in the next decade ranked social work schools primarily in terms of faculty scholarship. Regrettably, Columbia was not foremost in any of these studies. In fact, it was not among the top ten schools in some. One report placed CUSSW thirtieth in terms of per capita scholarly productivity for the period 1977 through 1981 and ninth for the period 1983 through 1987. Later studies, based on data collected in the mid- to late-1980s, placed Columbia seventh or eighth. By contrast, the four most recently published studies of faculty scholarship in refereed journals now rank Columbia at the forefront of social work education. Three place CUSSW first and one places CUSSW second.

Advances in faculty scholarship at CUSSW have gone hand in hand with success in acquiring extramural funds for research projects. Total grant monies in FY 1998 were $5,066,574. Fifty-four research proposals were submitted for extramural funding in FY 1998. Decisions were made on forty proposals; of these, thirty were funded. Hence, 75 percent of submitted proposals were funded (as opposed to a national average of only 20 to 25 percent). Equally impressive, eighteen of twenty-eight first-time research proposals were funded. This "success rate" of 64 percent compares very favorably with the national average of merely 20 percent.

The central issue in the next decade of social work education will be the mutual integration of practice-based research and research-based practice. CUSSW has made marked advances in this regard. Schools of social work will strive to educate their students in the most current and effective methods of intervention and of intervention evaluation. Research—whether quantitative or qualitative—will be essential to advance the profession's knowledge base, better educate students, and exercise more meaningful influence upon social work practice and public policy. Cutting-edge scholarship of many different kinds will be required if CUSSW is to significantly advance social work education in the coming years.

Curriculum Development

The overarching concern that must be addressed continuously by any school of social work is curriculum development. Here the fundamental question is, What constitutes the best possible practice curriculum for the second century of social work education? CUSSW's curriculum must enable its graduates to serve their clients effectively and also to demonstrate unambiguously the utility of their interventions.

CUSSW's curriculum is configured primarily in terms of two dimensions: practice methods and fields of practice. In the last decade there have been continuous efforts to improve and expand the curriculum. Much has been accomplished to augment the traditional strengths of professional education at CUSSW.

1. *Strong teaching.* Superior teaching is a time-honored hallmark of CUSSW. Student evaluations of teaching indicate that the quality of instruction at CUSSW now is stronger than at any previous period on record. However, student ratings alone are not sufficient to assess the quality of teaching. More creative ways must be devised to evaluate teaching.

2. *Sequencing of required practice courses, harmonizing the content for all sections of a given course, and integrating classroom and practicum content.* These, too, are valued hallmarks of the CUSSW curriculum. Their advantages are offset at least in part, however, by the difficulties of introducing major innovations into a curriculum that is highly integrated. Efforts to introduce change can generate unanticipated consequences elsewhere in the curriculum.

3. *Strong field advising.* Another characteristic of social work education at Columbia is the strong emphasis placed on field advising. This is reflected by substantial expenditures for field instruction personnel, faculty field advising, adjunct field advising, and, above all, favorable student evaluations of field advisors. A 1997–98 study indicates that CUSSW students are highly satisfied with the current system. Their mean rating for the quality of field advising was 3.4 on a scale of 1 to 4. To date, however, few experiments have been conducted to test alternative field advising models that might be more innovative or productive. This should be a priority for the future.

4. *Improved foundation and background content.* In recent years, CUSSW has introduced major changes to the foundation curriculum that have been

fruitful but expensive. Therefore, it may be advisable to seek even more cost-effective ways of delivering the requisite content. It may be productive, for instance, to offer considerably larger courses in selected background areas as long as they are staffed by outstanding lecturers and capable teaching assistants. Such a change might also improve the consistency and quality of certain courses. Moreover, by enabling doctoral students to serve as teaching assistants, it may be possible to strengthen their preparation for academic careers while providing financial support that could reduce attrition in the latter years of doctoral study. Space and fiscal pressures also would be eased by such a change.

5. *Major curriculum innovations.* The cardinal challenge for social work education inheres in how to best achieve significant advances in social work curricula. Even though the prospects for such advances are constrained somewhat by CSWE accreditation requirements, CUSSW has introduced major curriculum innovations in recent years. Among them are the following:

a. *Three new fields of practice.* New fields of practice have been introduced in School-Based and School-Linked Social Work Services, Contemporary Social Problems, and International Social Welfare and Services for Refugees and Immigrants. Each of these curriculum areas addresses significant and growing problems in the United States and abroad. They have been well-received by students and have greatly enriched professional education at CUSSW. To further build these curriculum areas, special efforts need to be devoted to the recruitment of key senior faculty members. Innovations in the international arena have been strengthened by operational linkages forged with the United Nations. CUSSW is the only school of social work to have a formal and ongoing working agreement with the UN. Yet, efforts need to be made to develop this relationship further and to assure that it yields maximum benefits for all of the participants.

b. *A new practice method.* Social Policy has been introduced as a new practice method. CUSSW is one of very few schools that are able to mount a strong M.S.W. concentration in this method. It already has proven to be of substantial interest to students.

c. *Required seven-week minicourses.* These courses are among the most innovative and successful at CUSSW. They permit considerable flexibility and choice for students to select from a menu of required courses concerning certain topics, and they are linked integrally with the student's practice method. Because these courses have been so well received in the Clinical Practice method, they now are being extended to Advanced Generalist Practice and Programming (AGPP) and to Human Behavior and Social Environment (HBSE). They offer the added advantage of enabling faculty members to teach courses in areas of their special interest and expertise. Given the constraints imposed on elective offerings by Council on Social Work Education (CSWE) accreditation requirements, such courses are especially welcome. The success of CUSSW's seven-week courses may account at least in part for the recent gains registered in the School's already impressive teaching evaluations.

   d. *Second research course.* Research content at CUSSW is more extensive and practice-relevant than in previous years. The addition of a second research course has facilitated CUSSW's ongoing efforts to link research and practice more productively. Such linkages are being demanded with increasing frequency by agencies as well as by CSWE accreditation requirements.

   e. *Social administration area.* With a tripling of full-time faculty in the Social Administration area, significant advances can be expected in this realm. These include growing curricular and research linkages with faculty colleagues from the School of Business, the School of International and Public Affairs, and other Columbia schools.

6. *Contemporary technologies.* One aspect of curriculum development that merits special attention is the growing utilization of digital technology and innovative modes of computing and information exchange. CUSSW has made vast strides in this regard through the creation of the new Office of Computing and Information Technology. Even though the School remains severely limited in this realm due to the deficiencies of McVickar Hall, much greater attention must be accorded to it in the near future.

   Finally, several additional curriculum initiatives are noteworthy. Course content on diversity has been strengthened greatly through the work of the Task Force on Diversity. The School's basic course on organizational change has been revised and updated as Advocacy in Social Work Practice. Two foundation practice courses have been expanded and accorded greater course credit and workload credit. Related initiatives that have influenced education and knowledge advancement at CUSSW include the Minority Leadership

Project, the New York City Social Indicators Survey Center, the Social Intervention Group, and the programs of the Center for the Study of Social Work Practice.

Administrative Developments

Numerous administrative developments have occurred at CUSSW in the last decade. For instance, the position of Business Officer was upgraded to Assistant Dean for Financial Administration in order to better link academic and fiscal planning. An early priority of this position was the establishment of a rigorous system of cost centers. Previously, CUSSW had no such system to guide budget planning or to monitor expenditures. Subsequently, administrative services also were subsumed into this office and the position of Senior Assistant Dean for Financial and Administrative Services was created. A newly appointed Director of Research and Grants was added to assist faculty with grant development and to ease the burdens of administering research and training grants once they are awarded. Also, a Director of Facilities and Purchasing was appointed in order to enhance the functionality and management of McVickar Hall, a daunting challenge for the University's most heavily utilized building.

Concurrently, the position of Senior Assistant Dean for Student Service Systems was established to better integrate the interrelated functions of admissions, student processing, and job and career development. This position coordinates all aspects of student enrollment and processing ranging from the point of application through admission, financial aid, all stages of graduate study, and into the job placement process. To support these activities, CUSSW appointed a full-time Director of Career Development, a Director of Student Recruitment and Retention, an Assistant Director of Enrollment and Student Service Systems, and a Dual Degree Coordinator. With faculty assistance, the admissions process has been objectified and greatly expedited, resulting in greater opportunities to identify and enroll especially strong applicants. Concomitant improvements in the quality of student life have been fostered through brown bag luncheons with students and faculty, construction of an atrium in McVickar Hall, and other initiatives.

The positions of Director of Field Instruction and Director of Development and Alumni Relations have been upgraded to assistant deanships, and these departments were expanded. In conjunction with the School's Career

Development Office, the latter department now offers a large variety of services to CUSSW alumnae/i. In June 1998, the Alumni Association inaugurated a CUSSW Hall of Fame which duly recognizes the achievements of distinguished alumnae/i. These initiatives have been instrumental in building alumnae/i support for the School and further strengthening the School's educational programs through the active involvement of alumnae/i in teaching, mentoring, job searches, and career development. And, importantly, the establishment of the Office of Computing and Information Technology has greatly improved administrative functioning at CUSSW while also advancing the quality of master's and doctoral education.

The Administrative Council meets regularly at CUSSW in order to promote interchange and planning among the School's administrators and to coordinate their efforts in the administrative and academic realms. CUSSW's administrative innovations also have had a major impact on the larger University by dint of the fact that the School has piloted major University-wide administrative initiatives in dial-up course registration, automated financial aid systems, computerized student data systems, and on-line gift processing.

Related improvements have been made in the School's faculty governance system. They assure greater integrity and confidentiality of faculty elections for key committees, more extensive and thoroughgoing procedures for evaluating candidates for promotion and tenure, and greater involvement of faculty at all ranks in promotional reviews and faculty search committees.

All major administrative and academic developments at CUSSW have been facilitated by the guidance, leadership, and hard work of extraordinary administrators and staff. Their efforts constitute the often invisible, but essential, underside of CUSSW's operations. Their accomplishments have enhanced professional education at the School by providing needed services, generating and conserving resources, increasing efficiencies, and improving the quality of educational, intellectual, and social life in a physical facility that does not lend itself readily to professional education.

Quality of Life

Currently, McVickar Hall is the key determinant of the quality of life at the School of Social Work. Perhaps more than anything else, consensus exists among faculty, students, administrators, and alumnae/i that McVickar Hall is not conducive to contemporary professional education. Even with $4 million in renovations, it impedes professional education as well as the quality of social interaction throughout the School of Social Work. Each student in McVickar Hall has available, on average, only 45 square feet of space. This is about one-third to one-fifth of the square footage available per student at most other Columbia schools.

In a school with nearly one thousand students, McVickar Hall offers merely seven classrooms. Only two can accommodate as many as forty to forty-five persons. Most rooms are L-shaped and/or have I-beams that impede sight lines and interaction. There is only one room where faculty and students together can attend a lecture, and it was not available until renovations were completed two years ago. Other than a newly constructed atrium, there are few spaces where students can socialize informally with fellow students, faculty can interact with colleagues or, above all, where faculty and students can interact with one another. There is limited space for student lockers and mailboxes, no dining facility, no library, no audiovisual laboratories, and not even sufficient space for coat hooks.

The dysfunctions of McVickar Hall have not been newly discovered. The Faculty of Social Work were informed in 1971 that they would be relocated to McVickar Hall for a one- to two-year "transitional period." Nineteen years later, the 1990 Reaccreditation Report of the Council on Social Work Education observed pointedly that "the School's facility is totally inadequate and might even contribute to difficulty in consensus building since there is no place where even the faculty can meet comfortably."

Nevertheless, with considerable assistance from benefactors and the central administration of Columbia University, this last major impediment to progress on the part of CUSSW is about to be addressed. Pending the completion of architectural plans and the attainment of fund-raising goals, the School of Social Work aims to construct a state-of-the-art educational facility by fall 2002. Until then, faculty, students, and administrators will need to be especially creative in seeking ways to alleviate the problems that flow from the School's inadequate physical facility. Student–faculty dinners, dean's forums, "Meet 'n' Eat" luncheons, and student-sponsored seminars and symposia constitute but a few recent initiatives in this regard.

ISSUES FOR THE FUTURE

Despite the gains enumerated above, much remains to be done in order to assure CUSSW's leadership in social work education throughout the next century. Accordingly, members of the School community must attend to a number of important concerns.

Finances and Student Enrollment

It is necessary to continue and even accelerate the School's fund-raising efforts. Faculty as well as administrative officers can play an important role in generating fiscal resources for the School while also advancing CUSSW's curriculum and knowledge development endeavors. It will be especially necessary for CUSSW to deploy more of its own fiscal resources toward building a strong in-house fund-raising apparatus.

Because CUSSW is highly tuition dependent, the best way to guarantee the School's financial health is by assuring that its students receive the best possible professional education. Among other things, faculty need to be readily accessible to students and well informed as advisors. Both at the master's level and the doctoral level, renewed attention must be directed toward raising funds for endowed student scholarships. Greater attention also needs to be paid toward "diversifying" the types of curriculum options available for students so that CUSSW is not overly reliant on a single revenue stream. For example, since advanced standing programs have proliferated nationwide, it may be advisable to consider increasing the number of advanced standing students who enroll at CUSSW. Likewise, as insufficient student housing becomes a potent barrier to enrollment, it may be advisable to revitalize the School's reduced residency program. To do so, however, might require expanded class offerings in the evening hours or, perhaps, on the weekend. Similarly, the number of international students enrolled at CUSSW has declined from peaks attained in the 1970s. Because the School's International Social Welfare field of practice may be of special interest to these students, it might be advisable to expand this segment of the student body. Finally, renewed efforts need to be made to increase enrollments at the School's Purchase Educational Site.

Faculty Workload and Salaries

Although significant progress has been made in reducing faculty workloads, even further advances would be desirable in this area. While it appears that the workloads of CUSSW faculty members are comparable to those at peer schools of social work, they remain higher than at other units of Columbia

University. And, even though faculty salaries at CUSSW are, on average, higher than those at peer schools of social work, it must be acknowledged that CUSSW faculty members are exceptionally competent and, therefore, highly competitive in the academic marketplace. Yet, even with gains in fundraising, enrollment increases, new revenue streams, and reduced operating expenses, it will be difficult to generate further workload reductions or significant salary increases in the near future.

Faculty Recruitment and Development

Numerous issues exist regarding the recruitment, development, and retention of CUSSW faculty members. Clearly, for nontenured faculty members, the prospects for attaining tenure are a paramount concern. Here, it is obvious that the tenure bar is rising significantly at Columbia University. Yet, this also is the case at peer institutions. Overall, tenure candidates from CUSSW have fared well over the years in an extremely competitive environment. Nonetheless, to facilitate optimum career development on the part of CUSSW faculty members and, correspondingly, to strengthen their prospects for tenure, it is essential to assure that their scholarship is regarded as original, cutting edge, and influential. Moreover, at CUSSW in particular, it is essential to assure that faculty are talented teachers and that they regard service to the School and the larger community as central to their career advancement.

To strengthen faculty members' research careers, it will be advisable for them to collaborate increasingly with colleagues from allied professions and disciplines at Columbia University or peer institutions. To date, few institutional mechanisms or incentives have been devised to promote such partnerships. This ought to be a topmost priority in the near future. Bona fide interdisciplinary linkages are needed to enhance faculty competitiveness in acquiring extramural research grants, advance the frontiers of social work knowledge, and become active partners in developments now taking place at Columbia University and other leading institutions of higher education. At the same time, CUSSW research centers and programs that promote interdisciplinary work should be supported by special efforts to build their endowments.

New procedures for reviewing faculty performance are helping considerably to prepare CUSSW faculty members for subsequent tenure reviews.

But, unquestionably, assistance at earlier stages of career development would be even more helpful. In this regard, a number of initiatives might prove beneficial. For example, research development and grant writing seminars ought to be offered more frequently at CUSSW. The School should schedule more "work in progress" colloquia where faculty members of all ranks can share their current and projected research or scholarly endeavors. And, above and beyond presentations by faculty candidates, many more colloquia should be scheduled at CUSSW where leading scholars from other schools of social work and from allied disciplines or professions can present their research.

To facilitate faculty research, two mechanisms that already are in place ought to be put to much greater use, namely grant proposal review teams comprised of experienced CUSSW researchers who provide feedback about draft proposals, and statistical consultants, for whom a modest fund already is available. To the extent possible, larger numbers of doctoral research assistants also should be made available to faculty.

Other mechanisms also can be employed to recognize and promote faculty development. The School could establish an annual teaching award and, if so, explore new ways of evaluating the quality of faculty instruction other than student evaluations. Faculty development can be enhanced by creating more opportunities for selected nontenured faculty members to teach in CUSSW's doctoral program. And, at a different level, it might be timely and appropriate for the School to consider periodic performance reviews of tenured faculty members as well as nontenured faculty members.

As noted previously, revitalized efforts must be made to recruit faculty members of color. CUSSW has attracted a large share of NIMH/CSWE Minority Scholars to the faculty and the doctoral program. Nonetheless, the School should strive even more vigorously to recruit talented students of color to the doctoral program and thereby increase the national pool of potential faculty members of color.

Certain curriculum areas are in particular need of priority attention for faculty recruitment. Above and beyond the perennial need for talented faculty members who can teach in the Clinical Practice and AGPP curriculum areas, it is essential to appoint one or more senior faculty members in International Social Welfare and the World of Work. To cope with the paucity of doctoral graduates in these areas and others, it may be advisable to consider the prospect of establishing clinical professorships at CUSSW. Likewise, to enhance interdisciplinary research and strengthen the School's curricular offerings, it may be useful to appoint increasing numbers of faculty members from allied disciplines and professions.

CUSSW also could experiment increasingly with alternative types of faculty appointments. Thus, for example, faculty exchange programs could take place with leading schools of social work in the United States and abroad. An innovative program in this regard is being launched in 2000 with the Hebrew University School of Social Work in Jerusalem, Israel. Also, leading practitioners could be invited to teach selected elective courses three or four weekends per semester.

Curriculum Development

A number of major initiatives need to be launched or strengthened to significantly advance professional education at CUSSW. In the coming years, digital technology will play a growing and essential role in social work education. Therefore, it behooves CUSSW faculty members and administrators to intensify their efforts to introduce advanced computing and information technologies to the curriculum. Consideration should be given to employing laser disc technologies for client interviews and assessments, digital technology to link the classroom and field instruction agencies, and skills laboratories and virtual cases for clinical education. It may be necessary to require that all CUSSW students own a laptop computer for these and related educational endeavors. Concurrently, it might be helpful to establish partnerships in this area with Columbia University's School of Engineering.

Even though CUSSW's mission requires that the preponderance of its resources be directed toward master's degree education, it must be recognized that the School's doctoral program constitutes an invaluable and indispensable resource for the School and the profession. Therefore, the quality of the School's doctoral program must be sustained and even strengthened. A superior doctoral program will enable the School to attract distinguished faculty and talented students, strengthen CUSSW's intellectual vitality, further improve scholarship and the curriculum, increase extramural funding, enhance the School's reputational standing, gain greater recognition and support from throughout the University, and exert greater influence upon social work education and the social work profession. To date, Columbia's doctoral program has trained two generations of social work educators, some of whom are current members of the CUSSW faculty. Columbia has educated more social work deans than any other school in the country. Because the School's doctoral and master's degree programs complement each other, each must be regarded as essential to the other's success.

To strengthen the School's doctoral program, it is essential to increase substantially the number of endowed scholarships for Ph.D. students. While considerable progress has been made in generating financial aid for doctoral students, much more remains to be done. It is timely for faculty to launch a wide-ranging review of all aspects of the doctoral program. Given the strong impetus toward interdisciplinary partnerships at Columbia University, as well as the great demand for graduates of joint degree programs elsewhere, it may be timely to explore the merits of establishing a joint degree doctoral program at Columbia. CUSSW also may wish to consider establishing a post-doctoral training program. Such programs not only enhance the quality of graduate education but, even more, create productive mechanisms for recruiting talented faculty members.

At the master's level, it may be advisable to expand linkages between the Social Administration area and relevant programs at the School of Business and the School of International and Public Affairs. It may be opportune, also, to consider establishing a dual degree program in international affairs. Concurrently, CUSSW ought to expand its partnership with the United Nations so as to strengthen the School's curriculum in International Social Welfare.

It is germane, too, to consider innovations or adaptations that could improve the School's financial strength while also enhancing the curriculum. Examples include more innovative ways of linking field instruction and the classroom, larger sections for selected courses, and revisions of selected programs. It also may be timely to consider the introduction of one or more third-year or post-master's training programs that could link CUSSW more readily with community agencies while also generating new revenue streams.

In the near future, it might be advisable to consider the formation of a series of faculty and administration task forces that examine core areas of social work education. Examples include field instruction where block placements, foreign placements, and digital linkages with practicum agencies could perhaps be examined. It also would be fruitful to explore special applications of digital technology in selected practice methods or fields of practice. It also may be productive to examine the impact of CSWE structures and requirements on curriculum development at leading schools of social work.

Finally, there would be benefit to discussions where CUSSW faculty have an opportunity to conceptualize truly significant innovations and advances in social work education. Possible topics might include extension of the master's program to three years, adding or dropping selected curriculum areas, reinstituting the D.S.W. as a practice degree, initiating a baccalaureate social work program, rescheduling classes and field instruction so that first-year and second-year students are able to interact more readily with one another, developing digital education linkages or consortiums with leading schools of social work elsewhere in the United States, and, even, establishing alternative accreditation bodies for schools of social work.

Administrative Development

At least three administrative areas will require substantial investments in the near future. To improve the School's ability to generate gifts, it will be advisable to add one or more major gift officers to the Office of Development and Alumni Relations and also to strengthen the School's public relations apparatus. Likewise, as CUSSW increasingly applies state-of-the-art digital technology to social work education, it will be necessary to invest more heavily in the Office of Computing and Information Technology. And, to facilitate funded research programs at CUSSW, it will be helpful to hire more staff in this area and possibly to establish an Associate Dean for Research.

Quality of Life

Unquestionably, the single most important means of improving the quality of academic and extracurricular life at CUSSW entails the construction of a new physical facility for the School of Social Work. The School is on the threshold of doing so. While the benefits of a new home for CUSSW will be profound, serious burdens will accompany such an endeavor, including additional debt service. Pending relocation to a new building, all members of the CUSSW community will need to be especially forbearing and, even more, will need to transcend the barriers to curriculum design, institutional development, and creative planning that have been imposed upon them for so many years by the limitations of McVickar Hall.

Finally, it is time for CUSSW to sponsor many more activities that bring together faculty and students. Examples include forums that can challenge the participants intellectually, such as major lectures or symposia, and activities that afford greater social and collegial interaction, such as sponsored coffee hours.

INTO THE SECOND CENTURY

As noted in the preceding essays, the history of the Columbia University School of Social Work has been a long and illustrious one. From its very origins, the School has shaped the nature and substance of social work education and, in turn, of the social work profession. At the same time, trends within the profession and the larger society have shaped the School's curriculums and the careers and social work activities of its graduates.

The preceding essays demonstrate that the present-day curriculum of the School of Social Work is a rich and a complex one. The School offers an outstanding master's degree curriculum and also a superb doctoral degree curriculum. In the course of their master's studies, all students must select both a method of practice *and* a field of practice. Options for the former are extensive. Students can select any one of five fields of practice: Clinical Social Work Practice, Advanced Generalist Practice and Programming, Social Administration, Social Policy, or Social Research. Concurrently, they also must select one of seven fields of practice: Family and Children's Services; Health, Mental Health, and Disabilities; Aging; World of Work; International Social Welfare and Services to Immigrants and Refugees; School-Based and School-Linked Services; and Contemporary Social Problems. In short, thirty-five different combinations of study are available to the School's master's degree students! At the same time, the doctoral program also offers extensive choices for students, namely concentrations in Advanced Practice; Social Policy, Planning, and Policy Analysis; and Social Policy, Planning, and Administration.

The great breadth and exemplary quality of the CUSSW curriculum have emerged over the course of a full century. Nonetheless, certain of the issues that confronted social work education at its birth in 1898 still need to be addressed by the School's faculty. From the beginning, there was the question of the proper mix among clinical practice, social advocacy, and scholarly research and publication. All three have been regarded as crucial hallmarks of the School since its inception. Yet, their relative roles have been debated con-

tinuously. Indeed, in some respects the discourse has intensified in recent decades as the School linked formally with Columbia University and integrated
its promotion and tenure review systems more thoroughly with those employed by the University. While teaching and community service are of great
importance for the School's faculty, research and scholarly publication have
become even more valued and salient in recent decades.

Faculty members now devote less time to field advising than in previous
years. While the quality of faculty teaching is as high or higher than ever before, the teaching loads for faculty have been reduced. Consequently, faculty
devote much more of their time and effort to preparing research proposals,
conducting significant programs of research, and publishing in a wide range
of scholarly venues. Faculty publications appear not only in the social work
literature but also in the literatures of allied professions and disciplines. In
fact, approximately one-half of faculty publications appear in allied literatures. Concurrent with the ongoing debate about the relative weight to be
accorded to teaching, research, and community service, there is discussion
about new organizational strategies for enabling all three functions to be per-
formed optimally by the School of Social Work. Thus, for instance, discussion is taking place about the advisability of establishing clinical professorships that evaluate selected faculty members primarily, if not solely, on the
quality of their practice instruction rather than scholarly productivity. Similar debates are occurring throughout all of social work education.

Related discussions also are occurring at CUSSW and elsewhere. What
should be regarded as the optimal size of the School? To what extent should
adjunct faculty members be employed even if, as at Columbia, rigorous evaluation procedures are utilized regularly and consistently to assure that only
the best instructors are hired and retained? What is the optimum blend of
classroom instruction and field instruction? And, of course, can social work
education—both in the classroom and at fieldwork sites—be improved or
delivered more cost-effectively through greater utilization of contemporary
information and communication technologies? Even more, can classroom
and field instruction be linked more effectively through such technologies?

Throughout its history, the overarching concerns at CUSSW have been
the quality, relevance, utility, and cost-effectiveness of professional social
work education. These concerns will prevail far into the future. Therefore,
as CUSSW progresses into the second century of social work education, it is
timely to ponder anew the School's collective vision for the future. As always,

the School's faculty will have the privilege and the primary responsibility for formulating that vision. Constructive input also will come from administrators, alumnae/i, students, University officials, the School's Advisory Council, and other sources. Clearly, CUSSW's social reform tradition must be honored at the same time that the School treasures professional interventions which are grounded in research and science. CUSSW faculty must educate the best possible practitioners at the same time that they develop the best possible knowledge base for the profession.

In the next century, many of CUSSW's most cherished attributes will not and ought not change. CUSSW will be a valued and esteemed unit of Columbia University. Promising students and able faculty will come to CUSSW from all over the world. CUSSW will judge itself by the highest standards. The drive for excellence will continue and even intensify. Each member of the School community will be valued for her or his own sake rather than the categories by which persons frequently divide themselves. Scholarship will continue to strengthen teaching and teaching will stimulate scholarship. These strengths will be employed to advance the profession and improve its quality of service to the community. Faculty, students, alumnae/i, and friends will maintain and even strengthen their commitment and sense of responsibility for the School's future.

Yet, as these treasured attributes are preserved, CUSSW also will change and evolve. Students, faculty, and administrators will more nearly reflect the diversity in American society. Planning will be more extensive and thorough as CUSSW strives to make the most effective use of its human, physical, and financial resources. Curricula and teaching will evolve so as to be at the cutting edge of a rapidly changing profession. Collaborative teaching and research will increase with other schools and departments. New technologies will improve communication, enhance education, and facilitate scholarship. Faculty and students will rely increasingly on current scientific knowledge. Continuing education will become more important and extensive. CUSSW will be more international in its outlook. The School will increase its fiscal strength due to the generosity of friends and the careful, disciplined use of resources. Financial aid will be more crucial and more expansive. And, a stronger sense of community spirit will be realized. With continued dedication, partnership, and care, the prospects for CUSSW are bright at the dawn of a second century of social work education.

REFERENCES

Bok, Derek. (1990). *Universities and the Future of America.* Durham, NC: Duke University Press.

Council on Social Work Education (CSWE). (1999). *Statistics on Social Work Education in the United States: 1998.* Alexandria, VA: Author.

Locke, Barry L. and Michael A. Patchner (1992). *Managing Faculty Workloads.* Paper presented at the semi-annual Conference of the National Association of Deans and Directors of Schools of Social Work.

INDEX

Americans with Disabilities Act, 48

American Welfare State, 25, 41

Arukh, Shulhan, 191

ASSA (American Social Science Association), 10, 13

Association of Labor-Management Administrators and Consultants in Alcoholism, 286

Association of Training Schools for Professional Social Work, 57, 91–92, 122–123

Associations for Improving the Conditions of the Poor (AICPs), 10, 12, 14, 34, 57, 83, 91

Austin, D., 208

Austin, David M., 186, 198

Austin, Lucille Nickel, 128, 129, 130, 131, 132, 137

Ayres, Philip W., 13, 27, 56, 64, 84

Baccalaureate Program Directors, 108–109

Bailey-Dempsey, Cynthia, 317

Bank Street College, Special Education, 46, 107, 108

Barker/Briggs Model of the Social Service Team, 256

Barker, Robert, 255–256

Bartlett, Harriet, 118, 148, 255

Behavioral science: and advanced generalist practice and programming, 154; and clinical practice, 123, 128, 131, 134, 139; and curriculum, 35, 36, 37; and faculty, 49, 55; and social work education, 17, 19, 20, 26, 46; and social work practice, 44

Bellevue Hospital Training School for Nurses, 254, 256

Bell, Winifred, 196, 198, 199

Berengarten, Sidney, 4, 38, 64, 110, 301–302

Berkman, Barbara, 222

Bermingham, Grace, 348

Bernstein, Saul, 4, 9, 28, 66, 67, 171, 185

Bieri, James, 37, 209, 215, 356

Bird S. Coler demonstration, 38, 40

Birtwell, Charles W., 230

Blau, Joel, 201

Blau, Zena, 276

Bloom, B., 269

Blythe, Ronald, 277

Bok, Derek, 388

Boston Children's Aid Society, 230

Boston School for Social Workers, 11, 119

Boysville Management Information System (BOMIS), 217

Brace, Charles Loring, 230

Bradshaw, J., 155

Brager, George, 40, 64, 151, 185

Brand, Morris, 283

Brandt, Lilian, 88

Breckinridge, S., 315

Brewer, Mrs. George E., Jr., 74

Briar, Scott, 137, 208, 210, 212, 215, 216, 357

Broadhurst, Betty P., 11, 12, 13, 27, 108

Brody, Elaine, 268

Bronx Defenders, 337

Brookdale Foundation, 269–270

Brookdale Institute of Aging and Human Development, 49

Brunner, J., 269

Bruno, Frank, 373

Bureau for Children's Guidance, 22, 124, 133, 229, 255, 256, 315

Bureau of Applied Social Research, 53

Bureau of Social Research, 27, 37–38, 56, 87, 208, 248

Burnette, J. Denise, 362

Burns, Eveline M.: and doctoral education, 348; and endowments, 49; and international social welfare, 299; and Public Services for Families and Children, 198; and social policy, 40, 185, 186, 194, 195–198, 199, 201; and Social Security, 36, 194, 195

Bush, George H. W., 45, 46–49, 177

Bush, Robert, 37

Butler, Nicholas Murray, 97

Cameron, Gary, 201

Cannon, Mary Antoinette: and clinical practice, 124, 125, 128, 129, 130; and health, mental health, and disabilities, 252–253, 257; and Milford Conference, 22; and Texas Relief Commission, 33

Carnegie, Andrew, 103

Carnegie Corporation, 36

Carroll, Nancy K., 269

Carstens, C. C., 228

Carter, James, 42, 48, 177

Casework: above poverty line, 30; and ad-

Cotton, Samuel, 75, 110

Coulton, C., 288

Council for International Exchange of Scholars, 301

Council on Social Work Education (CSWE): and advanced generalist practice and programming, 149, 151; and aging, 268–269; and centennial celebration, 108; and curriculum, 46, 386–387, 406, 407; and enrollment trend statistics, 72, 73; and social administration, 176; and social policy, 186, 197; and social research, 211–212; and workplace services, 285

Courtney, Mark, 129

Coyle, Joseph T., 109

Criminal justice: and advanced generalist practice and programming, 160–161; and curriculum, 21, 22, 23, 87, 189; and faculty members, 30, 37; as field of practice, 22, 44, 93; and fieldwork, 335; and health, mental health, and disabilities, 253, 331, 337; and homelessness, 328, 331, 336, 337; and juvenile justice, 29, 35, 40, 189, 192, 214, 310, 333; and prison work, 13, 35; and probation officers, 16, 35; and social problems, 326, 327, 330–331, 333, 334, 335; and social research, 214, 217; and substance abuse, 329–330, 331, 337; and treatment of criminals, 18

Cross-National Studies program, 42, 43, 49, 52, 201–202, 303–304, 306

CSS. *See* Community Service Society (CSS)

CSWE. *See* Council on Social Work Education (CSWE)

Cuellar, Benjamin, 357

Cupaiuolo, Anthony, 358

Curriculum: and advanced generalist practice and programming, 148, 150–151, 152, 155, 158–159, 407; and aging, 42, 266, 268–271, 274, 276–277; and casework, 22, 28, 43, 87, 106, 140n3, 229, 231; and child guidance work, 22, 23, 255; and child welfare, 22, 32, 35, 87; and client populations, 389; and clinical practice, 121, 202, 234, 407; and community organization, 35, 43, 93, 104, 106, 231; and Council on Social Work Education, 46, 386–387, 406, 407; development of, 7, 110–111, 405–408, 414–416; and doc-

toral education, 345, 414–415, 417; and faculty members, 19, 22, 24–25, 26, 34–35, 44, 403, 405, 415–416; and family and children's services, 227, 228, 229, 233–234, 240–241; and family casework, 22, 23, 30, 35, 87; and fields of practice, 3–4, 44, 48, 102, 106, 110–111, 171, 405, 417; and fieldwork, 85–86, 88, 92, 94, 96, 98, 99, 102, 405, 415; and Great Society, 41; and group work, 23, 31, 33, 35, 97, 104, 106, 231; and health, mental health, and disabilities, 247–251, 253–255, 256, 258; and immigrant and refugee services, 36, 50, 171, 188, 299; innovations in, 43–48, 54–55, 386, 417; and international social welfare, 194, 195, 293, 299–305, 306, 307, 406; and medical social work, 22, 35, 102, 256; and methods of practice, 3, 48, 106, 110–111, 405, 417; of New York School of Philanthropy, 15–20, 59–63, 87–90, 171, 172–173, 187–188; of New York School of Social Work, 20–24, 28–29, 31, 91–94, 97, 174; of New York School of Social Work of Columbia University, 34, 98, 99, 102–104; and psychiatric casework, 22–23, 35, 129–130, 254, 256; and public welfare, 32; and school social work, 35, 50, 309, 317–320, 406; and social administration, 169, 171–181, 407; and social policy, 35, 114, 186, 187–188, 190, 192–194, 197, 200, 203, 204, 406; and social problems, 44, 224–225, 324–326, 331–337, 338, 406; and social research, 35, 43, 87, 94, 97, 212–213, 231, 386, 407; and social science, 35–36, 37, 104; and student body, 76–77; and technology, 407, 414, 415; trends in, 383

CUSSW. *See* Columbia University School of Social Work (CUSSW)

Czechoslovakia, 30

Damron-Rodriguez, J. A., 274

Dauber, S., 312

Dawes, Anna L., 10, 14

Dear, Ron, 201

Deer, Ada E., 110

deForest, Robert W.: and Kennedy, 86; and New York School of Philanthropy, 1, 10, 56, 57, 83, 101, 369, 379